Come Help Change Our World

Books and booklets by Bill Bright

Come Help Change Our World

Bill Bright

CAMPUS CRUSADE FOR CHRIST INTERNATIONAL
San Bernardino, CA 92414

COME HELP CHANGE THE WORLD
by Bill Bright

A Campus Crusade for Christ Book
Published by
HERE'S LIFE PUBLISHERS, INC.
P.O. Box 1576
San Bernardino, CA 92402
Library of Congress Cataloging-in-Publication Data

Bright, Bill.
    Come help change the world.

    "A Campus Crusade for Christ book."
       1. Campus Crusade for Christ. 2. Students — Religious
life. I. Campus Crusade for Christ.
II. Title.
BV4427.B73   1985   267,.61   85-21931
ISBN 0-86605-157-0 (pbk.)

HLP Product No. 403493

FOR MORE INFORMATION, WRITE:

L.I.F.E. — P.O. Box A399, Sydney South 2000, Australia
Campus Crusade for Christ of Canada — Box 300, Vancouver, B.C., V6C 2X3, Canada
Campus Crusade for Christ — 103 Friar Street, Reading RG1 1EP, Berkshire, England
Lay Institute for Evangelism — P.O. Box 8786, Auckland 3, New Zealand
Great Commission Movement of Nigeria — P.O. Box 500, Jos, Plateau State Nigeria, West Africa
Life Ministry — P.O. Box/Bus 91015, Auckland Park 2006, Republic of South Africa
Campus Crusade for Christ International — Arrowhead Springs, San Bernardino, CA 92414,
U.S.A.

To those individuals who are and have been a part of the Campus Crusade for Christ staff family, I gratefully and affectionately dedicate this book. They are 20th-century Christian disciples who are committed to changing the world and fulfilling the Great Commission in this generation. This is their story.

Contents

Preface

Some time ago one of America's leading theologians and scholars wrote, "I am at Wheaton College where I am to speak at chapel tomorrow. I arrived late last night tired and eager to rest. However, before I went to sleep I decided to read the first chapter of your book, *Come Help Change the World*, which I had just acquired. It is now 2 A.M. and I have just finished reading the first eight chapters. I have gotten down on my knees to rededicate my life to the Lord Jesus Christ. Thank you for writing this book. It touched my life."

The revision of this book has been around the world in manuscript form many times since I began to rewrite my original book, *Come Help Change the World*. I have written on planes and trains, in hotel rooms and dozens of other places.

The reason that I have felt this book is important enough to sandwich my writing into an already overcrowded schedule is that God is doing so many dramatic, revolutionary things through this ministry that I feel the incredible story of Campus Crusade for Christ needs to be updated.

It is my prayer that God will speak to you, dear reader, and call you to be a part of this or some other similar movement dedicated to helping to change the world through helping fulfill the Great Commission — the greatest challenge ever given by the greatest Person who ever lived.

Bill Bright
Arrowhead Springs

Acknowledgment

I wish to express my deepest personal gratitude to the people who diligently labored with me in the production of this book. Their help has made it possible for me to tell the exciting story of the miraculous workings of our Lord through the ministry of Campus Crusade for Christ.

Chuch MacDonald was of invaluable assistance to me in this project as he spent long hours researching, updating and polishing the material.

Janet Kobobel's final editing was crucial to the manuscript. So were the efforts of Judy Douglass and other dedicated staff members in the publications department who aided me in revising the original *Come Help Change the World* book which was printed in 1970.

I am also grateful to Frank Allnutt for his wise counsel and for overseeing the entire project to completion.

Erma Griswold, my assistant, is another whose help was so important, as she provided detailed editing of the manuscript.

And finally, I am thankful to my beloved wife, Vonette, who has labored with me in this movement for the past 28 years and whose contributions of love, patience and dedication to the Lord have helped further the impact of this ministry around the world.

CHAPTER ONE

EXPLO '74 —
An Awesome Experience

My heart quickened as I stepped to the microphone. This was the most awesome responsibility and most exciting challenge of my life. I looked out upon an ocean of people stretching as far as I could see to the left of me, to the right of me and in front of me. Officials estimated 1.3 million people had gathered in Seoul, Korea, for this evening meeting of EXPLO '74, an international congress on evangelism sponsored by Campus Crusade for Christ.

My message was based on Ephesians 2:8,9, and I wanted to explain that salvation is a gift of God which we receive by faith. After each sentence that I spoke to the crowd, I paused, allowing Dr. C. C. Park, one of the leading pastors in all of South Korea, to translate my statements into Korean. At the completion of my message, I asked all of those who wanted to receive Christ, or who, as a result of my message, had gained assurance of their salvation, to stand.

All over Yoido Plaza, people began to stand from where they had been sitting on the asphalt of this converted airstrip. Grandmothers, teenagers, businessmen, farmers, merchants and children stood quietly as the EXPLO choir, some 8,000 voices in number, sang softly.

I could hardly believe my eyes as hundreds of thousands of people stood! I wanted to make sure they understood what I had said, so I repeated my invitation again, slowly. Still more people stood!

Midnight Call

About midnight, I answered a phone call from Dr. Joon Gon Kim to report on the evening's activities. Dr.

Kim is the director of Campus Crusade's movement in Korea and has been my beloved friend and co-laborer for Christ since 1958. He and his staff were responsible for calling together this remarkable gathering.

"I have exciting news," he said. "When you gave the invitation tonight, our staff determined that about 80% of the estimated 1.3 million people in attendance stood. Do you realize that more than one million people indicated tonight that they received Christ or that, for the first time in their lives, they were assured of their salvation?"

It was some time before I could respond, because I was so overwhelmed. Even now I cannot quite grasp it. I know it happened only because of God's supernatural, miraculous working, for what greater miracle is there than the miracle of a new birth?

This was just one of the many momentous moments I witnessed during EXPLO '74. Night after night I was filled with awe and praise to God as I stood on the elevated platform and looked out over a sea of faces.

I was deeply moved to learn that these were the largest Christian gatherings in recorded history. At least one of the evening mass rallies exceeded 1.6 million people, according to official police estimates.

Record-setting Gathering

Besides this amazing "first" in the history of the Christian church, Dr. Kim later told me of some 24 other firsts in connection with EXPLO '74, some of which, even five years later, were unmatched. They included:

1. The largest number of Christians trained in discipleship and evangelism during one week (a total number of 323,419 registered, representing some 78 nations).

2. The largest number of decisions for Christ in a single evening.

3. The largest all-night prayer meetings in the history of the Christian church (prayer meetings occurred six

nights in a row, with several hundred thousand in attendance each night). The night before EXPLO began, my wife, Vonette, spoke to more than 100,000 women gathered for prayer.

4. The largest personal witnessing campaign ever conducted (more than 420,000 heard the gospel in one afternoon and a record 274,000 indicated salvation decisions for Christ).

5. The largest number of Christians to appropriate the filling of the Holy Spirit at one time (an estimated 70% of the 1.5 million audience one night responded to this invitation).

6. The largest number of Christians to commit their lives to the fulfillment of the Great Commission at one time (a response of 90% was estimated among the final Sunday crowd of 650,000).

No number of human beings nor group of organizations could ever have accomplished what happened at EXPLO '74. All the glory, honor and praise must go to God.

Supernatural Living

I am reminded of the words of our Lord recorded in John 14:12, which have been a constant source of wonder and challenge to me since my early days as a Christian: "Truly, truly, I say to you, he who believes in Me, the works that I do shall he do also; and greater works than these shall he do; because I go to the Father."

From the beginning of my Christian experience, I have interpreted that verse to mean that God wants His children to live supernaturally, especially in the area of living holy lives and bearing much fruit, since that is the reason that our Lord came to this world. God's Word reminds us, "The Son of Man has come to seek and to save that which was lost" (Luke 19:10). Jesus explains in John 15:8, "By this is My Father glorified, that you bear much fruit, and so prove to be My disciples."

Through the years, I have prayed that my life and the ministry of Campus Crusade would be characterized by the miraculous and supernatural. I have prayed that God would work in and through us in such a mighty way that all who see the results of our efforts would know that God was responsible and give Him all the glory.

Now as I look back on EXPLO '74 — surely one of the most exciting and meaningful memories in the history of our movement — I remember earlier days which were also characterized by praise and glory to God, even though I was not privileged to speak to millions, or even thousands. At one point in our ministry, about the only understanding listener I could turn to was my wife.

But let me take you back to those days, to the beginning of the Campus Crusade story and that moment when God revealed to me the ministry I was to undertake for Him.

CHAPTER TWO

In the Beginning

It was the spring of 1951, my senior year at Fuller Theological Seminary. For two exciting and happy years I had been married to my home town sweetheart, the former Vonette Zachary. Vonette had accepted a teaching position in the Los Angeles school system, and we found ourselves living a busy and eventful life.

Once or twice a week, in addition to regular meetings at church, I had the privilege of leading a deputation group of more than a hundred dedicated college and post-college age young men and women who wanted to become disciples for the Lord Jesus Christ. We covered approximately 30 assignments each month, visiting the local jails and hospitals, skid row missions and wherever we felt we were needed. I soon discovered that we had to wait our turn to go to jail services and skid row missions because there were many other churches covering this area of service. One day it occurred to me that there were no waiting lines to reach college students or the top executives of the city. Here were the neglected leaders of our world, both today's and tomorrow's.

Contract With God

By this time Vonette and I had become increasingly aware that living for Christ and serving Him was our major goal in life. As a result of this awareness, we decided we would sign a contract with the Lord. No one had ever suggested this; it was just something we decided to do together. Both of us had been very ambitious and materialistic and had lived selfishly prior to becoming Christians. Now the Lord had changed us and had given us a love for Himself and a desire to serve Him and others.

One Sunday afternoon, Vonette went into one room in our home in the Hollywood hills and I into another, and we made a list of all the things we had wanted out of life. When I had first proposed to Vonette, we had once talked about a honeymoon in Europe, about securing the finest voice teacher to develop her already beautiful singing voice and about living in the fabulous Bel-Air district of Los Angeles. But now all that had been given to Christ. Such ambitions had become secondary for us, there was no longer a great appetite for them. So, we made a new list of the things we wanted.

Similar Lists

Our new lists, surprisingly alike, included: (1) to live holy lives, controlled and empowered by the Holy Spirit; (2) to be effective witnesses for Christ; and (3) to help to fulfill the Great Commission in our generation. We were also concerned for a Christian home, and we suggested two to four children (we have two sons). We thought it would be convenient to own two cars. Today we don't own any, but God has provided us transportation through the generosity of a friend who is also interested in helping to reach the world for Christ. And, we mentioned in our lists, if the Lord be pleased, we wanted a home nice enough for entertaining the President of the United States and modest enough that a man from Skid Row would feel comfortable in it.

By now we had begun to respond to the command of our Lord: "But seek first His kingdom, and His righteousness" (Matthew 6:33). We believed that God's will was better than our own. The more we knew of God's love for us, of His wisdom, power and grace, the more we could trust Him. So we signed our names to these lists as a formal act of commitment to Christ and His cause. This was an especially significant commitment

asmuch as we were doing it together as a young hus-
nd and wife. There was no particular emotion in-
lved. It was simply a transaction of the will. Of course,
e had been motivated to do this on the basis of the
irit of God working in us, as explained through the
ostle Paul, "For it is God who is at work in you, both
will and to work for His good pleasure" (Philippians
13).

What was to happen as a result of this commitment
e did not know, but I am sure that God did; and, within
few short weeks, as we continued studies, teaching,
putation work and business, His plans began to un-
ld.

rth of a Vision

One evening at about midnight, during my senior
ar in seminary, I was studying for a Greek exam. There
as nothing unusual about the setting or about the cir-
mstances. Vonette was asleep in a nearby room. Sud-
nly, without warning or without any indication of
hat was going to happen, I sensed the presence of God
a way I had never known before. Though it could not
ve lasted more than a few seconds, I suddenly had
e overwhelming impression that the Lord had flashed
the screen of my mind His instructions for my life
d ministry.

It is difficult to talk about such experiences for fear
being misunderstood or causing others to seek similar
periences; but I think I know a little something of what
e apostle Paul experienced when he met the Lord in
ch a dramatic way on the road to Damascus. In any
ent, this was the greatest spiritual experience of my
ristian life. At this time and in a very definite way,
od commanded me to invest my life in helping to fulfill
e Great Commission in this generation. I was to begin
helping to win and disciple the students of the world
r Christ. How to do this was not spelled out in detail;

that came later as the Lord gave additional insights fの
the implementation of the original vision. I awakene
Vonette, and together we praised God for His directic
and promised that with His grace and strength we wou
obey Him.

Counsel From Mature Christians

Though my heart was filled with praise ar
thanksgiving to the Lord for this remarkable revelatic
of what I was to do with my life, I still needed the couns
of more mature Christians. The next day I went to se
one of my favorite seminary professors, Dr. Wilbr
Smith, famous Bible teacher, scholar and author of mar
books. As I shared with him what God had revealed
me, he got out of his chair and paced back and forth
his office, saying again and again, "This is of God. Th
is of God. I want to help you. Let me think and pr
about it."

The next morning when I arrived for his seven o'clo
class in English Bible, Dr. Smith called me out of th
classroom into a little counseling room and handed n
a piece of paper on which he had scribbled these letter
"CCC" after which he had written "Campus Crusac
for Christ." He explained that God had provided th
name for my vision.

Since that spring night experience, it has been n
passion and concern to be obedient to the heavenly v
ion that God had given me. The first major decision
made was to drop out of seminary with only a few uni
remaining before graduation. I became convinced, ar
remain convinced today, that God did not want me
be ordained. Though I have a great respect and appre
ation for clergy, layman status has often worked to
great advantage in my ministry with students ar
laymen.

The next move was to look for an advisory board
outstanding men and women of God to advise and cou

sel me in the establishment of this ministry. Dr. Wilbur Smith was the first I approached. Then I asked Henrietta Mears, Billy Graham, Richard C. Halverson, Dawson Trotman, Cyrus N. Nelson, Dan Fuller and J. Edwin Orr, to serve in this capacity. All of them readily agreed to be part of this new facet of God's strategy.

The events of the days that followed were framed in prayer and meditation. "Lord, where do You want us to launch this ministry?" was a prayer that Vonette and I and our friends uttered frequently in the spring and summer of 1951.

The Target — UCLA

Increasingly, the University of California at Los Angeles became the focus of our attention. It seemed so right to begin there, at a university that in 1951 had a strong, radical minority which was exercising great influence and was causing a number of disturbances. It seemed that this would be one of the most difficult campuses on which to begin, and that if our venture for Christ could succeed there, it would be likely to succeed on any campus.

After our meeting with university officials to share our plans and request the necessary approval to work with the students, we looked for a place to live near the UCLA campus. Rents were high, and nothing was available in the immediate vicinity. But we kept searching and praying that God would lead us to the right location.

One day as I was going over the files with a local realtor, he turned past the listing of a large home only one block from the campus with a rental of $450 per month, which in 1951 was astronomical. Our budget indicated that we would be able to spend up to $200, though that was more than we could realistically afford to pay. Yet as the realtor flipped past the card of the listing of this house, I told him rather emphatically, "That's the house. I want to see it."

"Why?" he asked. "They are asking more than twice the amount you are willing to pay."

But I continued to press him. "How long has the house been listed?"

"For several months." Then he explained that two sisters who lived in the house were planning to take a South American tour. "As a matter of fact," he observed, studying the card, "they leave next week."

I asked permission to go to see them, and I found the house ideally suited for our needs. It was located approximately one block from sorority row and had plenty of room, in particular a spacious living room where I could visualize us holding large group sessions. I explained to the owners our interest in reaching the students of UCLA for Christ, and that we would not be able to pay more than $200 a month rent. They said that they would think about it and would call us. By the time I returned to our home in Hollywood, they had called. Impressed with our mission and wanting to have a part in it, they agreed to the $200 a month rent if we would pay an additional $25 a month for the gardener. This we agreed to do, and shortly thereafter we moved into our new home in Westwood.

Chain of Prayer

Our first spiritual effort was to organize a 24-hour chain of prayer divided into 96 periods of 15 minutes each and invite people to pray around the clock that God would do a unique thing on the UCLA campus. Next, we began to recruit and train interested students and to organize them into teams to visit the various fraternities and sororities, dormitories and other groups on the campus. The teams presented personal testimonies of their faith in Christ, after which I gave a brief message in which I explained who Christ is, why He came and how they could know Him personally.

I remember well our first sorority meeting. It was at

the Kappa Alpha Theta sorority, which was known then as the "house of beautiful women." Apparently the pledges were selected, among other reasons, for their good looks and personalities. In any event, when I finished my message and the challenge was presented to receive Christ, many girls remained behind to talk to us and ask further questions. It was a new experience for me. For more than a year we had gone into various fraternity and sorority houses on local campuses prior to the time that God gave the vision of this ministry; yet we had never seen one single person commit his life to Christ. To our knowledge, no one had ever received Christ as a result of any of our meetings.

Overwhelming Response

At the conclusion of the first sorority meeting following the vision God had given, I was amazed to see such a large group of young women standing in line to express their desire to become Christians. One after another they came (more than half of the original 60 girls present), communicating in various ways, "I want to become a Christian." It was a humbling experience, seeing God work in this marvelous way. This was a dramatic confirmation to me that the vision to help fulfill the Great Commission and to begin by going to the collegians of the world was truly from God. Unsure, stepping carefully, speaking reservedly, we had been cautious until then; but God seemed to be urging us forward, filling us with badly needed confidence and assurance that, having called us to this ministry, He was with us.

We invited the girls to join us the next evening for a meeting in our home nearby, and several of the young women brought their boyfriends. It was a memorable and exciting night. The men were skeptical, but they came with the girls from "the house of beautiful women," and many of them made decisions for Christ, too.

This, then, was the beginning of a movement which is now touching the lives of millions.

CHAPTER THREE

Growing Up

The days that followed demonstrated again and again the fact that God's hand was upon us and upon our ministry. In meeting after meeting — in fraternities, sororities, dormitories and with student leaders — the phenomenal response was the same as that at our first meeting. In the course of a few months, more than 250 students at UCLA — including the student body president, the editor of the newspaper and a number of the top athletes — committed their lives to Christ. So great was their influence for Christ on the entire campus that the chimes began to play Christian hymns at noonday.

By this time the news of what God was doing at UCLA had spread to other campuses, and students, faculty, laymen and pastors in various parts of the country were asking, "Will you help us? We would like to start Campus Crusade at our school."

At this point, I had to make a very important decision. The vision that God had given to me originally embraced the whole world. If I were to stay at UCLA and devote all of my own personal energies to reach only one campus, I would be disobedient to that heavenly vision. I loved the students and could easily have spent the rest of my life serving Christ on that one campus. Yet there was only one thing for me to do — recruit and train other people to help reach collegians of the world with the good news of God's love and forgiveness in Christ.

Search for Staff

As in any expanding business, we needed new personnel. We needed dedicated, qualified staff who could articulate their faith; and we needed many of them. I assumed that they would be available by the hundreds. The standards we established were high, of necessity. The first requirement for potential staff was that they be fruitful in their witness for Christ; second, that they be seminary graduates; and third, that they be sympathetic with what we were attempting to accomplish in winning, building and sending men to help evangelize the world for our Savior. Vonette and I prayed much about the urgency to expand to other campuses.

Finally, it was agreed that she would remain in charge of the work at UCLA while I went from campus to campus on a recruiting tour which took me to many of the leading Christian schools and seminaries of the nation, looking for new staff people.

Imagine my disappointment when I discovered that in those days there were just not many individuals, with or without degrees, who were fruitful for Christ and available. And there were practically none with bachelor of divinity degrees who were effective in their witness for Christ and who wanted to be a part of our ministry. Consequently, we were forced to change the requirements for our staff. We concluded that we would accept for campus staff those with college degrees who were otherwise qualified and who had teachable spirits and a willingness to learn how to introduce others to Christ.

New Recruits

After considerable recruiting, we did find six choice people. Two of them, Dan Fuller and Calvin Herriott, had been fellow seminarians and had just recently graduated. There were also Roe Brooks, a seminarian in his middle year; Gordon Klenck, who was just graduating from college; and Roger Aiken and Wayne Arolla, both of whom had college degrees.

Gordon Klenck was the first of these staff members to arrive in Los Angeles. He still needed to complete one

course, which he was doing by correspondence, before
he would receive his coveted degree. I had interviewed
him on campus and was impressed with his sincerity
and his dedication to Christ, though he did look extremely young. He was actually 20 years old but didn't
look a day over 17.

Somehow in our correspondence we had failed to give
him our telephone number and our home address. He
had only a post office box number for Campus Crusade.
Thus, when he arrived in Los Angeles, he didn't know
how to get in touch with us. We were still such a small
organization that we had not even listed Campus
Crusade in the telephone directory. Our dining room
was our office, and our dining room table doubled as
my desk. So Gordon checked in at the YMCA and mailed
a card to us, saying that we could find him there. He
told us that if he was not in the "Y," he would be in the
library completing his correspondence course. Following
his instructions, when we could not locate him at the
"Y," we proceeded to the library, where we spotted him
immediately in the main reading room.

Gordon returned home with us, and as soon as we
had walked into the house he asked for a card table,
insisting that he must finish his correspondence course
before we began our staff training. He must have sensed
that he would never get back to his own work once we
began to train him for staff. As he set his typewriter on
the card table and continued his studies, I remember
Vonette commenting to me, as she noted his youthful
appearance, "Do you expect to change the world with
people like that?" I am sure that Gordon must have
looked at us and wondered at the same time if he hadn't
made a serious mistake in coming to help us!

Family Atmosphere

Roe Brooks was the next to join us around the family
table. "Family" is the right word to use, because we were

a family, not only a family in Christ, but also a family in experience. We ate together and we shared together; and our love for each other was very real. Vonette tried to cook for all of us and was never sure how many guests there would be for dinner. But somehow we managed, cutting pork chops in two or adding a can of soup to the stew. Amazingly, no one ever seemed to go away hungry.

Among other things, since we held so many meetings in fraternities, sororities and dormitories, it was important that all of us observe proper etiquette, be well-mannered and understand proper eating procedures. Therefore, Vonette and I began to conduct a training course for the staff. Vonette was the chief drill instructor, and we had some very profitable (and often humorous) times together.

From the very beginning of Campus Crusade we have strongly emphasized the Lordship of Christ, assurance of salvation and the importance of the ministry of the Holy Spirit — how to appropriate by faith His power for a holy life and fruitful witness. We have also considered it very important that each staff member understand how to communicate his faith in Christ to the student world in the most effective way possible. So we began to explore together ways to accomplish these objectives. During that first summer, Vonette and I spent several weeks giving these young men intensive training, the pattern of which has been amplified and developed throughout the succeeding years.

In the fall of 1952, we established the ministry on additional campuses, including San Diego State, University of Southern California, University of California at Berkeley, Oregon State and the University of Washington.

Staff members were to be paid a salary of $100 a month for nine months only. During the other three months, they would receive no remuneration at all. Obviously,

they had not come because of a large salary, but because
they wanted to be part of something bigger than themselves; they wanted to help change the world. For the
first several years, Vonette and I received no remuneration from Campus Crusade; instead, we were giving of
our finances to help accelerate and expand the ministry.

New Housing

There were many opportunities to trust the Lord. One
day a wire came from Brazil from the owners of the home
we had leased for a year, stating that even though only
six months had passed, they were ready to return home.
Would we be willing to relinquish the house? As I was
sitting at the table reading the wire, the telephone rang.
Dr. J. Edwin Orr, internationally-known evangelist and
author, was calling to ask if I knew of anyone who would
be interested in living in his home during the next year
while he would be on worldwide evangelistic tours. It
just happened that I did know someone! We made Dr.
Orr's house our headquarters for three semesters, and
although it was two miles from campus, it proved to be
ideal for the next phase of our UCLA ministry.

But as we continued to hold many fraternity, sorority
and dormitory meetings, confronting thousands of students on several campuses with the claims of Christ,
many were responding. Once again we were pressed for
space.

Day after day, on my way to the campus, I passed a
large home of Moorish castle-style architecture with a
"For Sale" sign on the lawn. This home happened to be
located in the famous Bel-Air district of Westwood Village
directly across Sunset Boulevard from the UCLA campus.
I had promised Vonette when we were married that one
day we would live in fabulous Bel-Air, so I was tempted
again and again to stop and inquire about it. However,
I rejected the idea as being a personal, selfish desire until
one day I became convinced that perhaps God did want

us to acquire this property, inasmuch as it was located only about three minutes from the heart of the UCLA campus. I decided to stop and investigate the property. The price was far more than we could afford, so I decided to put the idea out of my mind.

Help From Dr. Mears

However, shortly after my conversation with the owner, our good friend, Dr. Henrietta Mears, learned of our interest in the property and told us that she had been interested in and had actually negotiated for the purchase of the house some years previously. Now, she would like to purchase the house, provided we would come to live with her, carrying our share of the expenses, of course. She explained that since the recent death of her sister, Margaret, with whom she had lived for many years in a large, two-story home near the UCLA campus, her house was much too big for her alone. Dr. Mears and Vonette accompanied me as I visited the "castle" again, and we unanimously agreed that this would be ideal for all of us — for Dr. Mears, for Vonette and me, and for the ministry of Campus Crusade. The house was large and so designed that we all had our privacy, yet could be together for our meals and whenever else we wished. Once again, God had provided for our needs!

The house was purchased, and soon we were happily and comfortably established in our new home and head-quarters. Within days, students were pouring into 110 Stone Canyon Road. As many as 300 students could be packed into the spacious rooms with all of the furniture pushed aside. Many students were introduced to Christ in our various meetings and especially in the little prayer room off the foyer.

Sharing the Bel-Air home with Dr. Mears was made all the more meaningful to us because she had played such an important role in introducing both Vonette and me to Christ.

Perhaps I should elaborate a bit more about Dr. Mears and the part she played in my life. Apart from my mother's life and prayers, Dr. Mears, more than any other person, was responsible for my becoming a Christian. Also, except for her, Vonette may never have taken that spiritual step through which I have had the benefit of her love, counsel and encouragement through the rich, exciting and fruitful years of this ministry.

Vonette and I grew up in the same little Oklahoma town, Coweta, a wonderful community of approximately 1,500 people. She was most attractive, intelligent and personable. She came from a fine family, and I was much impressed with her. She was also very active in the church, and I assumed that she was a vital Christian.

Decision to Enter Seminary

However, since she was four years younger than I, I had never had any romantic interest in her until I moved away and was established in business in Los Angeles. Then, through a series of rather unusual experiences, I got in touch with her, fell in love, proposed, and before I knew it, we were planning the wedding date. Yet, there was one thing that bothered me: the question of her dedication to the Lord. I had decided to enter seminary, and I remember a trip that I made to Oklahoma en route to Princeton Theological Seminary in the fall of 1946 in order to discuss this with her.

During our time together, I made the statement that God would have to come first in our marriage, and this annoyed Vonette. "I'm not sure that's right. I think a man's family should be his first concern," she bristled. I began to mount an argument but then dropped it, thinking that there would be plenty of time to iron out this difference later.

In the fall of 1947, I transferred from Princeton to Fuller Theological Seminary in California — in order to be closer to my business (a fancy food line called Bright's

California Confections) — and was proceeding toward a degree when the matter of Vonette's personal relationship with Christ began to trouble me again. I became increasingly concerned for her spirituality. Yet I was a young Christian and too immature to help her because of our emotional involvement.

Not a Christian

By this time, we had been engaged for more than two years, but a gnawing question persisted in my mind: Was it true, as I had originally been impressed to believe, that God had chosen Vonette to be my wife? If God rules in the affairs of men and nations, and not even a sparrow falls to the ground without His knowledge, it seemed to me that God does have one particular mate for us. Although I had dated many girls prior to our engagement and had been infatuated with some, I had never proposed to anyone else. I had been impressed, I felt, by the Lord and was confident even before our first date that Vonette was the one with whom I was to share my life and my ministry for Christ. Yet, since my proposal and her acceptance, we had both become aware that she was not a Christian. Since she had never received Christ as her Savior, she could not possibly share my vision and concern about introducing others to Christ.

This was one of the greatest conflicts of my life. What was I to do? I had committed my life to Christ and His service. My one great desire was to live and, if need be, die for Him. Now I was in love with and engaged to a girl who, though a good church member, was not even a Christian. Obviously, we could not marry if she did not become a Christian, and yet, I had been so sure. This conflict continued to persist until we decided that perhaps we should explore the possibility that God might have other plans for us. So we both began to date other people. I dated girls who were vitally interested in living for Christ; Vonette, I suppose, dated fellows who were less interested in the Lord. But we kept in touch through frequent letters and telephone calls from Los Angeles to Denton, Tex., where she was attending college.

California Visit

Finally, the day of graduation came for Vonette, and she received her degree in home economics from Texas Women's University. I suggested that she visit her brother, who lived in southern California. She apparently thought this was a good idea, a sort of do-or-die time when we would decide either yes or no. Vonette, as she later told me, confided in a girlfriend before she left college, "I am either going to rescue him from this religious fanaticism or come back without a ring." She did neither.

While in California, Vonette went with me to a meeting of several hundred students at a College Briefing Conference at Forest Home, the famous conference center for Christian leadership established by Dr. Mears. Even though I had been able to help many others find Christ, I felt inadequate in introducing Vonette to Him. Someone else would have to help me, and Dr. Mears was the logical choice. She had counseled with thousands of young people and knew how to communicate with individuals with inquiring and scientific minds.

By this time, Vonette had begun to doubt the Bible and even the existence of God, so I felt that she needed help from someone who knew more than I. Also, because of the emotional involvement, I was afraid that I might be able to get from her a verbal commitment to Christ but not a commitment of the will to Him. She might say yes to Christ with her lips in order to please me and not mean it in her heart.

We arrived at the beautiful mountain setting where thousands of lives had been changed by the power of Christ. Vonette could not help but be impressed with so many vibrant lives. She liked the quality of life they possessed but was bewildered by their expressions of faith. After a couple of days, she decided that they were enthusiastic about Christianity just because it was so new to them. After all, she had been reared in the church and did not see anything about Christianity to get excited about. She thought their enthusiasm would soon wear off. She did not want to stand in my way and suggested that since she felt this would not work for her perhaps we should break our engagement. It was then that I asked her to talk to Dr. Mears, who had played such an important role in my own spiritual birth and growth.

Joyful Reunion

While Dr. Mears and Vonette talked, I paced back and forth outside the cottage, praying. Time dragged — 15 minutes, an hour and more. Suddenly the door burst open, and Vonette came bounding into my arms. There were tears of joy on her cheeks and an indescribable look of joy on her face. She did not need to say a word. I knew what had happened, and tears of gratitude filled my eyes, too.

Vonette later wrote her impressions of that day:

> Dr. Mears was one of the most vibrant, enthusiastic personalities that I had ever met. She was waiting for me, and the entire conference staff, without my knowledge, had been praying for my conversion. Dr. Mears explained that she had taught chemistry in Minneapolis, and that she could understand how I was thinking. (I had minored in chemistry in college, and everything had to be practical and workable to me. This was one of the reasons I had questioned the validity of Christianity.) As she explained simply to me from God's Word how I could be sure that I knew God, she used terminology very familiar to me. She explained that, just as a person going into a chemistry laboratory experiment follows the table of chemical valence, so it is possible for a person to enter God's spiritual laboratory and follow His formula of knowing Him and following Him.
>
> During the next hour, she lovingly proceeded to explain to me who Christ is and how I could know Him personally. "Dr.

Mears," I said, "if Jesus Christ is the way, then how do I meet Him?" Dr. Mears responded, "In Revelation 3:20, Christ says, 'Behold, I stand at the door and knock; if any one hears My voice and opens the door, I will come in to him, and will dine with him, and he with Me.' Receiving Christ is simply a matter of turning your life — your will, your emotions, your intellect — completely over to Him. John, chapter 1, verse 12, says, 'But as many as received Him, to them He gave the right to become children of God, even to those who believe in His name.'"

When Dr. Mears finished, I thought, "If what she tells me is absolutely true, I have nothing to lose and everything to gain." I bowed my head and prayed. I asked Christ to come into my heart. And at that moment, as I look back, my life began to change. God became a reality in my life. For the first time I was ready to trust Him. I became aware that my prayers were getting beyond the ceiling. I found that I had control of areas of my life that I had not been able to control before. No longer did I have to try to love people. There just seemed to be a love that flowed from within that I did not have to create. God had added a new dimension to my life, and I found myself becoming as enthusiastic as Bill, Dr. Mears and other students were, and eager as they were to share Christ with others.

Soon after the purchase of our present headquarters at Arrowhead Springs, Calif., Dr. Mears came to see the property and participated in our first institute by offering a special prayer of dedication to the Lord for us and for Arrowhead Springs. This was especially meaningful to us because of the important role which she has played in our personal lives and in the ministry of Campus Crusade. Since Vonette and I had shared her home in Bel-Air for 10 years, both as our own home and as a headquarters and meeting place for our campus ministry at UCLA, and since she was now prepared to retire from her ministry with the First Presbyterian Church of Hollywood as director of Christian education, we invited her to come to live with us at Arrowhead Springs. This she was prayerfully considering when the Lord chose to take her home — a great loss to us and to the cause of Christ, yet we know that He does all things well and our confidence is in Him. Multitudes from around the world have been spiritually blessed and have benefited, even as we have, through the great ministry of Henrietta Mears.

CHAPTER FOUR

Moving Out

From UCLA, our training headquarters was moved to Minnesota. In the fall of 1956, a long-distance call came from Mound, Minn., from Bill Greig, chairman of the Midwest Keswick. He wondered if Campus Crusade would be interested in receiving a gift of a five-acre tract of land in Mound, on the shore of beautiful Lake Minnetonka. Since his group could no longer use the property, they were looking for an organization that would utilize it effectively for the glory of God. "Come out and look it over," Bill said. "If it fits your needs, it's yours."

I expressed gratitude for the offer, but only when I saw the site did I fully appreciate the gift. Though the buildings were old and mostly run down and there was only a rough foundation for a new chapel-dormitory building, the place offered great promise. It was a breathtakingly beautiful site. I knew it would be ideal for a training center for our staff and students, so we gratefully accepted title to it. In the summer of 1958, we completed a beautiful chapel and dormitory combination which, together with existing facilities which we had also remodeled, enabled us to train approximately 150 people at one time.

That first summer we had that number and more. We also had our troubles trying to get the buildings completed. Carpenters, masons and electricians were everywhere. The staff and local volunteers were still painting and building partitions in the dormitories when the students arrived. As a matter of fact, the students joined with the staff in finishing the job. There were problems, too; more than I care to remember. But even these problems served to draw us closer together, so great was the challenge and excitement of moving into our beautiful new training center.

A Successful Pitch

One of our speakers for staff training that summer was a Christian layman who was an outstanding sales consultant, a man who had taught thousands of salesmen how to sell. One of the main points of one of his addresses was that to be a successful salesman a man must have a pitch. In other words, a man who is a good automobile salesman tells every potential customer basically the same things, and the better he communicates, the more successful he is as a salesman. But the danger, he explained, is that when a man becomes weary of hearing himself make the same presentation, he develops presentation fatigue. When this happens, he often changes the message and loses his effectiveness.

Zeroing In

He compared the witnessing Christian to the secular salesman. To be effective in our ministry for Christ, we must have, in his words, "a spiritual pitch." He illustrated his remarks by telling how several well-known Christians had their own special pitch. He spoke of a famous minister who always said basically the same thing; no matter what the problem, his emphasis was the same. He told of a woman, an outstanding Christian leader, who always prescribed the same spiritual solution for whatever problem was presented. He cited successful evangelists who always preached the same basic message under different titles. Then he zeroed in on me and said, "Bill Bright, who works with students and professors and outstanding business executives, as well as with prisoners and men on Skid Row, thinks that he has a special message for each of them. But the fact of the

matter is, though I have never heard him speak or counsel, I would be willing to wager that he has only one
pitch. Basically, he tells them all the same thing." To say
that I objected to such a suggestion is to put it mildly.
The very thought that a man needed to resort to what I
considered Madison Avenue techniques to do the
spiritual work of God was repugnant and offensive to
me.

The longer he spoke, the more distressed I became. I
resented anyone suggesting that I or anyone else who
truly desired to serve the Lord had to depend on gim-
micks, or that we were not led of the Spirit in such a
way that the Holy Spirit was able to be original through
us to the various individuals with whom we worked,
according to their various needs. Furthermore, I resented
his using me as an example before the rest of the staff.

So, when it was all over, and I was licking my wounds
(the most serious of which was a lacerated ego), I began
to reflect on exactly what I shared with the various ones
with whom I worked, young or old, management or
labor, Episcopalian or Baptist, students or professors, or
the men in jails or on Skid Row. That afternoon, I wrote
down my basic presentation and, to my amazement, my
friend was right. I had been sharing fundamentally the
same thing with everyone without realizing it!

God's Plan

What I wrote that afternoon (and later polished) is
now known as "God's Plan for Your Life," from which I
later wrote "The Four Spiritual Laws." I asked each staff
member to memorize it. We all began to share this presentation in personal interviews and in various team meetings on the college campus. Because of this one type of
presentation alone, our ministry was multiplied a hundredfold during the next year.

For those who are not familiar with God's Plan, I
should explain that it is a positive, 20-minute presenta-

tion of the claims of Christ: who He is, why He came and how one can know Him personally. It does not contain any startling new truths. It is a simple statement of the gospel. However, God has used its presentation by our staff, in the power and control of the Holy Spirit, to draw countless thousands more to Himself.

God's Plan was our first written how-to evangelistic material. The how-to approach spells out the specific steps involved in a concept or activity of the Christian walk. There has been a tendency in certain academic and theological circles to play down the simple approach to living the Christian life and sharing our faith with others. "Such an approach is simplistic and anti-intellectual," some have said. It required several years and considerable front-line spiritual combat experience in my work with students, professors and laymen, for certain great concepts to begin to come into focus. The longer I worked with the intelligentsia, the more I realized the necessity of developing simple how-to's for the Christian life.

Need for How-to's

For five years, shortly after I became a Christian, from 1946 to 1951, I studied in two theological seminaries under some of the greatest scholars of the Christian world, to whom I shall always be indebted. I learned many things about the Christian life. But like many other seminarians — and other Christians, for that matter — I was unable to put together the pieces of the spiritual jigsaw puzzle. I did not know the how-to's of the Christian life.

As Campus Crusade grew and how-to materials were developed, we found that the 20th century counterpart of "the masses who heard Jesus gladly" responds with great joy and enthusiasm to our presentation of certain how-to's (or "transferable concepts").

Four Spiritual Laws

Though we had found the 20-minute presentation of God's Plan to be extremely effective, we realized that we needed a much shorter version of the gospel in order to communicate quickly, clearly and simply to those whose hearts were already prepared to receive Christ. I prepared a condensed outline of God's Plan, complete with Scripture verses and diagrams and asked the staff to memorize it. For several years, we wrote it out as we were sharing Christ in witnessing experiences. Then, as more and more people became involved in the training program of Campus Crusade, it became apparent that we needed to make the Four Sprirtual Laws presentation available in printed form to insure faithfulness to the content and uniformity of presentation. Thus, the booklet was born.

As the name suggests, there are four basic truths to the Four Spiritual Laws: (1) God loves you and offers a wonderful plan for your life. (2) Man is sinful and separated from God, thus he cannot know and experience God's love and plan for his life. (3) Jesus Christ is God's only provision for man's sin. Through Him you can know and experience God's love and plan for your life. (4) We must individually receive Jesus Christ as Savior and Lord; then we can know and experience God's love and plan for our lives.

Originally our first law emphasized man's sin. but the Lord impressed me to emphasize God's love. This change was made just before we went to press. I had done my final editing and had left Vonette and the girls to finish the typing. As I had been traveling a great deal and it was quite late, I had gone upstairs to bed. In fact, I was in bed just at the point of going to sleep, when suddenly there came clear as a bell to my conscious mind the fact that there was something wrong about starting the Four Laws on the negative note of man's sinfulness.

Last-minute Revision

Why not start where God starts, with His love? I had been drawn to Christ originally because I was overwhelmed with God's love. The love of God had been the basis for my presentation of the gospel ever since I had become a Christian. I wanted everyone to know how much God loves him and that God offers a wonderful plan for the life of everyone who will accept His plan. I felt that few people would say "No" to Christ if they truly understood how much He loves them and how great is His concern for them.

So, I got out of bed, went to the head of the stairs and called down to Vonette and the girls to revise the presentation so that the first law would be, "God loves you and has a wonderful plan for your life," instead of "You are a sinner and separated from God." We moved the statement of the fact of man's sin and separation from God, making it Law Two. Thus, the Four Spiritual Laws started with the positive note of God's love and plan.

Some time later, one of the girls said to me, "I was so distressed over your change in the presentation that I wept that night. I was afraid that you were beginning to dilute the gospel and that you were no longer faithful to the Lord, because you placed such a strong emphasis on the love of God rather than on man's sin. Now in retrospect, I realize of course that this is one of the greatest things that has ever happened to the Campus Crusade ministry." Now many millions of people all over the world are being told, through the presentation of the Four Spiritual Laws, that God loves them and offers a wonderful plan for their lives. At last count, more than 250 million copies have been printed in 100 major languages of the world. It is believed that many millions have received Christ as a result of the Four Spiritual Laws.

Each of these four laws is illustrated by portions of
Scripture and diagrams. We have discovered that most
people believe the first three laws. However, many
people need counsel and assistance in regard to the
fourth law. Though most people believe that Jesus Christ
is the Son of God and realize their need of Him as Savior,
they do not know what to do about it. So, the simple
presentation of the Four Spiritual Laws helps honest in-
quirers, which most people are, to know what to do.

Impact of the Booklet

This little booklet is so simple that one marvels at its
effectiveness. I could tell hundreds of stories — thrilling
stories — of how God has used it to reach people who
have not responded to previous presentations. I think,
for example, of an assistant minister whose senior pastor
had come to Arrowhead Springs for training. The senior
pastor was very excited about the Four Spiritual Laws
presentation. He went back to share his enthusiasm with
his church and with his assistant minister.

The assistant minister was turned off by the Four
Spiritual Laws booklet. He had a dislike for tracts, and
this looked like just another tract to him. He tossed the
booklet aside on his desk.

A few days later a woman who was a city official came
by to inspect the facilities of the church plant. As the
woman was about to leave following the inspection tour,
it suddenly occurred to the man that he had not talked
to her about Christ. He looked around quickly, and the
only thing he saw was this little Four Spiritual Laws
booklet, which he had tossed aside in disgust some days
previously and had not bothered to read. He reached
for the booklet to give it to her, as the pastor had
suggested, thinking it would certainly not do her any
harm.

"Read this," he said, meaning that she should read it
when she got home. She misunderstood, however, and

began to read it aloud in his presence. She read every word, and by the time she got through Laws One, Two and Three and began to read Law Four, tears were streaming down her cheeks. She came to the prayer and prayed aloud, leading herself to Christ.

By this time, the assistant was so overwhelmed that he vowed to go to Arrowhead Springs and to find out for himself how he could use the Four Spiritual Laws. He decided that it was far more effective than anything or any other method he had ever employed.

The Town Atheist

A missionary friend in Japan shared a heartwarming experience of his use of the Four Spiritual Laws. There was a man who was greatly admired in his home town, though he was not a Christian. In fact, he was known as the town atheist. Whenever there was any kind of evangelistic meeting in his city, the pastors, evangelists and laymen would "witness" to him, but he would never respond. My missionary friend, whose parents had been befriended by this man, felt indebted to him and was also concerned for his soul. After obtaining a Four Spiritual Laws booklet, the missionary decided to call on his friend and read it to him.

As he finished reading, he asked, "Does this make sense?"

The atheist replied in the affirmative.

"Is there anything that would keep you from receiving Christ?"

"No," was the reply.

The two men knelt together and prayed, and the "atheist" invited Jesus into his life. When they arose, my friend was rejoicing with the man, who then stunned him with this question, "Chuck, is this what you and all the other Christian leaders have been trying to tell me for years?"

When my missionary friend nodded affirmatively, the man continued, "Well, why didn't you tell me? Any man would be a fool not to receive Christ if he really understood what is involved."

Obviously, others had been trying to communicate the gospel but had been unsuccessful. The Four Spiritual Laws presentation had cut right through the barrier of skepticism and indifference so that the professing atheist got the message.

We have found that the average person does not need to be convinced that he should become a Christian; he needs, rather, to be told how to become a Christian. I should hasten to explain that it is the Holy Spirit who uses this presentation as He empowers the one giving the witness and enlightens the one who hears and responds.

There is no magic in the Four Spiritual Laws booklet. God blesses its use because it contains the distilled essence of the gospel, especially when it is used by men and women who are controlled and empowered by the Holy Spirit.

Being Filled With the Spirit

The second most important how-to in our training explains how to be filled, controlled and empowered by the Holy Spirit. Like many other sincere seekers after the "deep things of God," I had sought for many years to understand the Person and work of the Holy Spirit. For many days at a time, I had fasted and prayed in my attempt to discover new depths of meaning in my Christian experience. Though I had on numerous occasions enjoyed a wonderful fellowship with the Lord and even had several experiences when I knew the Holy Spirit had touched my life and used me, I knew nothing of how to appropriate the fullness and power of the Holy Spirit by faith, nor of how to live under His control. I made a special study of the Person and work of the Holy

Spirit, which included almost every book on the subject on which I could lay my hands. I was hungry for all that God had for me. I longed to be a man of God, whatever the cost, and I knew that this desire could be fulfilled only through the ministry of the Holy Spirit in my life.

One summer in the early years of the Campus Crusade ministry, Vonette and I were invited to spend a few days in the Newport Beach home of Dr. and Mrs. Charles Fuller. Dr. Fuller, a famous evangelist, conducted the "Old Fashioned Revival Hour" on the radio and was the founder of Fuller Theological Seminary. He and his family were very dear to us, and we accepted the invitation gratefully. Vonette and I were both very tired. Our schedule had been extremely busy and crowded, with no vacation for several years, and we could think of nothing more inviting than having a few days to sleep, lie in the sun and swim in the ocean. The midnight hour had come and gone by the time we had arrived and unpacked. Some time near one o'clock in the morning we wearily climbed into bed and fully expected to be asleep by the time the light was out.

Midnight Revelation

But God had other plans. As I turned over to go to sleep, I found my mind flooded with truths concerning the Holy Spirit. Fearful that I might forget them if I didn't write them down, I got up to look for pencil and paper and found several shirt boards. After filling the shirt boards, I found some brown wrapping paper and continued to write furiously.

That night God gave me the truths concerning the Person and work of the Holy Spirit that have been basic to the ministry of Campus Crusade through the years. This material has now been incorporated into our Bible study course, Ten Basic Steps Toward Christian Maturity, and the Transferable Concepts, which are being used by many churches and various Christian organizations around the world.

This basic and revolutionary concept of how to be filled with the Holy Spirit has been condensed into a small booklet comparable to the Four Spiritual Laws presentation and entitled, "Have You Made the Wonderful Discovery of the Spirit-filled Life?" This Holy Spirit booklet has also been printed by the tens of millions and is being used by many thousands of Christians all over the world to help lead carnal Christians into an abundant and fruitful life in the Spirit as well as to help new Christians understand their spiritual heritage in Christ. Like the Four Laws, this brief presentation of the ministry of the Holy Spirit is having revolutionary results.

CHAPTER FIVE

Arrowhead — A Fabulous Dream

By 1960 our staff numbered 109, and we were serving Christ on 40 campuses in 15 states. Furthermore, we had established ourselves in Korea and Pakistan. We had also begun a weekly radio broadcast which was carried on several local stations without any cost to Campus Crusade.

It had long since become obvious that we had outgrown our facilities at Mound, Minn., and we had begun to intensify our search for a solution to our expansion problem. We knew that we must either build or purchase larger facilities in the Lake Minnetonka region, or find more adequate facilities elsewhere. It was then that word came from a long-time friend, George Rowan, president of the R. A. Rowan Company in Los Angeles, that the famous Arrowhead Springs Hotel and Spa which had been closed most of the time for four years was for sale at "a greatly reduced price."

I agreed to look at Arrowhead Springs in the foothills above San Bernardino, Calif., assuming that this beautiful hotel would have deteriorated considerably from the plush days when it was hosting some of the biggest names in the entertainment and business world. To my surprise, it was all in amazingly good condition. Except for a little peeling paint on the outside of the six-story building, there seemed to be little wrong with it. One could not haggle too much over a little paint!

"This is a fabulous place, and it would be an ideal headquarters and training center for us," I told George, "but I am sure that it is far beyond our means. What is the lowest price the owner would take?"

Two Million Dollar Price Tag

"He is asking two million, firm," George replied. I swallowed hard. This was an incredible amount for our organization, which had never had an extra dollar in its 10 years of existence. Now, even though we had expanded to the point that we had to have more and larger facilities, I could not truthfully conceive of any way that we could raise the kind of money that would be needed to make such a large purchase.

The two million dollar figure was a good one — only a fraction of the property's true worth. It had been appraised at $6,700,000. The beds were even made; spare linens were in the closets; china, silverware and cooking utensils (about $450,000 in inventory) were ready and waiting for guests. "All we would have to do would be to move in," I thought. The place didn't look as though it had been closed most of the time for four years.

Meanwhile, I did a little research and learned several interesting things about the famous resort. For example, I learned that various Indian tribes had come to this spot through centuries, bringing their sick and wounded for healing in the natural hot mineral springs. They called the place "holy land," and all weapons of warfare were laid aside here.

The first hotel and spa was built on the property in 1854 by Dr. David Noble Smith and was widely advertised as a health resort. When the original hotel was destroyed by fire, two others followed.

They too, in turn, were destroyed by fire, and the present structure of concrete and steel was built in 1939, financed by a group of Hollywood film stars. It opened in December of that year. Present for the gala opening were some of the biggest names in Hollywood and the business world. Rudy Vallee, Al Jolson and Judy Garland entertained on that first night.

Arrowhead Springs became a popular retreat for the

movie colony and for top executives in the business world. Only a short distance from the heart of Los Angeles, world-famous movie stars streamed toward Arrowhead Springs for relaxation and revelry.

White Elephant

However, when transportation developed to the point that the stars could easily travel further afield, they were attracted to Las Vegas and Palm Springs, and Arrowhead Springs turned into something of a white elephant. Several different owners tried to restore the property to the status it had once enjoyed but without noticeable success. Finally, Benjamin Swig, owner of the Fairmont Hotel in San Francisco and the historic Mission Inn in Riverside, Calif., acquired it from the Hilton Foundation. He operated it briefly before concluding, as had his predecessors, that it had limited profit potential, and then he closed it down. Though different groups tried to purchase it from Mr. Swig, and one or two parties used it for a brief time, it was closed more than it was open during the approximately four years before my visit.

I was immediately enchanted by the remoteness and beauty of the property. Following a winding road into the hills above San Bernardino, I was reeling with the grandeur of this famous place before I ever stepped out of Mr. Rowan's automobile. I was even more impressed as I walked about the spacious grounds and examined the many buildings.

Below me, a couple of miles away, spread the populated valley, feverishly at work — industry clanging and pounding, cars and trucks rumbling in every direction. But all I could hear was the song of birds, the rustle of date palm leaves as the wind filtered gently through them and the sound of rushing water from a stream as it made its way from many artesian springs, tumbling wildly down over the rocks into Strawberry Canyon. But even these sounds were muted. In a way, an ethereal quality permeated the place, and more than once I found myself almost whispering to Mr. Rowan as we walked the grounds, 1,735 acres in all. There were 10 private bungalows, dormitory facilities for several hundred, an auditorium which could accommodate 700 people, a recreation house, four tennis courts, a stable, two big swimming pools and the 136-room, six-story, concrete and steel hotel. Without too much imagination, I could see as many as a thousand people here at one time. This was breathtaking in comparison to Mound, where approximately 150 people were all we could crowd in at one time, even with wall-to-wall people.

Talking With the Lord

Could this be the answer to our dilemma — our need for larger training facilities? I wondered. Constrained to be alone to talk with the Lord, I asked Mr. Rowan and the caretaker of Arrowhead to excuse me while I went into the hotel.

Past the unattended reception desk, through the empty lobby, out into the glass-enclosed Wahni Room I moved, the click of my shoes echoing as I walked. There was a shiny bar, empty of customers. Behind it the glasses were neatly stacked, awaiting business. The shelves, where a goodly supply of bottles once stood, were now empty. Tables and chairs were grouped in intimate clusters so that holiday visitors could look out on the city, which I could imagine would be a starry wonder at night. But it was broad daylight at that moment, and I had not come there for a drink or to see the panoramic view, but to share with the Lord the dream that was working overtime in my head.

Falling to my knees, I bowed my head and began praying and listening, "I am overwhelmed, Lord. This place is so big and beautiful. True, we've been asking You to direct us to new facilities, the best place in the country, and I know that You will; but if this is it, where

ill we get two million dollars to buy it? It seems too
npossible to even consider. Yet I keep hearing in my
eart Your voice, and it suggests that this is the place
ou have chosen for us. If it is, then You are going to
ave to make it crystal clear. How can I know for sure?"

Then, though not in an audible voice, God spoke to
ie as clearly as if there had been a public address system
 the room. Unmistakably I heard Him say, "I have been
iving this for Campus Crusade. I want you to have it,
id I will supply the funds to pay for it."

With tears running down my face, I said, "God, I don't
how how You intend to work this miracle, but I know
ou can, and I thank You for this gift. I claim this property
 Your name."

CHAPTER SIX

Story of a Miracle

I came away from that memorable visit to Arrowhead Springs convinced that Campus Crusade would one day occupy those beautiful facilities. The impression that God wanted this facility for Campus Crusade was so real that almost every day I found myself expecting a telephone call from some person saying that he had heard about our interest in Arrowhead and that he would purchase it for us.

I felt certain the Lord did not want me to write letters inviting people to invest, believing instead that God had a plan already working. Vonette and I and other members of the Campus Crusade staff purposely limited our concern to prayer. For 14 months, we prayed that if God wanted us to have Arrowhead Springs, He would provide the funds in some supernatural or unusual way.

Increasingly, I knew that God wanted us to move to Arrowhead, though there was no tangible evidence of that fact. That is not to say that our faith never wavered. Sometimes the thought came, "What if someone else buys the property?" Then deep down in my heart I knew that it would eventually be ours. Still, I frequently prayed that God would not let us have Arrowhead Springs unless it was His perfect will for us. I well knew that unless this was truly God's will, to become involved in raising money for such a big project could well sabotage our spiritual ministry and destroy Campus Crusade in the process.

While we were praying, we were also working. Among other things, we did a feasibility study of the property, a careful cost analysis of what was involved in operating the grounds, figuring the cost of maintenance and repairs and the operation of the various facilities. After several weeks of careful analysis, various factors convinced us that if money could be raised for the capital investment, we could carry the load and operate in the black from the very beginning. The factors included such items as our office rental in Los Angeles, our expenses for the various training conference grounds which we rented from time to time, and the fact that the headquarters staff would be living on the Arrowhead Springs campus and thus would pay rent there. Our conviction was strengthened by a dedicated staff willing to work long hours and without thought of personal remuneration or glory.

Negotiations Begin

Then it happened. The telephone rang. Henry Hanson, the father of two students who had been influenced for Christ through our ministry, was on the line. Through him negotiations were begun with the owner, Benjamin Swig. Mr. Swig proved to be most cooperative, helpful and generous.

Though we had not asked for financial help from our supporters during the 14 months of waiting and praying, I now felt, after my conversation with Mr. Swig, that the Lord wanted me to share this opportunity with some of my close friends. Outstandingly successful men who were also dedicated to Christ and vitally interested in the ministry of Campus Crusade came to look over the property and talk with me. Many of our close friends, however, were far from being of one mind concerning the wisdom of making the purchase. Some were convinced that it would be a foolhardy move and poor stewardship of the Lord's money, while others believed that Campus Crusade needed training facilities such as Arrowhead Springs would supply. On the basis of God's previous blessing on the ministry, this was another opportunity for us to trust Him for even greater things. A few individuals supported their convictions with offers to help make the down payment.

Property Purchased

After careful and prayerful consideration of loans and gifts, the board of directors, acting upon the advice of these men who were interested in helping us, advised us to make an offer to Mr. Swig. The offer was a $15,000 deposit toward a two million dollar purchase price, with an additional $130,000 to be paid within 30 days after we signed the contract. Amazingly, the offer was accepted. With an empty bank book we were buying a two million dollar property! It was the greatest act of faith I had ever seen or in which I had ever had a part. We borrowed the $15,000 needed for the deposit, and on the weekend of December 1, 1962, Campus Crusade for Christ International moved from its Westwood headquarters in Los Angeles to Arrowhead Springs.

We still did not have the necessary $130,000 for the next payment, but several friends had agreed to help and, interpreting this as God's will, we took the first step by advancing the $15,000 as a deposit. Thirty days later at the last minute an additional $130,000 had been given by interested friends. I dashed off to San Francisco to see Mr. Swig and make the payment to consummate the purchase. The monthly payment schedule was a very stiff one, and there followed a series of financial cliff-hanging experiences that forced us to depend wholly upon the Lord. Every financial move was a precarious one for months — indeed, for several years. God used the faith, work and prayer of a dedicated staff to make Arrowhead Springs possible.

Lives Transformed

From the start, God blessed and used the headquarters in a spiritual way that surpassed all our expectations. Hundreds of young men and women, and adults as well, came to Arrowhead for training that first year, and their lives were transformed. We had the assurance that the day would come when God would send a thousand people per week to Arrowhead Springs for training. That goal was soon exceeded, and so many staff, students and laymen began to respond to our training that scores of conferences are now held each year not only at Arrowhead but also on university campuses, in conference facilities and in hotels across America.

The decision to acquire Arrowhead Springs as our international headquarters and institute for evangelism for our worldwide ministry was to be one of the most significant ones that we had ever made.

When Arlis Priest, outstanding Phoenix businessman, visited Arrowhead prior to its purchase, he volunteered, "If God should make this property available to you, I would like to give my services for one year without salary to help you get the headquarters operating efficiently." His life had been greatly affected in one of our day-long institutes in Phoenix, and this was his way of thanking us. Imagine his surprise a few weeks later when I took him up on the offer. "How soon can you come?" I asked over the phone. "We are now ready to move to Arrowhead Springs, and we need a manager."

"I'll call you back later today and give you an answer," he said. Within a matter of days he was with us; God used him mightily to help organize the offices and get the long-closed facilities operating efficiently. I do not know how we would have done it without him and his lovely wife, Nadine, who was not only a great help herself but also was willing for Arlis to work day and night to help us get into operation. The dedication of the entire headquarters staff was a joy to behold. A normal day ran 10, 12, 15 hours — all with a joyful spirit — as we all were responsible for many different jobs.

Dedication Service

May 17, 1963, found several hundred friends of Campus Crusade gathered for our dedication of Arrowhead Springs as our international headquarters and conference center. Dr. Walter Judd brought the dedication address, which was one of his characteristically inspiring and challenging messages. The mayor and many outstanding local officials were present. The mayor stated, "The finest thing that has ever happened to the city of San Bernardino is the coming of Campus Crusade for Christ to Arrowhead Springs." Participating in the program were Dr. Bob Pierce, president of World Vision; Dr. Dick Hillis, president of Overseas Crusade; the Rev. Armin Gesswein, director of Pastors' Revival Fellowship; Dr. Walter Smyth, vice-president of the Billy Graham Evangelistic Association; Dr. Carlton Booth, professor of evangelism, Fuller Theological Seminary; Dr. Roger Voskyle, president of Westmont College; and Dr. John MacArthur, Sr., leading evangelist and radio pastor.

Also present at the dedication service that day were Mr. and Mrs. Guy F. Atkinson. Mr. Atkinson was one of the world's leading builders of roads, dams, bridges and other multimillion dollar construction projects. He was then 89 years of age — sharp, alert and very astute — and had come primarily to hear Dr. Judd. He inquired what we planned to do with the property and asked more questions about the ministry of Campus Crusade at Arrowhead Springs than any group of people had ever asked me in its history.

Some months later he expressed interest in helping, but before he did anything he wanted to send his attorney to look over our financial records and our corporation structure, including the bylaws. Of course we were very happy to have him do this. After several days of careful study of the organizational structure, policies and financial records by himself and his attorney, Mr. Atkinson announced that he would like to give $300,000 if we would raise the balance of the then $1,570,000 still due on the two million dollar purchase. This was an exciting challenge. He gave us exactly one year to raise that amount, and we set forth with great enthusiasm and determination to raise a sum so great that I could hardly even comprehend the amount. It might as well have been a billion dollars. Yet, we were confident that God would help us.

Slow Progress

With the passing of the months, however, it seemed that we were not going to be able to reach our goal of $1,570,000 to qualify for Mr. Atkinson's $300,000 pledge. We had an additional challenge of an offer from Mr. Swig to discount $100,000 from the balance due, plus a savings of $120,000 in interest. All this meant, with Mr. Atkinson's pledge of $300,000, a total gift and savings of $520,000. But we were becoming aware of the fact that we were faced with an impossible task. We asked Mr. Atkinson if he would still be willing to pledge his $300,000 if we raised part of the balance by selling some of the land. He agreed to do this with the understanding that we would not sell more than 400 acres of our 1,735-acre total.

Arlis Priest and I had interested a group of 20 laymen in the idea of purchasing one million dollars worth of our land from us. It was estimated that by selling approximately 400 acres we could raise that amount. When Mr. Atkinson agreed that we could sell one million dollars worth of land and raise the balance through gifts, we took new courage and approached the deadline of June 30, 1965, with confidence. In the meantime, we were devoting considerable time to contacting potential contributors in an attempt to raise the balance.

In spite of the additional encouragement, we found that we would still fall short of the amount needed. I had made a commitment to the Lord that I would not

allow Arrowhead Springs or the raising of funds to inter-
fere with my spiritual ministry or the ministries of any
of our campus staff. In fact, none of the field staff were
ever asked to become involved in raising funds at any
time, because we felt that it was a tangible expression
of our trust in the Lord to put our spiritual ministry first.
We were confident that if we sought first the kingdom
of God, the Lord would meet our financial needs.

One Week Left

Thus, in the last week prior to the deadline, I found
myself speaking at very important conferences several
times a day and unable to make any significant contribution to the raising of funds. Dr. Raymond V. Edman,
president of Wheaton College, came to speak for an
educators' conference at the same time a Campus
Crusade student conference was in session. He shared
with Vonette and me a very meaningful verse that God
had given him that morning while he was praying for
our needs. The verse was especially appropriate: "He
that putteth his trust in Me shall possess the land, and
shall inherit My holy mountain" (Isaiah 57:13). We will
always be grateful to Dr. Edman for his special concern
and prayers for us during those urgent days of crisis, as
well as for the great ministry of his life and witness with
us.

On the evening of the deadline, I met with Arlis
Priest, just before I was to bring a message to the conference then in session. He informed me that we still needed
$33,000 and that every possible source of revenue had
been exhausted. There was nothing more, humanly
speaking, that we could do. After the completion of my
message at about 9 in the evening, I inquired again as
to our progress. Though several members of the staff
were gathering and praying, working and hoping, the
situation remained unchanged. I assumed that there was
nothing more I could do personally so I went to our

cottage, too weary to give further thought to the matter.

Deadline Approaches

I was dressing for bed when Vonette returned with the boys from a youth meeting. "All of the money must be in or you wouldn't be going to bed," she said.

I told her that was not the case, adding, "I've done all I know to do. I will have to leave the rest in the Lord's hands."

"Honey, I have never seen you give up so easily," Vonette said.

"If the miracle is going to happen, the Lord will have to do it right away," I replied.

It was then about 10 p.m., and we had two hours to go before the deadline. We had been praying for months, but as Vonette and I now knelt with our two sons, Zachary and Bradley, we prayed with a new urgency. I prayed first, then Vonette and then Zac. But it was Brad's prayer that I remember. He was only seven years old, but he spoke to the heart of the matter. "Lord, we need this money, and we ask You to send it right away."

After all of us had prayed and the boys had gone to bed, I reached for my Bible to read before turning out the light. As I did so, I saw a scrap of paper I had brought home from my office. It had memos on both sides. I had read only one side; now I saw the other side. There was a telephone number on it. Gerri von Frellick had called me the day before and had asked me to call him back. I had failed to get the message.

More Help

I checked my watch and by now it was 10:30, which meant that it was about 11:30 at his home in Denver, Colo. I debated whether I should return his call at such a late hour. "Maybe Gerri wants to help," Vonette suggested. I finally decided to call him even though it was very late. He answered the phone sleepily, and I apologized for waking him up. "How are you getting along with your fund-raising campaign?" he asked.

I told him that we had an hour and 30 minutes to go and still lacked $33,000. He said that he wanted to send us $5,000 if it would help us meet our goal and would send it the next morning. Gerri had already given generously when we first moved to Arrowhead Springs; now he was giving again. This, of course, was encouraging, and yet at that point I did not think that $5,000 was going to make much difference, but I thanked him warmly and hung up. "You were right, Vonette," I said. "He did have some money for us. Now we need only $28,000."

Property Offered

Suddenly it occurred to me that a month or so before, a businessman in Arizona had given us a piece of property not far from Denver, for which we had been offered $17,000 by a local attorney. If he would pay us $20,000 for the property, that would reduce the balance to only $8,000, and there was still a possibility that we could meet that amount. The more I thought about it the more excited I became, so I placed the call to the attorney in Colorado, who I realized was also probably in bed asleep.

Shortly the attorney was on the line. I reminded him that a month ago he had offered $17,000 for the property and that we would be willing, because of a particular need, to take $22,000 for it. He countered with $18,000 and said he would wire it the next morning. I accepted his offer. Now we were within $10,000 of our goal.

I called the switchboard at the hotel and reported the good news. I heard a big cheer when staff and friends who were waiting prayerfully and expectantly learned we were within sight of our goal.

In the meantime, members of our staff were gathered in the lobby of the hotel, praying and giving generously of their own limited funds — not because they were asked, but because they were impressed by the Lord to do so. Arlis Priest recalls that dramatic evening: "It was getting late. Nadine and I were both in bed when some of the staff began to knock at our door. This happened several times. Each time some staff member would hand me an envelope with money in it. The first few I looked at were $25, $200 and $250. A peace came over me, for I knew God was doing something special. These dedicated staff members who had hardly enough money to live on were giving the widow's mite."

Final Minutes

With less than 30 minutes before the deadline, we had $10,000 more to raise. We were all getting increasingly excited. Surely God was going to answer our prayers and meet our need.

About 15 minutes before midnight, Dr. Walter Judd, who had come to Arrowhead Springs to address one of our conferences, returned from speaking at a local medical association meeting and called to inquire as to the progress toward our goal. "Have Bill call me," he told the switchboard operator.

When I called, he said that he would like to give the last $5,000, and I should call him back if his money was needed. In the meantime, Vonette (her mind working overtime) reminded me that Al Curtis, our business manager, at my request, had put aside some months previously a $5,000 gift from Mr. Atkinson, money which had been given to be used wherever we felt it was most needed. We had agreed then that the money should be held for this very deadline in case of need. Yet, at the moment I had temporarily forgotten about it. I called Al, who had just returned to Arrowhead from Los Angeles and a futile attempt to raise funds. He verified the fact that we had $5,000. "Get it ready," I told him.

This meant that we only needed Dr. Judd's gift of

$5,000. At two minutes till midnight and our deadline, I called him to make sure that I had understood his offer. "I will pledge that amount," he repeated, and a minute later I called the hotel lobby and an anxious, waiting staff to announce that God had worked another miracle.

By this time Vonette and I and the members of the staff were so excited and filled with gratitude to the Lord that we decided to meet immediately in the International Theater to thank Him for this miracle. We quickly dressed and rushed to the hotel. The International Theater was packed to overflowing with grateful staff and friends.

For the next couple of hours we sang and worshipped the Lord. The office girls, some of them in pajamas and housecoats with their hair in rollers; faculty, who were there for an educators' conference; and other workers all came together. It was a beautiful experience, one of the highlights of my spiritual life. Never have I heard the doxology sung with such vigor. Never did the lyrics, "Praise God from whom all blessings flow. . ." hold so much meaning.

CHAPTER SEVEN

The Trial of Faith

The good news of what God had done had to be told. I could hardly wait to inform all of our friends of the miracle God had performed. Soon a letter was dispatched to thousands on our mailing list and to personal friends and supporters, telling them that the deadline had been met and that Campus Crusade had been able to pay off the total indebtedness against the Arrowhead Springs property. In part I wrote:

> Rejoice and give thanks to the Lord with us. The miracle has happened! God has answered prayer! Exactly two minutes before the June 30 deadline, at 11:58 p.m., the goal of $1,570,000 was reached which qualified us for a $300,000 pledge, and the future of Arrowhead Springs as our International Headquarters and International Institute of Evangelism was assured (sale of the land involved in the transaction is to be consummated in approximately sixty days). The details of how it happened are far more dramatic than words could ever describe. We had prayed that God would provide the needed finances in such a way that the end result would cause all men to acknowledge His supernatural provision and that all honor, glory and praise would go to Him. God has answered this prayer, for no man could have planned the final days prior to the deadline as exciting, dramatic and fruitful as He had arranged them . . .

The letter was sent, and calls and letters of congratulations came back from all over the country.

Disturbing Development

But the story was not ended. Ten days later the appraisers announced that the acreage required for the one million dollar sale of the property was approximately 120 acres more than we had thought would be needed. The 20 friends who had agreed to purchase the land were

51

going to borrow the one million dollars from an insurance company, purchase the land and later sell or develop it and give any profits to Campus Crusade. But to borrow that amount, it was necessary for the value of the land to be at least double the amount of the loan, which meant that two million dollars worth of land had to be made available to the men to secure a one million dollar loan.

When I informed Mr. Atkinson of these developments, he was disturbed. He said he wanted to see me immediately. When he arrived from his La Canada home, he reminded me, as we sat in my office, that his original agreement called for our raising in contributions and pledges the entire amount of $1,570,000 to match his contribution of $300,000 in cash. When it was discovered that we were not going to be able to raise that amount, he had agreed to our selling 400 acres of land.

"I remember when land in nearby Orange County was selling for a few dollars an acre and some of it is now selling for as much as $50,000 an acre," he said. "You would be foolish to sell at this price. Whatever you do, don't sell it. And if you do, I withdraw my pledge of $300,000." I realized that Mr. Atkinson, because of his warm friendship and interest in the ministry, was seeking to prevent us from making an unwise move. Nevertheless, this was a crushing blow, and as I took him from my office to his car, I could hardly wait to get back to my office before my emotions took charge. Back in my office, I closed the door behind me, fell on my knees and wept.

Crumbled Dreams

The miracle had become a mirage. All of our hopes and dreams had suddenly crumbled. In the attempt to meet the challenge of Mr. Atkinson's pledge, all of our fund-raising efforts were designed to raise the money for this project. Now, since we had failed to meet this goal, we were in an impossible position financially. Not only could we not write off the debt, but also we would actually lose the property unless God intervened immediately. This possibility seemed rather remote in those bleak moments of discouragement. Furthermore, I would have to write the thousands of friends who had read only a few days before that God had worked a miracle and tell them that there had been no miracle at all. There was personal humiliation involved, of course. But worse than that, the cause of Christ would suffer, and many Christians would be confused.

What was I to do? I got out my Bible and looked for help and assurance. We are admonished and assured, "God causes all things to work together for good to those who love God, to those who are called according to His purpose" (Romans 8:28). I read, "Without faith it is impossible to please Him" (Hebrews 11:26), and "The righteous man shall live by faith" (Galatians 3:11). I read a command from God which I had discovered some years before and which on various occasions had proved very meaningful to me: "In everything give thanks; for this is God's will for you in Christ Jesus" (1 Thessalonians 5:18).

"Thank You"

Since the righteous are to live by faith and since "all things work together for good to those who love God," I didn't know of a better way to demonstrate faith than to say, "Thank You." So I got back down on my knees and thanked God for what had happened. I thanked Him through my tears. I thanked Him that in His wisdom and love He knew better than I what should be done and that out of this chaos and uncertainty I knew would come a far greater miracle. There on my knees while I was giving thanks for this great disappointment, God began to give me the genuine assurance that this greater miracle really was going to happen.

Even so, the next day I began drafting the letter that

would inform our friends that "our miracle" had been only a mirage. For some reason, however, I felt strongly impressed to delay mailing the letter.

Saving the Land

A week passed. Ten days. Then Mr. Atkinson called and said that he would like to see me again. He said he had been talking to Arlis Priest and had an idea he thought might solve our problem. As soon as he arrived at Arrowhead Springs, he came directly to my office. "I would like to suggest," he said, "that Campus Crusade borrow the money as an organization from the same insurance company that had offered to loan the money to the original 20 men. Then we should invite the men who had originally agreed to purchase the land to sign the notes as guarantors. If you like this idea, I will still give Campus Crusade the $300,000 originally pledged."

I was overjoyed at his offer. This meant that we would not have to sell our prized land, which we would one day no doubt need because of our rapidly expanding training program. The 20 men agreed to this new arrangement, for they had no interest at all in promoting their own financial gain, and they signed the note. Jess Odom, the president of the insurance company, a wonderful Christian and good friend of Campus Crusade, approved the loan at the lowest legal interest rate allowable.

The second miracle proved to be greater than the first. We still saved a large portion of the interest. Mr. Swig generously discounted his note $75,000 instead of $100,000 as he had originally offered because of the lapse of time which now had taken place. So I tore up the letter of apology to our friends and supporters and in its place sent another explaining all that God had done.

I shall be forever grateful to the Lord for Mr. and Mrs. Atkinson and for their encouragement in so many ways. After Mr. Atkinson went to be with the Lord, memorial gifts from his family and friends were used to build the beautiful Guy F. Atkinson Memorial Chapel at Arrowhead Springs which has been dedicated to his memory.

Prior to and following the purchase of Arrowhead Springs, it has been our prayer that everything God would do through Campus Crusade and through our own personal lives would be characterized by the supernatural and the miraculous. We have asked Him to do things in such an unusual and wonderful way that men would have to say that He was responsible, and that they would give the glory to Him instead of to man. God has answered that prayer on many occasions.

Exhausted Water Supply

A few months after our arrival, we faced a particular crisis that demanded a miracle. I received a call early one morning from Arlis Priest, stating that our large water reservoir was exhausted, that the water had disappeared mysteriously overnight, and that now, with a large staff and student group of 450 gathered for several weeks of training, there was absolutely no water for them. When we purchased the property we had been assured that there was plenty of water, but now we discovered that there was not enough water, at least not for us. This was one of the greatest of all the crises that had arisen for us at Arrowhead Springs.

The students and staff had paid thousands of dollars to come from far distances to be present for the training, and now our only alternative would be to send them home unless God worked a miracle to supply water. To return the students' money would be financially disastrous, for we had actually anticipated the revenue of the summer in making preparations for their coming. The maintenance and repairs for the facilities and the purchase of food took all the money; there was none left with which to reimburse them. Once again we were faced with the kind of crisis that could have meant the loss of this property and quite possibly the destruction of this ministry.

My first impulse was to panic; then, remembering again the admonition to give thanks in all things as an expression of faith, I fell on my knees, saying, "Lord, thank You for this crisis. I thank You that You will again demonstrate Your power and wisdom in our behalf."

While on my knees, I felt impressed to call George Rowan, who in drilling for steam had discovered large quantities of hot water on the property, and to ask him if he had any idea of how we could convert the hot water well into drinking water. We had not used any of the hot water from the big well because we had been told that a cooling tower would cost at least $20,000; and since we didn't have even $20 extra, this expense was far beyond our capabilities.

George informed me that he did not know how to cool the water but that he would check immediately with a friend of his, the president of a large geothermal corporation, who very likely could give us the information we needed.

Cooling Tower

Within a matter of a few minutes, his friend called me and told me over the telephone how a simple, inexpensive wooden cooling tower could be built. With the most rudimentary blueprint in hand, I rushed to the maintenance department and explained how the cooling tower could be built. Immediately, several staff members and a host of other volunteers, professionals and amateurs alike, began to work. By two the next morning, cool water was running through the tower. Again God had heard our prayers.

One of the most beautiful parts of the whole experience, however, was the attitude of the staff and students about the crisis. They gathered in meetings, large and small, to thank God as an expression of their faith for this crisis in obedience to the command of 1 Thessalonians 5:18. During the next 24 hours, a most remarkable spirit of cooperation and of cheerfulness pervaded the entire campus. Individuals were going to San Bernardino to buy small jugs of water and supplying their own needs and the needs of others. It was a beautiful experience of what happens to men who trust God and of how God honors faith. What better way to demonstrate faith than to thank God for whatever He does.

Growing Faith

But these have not been the only times of testing. Such times are still frequent and almost continuous. But faith is like a muscle; it grows with exercise. The more we know of the trustworthiness and faithfulness of God, His grace, love, power and wisdom, the more we can trust Him. I think of my own faith; how, in the beginning years of the ministry, I could believe God for a few dollars and, on occasion, a few hundred. More recently I have been asking God for millions.

For example, early in the ministry I discovered one day that we had an urgent need for $485. It was a Saturday morning, and I was alone in the office. I was on my knees praying for this $485 when the mailman came knocking on the door with a registered letter. I reached the door just as he was leaving, and he said, "It's a good thing you were here, or I wouldn't have been able to leave this letter." I signed for it, went back into my office to pray, but decided I would open the letter first. Inside, I discovered a bank note for $500 sent by a friend from far off Zurich, Switzerland, whose entire family had become Christians through our ministry.

Need for $48,000

At another time, an additional $48,000 was desperately needed to meet one of our annual payments on the loan. This kind of money does not come easily. We had prayed much and worked hard to raise the money but to no avail. Our deadline was only days away when a lawyer friend who knew of our need introduced me to a friend who agreed to loan the amount needed for 60 days. I was in the lawyer's office ready to sign the necessary papers when my office called to tell me that Dean Griffith had called from Chicago and wanted me to contact him right away. Within minutes I reached him at his Chicago office. "I have been praying about your need for $48,000," he said, "and my father and I would like to send you a check for that amount today." Needless to say, I was grateful. As a matter of fact, I got down on my knees and thanked the Lord that He had answered our prayers, and then I went out to share with our friends the good news that the loan was no longer needed. I offered to pay for the costs and inconvenience involved, but my offer was refused.

The purchase of Arrowhead Springs was a giant leap of faith. This facility accommodated several times as many as could be housed at our training grounds on beautiful Lake Minnetonka in Minnesota. However, we soon found that it was not big enough. The first summer of 1963 found the big hotel and most of the other facilities filled, and by the second and third summers, we were overflowing during the summer peaks. By 1966, we knew we would have to expand our facilities. Projections indicated that we would one day be training many thousands each week during the summer months, and there was no place to train them, as present facilities were already taxed to capacity.

Facilities Expansion

What were we to do? I called together a group of outstanding businessmen, planners and builders for counsel. Norman Entwistle, our very able architect, drew up elaborate plans. One member of the board of directors agreed to chair an emergency fund-raising campaign called Operation Explosion. We needed large sums of money to provide these new facilities as well as to meet other emergency needs resulting from the rapid growth and expansion of the ministry. Warren Bradley, an outstanding Los Angeles building contractor and dedicated Christian, agreed to construct whatever facilities we chose to build without profit to himself or to his company. We were under the pressure of deadlines. If we did not start building at once, it would not be possible to complete construction in time for the summer invasion of thousands of students.

So it was decided by the committee and the board of directors, that, for emergency needs, we would build a simple, inexpensive board-and-batten frame construction with a tar paper roof. We soon discovered we were building in an area where fire insurance premiums would be extremely high, and upon the recommendation of Warren Bradley and his brother, Elmer, it was decided we would be well advised to build with slump stone and a tile roof. Norman Enwistle designed a beautiful complex of four dormitories and a dining-auditorium area that would accommodate a minimum of 480 and a maximum of 640, depending upon the number of people assigned to each room.

Though no funds were available for the construction of these buildings, the urgency of their completion was upon us, and after much prayer, we felt impressed to proceed with the building in the assurance that God would supply the funds to pay for their construction. The bulldozers had cleared the site, the foundations were being poured, and some of the walls were beginning to rise when a newcomer (who has since become a very good personal friend and strong supporter of Campus Crusade) appeared on the scene. He and Arlis Priest visited the building site, and as they surveyed the hustle and bustle of the busy scene with workmen rushing to and fro hastening the construction of these urgently needed buildings, my friend turned to Arlis and said, "Who is going to pay for these buildings?"

Funding the Program

Arlis said, "God impressed me to share this need with you."

Our friend dropped his head as if in silent prayer and meditation and then said, "I think I would like to be responsible to provide the funds for the building of these four dormitories. I need to talk with four of my associates and see if they are in agreement."

A short time later he came excitedly into my office to share his idea. He explained that he had been down to look over the site of the new Arrowhead Springs Village development and that he had felt impressed of the Lord to encourage his associates to join with him in paying for the project. "How much money will it take?" he inquired. "Approximately $550,000," I responded. "I think we can swing it," he said, "if we can work out a plan which will enable us to pay a certain amount each month over a period of years."

Soon he was on the telephone contacting his associates, and before long they were in unanimous agreement that this would be a good investment for the Lord's money which He had so graciously and so generously given them. They were being good stewards. Here they saw a chance to multiply their dollars a hundredfold so that the tens of thousands of men and women who would be trained in this beautiful new addition would join with them to help take the claims of Christ to the entire world.

Giving God the Glory

Later, I said to my friend, "What you are doing is such a challenging and inspiring example of Christian stewardship that I would like to prepare a plaque so that other friends of Campus Crusade will see what God has done through you and your associates. How would you like the plaque to read?"

Whereupon he responded, "My associates and I want to give God all the glory for the gracious way He has met our needs. Therefore, we would like the plaque to read. ARROWHEAD SPRINGS VILLAGE, DONATED BY FIVE BUSINESSMEN WHO WANT TO GIVE GOD ALL THE GLORY."

Later, a beautiful dining-auditorium building was constructed at a cost of $286,236, which amount our anonymous friends asked the Lord to enable them to underwrite as well. Thousands of students and laymen from as many as 50 countries have been trained to be disciples for the Lord Jesus Christ in these beautiful facilities.

This gift is a true example of Christian stewardship — an example to other Christians to "lay up . . . treasures in heaven, where neither moth nor rust destroys, and where thieves do not break in or steal" (Matthew 6:20).

CHAPTER EIGHT

Training: Repeating the Basics

I believe that there are three basic reasons why God has blessed the Campus Crusade ministry in such a phenomenal way: (1) dedication to exalting Jesus Christ and His cause in every circumstance; (2) a strong emphasis on the ministry of the Holy Spirit in the life of the believer; and (3) special, detailed, comprehensive training for every staff member, student and layman in how to live holy lives and share their faith in Christ with others.

The training ministry of Campus Crusade insures that the staff, students, laymen, pastors and all persons associated with the ministry receive adequate instruction in the various training programs in which they are involved. The instruction includes principles of Christian living, principles and methods of evangelism and follow-up, as well as biblical and theological training.

Importance of Repetition

In this ministry, a strong emphasis is placed on the basics, which are reviewed again and again without apology. Repetition is one of the major factors in learning.

Some time ago I had occasion to explain to our staff why we repeated the same basic messages and materials again and again as a part of our training. At the close of the meetings, one of our directors, a seminary graduate and former Presbyterian pastor, said, "I would like to share with you a good illustration to help support your emphasis on the necessity of repetition. Years ago I was a member of a good church where the pastor repeated the basic Christian doctrines several times each year, much to the benefit of us all. Recently, after nine years away, I returned for a visit and was encouraged to know that the pastor is continuing to preach and teach these same basic truths which made such an impact on my life.

"Later," he shared, "I was associated with a very scholarly minister who polished each message like a beautiful gem. He never spoke on the same subject twice. You will be interested to know that I could not tell you one thing I learned from this great, eloquent preacher, but much of what I know about Christ and the Bible I learned from my first pastor who believed in and practiced repetition."

Training Makes the Difference

We have discovered that when we truly train people, they are inspired to a height of dedication that one cannot possibly experience through inspiration alone. It is my strong conviction that true inspiration is the result of a very strong training program. From the inception of this ministry, our major thrusts have been to first build disciples and then, after training, to send them forth for Christ. Even in a conference in which a number of non-Christians are present, if the majority of those present are Christians, almost all of our messages are designed to build the Christian in the faith and challenge him to become a disciple. We train defeated, discouraged, unfruitful Christians to become spiritual, joyful, fruitful Christians, teaching them the difference between walking in their own power and walking in the power of the Spirit. We show them how to share their faith in Christ more effectively with others. The end result is that within a matter of a few hours after the carnal Christians have become spiritual Christians and have learned how to communicate their faith, they begin to share Christ with the non-believers at the conference or institute. Soon they, too, receive Christ. Thus, more people come to Christ through the awakened Christians than we could ever hope to reach for Christ through directing all of our messages toward non-Christians. Of course, the Christians are forever changed through their experience of introducing others to Christ.

These basics of training are repeated again and again in each of our ministries. But although our experience and tested methods are transferred to each kind of outreach, every ministry is also unique — with a special appeal to each unique group of people.

Initial Training Program

With this basic commitment to training and building disciples, Campus Crusade has first of all placed a strong emphasis on training the staff. We began this during the second year, when Vonette and I met with our six staff members at Forest Home and planned our training program for the coming year. There we began the preparation of materials for evangelism and follow-up. The second and third years our training program was held in the Campus Crusade lodge at Forest Home. Then we graduated to the beautiful campus of Westmont College. As the staff continued to grow, however, we found it necessary to secure still larger facilities, and in 1956, our training was conducted near the UCLA campus. Ultimately, of course, the training has been given at Arrowhead Springs, and now additional conference sites across the country are being utilized.

Our commitment to the necessity of training has led to the establishment of several effective programs, including:

Institute of Biblical Studies: This is a three-summer course of study, lasting four weeks each summer. The entire curriculum is centered on the Bible and has been developed to provide solid biblical training that will help to equip Christians for roles in spiritual leadership in a world of crisis.

Leadership Training Institute: Hundreds of week

long and weekend training sessions held around the world each year are designed to teach students how to experience a revolutionary Christian life and how to communicate it effectively to others in the power of the Holy Spirit.

Christian Living Seminar: Laymen are encouraged to become more vital and fruitful in their lives and witness for our Savior in their local churches, families, businesses and professions.

Through the years we have developed an entire series of how-to's or transferable concepts, which have helped to make this a dynamic ministry. These concepts contain the distilled essence of the Christian life. For example, our experience has proved that we can teach these transferable concepts in a very short period of time to any sincere Christian who wishes to know them.

A transferable concept is a truth that can be communicated to another, who, in turn, will communicate the same truth to another, generation after generation, without distorting or diluting the original truth. This is what the apostle Paul was saying to Timothy, his spiritual son in the faith, when he wrote, "For you must teach others those things you and many others have heard me speak about. Teach these great truths to trustworthy men who will, in turn, pass them on to others" (2 Timothy 2:2, Living).

A "transferable technique" is the vehicle, such as a tape, film or booklet, which is used to communicate a transferable concept. For example, the Four Spiritual Laws booklet is a transferable technique. The message contained in the Four Spiritual Laws booklet is a transferable concept.

When Jesus gave the disciples the command to "Go therefore and make disciples of all the nations, baptizing them . . . teaching them to observe all that I commanded you" (Matthew 28:19,20), He was referring to certain truths which would enable His disciples to be more vital in their lives and more fruitful in their witness for Him.

Since like begets like and we produce after our kind, we cannot disciple others until we ourselves grasp certain important principles. I do not know how one can build a disciple without including all of the following transferable concepts:

1. How to be sure you are a Christian.
2. How to experience God's love and forgiveness.
3. How to be filled with the Holy Spirit.
4. How to walk in the Spirit.
5. How to witness in the Spirit.
6. How to introduce others to Christ.
7. How to help fulfill the Great Commission.
8. How to love by faith.
9. How to pray.
10. How to be an effective member of the Body of Christ.

It is true that no one can ever master these transferable concepts. I feel like a beginner myself after all of these years. Yet, it requires only a few weeks or months for any one who desires to be used of God to learn these concepts and techniques well enough that they begin to be a part of his own life and he is able to pass them on to others. It is our objective to help train tens of millions of Christians around the world to experience and share the abundant life in Christ so that they can help to fulfill the Great Commission. These transferable concepts will help to accomplish this objective.

Today, the title "Campus" Crusade for Christ is, in a sense, misleading. From our beginning in the early 1950's, the need for more expanded and specialized ministries has been seen again and again. In response to that need, our field ministries have grown over the years to include college, executive, high school, international, lay, military, athletic, music, prayer, prison and special ministries both in the United States and overseas.

Each of the U.S. field ministries is staffed by godly men and women who are committed to the same objective: to help saturate the United States with the claims of Christ on a continuing basis. Throughout the world our goal is to bring this good news to everyone in our generation.

Now, I should like to spell out more about the individual development and strategies of the field ministries to show how they each fit into Campus Crusade's objective of becoming "all things to all men" that we might be used to "save some" in order to help fulfill the Great Commission of our Lord.

CHAPTER NINE

A Strategy for Colleges

Upon my arrival at a large midwestern university, it was announced that I was to have dinner and speak in the leading fraternity on campus. There was no time to check into the hotel nor to get ready for the meeting. I was already late, and consequently I rushed to the fraternity house.

As I entered the living room, the fellows scattered as though I had leprosy. I wondered what was wrong and was puzzled by the coldness and indifference of the men who remained in the room. Apparently someone had invited me without knowing who I was or anything about the nature of my message. No doubt they had decided in a subsequent fraternity bull session that they had no interest in a religious speaker, and my invitation to speak had been a mistake.

The president of the fraternity hardly spoke to me during the dinner hour. Obviously, he did not want any of his brothers to think that he was interested in religion. Finally, it became his painful duty to announce that there would be a "religious" meeting upstairs in the living room following the dinner hour. Without introducing me, he simply mentioned (in a tone that indicated he was not interested, and anybody who was, was foolish) that a speaker from California would be speaking to those who were interested in religion.

Not a Religious Speaker

I knew, as I observed the attitudes of the men, that there would be no one present to hear me unless I acted fast. So I asked the president for permission to say a few words. Reluctantly, he granted me a few moments, and I said to the men, "I have observed from your reaction that you are no more interested in religion than I am, and I want to put your minds at ease at once. I am not a religious speaker, nor am I here to talk to you about religion. As a matter of fact, I am opposed to religion. History records that religion has done more than any other one thing to keep man in ignorance and fear and superstition through the centuries."

This group of cold, indifferent, even antagonistic men had suddenly come alive. Some of them were dumbfounded. A few well-chosen words had captured their attention. By this time, the men appeared ready to listen to anything I had to say, so I invited them to meet with me upstairs in the living room if they wanted to hear more.

Some of the men began to quiz me. "We thought you were a religious speaker," they said. "You don't sound very religious. What are you going to say?" Others, I discovered later, rushed to the telephone and called their friends in other fraternity houses and dormitories. They invited them to come and hear me speak, saying, "We have a religious speaker at our house tonight who doesn't seem to be very religious. Come on over." By the time we gathered upstairs for the meeting, the room was packed. Many additional men had come out of curiosity to learn what I had to say.

"As I mentioned earlier," I began, "I am opposed to religion. But let me explain what I mean. By way of definition, religion is man's best effort to find God through his own good works, whereas Christianity can be defined as God's search for man and the revelation of Himself in Christ. Because of man's many efforts to find God through the centuries, he has even resorted to criminal means, such as the Inquisition and the Crusades. The superstition of reincarnation and the belief that certain animals are sacred beings have caused masses of human beings to starve while animals survived.

"I am not here to talk to you about religion, but I am here to tell you how God became a man and visited this planet in the person of Jesus of Nazareth. I am here to share with you how you can have a personal relationship with God made possible through the most remarkable Person who ever lived — the God-man who changed the course of history: B.C., before Christ; A.D., *anno Domini*, in the year of the Lord."

Speaking About Jesus

For the next 45 minutes, I talked about Jesus — who He is; why He came to this earth; what He taught; the miracles He performed; His death on the cross for our sins; His resurrection; His message to men through the centuries; and His relevance to the collegian of today. When I finished, no one seemed to want to leave. As usual, a good percentage expressed their desire to receive Christ.

Multitudes of students in fraternity, sorority and dormitory meetings on campuses across the country respond similarly when staff members of Campus Crusade present the Person of Christ — not religion, not Christianity in the broad general sense, not even the church, but a living, dynamic Person.

How do we account for this remarkable response on the part of students? In addition to the spiritual emphasis, part of the answer is planning and strategy. Since the inception of this ministry, our slogan has been, "Win the campus to Christ today, win the world to Christ tomorrow." Our strategy for accomplishing this is to expose men and women to the gospel, win them to Christ, build them in the faith and send them forth to proclaim with us throughout the world the good news of the gospel.

For example, many years of experience have shown

us that an average of one-fourth to one-half of the non-Christian students in "team" meetings are interested in making their commitments to Christ. Though not all of the ones who offer to pray a prayer of commitment give evidence of new life at that time, many thousands do.

Interested in Christ

Many adults automatically assume that college students are not interested in religion and in the church, and in this assumption they are correct. However, the average student is interested in the Person of Jesus Christ, and for many years we have made this distinction in our presentation.

We do not talk about religion or the church, though we believe in the church and require that every staff member become an active member of a local church within 90 days after arriving at his permanent assignment. We also encourage all the students to become active church members.

However, at our first encounter our message emphasizes the Person of Jesus. Students are sometimes antagonistic when we first arrive, assuming that we are going to give them the bit about religion and the church, which they have long since rejected.

I remember one such experience when I arrived with a team to speak in an outstanding fraternity house. We arrived in time for dinner, as per the invitation, and it was arranged that we would make our presentation following the dinner hour. While I was sitting beside the president during the meal he revealed to me that he was faced with a very serious problem. Though he was not a Christian, he was sympathetic with our cause and felt that he should warn me that several of his brothers were planning to embarrass us and cause us to leave the fraternity house in defeat and humiliation. The ringleader of this plot was one of the outstanding students on campus, a moral reprobate who had an unholy disgust and dislike for anything religious or Christian. He was determined to make us the laughingstock of the campus and had rallied several of his fraternity brothers to his cause over the objection of the president.

As the president and I conferred, I felt impressed to recommend to him that he exercise his authority as president and require that every member of the fraternity attend the meeting and that he leave the rest to us. Though I did not tell him so, I was leaving the rest to the Lord. The brothers were somewhat disgruntled when the president announced that their attendance at the meeting was required.

Anticipating their disgruntlement and unhappy presence, we greeted them with a bit of humor then proceeded to explain to them that we were not there to play games. We were there to talk about the most revolutionary Person the world has ever known, a Person who made revolutionary claims for Himself and revolutionary demands upon all who would follow Him. We made it clear that there were a lot of people who did not have the intestinal fortitude to be His followers and asked all of those who felt that they had the potential to be His followers to put aside their preconceived ideas and listen to what was being said as though their lives depended upon it, as indeed their eternal lives did.

Responsive to the Gospel

The whole atmosphere of the house changed. The men responded to the challenges, and when the opportunity was given for those who wished to receive Christ over half of the men, including the president and the leader of the original plot to embarrass us, marched with me into the fraternity den. There we had the opportunity to explain to them further how they could know Christ. We had prayer with them and made plans for the beginning of a weekly Bible study. Different members of the team made appointments with those who had responded, as well as with other members of the fraternity who had attended the original meeting. Throughout the remainder of the week these appointments were kept, and further commitments to Christ were made.

Appointments for subsequent personal interviews are usually made by a member of the team approaching a member of a house and asking, "What did you think of that meeting?" The response is usually, "Great! Wonderful! I've never heard anything like it." The next questions is, "Did it make sense?" "It sure did," is the reply. "Would you like to get together and talk about it?" The answer is almost always in the affirmative.

Often, when there is no rush to leave, a team member will pursue the matter further, if the individual responds that what he heard made sense. The team member will ask if he would like to talk about it at that point, and together they consider the Four Spiritual Laws and then pray together. Thousands of students have been introduced to Christ following meetings of this kind. It is also an approach that many laymen use following church services or similar meetings which non-Christians are invited to attend.

Saturated With Prayer

A meeting of this kind is always bathed in prayer. The team members meet one hour before the time of departure for a special briefing on what each team member is to say and how he is to say it; to check each other on the way they are dressed; and then, finally, to pray for God to work in the hearts of the students. They are conscious of the fact that unless God speaks through their lips there can be no spiritual harvest, for Jesus said, "No man can come to Me, except the Father, who hath sent Me, draw him." By faith, each team member acknowledges his dependence upon the Holy Spirit and appropriates the fullness of God's power, and the group is on its way, in joyful anticipation of what God will do.

In addition to these thousands of team meetings, individual students are also contacted by staff through random surveys taken casually over a cup of coffee or a Coke in a dorm, student center or fraternity. The random survey is an evangelistic tool containing questions which provide an opportunity to share the Four Spiritual Laws.

Unpressured honesty characterizes all appointments. Staff are not so concerned that a student make an immediate decision to accept Christ as they are that each student has a clear understanding of how he can establish a personal relationship with Him.

College Life meetings are another evangelistic opportunity, as they give staff a chance to interact with students. Held each week on hundreds of campuses across the nation, these meetings are attended by as many as 300 on some campuses and on special occasions by several thousand. The program includes singing, entertainment, a main speaker — usually a Campus Crusade staff member — and refreshments. Afterwards, trained staff members and students are on the alert for visitors and guests who are interested in Christ's promise of new life.

"Aggressive" Evangelism

Campus Crusade is committed to "aggressive" evangelism. By aggressive evangelism, I mean going to men with the good news of our living Christ and His love and forgiveness, not in argumentative tones nor with high pressure techniques, but taking the initiative to tell (as the apostle Paul wrote) all men everywhere about Christ.

We realize that this can best be accomplished by multiplication (teaching witnessing disciples to make other witnessing disciples) rather than through addition (simply leading others to Christ one by one). This is the reason training is so important and has been since the inception of this ministry. Each week on hundreds of campuses, Leadership Training Classes are held in which thousands of students learn how to share their faith, how to study the Bible and how to disciple other students.

Those who participate in the classes are encouraged to become involved in smaller action groups. It is the purpose of these action groups to put into practice the training received in the Leadership Training Classes. As these groups of a half dozen or so encourage one another in their Christian walk and witness, their lives are enriched for Christ and their relationship with one another is beautifully enhanced. Because of these small action groups and Leadership Training Classes, there develops a great bond of Christian love and camaraderie reminiscent of first-century Christians, whose love for one another has been extolled.

Thousands of students are being introduced to Christ through team meetings, personal appointments, College Life meetings, and through special meetings with Andre Kole, Josh McDowell, and our various athletic teams and singing groups. It all adds up to a busy schedule for our more than 1,200 campus staff members who are presently working on hundreds of campuses across the United States.

Bal Week

An additional strategy that has proved tremendously successful in working with college students has been to involve them in a ministry during times when they are not in school. This strategy was first put into practice in 1965 during Bal Week, Easter vacation at Balboa and Newport Beaches in southern California.

Approximately 30,000 students from California and surrounding states crowded the sunny beaches during this time of year. For years Bal week had been one of the biggest headaches for the local police as thousands of students became involved in all kinds of delinquencies, including sex, drugs, drunken brawls and vandalism.

The staff believed that something should be done about taking the claims of Christ to these thousands of students. So a strategy was developed. It called for taking several hundred of our staff and students into the Balboa area where they would live in the homes of adult friends. The morning hours would be spent in training the students to understand how to live in the control and power of the Holy Spirit of God and how to communicate their faith in Christ effectively with these thousands of beach-goers. The afternoons and evenings were to be spent in personal and group contacts with the students.

Startling Results

The results were startling and phenomenal. Contacts were not hard to make. There were plenty of people who had nothing to do but sit and listen. Trained students with clipboards, student surveys, evangelistic booklets, Van Dusen letters and Four Spiritual Laws booklets would sit down in their swim trunks and proper beach attire next to a sun-baked coed or young man. Thousands of students responded. The impact was so great that delinquency and vandalism were greatly lessened, and before the end of the week, the police were giving the violators of the law the alternative of going to jail or talking with a member of the Campus Crusade team.

In a converted bar called The Hunger Hangar, several members of the team were available to provide refreshments and to give personal counsel to hundreds of lonely students who were looking for someone to talk to about the things of God. Across the front of the temporary summer headquarters was hung the banner, CHRIST IS THE ANSWER. On the other side of the street, a group of fraternity men reacted to our banner by hanging a sign from their apartment which read, BOOZE IS THE ANSWER. But in the course of the days that followed, these men made their way one by one to our headquarters, at first out of curiosity and then from a genuine interest that developed as members of the team talked to them about Christ and introduced them to the Savior. Eventually all of the young men met Christ, and the BOOZE IS THE ANSWER sign came down.

From its beginning at Balboa and Newport Beach, the ministry soon spread to other beaches. Daytona Beach, Ft. Lauderdale, Panama City, Ocean City, Lake Tahoe, Cape Cod, Santa Cruz, Colorado River and other resort areas became the scene of Campus Crusade activity, as thousands of staff and students invaded these areas to give witness to the living Christ.

Modern-day Prodigal Son

One day, just after I had arrived at my hotel room, where I was to speak to the students at Daytona Beach, a young man knocked on the door of my room and asked if he could retrieve his key. It seemed that he had tossed his key from the patio area on the ground to the third floor, but he had missed the third floor, and his key had fallen on my terrace on the second floor. Knowing that God makes no mistakes and sensing that here was a lad whom God had prepared, I invited him in and he found his key. Then I asked him if he had a few moments to talk. As we chatted together, I explained to him the love of God and His forgiveness made possible through faith in Jesus Christ, as contained in the Four Spiritual Laws booklet.

When I finished, he told me this moving story: "I grew up in the church. My mother and father are very devout Christians. But I have rejected Christianity. For some reason I have not found satisfaction and fulfillment in the church. My parents did not want me to come to Daytona. They knew I would be involved with the wrong crowd. But, in violation of their wishes, I came anyway. And now, of all the places in the world, you should be here to confront me with what my mother and father have told me all these years. Surely, God has arranged this meeting."

We knelt together and prayed, and this young modern-day prodigal who had been running from the Lord surrendered his heart to the Savior.

Expansion to Other Resort Areas

The success of these outreaches prompted the expansion of the format to involve students in a similar type of program for an entire summer. The summer projects gathered students together in various vacation spots around the country to help them grow in their Christian walk. The plan is a simple but effective one. A selected team of students comes to the resort area, locates jobs and settles into a normal work routine. At the same time, a Campus Crusade staff team comes to live with the students for a portion of the summer months. Often the Christians find housing together. Usually they secure a common meeting ground to sponsor outreaches.

After work hours, the staff members spend time with the students, helping them acquire effective evangelistic skills. The constant influx of tourists and vacationers in most spots provides ample opportunity for students to practice one-to-one evangelism.

"The lasting impact this project makes is phenomenal," commented one staff member from the South Lake Tahoe project. "Church members are ecstatic to see us back each summer. Employers beg us to send students to work for them because of the quality of life evident in these young Christians. Scores of people at work, on the beaches and in the parks come to know Christ personally each summer through the witness of the students."

Projects Overseas and in the Inner-city

Summer projects are also held overseas and in the inner-city. In Detroit's inner-city, students and staff capitalized on a city ordinance that permitted city streets to be roped off for parties, with the consent of the residents. They moved a truckload of recreational equipment like basketball hoops, volleyball nets, ping-pong tables and other sports equipment into the area. "The street was turned into a playground," said the project director, "and we found the atmosphere very conducive to sharing the gospel."

In addition to ministering to American college students, a number of our staff work almost exclusively on campus with international students. There are some 260,000 international students studying in the United States, representing nearly every country in the world. Students studying in the United States are generally more open to the gospel than they are in their home countries. Also, they represent the potential leadership of the countries from which they have come. International students reached for Christ and discipled for Christ here in the U.S. can return to their home countries where they can be a powerful influence for Christ.

One man whom I met during a recent tour of the Middle East had earned his Ph.D. from a midwestern university where he was very much involved in the Campus Crusade ministry. He now plays an important role of leadership in the business and Christian communities of his country, where Christians are in a decided minority.

Our campus staff also minister to people of varying ethnic backgrounds including blacks, Mexican-Americans and American Indians. One of our staff members began ministering to Asian-American students on the campus of the University of California at Berkeley. His ministry expanded to the point where he had a direct or indirect influence for Christ on the lives of 60 Asian-American students. We also have staff ministering full time on a number of black college campuses.

Many thousands of students are being led to Christ

and discipled by our staff on the college campuses. These dedicated men and women are committed to the objective of helping to fulfill the Great Commission in this generation. And they realize that the college campus represents the greatest source of manpower immediately available to accomplish this objective.

CHAPTER TEN

Berkeley —
A New Kind of Revolution

In 1967, Berkeley was synonymous with worldwide student riots, demonstrations and radical movements of all kinds.

As Christians and as members of the Campus Crusade staff, we became concerned that so little was being accomplished for Christ on this campus, the fountainhead of the radical movement. So, at one of our campus strategy sessions, we decided to call together 600 of our staff and students from across the nation and saturate the University of California with the good news of Christ through a week-long convention. Our theme was "Solution — Spiritual Revolution."

A syndicated news release from Berkeley carried this story:

> A new kind of revolution talk was heard today on the steps of Sproul Hall on the campus of the University of California at Berkeley. This site has been the scene of student protests and demonstrations and unrest for several years, but today about 3,000 students gathered to hear about a different kind of revolutionary leader — Jesus Christ. The occasion was a rally put on by the Berkeley chapter of the Campus Crusade for Christ, an organization which is having its national convention this week in the Berkeley student union building. While other students passed out handbills for and against the firing of the University of California president, Clark Kerr, and others distributed buttons reading "Impeach Reagan," a folk singing group sang gospel songs with a contemporary sound and the Campus Crusade leader proclaimed a new kind of revolution. The students were asked to trust Christ as the One who has the answers to all the problems of today and the One who can bring spiritual revolution and change to the world. They claimed that the Christian message is revolutionary because it has changed history, creating vast social reforms through reshaping the lives and

attitudes of individuals. The Campus Crusade rally on the Sproul Hall steps came at a time of special turmoil and tension on the Berkeley campus because the day previously the Board of Regents had fired President Clark Kerr. As a result, newsmen and television cameras were on hand for the rally assuming that students were planning a major demonstration over the firing of Kerr. Instead, they were greeted by the Campus Crusade revolutionaries who had reserved this area some weeks prior to the firing of President Kerr. Inasmuch as they had the use of the air, it was impossible for the radicals to drown out the demonstration, and both of the major television networks commented on the fact that Berkeley was the quietest campus in all the University of California system because of the influence of the Campus Crusade for Christ on the Berkeley campus.

Student Leaders Respond

The week at Berkeley began Sunday afternoon with an athletic banquet. All Cal athletes were invited, and some 400 responded to hear famous athletes give their testimonies. I presented additional good news of Christ to these men and invited them to receive Him as their Savior. A number of Berkeley's outstanding athletes responded to the invitation.

The following morning 125 student leaders of the university's student government attended the student leadership breakfast where two leaders shared their faith in Christ, and I followed with a salvation message explaining who Christ is, why He came and how to know Him personally. A number of these leaders also responded.

During that week, many additional meetings were held on and off campus. Christ was presented at 28 separate dinners given for international students, and many of these were introduced to Christ. Meetings continued from noon until after midnight in the Forum of Telegraph Avenue, a hangout for the radical students, the street people and the hippies at Berkeley. Approximately 40 of these radicals received Christ during that week. In addition, each evening another 1,400 students gathered in the Berkeley Community Theater to hear Campus Crusade staff present the claims of Christ.

Billy Graham was with us for the last day of the meetings. That last Friday morning a special breakfast was held for approximately 300 of the faculty in the Student Union. Billy gave a powerful presentation of the gospel, and I explained the purpose of our week at Berkeley.

Threat of Cancellation

We had scheduled a great rally at noon at the Greek Theater, where Dr. Graham and I would both be speaking. Dawn had greeted us with a downpour of rain that continued all morning. As we met in our various sessions, we prayed God would stop the rain in time for the noon rally. There was no other place to meet, and the Greek Theater had no roof. Thus, thousands who would otherwise come would be forced to miss hearing the gospel through Dr. Graham's message. As we continued to pray, the rain continued to pour. What were we to do? Surely God had not brought us to this great week of witness for Christ and finally to the grand climax meeting for us to fail.

"Whatever we ask in prayer believing we shall receive . . . If we ask anything according to His will, He hears, us, and if He hears us, He answers us . . . God is not willing that any should perish but that all should come to repentance." These and many other promises of Scripture were claimed as we asked God, the Creator of heaven and earth, the One who controls men, nations and nature, to intervene for the salvation of souls. As we prayed, dramatically and abruptly it happened — the rain stopped. A spontaneous song of praise flowed from our hearts, for we realized that the rally in the Greek Theater would take place as planned.

More than 8,000 students and faculty joined us in the Greek Theater. I greeted them with a brief message and introduced Dr. Graham. Following his clear-cut presentation of the gospel, he invited the students to commit their lives to Christ. Long after the meeting was over, 600 staff and students counseled and prayed with those remaining behind to learn how to become Christians. God had done a mighty work at Cal, but this was only the beginning.

Follow-Up Program

After most of us left Berkeley, those remaining began a follow-up program designed to preserve and increase the impact that had been made. All the students who had invited Christ into their lives, and those who expressed interest in knowing more, were contacted during the first week after the convention. Approximately 200 of those who had just received Christ attended a retreat to learn more about how to live the abundant Christian life. Many of those who expressed interest in Christ also responded.

One local newspaper described the "invasion" at Berkeley this way:

> Unparalleled organization. Campus radicals, accustomed to being hailed the best student organizers, looked on in amazement as the extensive Campus Crusade for Christ campaign got under way in an attempt to evangelize the entire student body at Berkeley. Teams of delegates spoke and shared their faith in Christ in more than 70 dormitories, fraternities, sororities and nearby student residences. Other groups spoke and sang in restaurants, coffee houses and similar gathering places for "free speech movement" advocates, and other teams of delegates conducted a door-to-door campaign in the entire area adjacent to the campus just to make sure that no one was overlooked in the crusaders' effort to give each of the 27,000 students an opportunity to hear the claims of Christ on their lives.

> In addition to the regular convention schedule of morning and evening addresses, daily Bible exposition and prayer sessions, staff members also spoke in nearby churches and in church related meetings.

> More than half of the students in most of the fraternities, sororities and dormitory meetings indicated that they would

like to know how to become Christians. A young man from Hawaii who was visiting Berkeley made his decision in a restaurant after a third Crusade delegate, during that one week, had talked to him about his personal relationship with Christ.

During that week at Berkeley, I met by appointment with one of the leaders of the radical movement on campus — a brilliant, dynamic, personable individual. Reared a Jew, more recently this person had become a dedicated atheist and card-carrying Communist. It has been my practice for years to ask Muslims, Hindus, atheists and Communists, "Who is the greatest person who has ever lived?" When I asked the radical leader this question, there was a long, awkward silence. "I guess I would have to say Jesus of Nazareth," was the reluctant reply. This leader was one of thousands who came face to face with the Master that week.

Radical Movement Broken

Dr. Hardin Jones, a well-known scientist and professor at Berkeley for 40 years, shared with me that the back of the radical movement was broken at Berkeley that week. He also said that since then there was more talk about Jesus Christ on campus than about Karl Marx. There is power in the gospel. Satan cannot withstand it. When he is confronted with men and women who trust and obey God, he releases control of occupied territory.

By the time the week-long convention had ended, more than 700 had made commitments to Christ, and approximately 2,000 other students indicated that they would like to know more about Jesus Christ and how they could also commit their lives to Him.

On another campus, a similar "invasion" of our staff and others confronted a strong group of student activists. It was the fall of 1970 at the University of Texas that brought us another tremendous opportunity to bring glory to God.

Operation Alternative

Campus radicals planned anti-war rallies on the Austin campus that week in October, as we sent 400 Campus Crusade-trained students and staff, working with 100 Navigators, to present an alternative plan for peace. The main thrust, called Operation Alternative, centered on two big free speech rallies during the weekend, but also included two marches on campus, massive use of literature and radio and TV news coverage.

As Christian students and staff began to arrive from Arkansas, Oklahoma and throughout Texas, they took speaking assignments in every campus dining area.

The next morning everyone went on campus to distribute flyers, carry signs, mass for a march and hold a rally on the Main Mall, which Campus Crusade students had reserved weeks before.

About 1,000 gathered as Josh McDowell, traveling representative for Campus Crusade, began telling what Christ meant to him. Other speakers and a number of students followed him.

During the free speech time, students and some professors blasted Christianity and proclaimed political radicalism. At the close, a Cuban student strode to the mike and said, "You don't know what you're talking about. I've been through two revolutions — the one on Cuba and now the one in Jesus Christ." As this student described both, he pointed out that only Christ is the answer.

On Saturday, several thousand students and visiting parents witnessed a similar rally on the West Mall. "The atmosphere was electric," the Campus Crusade director at UT later told us. "Hundreds stopped and listened on their way to the football game. Among other results, Christians at UT have never been as bold or as united as they are now. And students at UT really know that the Christians are alive!"

One radio station described the week on its news broadcast, "Campus Crusade for Christ smashes Student Mobilization Committee."

These wonderful experiences of God's power have been high points in our Campus Ministry. They have revealed to the world that the light of Jesus Christ is more powerful than darkness. As I think back on these times, my prayers increase for God to do it again and again throughout the entire world. Wherever the light of God's love and forgiveness meets the darkness of atheism head on, His light overcomes.

CHAPTER ELEVEN

Here's Life America

A dentist from Cape Kennedy, a businessman from New Jersey and a man with a young family in California — all have been a part of the Here's Life America ministry of Campus Crusade. What brings them together? As one staff member explains, "My wife and I were typical church members. We were traditional, mediocre, a lukewarm kind of Christian. Now that we have experienced a vital personal relationship with Christ, have helped others to find this same exciting relationship and seen entire churches come alive, we want to spend the rest of our lives serving Him." That same desire unites the 320 Here's Life America staff across the United States and Canada, in spite of the variety of backgrounds and education. Directed by Alan Nagel, this ministry is having a dynamic ministry across this country.

This ministry to lay men and women began as a direct outgrowth of the Campus Ministry. As God continued to do a mighty work in the lives of thousands on many college campuses, laymen began to ask, "How do you account for the miraculous results of the ministry of Campus Crusade among students? Can't you give us the same kind of training you give your staff and students?"

Day-long Institutes

Thus it was that in 1959 I began to speak at many day-long Lay Institutes for Evangelism (since renamed Christian Living Seminars) in various cities throughout the nation. From early in the morning until late at night, I presented the basic messages and seminars on how to live the Christian life and share our faith in Christ more effectively. Hundreds of laymen and pastors came for the entire day to hear this seminar presentation. Shortly after that, the Lay Ministry (now Here's Life America) was born, and it has since produced some of the most exciting results that we have seen.

The day-long institutes for evangelism soon became week-long and spread city-wide, encompassing hundreds of churches and thousands of laymen who responded to training.

The greater the response to the training, the more we realized the need for our Lay Ministry to become more than a training institute. From the beginning, the local church has been the most important part of God's strategy to help fulfill the Great Commission. Now we were discovering how to serve the local church more effectively. We became even more committed to the fact that local pastors and laymen are the key to evangelizing communities. If properly trained with an understanding of how to share their faith in the power of the Spirit, they could be used of God in a revolutionary way, even as were the first-century Christians.

Assisting Church Leaders

Here's Life America staff function in two areas to serve the local church. First, they assist pastors and laymen in developing discipleship ministries. Second, they develop movements of spiritual multiplication within some of the leadership groups of the community such as business and professional people, lawyers, doctors, educators and entertainers.

In their church-related ministry, lay staff assist church leaders in causing discipleship methods to become a way of life. In addition to this plan, national conferences called Christian Living Seminars are made available to pastors and laymen. These seminars include courses on discipleship, Lay Institutes for Evangelism and management training. The management course helps pastors break away from the "I don't have time" syndrome and provides pastors and church leaders with priority-oriented administrative procedures as well as training in discipleship and evangelism.

As one pastor put it, "Management training filled the missing place in my church work and in my life. To know the how-to's — how to set clear goals and objectives, set priorities, write job descriptions and divide the work load — will help us succeed in building a Christian community."

Witnessing Assignments

An integral part of our Christian Living Seminars is a laboratory training program. Less than 24 hours after the delegates arrive for an institute, they have already been told how to witness and have spent a few hours in the field seeking to communicate their faith to others. The results are startling and revolutionary.

Many, and one could probably say most, go out on this first witnessing assignment with their fingers crossed. Many are frightened. As one woman said to me, "I won't go. I refuse to go." I assured her that she did not have to go, that it was strictly voluntary, and that she should not feel under any pressure to go. She kept saying, almost as though she were in a state of shock, "I won't go. I won't go." And I kept assuring her that she didn't have to go.

Finally, I suggested that maybe she should go with someone and listen. Reluctantly, and with a face white with fear, she agreed to accompany a staff member. Two hours later she returned bubbling with enthusiasm, overjoyed. She took my hand in both of hers and said, "I'm so glad that you encouraged me to go. What a great loss if I hadn't. My life was forever changed this afternoon when I saw God transform the lives of those who received Christ."

Renewed Life

In one large city, I was speaking at a meeting to which several hundred laymen and students had come from throughout the entire state, some from as far away as 500 miles. At the conclusion of one of my lectures, a leading layman came running down the aisle. He said, "This is the greatest thing I have ever heard in my life. Today I have been liberated. I am now on 12 boards of various Christian organizations, including a couple in my church. I have been trying to serve God so diligently that I practically ignored my business and my family.

"Now you tell me that the Christian life is not what we do for God, but what we allow Him to do in and through us. You say the Christian life is a supernatural life, that no one can live it but Christ, and that this life is by faith through the power of the Holy Spirit. I have been trying to serve God in the energy of the flesh. I understand now why I have been so miserable and so unproductive!"

He telephoned his wife, explained to her how he had made the discovery of being filled and controlled by the Holy Spirit by faith and insisted that she come at once to join in the training. Even though she had made previous commitments, she canceled all her engagements and came. That night at the banquet, following my final lecture, they both stood to tell how the course of their lives had been dramatically changed that day through the new concepts they had heard.

At another institute, I had just finished one of my lectures on the ministry of the Holy Spirit when a pastor approached me. He was rejoicing in the fact that he now knew he was filled with the Holy Spirit by faith, but he was also distressed by the fact that with all of his theological training and his years of preaching, he had never once personally introduced a person to the Savior. He was rightly concerned. As we talked and prayed together, I felt impressed to ask him if he would like to be used of God that very day to introduce someone to Christ. He looked at me in amazement as if to say, "How foolish! I've never led anyone to Christ in all these years. How could I possibly expect to lead anyone to Christ today?"

I suggested that we pray together and then that he go door-to-door in the area where his church was located, using our Community Religious Survey, and present the gospel as explained through the Four Spiritual Laws. This he agreed to do. We asked God that He might honor his efforts.

Imagine his elation and my joy when he returned that afternoon so excited he could hardly speak. In the very first home he visited, he met a 19-year-old student who was rope for the gospel, and upon the simple presentation of the Four Spiritual Laws, this person invited Christ into his life. Needless to say, this was a revolutionary experience for this young pastor.

Mediated Training

A giant step forward in the Lay Ministry was taken in 1974, when this key training that had been used to revolutionize the lives of hundreds of thousands of people was put into an exciting new format, developed by Dr. Norman Bell, a Christian professor of communications at Michigan State University. Dr. Bell is an active adviser, consultant, teacher and friend of the Campus Crusade ministry. During one of my visits to the campus to speak to the students, I met Dr. Bell and learned of this revolutionary new concept in communications called mediated training. As we discussed the concept, it became apparent that it applied to our basic training. We could train tens of millions of Christians around the world — instead of the tens of thousands whom we were then training. So I asked Dr. Bell and Chuck Younkman, then the director of our Mass Media Ministry, and his staff to help me adapt the basic training which had been so effective for more than 20 years into this new format.

This format utilizes slides, 16mm film and cassette sound track. Tests have shown that in similar training sessions 80% of the people who attend retain 80% of the material, as compared to the customary lecture method where retention is frequently no more than five percent.

At the time that God impressed us to pray toward the goal of seeking to help saturate America with the gospel by the end of 1976, we didn't understand how He would do it. We had the capability to train many people to be effective in reaching others for Christ through the staff of Campus Crusade, but we saw no way to be able to train the hundreds of thousands of workers who would be needed to help reach our nation for Christ.

When I first heard the idea of putting our training into the mediated format, the Holy Spirit confirmed that this was a portion of the answer to my prayer for the salvation of millions in the United States. Such revolutionary concepts as "How to Be Filled With the Spirit" and "How to Witness in the Spirit," plus how-to's of evangelism, could now be made available to millions of Christians. We would no longer be limited to our staff as trainers, but laymen and pastors could train others by using the mediated training presentation.

Training Produces Results

At first there were many questions and much skepticism. Many wondered if mediated training could really communicate better than a live teacher. Larry Marks, a Methodist layman from Athens, Ala., expressed the feeling of the people who have taken the training. "I was amazed at the amount of information I gained and could recall when I needed it," he said.

Marks also tells the story of Jack, a layman in his

church, who had always thought that he could witness only by his style of living. After taking mediated training, however, his mind changed. He made a list of 10 friends whom he wanted to introduce to Christ and soon saw six of them receive Christ as Savior.

Ken Kirby, pastor of Bryant Street Baptist Church in Yucaipa, Calif., has also been enthusiastic about the benefits of mediated training. "It gets results," he says. "I couldn't recommend it if there hadn't been any real change in my laymen's lives, but there has. I've seen the Lord use mediated training to equip my men boldly to share their faith."

Those people who have been trained through the mediated training in a Christian Living Seminar do not go out to convert people to their way of thinking or to their philosophy of life or even to their religion. They go with new boldness to share the most important news the world has ever received: the good news of God's love and forgiveness in Christ Jesus. As thousands respond — not to their words but to His Spirit — they have the joy of knowing that their lives are truly counting for eternity.

It occurs to me that there are many, like Peter and John of the Bible, who have "fished" for men for years and are wearied and discouraged. They have never caught anything, never introduced another person to Christ. There is a solution. One needs simply to bow in prayer and ask the Holy Spirit to control and empower his life as he surrenders it to Christ and then receive training in the how-to's of sharing one's faith. The Holy Spirit provides the ability to learn how to communicate Christ more effectively with others.

The time is now: Men and women have never been more ready to hear the good news of our Savior. And the opportunity is now: Christian Living Seminars are held each year across the nation to help lay men and women and pastors fill their nets and to challenge them to forsake all and follow Him.

CHAPTER TWELVE

Special Ministries

Of all the outreaches Campus Crusade employs to reach men and women everywhere, there is probably none so unusual as the methods of our special representative, Andre Kole. As America's leading illusionist and foremost inventor of magical effects, Andre has spent the last 20 years pulling coins from the air, sawing his assistant in half, turning flaming scarves into canes and escaping "The Table of Death."

But his most recent 22 years of performances around the world have been for the sole purpose of using the fantasy of illusions to gain a hearing for the reality of Christ.

At the age of 25, Andre was a success in the fields of business and magic. He was married, had a family and owned a new home and car which were paid for. In addition to doing between 20 and 30 shows each month, he was in charge of the state-wide operation of one of the largest corporations in Arizona, was co-owner of a ranch and a number of real estate buildings and directed several enterprises in show business.

Then he was challenged to consider the miracles of Jesus Christ and what He had to say. "At that time, I took great pride in my reputation as a magician," Andre recalls. "I have never been fooled by any other magician, and I had no intention of being deceived by any first-century trickster — if this was all that Jesus really was."

Unshakeable Proof

The fulfillment of biblical prophecy, the evidence for the resurrection and the dynamic Christian lives that he

saw finally compelled Andre to let Christ take control of
his life. But it wasn't until he spent two days on campus
with the late Elmer Lappen, then our staff director at
Arizona State University, that Andre caught a vision of
the intriguing new life that lay before him. He developed
a presentation to illustrate the Four Spiritual Laws with
illusions and convinced that it would work, Andre joined
the staff of Campus Crusade in 1963.

Today, he spends more than 60% of each year on
tour, has performed in person in 73 nations and has been
seen by more than 78 million on television in one year
alone. To date, he has addressed more than 2,600 separate university audiences, and some 400 copies of his
two films are now circulating worldwide.

Wherever Andre goes, his performances and message
never fail to capture the minds and hearts of his audiences. In a recent three-month Asian tour, he found that
"the people were open everywhere. I performed 100
times before 110,000 people, and as a result over 10,000
responded to the gospel. Now, staff, students and
laymen in that area are following up the young Christians."

A three-week tour through Latin America in 1973
resulted in 14 invitations for Andre to perform on TV
programs — nine of which were over national television
and all of which were aired free of charge as a public
service. Simultaneously, capacity crowds jammed each
stage performance.

His popularity continues to grow on American campuses, too. During a recent school term, he appeared
before an average of one million people each week
through stage and TV performances. Among the
thousands who have come to Christ through Andre
ministry is a student leader in Taiwan who said, "Mr
Kole, when you mentioned that most people are laughing on the outside and crying on the inside, you described me perfectly. Not only is this a picture of my life

but of the life of every student I know on this campus. I only wish I had heard you a week ago or even a day ago." Another said: "I have been a Christian for 11 years but I closed Christ out of my life when I came to college. About a year ago I attempted suicide. I saw nothing worth living for. Since then I have been seeing a psychiatrist, but after tonight I won't need him any more. Thanks to you, I now know I have Christ. Thank you for showing me my need."

From his investigations in 73 countries of the world, Andre has learned that most tricks and illusions attributed to the supernatural (witchcraft and occult) are produced by very natural means. The one thing Andre has found that men can't reproduce, though, is the exciting reality of a personal relationship with Jesus Christ. That is why he is thrilled to be able to use his magical medium for an eternal purpose. Everywhere he goes, he challenges men and women in all walks of life to let their lives count for Christ. "I've always felt that God is likely to use those whom the world considers the most unlikely," he says. "After all, if God can use a magician to accomplish His purpose, He can use anybody."

Ministering to Large Audiences

Like Andre, God has used the ministry of staff member Josh McDowell to minister to large audiences. During a 12-year period, Josh traveled to 539 campuses in 53 countries and spoke to an estimated five million people.

A graduate of Talbot Theological Seminary, Josh keeps the students interested in his message with well-documented historical, scientific and biblical evidences for the Christian faith. And he puts his whole personality into his delivery. Roaming the platform and gesturing enthusiastically, he'll treat his listeners to a joke or let them in one a personal incident from his past. His rhetoric is direct, and he doesn't mince words when exposing faulty thinking.

His messages rarely miss their target. Commented one student after hearing "Maximum Sex," "It presented dating and sex in a healthier light than I've ever heard it before."

On one occasion, 4,500 students came out to hear Josh speak on "Maximum Sex" at Kansas State University. This crowd represented approximately one-third of the student body. Some 400 students checked comment cards indicating that they had invited Christ into their lives that night.

At Louisiana State University, a total of 9,000 students came out to hear Josh during his stay on campus, with 900 of them marking comment cards that they had accepted Christ.

Preparation and Prayer

Successful outreaches like this do not come without a large amount of student participation and prayer. LSU students staged a campaign to build momentum for Josh's appearance on campus by entering a classroom, writing "Josh is coming" on the blackboards, then walking out. This went on for nearly two months before he actually arrived on campus to speak.

The blackboard campaign was followed by ads in the local newspaper announcing "Josh in January." Then, following Christmas, as registration for the next semester's classes took place, students posted 150 hand-painted signs and hung banners saying, "Josh is Coming January 21, 22 and 23."

Several days before Josh arrived, his identity was revealed. Teachers were contacted about speaking engagements in classrooms, student leaders were invited to a banquet, and all the details of his visit were publicized.

Despite the organization, last-minute problems provided the workers with numerous opportunities to trust God for the seemingly impossible. A scheduling error for the athletic field house appeared to thrust the Wisconsin series out in the cold. As others prayed, the student in charge of coordinating the lecture series spoke with the athletic director who decided to cancel women's basketball and junior varsity basketball so Josh could use the facilities. The contract was signed just two days before he arrived.

At the University of Illinois, the assembly hall was already booked for another event, and the rental price of $1,000 a night was far in excess of the budget for Josh. Yet there was no other facility on campus which could accommodate the expected student turnout. Prayer proved to be the answer.

"As we prayed about the situation," said an Illinois student in charge of the physical arrangements, "God unbooked the assembly hall, and He got it for us free! We simply had to say, 'Okay, God, You do it' and that's what He did. It was a real faith builder for me."

In addition to his campus lectures, Josh now speaks frequently to lay audiences. He has written several books, including *Evidence That Demands a Verdict* and *More Evidence That Demands a Verdict* which have both been on the Christian books' bestseller list. Also, he has been involved in the production of an inspirational film, "The Secret of Loving," which was broadcast on television in a number of cities across the nation.

Drama Ministry

Another of the specialized ministries of Campus Crusade is the drama ministry. Formed in 1974 by staff member Jeff Taylor, the drama ministry performs in churches, on campuses and in street theater evangelistic outreaches. Past productions include "Changing Faces," a testimonial performed by one of the drama staff; "O Virginia," which portrayed the life and Christian faith of Revolutionary War patriot Patrick Henry; "The Toy Shop" and "The Pandemonium Parables," a dramatization of several New Testament parables.

Drama ministry staff performed before some 3,000 students during a month-long tour of Ireland in 1978. The performance of "The Pandemonium Parables" at Carysfort Teacher Training College was one of the highlights of the tour. Nearly one-third of the college population attended the Thursday evening presentation. The show was stopped several times by applause, and all available copies of the Four Spiritual Laws were used. There were many opportunities to talk individually with students, and some of the discussions continued for several hours.

Presenting the Gospel by Multimedia

The Paragon Experience is another ministry that reaches large groups of people. A 45-minute multimedia production, Paragon is an effective presentation of the gospel and a dynamic tool for evangelism and follow-up. Nine projectors flash rapidly-changing images, synchronized to the lyrics of contemporary music, on three screens.

Because they are "still" shots rather than a moving picture, they can be more abstract, jumping from one scene to the next, allowing the viewer to fill in the gaps with thoughts and experiences from his own background.

The shows confront audiences with questions of life, death and Jesus Christ. "If I Should Die" tells the story of a young couple's carefree existence suddenly shattered by a head-on collision with death. "How's Your Love Life?" begins by laughingly commenting on the games of love. The story traces a student's agonizing search for fulfillment in life from the break-up of an "ideal" love relationship to the resulting depression that culminates in suicide.

Together, "If I Should Die" and "How's Your Love Life?" were presented to more than a quarter of a million people in the first three and a half years of Paragon's existence. More than 27,000 viewers indicated first-time commitments to Jesus Christ during that time.

Fulfillment of a Dream

Helmut Teichert first dreamed of evangelistic slide shows after becoming a Christian during his freshman year of college. During his junior year, with the help of three others, Teichert set to work on his production. The slide presentation dealt with the topics of Vietnam, drugs and ecology — and offered a solution in Jesus Christ. The following summer the Paragon Experience crew worked hard to produce a second show, which was the backbone of the current "If I Should Die." After college, the group premiered a third show at EXPLO '72 in Dallas to a crowd of 5,000.

Teichert and his wife, Laney, continued to develop Paragon at home while working on their dairy. At many of their showings they saw 25% of the audience respond to Christ. Seeing the great need to begin discipling these Christians, which Helmut and Laney could not do alone, they realized that Paragon needed to be part of a ministry like Campus Crusade that could provide the essential follow-up.

After applying for staff and being accepted, the Teicherts were assigned to Special Ministries to work on their own Paragon Experience. Since the development of the shows, they have toured the United States and Canada with presentations being viewed not only on several campuses but also in churches, high schools, camps, prisons and on military bases.

Individuals come to grips with the issues presented during the shows. One student commented, "For 19 years I've been looking for someone to love me. Tonight I know I finally found it. I know that Jesus has come to live in me now." Another responded, "As a Christian I had always known what I was saved for, but I never thought about what I was saved from! I realized tonight I've got to start telling the people I love about Jesus, even though it's not easy for me."

CHAPTER THIRTEEN

Student Venture — A Ministry to High School Students

Scott Phillips was an enthusiastic, outgoing, rambunctious high school student at Princeton High in Cincinnati, Ohio. In most people's eyes he was a success. A ferocious goalie on the school's soccer team, Scott also played on Princeton's tennis team and was involved in other school activities.

But he was involved in less desirable activities, too, including frequent use of alcohol and marijuana.

"I was pretty wild," Scott says. "When I was almost arrested for possession of marijuana, I became disillusioned with my lifestyle. I saw that I wasn't headed in the right direction."

Some of his friends came to Christ through the high school Campus Crusade Student Venture group, and he began to take notice. After a period of five months he grasped the fact that he did not know Christ.

"It took me a month after that to let go of everything and come to Christ," Scott says.

Student Venture staff member Russ Bannister began to help Scott lay the foundation for Christian growth in his life. And he took it to heart. In later years Scott would return home from college each summer and take on leadership in a ministry which included sixty high schoolers. He led a delegation of students to a Student Venture conference in the Rocky Mountains, and he discipled several students, including his brother.

Individuals like Scott reveal the potential of high school students in making an impact on their world. And it's a world with grim realities: More than 5,000 teenagers commit suicide each year. A survey conducted by the University of Michigan revealed that nearly 62 percent of the teens are involved in some kind of drug use, while 38.7 percent reported having five or more drinks in a row within a recent two week period. According to the Guttmacher Institute, 49 percent of all 15-to 19-year-olds are sexually active.

After fifteen years of fruitful ministry with college students, Campus Crusade's official entrance into this troubled, turbulent mission field occurred in 1966. At this time many college students who had been reached for Christ through Campus Crusade were returning to their home communities and seeking to start Campus Crusade meetings among the high school young people. Thus, across the nation, high school Campus Crusade groups were starting unofficially. We had no control over them nor any opportunity to serve them unless we developed a special organizational program.

To avoid possible conflicts and misunderstandings, I met with Bill Starr, president of Young Life, and Sam Wolgemuth, president of Youth for Christ. They were warm and gracious. I remember Bill Starr's statement which I believe expressed Sam Wolgemuth's thinking as well. "Bill, let me say to you that we are reaching perhaps only one percent of the high school students of America. It would be naive of us to say that there is no room for Campus Crusade to reach high school young people. We just ask that you cooperate with us, that you work with us, that you move carefully into what you are doing so as not to make unfortunate mistakes."

We had prayer together and from that time on Campus Crusade began a great effort to expand this ministry to help reach the millions of high school students.

So the High School Ministry, since renamed Student Venture, was launched under the direction of Carl Wilson. The strategy then, as today, calls for the staff to focus on a broad spectrum of students on the campus. It is also a part of the Student Venture strategy to reach out to the campus leaders — the athletes, student council officers, club presidents, cheerleaders, etc. As the staff reach a few of the leaders, other students will follow. One of the biggest things that keeps students from coming to Christ is a fear of rejection. But when a student knows that the peers he respects are taking a stand for Christ, he has the freedom to respond.

Staff members contact students before and after school and, in some cases, minister on campus during the lunch hour. At an all black high school in Atlanta, a staff member had so many students wanting to talk with her after school that she asked Carla, a new Christian, to meet with two of the girls. Carla read the Four Spiritual Laws booklet to them, and they received Christ. Thinking that the students were loitering in the hall, the assistant principal asked them what they were doing. Carla explained that she had shared with the girls a booklet about Jesus Christ and asked if he would like to know what it said. "It wouldn't hurt me to listen," he said, and in the hall outside his office, he asked Christ into his life.

Staff members also often take surveys or hold meetings with entire sports teams or clubs, thereby exposing several students at once to the issue of Jesus Christ.

These staff are seeking to win and disciple students who will be faithful in their walk with God and bold in their witness to their classmates. Mike, a student in Chattanooga, Tennessee, was one such student. He stood before fifty football players and cheerleaders and invited each of them to get together with him personally to discuss their relationship with God. Mike said, "I know a lot of you use God as a good luck charm before every game, and some of you pray to Him when you're in trouble, but I want you to know that knowing God is much more than that. I want to meet with any of you who are interested in developing a personal relationship with Jesus Christ."

Currently, Student Venture's 225 staff and their volunteers are ministering at more than 175 high schools in 18 metropolitan areas across the country, reaching out to more than 100,000 students each year. "Our ultimate goal is to help communicate the message of the love of Christ to every high school student in America," says Chuck Klein, Student Venture's director. By the year 2000 the ministry plans to help field outreaches at 3,800 schools.

Student Venture staff members help build Christian students in their faith through personal follow-up, discipleship groups, retreats and conferences. Conferences, called "Getaways," gather students each summer for a week of challenge, fun and training for action at four regional sites across the country. Some of the Getaways have attracted as many as 1,000 students and their leaders.

Kathy Schmid, a physical-education teacher, brought students to a Getaway for three consecutive years.

"The Getaway offers an environment where students can get to know God beyond a surface level," she says. "The Getaway offers an environment where all the other clutter in their lives — the stereos and other distractions — are gone."

Student Venture's "VITAL People" strategy involves volunteers, interns, teachers, affiliates and lay people in ministry. Student Venture helps these VITAL People assume more and more responsibility in reaching high schoolers with the gospel. Conferences such as the National Convention of High School Discipleship offer the kind of resources and training necessary to equip individuals to minister to high school students.

In 1985 Student Venture staff, working with Youth for Christ staff, sponsored a conference of another kind. Titled Youth Congress '85, the convention brought 20,000 students to the nation's capital to motivate them and equip them for the task of reaching their schools — and their world — for Jesus Christ.

Student Venture is committed to working with other Christian organizations, churches, volunteers, teachers and parents. The commitment is great, but the cause is greater — to reach a generation. Chuck Klein describes high school ministry as "an investment in the future of our culture. We're dealing with people at an age when they're formulating values for all of life. For any movement seeking to change the world, young people have been the main target."

Not only are we finding that we can make a difference in the lives of the young people, but sometimes whole families are influenced. At a March, 1984, program in San Diego, 1,300 students and parents attended a performance by André Kole, one of America's leading illusionists. The performance was sponsored by Student Venture. A total of 258 people turned in comment cards indicating that they had prayed to receive Christ. One of those was Rob, a junior at one of the high schools in the area. When one of the staff came to follow up with Rob, he discovered that Rob's mother and two sisters had also indicated decisions to accept Christ that same night.

Parents notice when their children's lives are transformed by Christ.

"Pete really has begun to live the Spirit-filled life," said one mother.

Kenny's parents were a bit concerned at first that he would "get so involved with Campus Crusade that he wouldn't be faithful to his own church." As it turned out, Kenny and several other students, motivated by a desire to transfer to others the truths they had learned, took on increased responsibilities in their local churches.

One mother remarked, "I have never before seen kids such as these — standing up for what they believe. The high school staff are certainly sending out missionaries for eternity!"

CHAPTER FOURTEEN

"Basic Training" for Military Personnel

We have the prediction of the Bible that we will continue to have wars and rumors of wars. With world conditions as they are, we know that as one hot spot cools off there will be another one to take its place, requiring a constant need for our armed forces personnel. They deserve to hear a clear presentation of the gospel.

The Military Ministry began in 1966, shortly after I was invited to address the congregation of a community church established by a local businessman with investments in real estate. This very gracious southern gentleman was Col. John M. Fain, USAF, Retired. During World War II, he had served on General Douglas MacArthur's 5th Air Force staff in the Pacific, and now he was devoting most of his energies to introducing others to the Savior.

After I had spoken in his church, where a number of people responded by committing their lives to Christ at the invitation, Col. Fain related how in the middle of the night he was awakened and felt strongly impressed of the Lord to ask me to start a new division of Campus Crusade for the military. He added that he would be available in whatever capacity the Lord would have him serve.

Reaching Military Personnel for Christ

This rang a bell with me, for I had long been interested in reaching the military and had on different occasions personally spoken at meetings for military personnel. I had always found servicemen very open to the gospel. Later, I suggested that Col. Fain come to Arrowhead Springs to head up a military division of the expanding ministry of Campus Crusade.

The Military Ministry now has a worldwide outreach. Among other things, it has distributed hundreds of thousands of Van Dusen letters and Four Spiritual Laws booklets in various army bases across the nation and around the world.

Many people who have not been in the service think of the military as uniforms and sophisticated weapons. Our staff see the military installations as very special communities. They are cities in themselves, with their own libraries, recreation areas, police forces, medical facilities and shopping centers. Some even have schools.

The real challenge, though, comes in reaching each individual there with the claims of Christ. The population includes more single men than most civilian communities and has a growing contingent of young, single women. It also includes neighborhoods filled with couples and their children.

Besides living in a diverse and challenging community, Christians in the military have a unique opportunity to reach beyond their bases to the world. The United States has military installations throughout the world which allow a trained man or woman to become an overseas missionary for the Lord at the expense of the government. Also, many countries of the world send their soldiers to the U.S. for special training, giving American soldiers another opportunity to exercise a worldwide influence for Christ.

Because of these factors, the Military Ministry emphasizes training military personnel. When a man leaves a base, we want him to have a vital relationship with Christ. When he arrives at his new base, we want him to be able to formulate his own strategy for winning the men there to Christ and discipling them.

Under the leadership of Col. Glenn Jones, former executive assistant to the chairman of the Joint Chiefs of Staff, our military staff are making an impact on military installations as they take the gospel to America's 2.1 million servicemen.

Our staff work on a specific base with the permission of the chaplain. Most chaplains welcome the assistance, and together with the staff, they develop a strategy to reach their base with the claims of Christ. Bible studies, action groups, prayer, planning and personal witnessing fill the days of the staff members as they work with the already committed Christians to train and build them in their faith.

"I thank the Campus Crusade for Christ staff members for helping us fill in a fundamental and necessary foundation of our chapel program," says Chaplain James Eastland.

Army Chaplain John De Seager explained that the Military Ministry staff work is an extension of his chapel program. "Because of my busy schedule, they often become my eyes and ears and hands and feet."

Evangelistic mass outreaches are also used in this ministry to expose hundreds of men and women to the gospel at one time. Singing groups perform often at military bases, and the Athletes in Action track teams give frequent athletic demonstrations and relate their faith in Christ. After these outreaches, those who receive Christ or express a desire to learn more about Him are contacted for follow-up.

Often, Lay Institutes for Evangelism are held to follow up interested service men and women. Skip Cannevit, a non-commissioned officer, came to a LIFE after attending a Campus Crusade music group's performance: "I was at the concert," Cannevit relates, "when one of the staff members came up to talk to me. I told him that I was a Christian, but that I was frustrated in my faith. He invited me to the LIFE, and there I saw that I hadn't understood what the Christian life was all about. I was trying to walk with the Lord on my own strength and on my own terms." Skip then became active in an action group on his base and reached out to other frustrated Christians and non-Christians.

Weekend Retreats

Weekends on base are times of recreation and intensive training in the Military Ministry, especially if the chaplain and staff members have organized a "Getaway" or retreat. Following one weekend retreat, nine people accepted Christ as their personal Savior, 32 rededicated their lives to Christ and 13 expressed a desire to enter full-time Christian service. Through these and other activities, thousands of servicemen are responding to the claims of Christ.

Military staff also offer assistance to the chaplains in making chapel programs as effective as possible in discipling the congregations and equipping them to be effective in reaching others for Christ. During the Here's Life, America campaigns in 1976, many chapels participated in helping to saturate their bases with the gospel message. This is also being implemented on overseas bases in conjunction with Here's Life movements which are being carried out in the area.

Possibly nothing illustrates the effectiveness of this work so dramatically as the story of one changed life. "All of my life I have searched for adventure," said one man. "Flying jet fighters as a naval officer seemed to be the answer for a while — with the added bonus of prestige and material security. But my craving for real action wasn't filled by combat missions and world travel. So my wife and I began a practical, realistic search for the most effective way to invest our lives for our Lord Jesus Christ. Exposure to Campus Crusade for Christ, to the changed and exciting lives of some staff couples, gave us the answer. We have found the action we sought on the full-time Campus Crusade staff."

CHAPTER FIFTEEN

The Message in Music

Music is a universal language, and tens of thousands are receiving Christ and committing their lives to His Lordship around the world through our music ministry.

The desire to be all things to all people brought about the birth of The New Folk, Campus Crusade's first singing group, and the beginning of the music ministry.

In 1966, 200 of our staff and students convened at Ohio State University for Operation Otherside, which was designed to saturate the campus of some 40,000 students with the claims of Christ. There I heard an outstanding singing group known as the Christian Minstrels, who had come from the University of Minnesota as a part of the Campus Crusade staff and student group under the direction of Ted Martin, then the director of the campus ministry for that area. The members asked me if I thought there might be a place for them in the ministry of Campus Crusade. As we talked and prayed together about such a possibility, I felt impressed to invite the entire group to come to Arrowhead Springs for training that summer.

During the course of that summer, the name was changed to The New Folk. After their training, the members took off for their first year of traveling and visited 125 colleges and university campuses in 27 states, singing before 250,000 people. God blessed their ministry in remarkable way, and many thousands of students were introduced to the Savior through their concerts.

Overseas Outreach

From that beginning of eight New Folk singers, the music ministry grew to include at one time more tha

10 singing groups that performed not only in the United States but also overseas.

The Forerunners, called the most outstanding singing group in Europe by secular and Christian leaders, presented concerts from 1967 to 1974. During one of their tours through Finland, the Forerunners performed before an average of 1,000 to 2,000 people every day. Those in the audience eagerly questioned the group members concerning their faith in Jesus Christ after the concerts. The leader of a large humanistic youth movement confessed that despite all of his attempts to find reality and meaning in working for the betterment of all men, he still found that there was a gaping emptiness within. After he received Christ into his life, he wrote, "You and your music got across to me like nothing has ever done before. It's a wonderful relief to have found the answer."

The Crossroads traveled throughout Asia, presenting evangelistic concerts. In Malaysia they drew 18,000 people to two concerts — making them the largest Christian gatherings in that country in the last 100 years — and performed to a total of 72,500 Asians during a seven-week tour.

After one of the Malaysian concerts, a Muslim girl named Nari asked a Crossroads member to explain to her the difference between Christianity and Islam. They discussed the uniqueness of Jesus, and the next day she talked to another Crossroads member who explained to her why he had become a Christian even though he, too, was from a Muslim nation. After three long talks, Nari received Christ. Later the Crossroads received letters from Nari in which she told them about the changes she noticed in her life since she accepted Christ as the only way to God.

At the same concert, a Buddhist student who was "tired of praying to a wall of stone statues" received Christ with a Crossroads member. Just before the Crossroads left to continue their tour, he expressed his eagerness to share his experience in Christ with his Buddhist parents.

The group's phenomenal impact for our Lord was evident through the results of a 22-month Asian tour. Visiting eight nations, the Crossroads performed 300 concerts, presenting the gospel to 256,000 people and saw 20,413 people indicate decisions to accept Christ as their Savior.

In international thrusts, American music ministry staff have traveled to other countries to give evangelistic and promotional concerts. The promotional concerts are designed to recruit workers who would help saturate a city or a country with the gospel.

On one such trip to the Philippines to assist in the Here's Life, Manila campaign, in personal witnessing after concerts and in random witnessing, music ministry staff talked to more than 900 people. About one-third of these individuals indicated decisions for Christ. In one instance, a staff member began reading aloud the Four Spiritual Laws booklet to a small group after a concert, and eight of the 14 students listening to him asked Christ to be their Savior. A combined total of more than 12,000 attended the 24 concerts, and of these, more than 2,000 signed up for campaign workers' training for Here's Life, Manila during the staff members' 19-day tour.

Hungry for God

Singing groups in the United States also find that people are hungry for God as they see thousands of individuals respond to His claims. At one New Folk presentation in a high school, 260 of the 600 students received Christ, with 125 others wanting to discuss the matter further.

Each of the music groups has developed a different style to communicate with various audiences of laymen, high school and college students, military personnel and prison inmates.

Besides the importance of evangelism in their ministries, stress is also placed on discipleship. Groups travel within specific regions so that performers have opportunities to personally follow up some of the people they lead to Christ during their concerts. Also, to insure discipleship, a follow-up program is set up with the local director of Campus Crusade to be carried out after the concert is over.

Part of the discipleship program also involves teaching others how to use their talents to share Christ. Music Institutes for Evangelism are conducted by staff members who teach individuals interested in music how to share their faith and how to put on an evangelistic music program.

It is the objective of the music ministry to present the ageless love of God and the exciting message of Jesus Christ to individuals through the medium of music. This method of creative expression has an appeal that crosses barriers and communicates throughout the world.

Each music program is designed to present Christ through a sound the audience is accustomed to, whether that be folk, soft rock, contemporary or classical. Communicating the reality of Jesus Christ to each individual in the audience is what the music ministry is all about.

As one student commented after a musical concert, "All the top professional groups have exploded my mind with questions. This group has satisfied me with the answers."

CHAPTER SIXTEEN

When Winning Is Secondary

Athletes have played an important role in the ministry of Campus Crusade since its inception. From the early years, all-Americans Donn Moomaw, Bob Davenport, Don Shinnick, Olympic decathalon champion Rafer Johnson and many others across the nation have been active participants in helping to reach for Christ other athletes and through them an even greater segment of society.

One of the first athletes to receive Christ and to become active in the movement was Donn Moomaw, UCLA's All-American linebacker of 1952. He passed up a promising career in professional football to study for the Presbyterian ministry. In explaining his personal decision, Moomaw said, "I am playing on God's varsity now. The temporary thrills of athletic achievement and the applause of the crowds cannot begin to compare with the challenge and the thrills of sharing Christ with others."

Donn's influence for Christ is worldwide. I met one outstanding young businessman, a member of Donn's church, whose business takes him all over the world. "I was an atheist," he said, "until I met Donn Moomaw. Through his life and ministry I became convinced that Christ is the only way to God."

The December 27, 1954 issue of the Los Angeles Examiner contained a full-page spread with testimonies of nine members of UCLA's great football team, the number one team in the nation that year. These nine first stringers were active in Campus Crusade. Four of them received All-American honors during their college careers.

Warner Award

One of the highlights of my experiences with these athletes was the day that Bob and Barbara Davenport handed me a little gift-wrapped box. Bob was one of UCLA's greatest athletes — a two-year All-American and student chairman of Campus Crusade. Upon opening the box, I discovered a beautiful watch with an alarm on it. I was very pleased, but could not understand why they were giving me such an expensive gift. Then Bob told me to turn the watch over and read the inscription on the back. It read: "Bob Davenport, Warner Award, 1955, to Bill, from Bob and Barbara."

I looked at Bob in amazement because this meant that he was giving me his most coveted award, one of the most prized awards, apart from the Heisman trophy, that an athlete on the West Coast can receive. I said, "Bob, I can't accept it. This is something that you should save for yourself or give it to your son."

But he insisted that because God had used Vonette and me in helping him and Barbara come to know Christ in a vital way, they wanted me to have the watch as an expression of their gratitude and love. You can well imagine how moved I was. In fact, I did what I always do when my heart is filled with joy and gratitude and I have no words to express it: I suggested that we pray. We all knelt together and prayed that, as I traveled around the country, God would use Bob's watch as a means of telling others the good news of our Savior. God has answered that prayer many times.

For example, as I was visiting Michigan State University, I met a junior who was a star football player and who had won All-American honors in both high school and junior college in California. The first thing the young man asked me was, "Do you know Bob Davenport?"

I assured him that I did and asked if he knew Bob.

"No," he replied, "but I have been one of his admirers for many years."

Bob Davenport had once spoken in his high school assembly, he explained, and had given such an inspiring and challenging talk that it had made a lasting impact on the athlete before me. Knowing that Bob never spoke unless he could give his witness for Christ, I asked this young man if Bob had spoken of his faith in Christ, and he said he had. Then I pulled off the watch Bob had given me, and the young man looked at it in wide-eyed amazement. After explaining why Bob had given it to me, I asked him if he had made the wonderful discovery of knowing Christ personally. He said, "No, I have gone to church almost every Sunday since I heard Bob Davenport speak in my high school assembly some years ago, but I have not yet made this decision. I don't know how."

Very quickly I explained how he could know Christ personally, and as we knelt together, he prayed and committed his life to Christ. All of this happened in a matter of minutes because God had already prepared his heart and had used Bob Davenport's watch in answer to our prayer.

Because of the influence that athletes can have, it became increasingly evident that a special emphasis needed to be directed toward athletes. In 1967, I asked Dave Hannah to direct the athletic ministry of Campus Crusade, which later became Athletes in Action. Dave played football for Oklahoma State University, where he led the team in scoring as a kicker. After graduation he tried out for the Los Angeles Rams, but painful leg injuries curtailed his career.

"I had an unquenchable desire to play pro football," Dave said, "but God suddenly took that desire away. Instead, He gave me a vision for challenging athletes to help reach the world for Christ."

A Platform to Share Christ

Dave believed that athletes could be an effective tool

or reaching the world with the gospel. He reasoned that since athletes are some of the most admired people in the country and the world, if they were won to Christ and discipled, they could use their position and fame to share the gospel of Christ with many who might never listen to a pastor, parent or teacher. He felt that an Athletes in Action ministry could establish teams in various sports and compete against colleges and athletic clubs. This would provide ready-made audiences with whom the athletes could talk about their experiences with Christ.

Dave's initial inspiration was a basketball team. By all worldly standards, Dave's idea for an Athletes in Action basketball team had no chance of succeeding. First, he had to get permission from the NCAA to play major colleges and universities as an extra game in their season schedules. Then he had to find schools willing to play an unknown, untried team of former college ballplayers.

Against all odds, permission came from the NCAA, and in 1967 Dave contacted more than 40 major universities who were interested in playing AIA. He ended up with a 29-game schedule for the 1967-68 season. Fortunately, no one ever asked Dave how many players he had or who his coach was. Because at that point, he had only one player. And no coach.

But that one player was the former captain of the number two-ranked University of Michigan team, Larry Tregoning. And by the time the season had opened on December 1, Tregoning had helped recruit nine other players and a coach, Fred Crowell, former head mentor for the University of Alaska.

Opening Games

Dave remembers how they opened their first season on consecutive nights against Utah and Wichita State. 'Our scouts reported that while Utah's team was good, Wichita's was tremendous. In our first game, Utah won by more than 20 points.

"As we trailed by 18 points at half-time, I'll never forget the challenge it was for our ballplayers to get up and say, 'Christ is the answer to all the problems of life.'"

After an all-day flight, the new team arrived in Wichita, Kan., dead tired. Their prospects were not promising against the nationally-ranked Shockers. Before 10,000 screaming fans, AIA fell behind 23-5 after the first five minutes. Then a miraculous turnabout took place and by half-time, AIA was ahead 46-44.

Athletes in Action lost that game, too, but only after a close struggle that went down to the final minute. Coach Fred Crowell recalled his thoughts after the game as the team presented its program. "Standing there lamenting the lost game, I heard Mack [Crenshaw] ask anyone interested in receiving information about how to mature in his relationship with Christ to turn to the back page of the program. Thousands of people responded. God was showing me that winning the basketball game was insignificant compared to our ultimate purpose."

Though winning games is not their ultimate purpose, AIA teams have compiled a fine record over the years. In their first season they finished with a 15-14 record, remarkable when you consider the fact that all of their games were played on their opponents' home courts. Even more important, however, the team spoke to more than 75,000 people about Christ. Dave and I both feel it is important to assemble the best teams possible for AIA. People respect you and listen more attentively to you when you are a winner.

Aiming for the Top

Dave set a very high standard. "If we could put together the best amateur team in the world," he said, "more people would listen to us share our faith in Christ."

Since that first year, the AIA basketball team has defeated many top-flight amateur teams throughout the United States. In 1972, the basketball program expanded to two teams, one located in the eastern section of the United States and one in the west. The teams later became known as the USA team, which played mostly major college competition, and the Challengers, who scheduled their games primarily with small college opponents.

In 1975, AIA began to take steps toward fulfilling Dave's dream about being the best amateur team in the world. During that year, Bill Oates, a successful coach at Santa Ana (Calif.) Junior College, took over the reins of the AIA USA team. Bill prayed often with Dave concerning potential new players.

Big things began to happen. Again and again Oates rushed into Hannah's office with the news that another player had been signed. Eventually, every player the two had prayed for decided to join AIA.

Oates meshed these new players into a unit that brought about a stark reversal of the team's fortunes. From a 30-13 record the year before, the AIA USA squad spurted to a sparkling 37-8 mark. Included in the wins was an 86-61 victory over the tough Cincinnati Bearcats. It was the first loss for Cincinnati on their home court in 33 games. The USA team closed the year by winning the National Amateur Athletic Union championship.

Turning Down Pro Offers

The 1976-77 season marked the arrival of several more talented basketball players. Two of them turned down offers to play in the National Basketball Association, and both are committed to the cause of Christ. UCLA's Ralph Drollinger was one of them. He turned down an offer from the Boston Celtics that year and another offer from the New Jersey Nets a year later for a three-year no-cut contract of $400,000. Ralph turned down these offers because, "I saw that the biggest challenge in my life is to know the character of Jesus Christ — to know Him and the power of His resurrection," he said. "One of my objectives is to help reach the world for Christ, to help fulfill His Great Commission."

Center Bayard Forrest turned down a Seattle Super-Sonics guarantee of $230,000 over two years. "I'm more excited about laying up treasures in heaven," said the former star of Grand Canyon College. With Bayard and Ralph anchoring the center position, the USA team roared to a 54-7 record. Included in those wins were two games that rocketed the team into national prominence.

The first of these games was with the undefeated University of San Francisco Dons, the top-rated team in the country. The game marked the first time in AIA's nine and a half year history that the team would be playing a home game.

They responded to the situation by dominating the powerful Dons, stretching an 11-point half-time lead to a 19-point victory, 104-85. All of a sudden, sports fans across the country began to hear about Athletes in Action. Daily newspapers devoted big coverage to the win, *Sports Illustrated* scheduled a special story and NBC-TV's *Grandstand* carried action spots from the game.

No Fluke

Within two weeks, AIA erased any thoughts that their win had been a fluke. They proved it by demolishing the fifth-ranked team in the country, the University of Nevada at Las Vegas, 104-77. Las Vegas' highly successful coach Jerry Tarkanian expressed his respect for AIA in post-game interviews. "They whipped us in every way . . . they totally dominated us. We got thoroughly whipped by a much better basketball team. They could stick with any team in the country." In addition to the credibility these two wins gave AIA, they also gave the 13,706 fans who attended the two games a chance to hear the gospel through their half-time presentation.

These two games set the stage for the season-ending encounter with the Soviet Union Red Army team, one of the best amateur squads in the world. In a thrilling battle before 10,239 enthusiastic fans, AIA lost 108-106. Clearly, Athletes in Action had made giant strides toward the fulfillment of Dave's dream of putting together the best amateur team in the world. In averaging 95 points per game over the year, AIA had outscored their opponents by an average of 21 points per game, an impressive showing. The team was also able to communicate the claims of Christ to 165,000 people who attended the games during the season.

The team started off the next year by downing the Russian team, 93-84. They went on to defeat Maryland, Michigan, San Francisco, Syracuse, Las Vegas and the coaches' All-American team, a team comprised of some of the year's finest college basketball players. They compiled a 35-game winning streak against college competition stretching over two years. "It's possible that the best non-professional team in the world might be a team of committed Christians who are using the game of basketball to help take the gospel to the world," observed Hannah.

The morning after their final regular season game, the team boarded a plane and flew to South America to join six other Western Hemisphere countries in the Christopher Columbus Cup. Representing the United States in the tournament, AIA defeated Argentina 81-69 in the finals to bring the championship home to this nation. This victory brought the season's record to 37-4, the best ever for the team.

AIA again was honored in the fall of 1978 as they were selected to be a part of the United States team in the World Basketball Championships in the Philippines. We praised God for the chance AIA had to represent the United States. To our knowledge it was the first time in the history of the tournament that a team committed to

Jesus Christ had represented its country.

Although the team struggled hard to win the championship, its efforts fell short. AIA managed to win six games and lose four in the tournament, placing fifth among 14 nations.

AIA's second basketball team, the Challengers, has also had its share of successes over the years. Playing mostly small colleges while the AIA USA team took on major college powers, the Challengers team moved to Canada to set up its headquarters and began playing Canadian colleges and universities. During that year, the Challengers pulled off perhaps the biggest victory in the team's existence by upsetting the Soviet National team, 79-71.

Wrestling Teams

Like our basketball teams, our wrestling squads have been blessed with success. Since the team was launched in 1967 with a tour of Japan, it has rapidly improved to the point where it rates among the top amateur wrestling powers in the United States. In 1971, the team won the Unites States Wrestling Federation Championship, symbolic of being the best amateur wrestling team in the nation.

Several of our wrestlers are former national collegiate champions, and many have been selected to travel overseas as representatives of the United States. Frequently they have had opportunities to share the gospel in foreign countries because of these honors they have received. In the 1976 Olympic Games at Montreal, two of our wrestlers represented the United States and won medals. John Peterson won the gold medal in his weight class, and Gene Davis was awarded a bronze.

Jim Axtell is a living testimony to how the Lord has used the AIA wrestling team to cause people to turn to Christ. During Jim's junior year at the University of Minnesota, he and his teammates wrestled the AIA team.

"After the match the man I wrestled shared with me what Jesus Christ meant to him," Axtell said. "As I talked to him, I could see in him a vital relationship with a living God."

A few days later, Jim decided to give his life to Jesus Christ. He began to see changes in his life over the following weeks and months. After graduating from college, Jim joined the AIA wrestling team so he, too, could use his talent as a means for explaining his faith to others.

Weightlifting

In the fall of 1969, AIA expanded into still another sport, weight- lifting. Russ Knipp, a man who has set nine world records and 30 American lifting records, helped the program get off the ground.

Over the years, the lifters who have made up our weightlifting teams have given exhibitions around the country in high schools, colleges, churches, civic clubs and military bases. During those exhibitions, the weight that they lift often surpasses existing records. Essential to the program is the presentation of the gospel. The lifters share their testimony, telling people how God has changed their lives and how they can allow Him to change theirs.

A track team was added to the list of AIA teams in 1971. Each fall the runners compete in top cross-country meets around the United States. Then they take to the indoor circuit to run against the leaders in amateur track. Several all-Americans and one world record holder have competed for the AIA track team. AIA also has a fine cross-country team, one which has won four national team titles since its inception.

Also touring the country and giving exhibitions at high schools and colleges is the gymnastics team. These athletes, too, take advantage of their exhibitions to present Christ to those in attendance. In addition to exhibitions, the team competes against top college and university teams.

AIA also fields soccer, softball and volleyball teams, has staff who minister to high school and college athletes and coaches, has radio and television programs and ministers to professional athletes.

Part of AIA's ministry to professional athletes has taken the form of training them how to share their faith and helping them to have an impact for Christ through Pro Week, a concentrated evangelistic outreach in one area. In 1973, 20 athletes participated in the first Pro Week in Atlanta, Ga. During that week the players spoke to high school assemblies, college campuses, civic clubs and church groups. As a climax to the week, the pros played an all-star team composed of football players from Georgia and Georgia Tech in a flag football game. When the final tabulation was taken, more than 73,000 people heard the claims of Christ with 10,000 making decisions. Since the Pro Football Week in Atlanta, teams have traveled to many cities and military bases throughout the United States and Canada.

Why AIA?

Much of AIA's incredible success story is told in the lives of the key athletes who make up these winning teams. People often ask the AIA members why they participate in the ministry, especially when there are greater financial rewards to be realized elsewhere. West wrestling coach Gene Davis, who has lost only two dual-meet matches in his 10-year AIA career, explains that he became a member of Athletes in Action "because I saw what a terrific impact AIA and Campus Crusade were having on different people throughout the United States and the world."

One professional football player said he has worked with AIA because of the need people have to hear about Christ. "Somebody was interested enough in me to come and tell me about Christ. And so I feel need to take advantage of the platform God has given me as a football player to tell young people about an answer to their needs."

More than five million people in live audiences have heard individuals on the AIA teams share the gospel through the first decade of the ministry. Millions more have heard the message over radio and television. "There's no way of knowing how many lives have been changed as a result of this ministry," Dave Hannah said. "Numbers can be misleading. But we collect comment cards after many of our appearances so that other Campus Crusade ministries can follow up those who receive Christ." More than 335,000 specified on their decision cards that they received Christ during the ministry's first 10 and a half years.

Through Dave's leadership, the athletic ministry of Campus Crusade has had a worldwide witness for Christ. The joy comes as the athletes hear what happens when they share the love and forgiveness of Christ with audiences. One student wrote after the basketball team played North Carolina State, "I used to be a drug addict and had sex problems. But now I want to live a Christian life. Write and tell me how."

One of the fans who attended an AIA game commented, "What you said tonight needs to be said more often to more people." Toward that end, Athletes in Action teams will continue to travel and compete around the country and the world, telling people about the life-changing promises of Jesus Christ.

CHAPTER SEVENTEEN

Multiplying the Message

Never before in history have we had such unlimited opportunities to reach the world with the good news of God's love and forgiveness. The diversity of the media — radio, television, newspapers, magazines, literature — provides us with the means to communicate to many individuals in the world how they can know Jesus Christ as Savior and Lord.

Bob and Amy George and their family provide a striking example of how the Holy Spirit can use the media to bring people to Christ. One of our earlier films, *Revolution Now*, which showed how God was using college students involved in our movement, was being shown on nationwide television. The Georges, watching the program in their home, were very moved by its conclusion — that Jesus Christ is the world's only hope. They later came to Arrowhead Springs for a personal appointment, and I had the joy of introducing both Bob and Amy to Christ.

Sharing Their Faith

The Georges promptly began to share their faith and joy in Christ with others — family, friends, business associates and employees — and saw many come to Christ. Desiring to know more about effective evangelism, Bob attended three Lay Institutes for Evangelism. Talking with me after one such training session, he asked about the some 2,500 people in the Los Angeles area who, like himself, had responded positively to the television program. I explained that each individual had been put on our mail list for our series of follow-up letters and materials, but due to limited personnel, we were not able to follow up each one personally.

Bob shared his burden for those people with me, stating, "I have felt strongly impressed of the Lord in the last few days that I should be personally responsible for following up all of these other 2,500 people. Would you allow me the privilege?"

I was overwhelmed. Only four months old as a Christian, yet he already desired to build other new Christians and pass on the training and knowledge he had learned. We gave him the assignment, and he immediately began organizing others he had introduced to Christ. Together, they began a program to follow up those in their area who had responded. A few years later, Bob and Amy joined our staff to work full time, and Bob played a major role in the overall success of Here's Life, America as director of the Dallas campaign.

What better way to do so than through the mass media?

The Impact of Mass Media

The communications media — newspapers, radio, motion pictures and television — have made a tremendous impact upon our society. They influence public opinion, keep us better informed than ever before in history, help mold character (usually in a negative way) and touch almost every phase of human existence. I am convinced that we, as Christians, should be utilizing the media for the proclamation of the gospel.

In a sense, proclaiming the gospel is like a military offensive, with the mass media serving as the air force — softening up the objective — so that the ground forces can come in and capture an area. The ground forces are those people making individual presentations of the gospel. The mass media play an important role as they prepare the way for those personal challenges to accept Christ.

Our commitment as a movement to utilize mass media tools to the fullest advantage to communicate Christ acts as a supplement to our commitment to personal evangelism. In many ways, our Mass Media Ministry serves and supports our entire movement, as well as churches across the nation. Our field staff make wide use of our evangelistic publications and materials in their ministries with individuals. Our radio and TV broadcasts reach individuals in areas where we do not have staff. And our staff use our tapes and training films to minister to many people simultaneously, thus increasing the scope and effectiveness of their personal ministries.

Chuck Younkman, who directedof our Mass Media Ministryfor a number of years, explains its importance this way: "Television, radio, films, tapes, audiovisuals and literature provide opportunities to reach millions of people at one time, as well as to increase our effectiveness in one-to-one situations."

Communicating to College Students

Our use of mass media began in response to a scarcity of evangelistic materials to attractively communicate to college students the claims of Christ. We began to publish the *Collegiate Challenge* magazine in 1967 to help meet that need, and since then, our staff and Christian students have used millions of copies across the nation and in other countries.

Thousands of students have made commitments to Christ through the influence of this magazine. One young woman picked up a copy in her sorority house. As she was reading it, a member of our staff dropped by, saw her reading it and began to talk with her about it. Before their conversation ended, she asked Christ into her life. After graduating from college, she joined the Campus Crusade staff and was used to introduce many others to the Savior.

Revolution Now!, a book containing my basic messages and content of our training, was published in July, 1969. The title *Revolution Now!* attracted a rebellious young radical who thought it had something to do with political revolution. As he read, he was surprised but not disappointed, for in the process of reading the book, he received Christ. After several years of exposure to our staff during which he received in-depth training, he made application for staff, was accepted and had a very fruitful ministry for our Lord.

Van Dusen Letter

One of our most popular pieces of evangelistic literature, the Van Dusen letter, came into being when a businessman who had expressed an interest in knowing Christ asked me to discuss the matter. Since he lived in New York and I lived in Los Angeles, it was not possible for me to visit him personally at that time. Instead, I wrote him a letter explaining the basic facts concerning Christ and the Christian life.

After mailing the letter, it occurred to me that this was the kind of letter that I could write to almost anyone whom I wanted to introduce to our Savior. So several thousand copies of the letter were mimeographed with the fictitious name of Van Dusen replacing the name of the friend to whom I had originally written. These mimeographed copies were used by members of the staff with students. The response was so encouraging, in some cases even phenomenal, that we decided to print it. Today, millions of copies of the Van Dusen letter are being used all over the world and are available in most major languages.

A Bible study series, The Ten Basic Steps Toward Christian Maturity, and our series of Transferable Concepts booklets, communicating basic truths of the Christian life, are widely used by all of our ministries. Thousands of local churches and other Christian groups also utilize these materials as they build those who have responded to the gospel and those who have been Christians for many years.

Our *Worldwide Challenge* magazine, sent to more than 100,000 readers each month, is designed to communicate the news about what God is doing worldwide as well as to encourage readers in their relationship with the Lord. Since its beginning in January, 1974, many readers have written that it has helped them to understand our ministry in greater depth in addition to encouraging them spiritually.

Here's Life Publishers

One of our most rapidly growing ministries is Here's Life Publishers. As a publisher, we are now releasing more than thirty new books a year. As a training resource, we are involved in training media staff, writers and other publishing personnel, on an international level. And we are directing translation and international distribution of books and Campus Crusade training materials in 150 countries. Through coordinating the publishing and distribution of these books, audio and video tapes, evangelistic tools and other products, Here's Life Publishers is making a life-changing impact worldwide, fulfilling the goal of moving people to ministry, helping them become active, involved Christians, and equipping these ministering Christians with the tools for evangelism, discipleship and leadership.

Film Ministry

Another branch of the Mass Media Ministry that is having a positive impact is our film department, now called Paragon. Our films are created for one purpose: to communicate the resurrected Christ, thus encouraging individuals to receive Him as Savior and Lord and to commit their lives as His disciples to helping fulfill the Great Commission. These films are shown in a wide variety of places — churches, youth camps, college campuses, reform schools, prisons and military bases. Through film we have communicated the story and miracles of EXPLO '72, ministered to the black community about Christ's relevancy to its needs, exposed the dangers of the occult, and shown Christians how to experience the joyous, fulfilling life Christ offers and how to communicate the good news to others.

One man, writing to tell us how God used *Too Late to Wait*, a film designed to communicate the gospel to minorities, shared with us the excitement of watching God work in his church after they showed the film in a secular high school sociology class. He wrote: "One of the teachers was very moved and thought the film was excellent. . . .As a result of this one film and other evangelical tools used in our congregation, the high school youth group has grown from three to over 30 witnessing Christians."

Other films on the Christian home and the role of the pastor are also available through our film lending library.

Our tape library also makes available hundreds of messages that have been part of our training programs over the years. With the compact, inexpensive, playback equipment now available, many are finding that they can listen to tapes anywhere. Messages available include the ministry of the Holy Spirit, training for evangelism and family living, evangelistic messages and a series of studies of several books of the Bible. In addition to these training tools, our Mass Media Ministry also supplies a variety of visual aids for our training institutes, classes and the School of Theology.

Television broadcasts of selected Athletes in Action basketball games have also reached many people. In addition to being treated to fine sports entertainment, the audiences have been presented with the claims of Christ through half-time programming.

CHAPTER EIGHTEEN

JESUS Film

Beneath a cool, starlit sky, Pakistanis of all ages sauntered out from pitch-dark corridors, finding a place to sit before the movie screen. Women dressed in flowing saris sat on woven mats, several rocking discontented babies slowly to rest. A horde of wide-eyed children squeezed close to the screen, their heads cocked uncomfortably back to look up at the picture. A wall of men stood around the dark perimeter of the gathering.

For most of the people in the small village of Korungi, this would be the first movie they had ever seen. The film was *JESUS*, a portrayal of the life of Christ based entirely on Luke's gospel.

The crowd swelled to about three hundred as the show began in Urdu. As the film unwound through four reels, the people remained hushed and transfixed. During the crucifixion scene, several faces contorted in anguish. Many people sobbed aloud. But when the risen Christ appeared to His disciples, sighs of relief whispered throughout the crowd.

"Tonight I have a new relationship with Jesus," said Mustaq, an 18-year-old street sweeper. "To think that He did all that for us — all that pain He suffered. Now I want to do something for Him."

This scene has been repeated across the globe as more than 250 million people have seen the story of *JESUS* and tens of millions of people — like Mustaq — expressed their desire to receive Christ as their Savior. The film has been translated into more languages than any other movie in history and has been called by some missions leaders "the greatest tool for evangelism in the history of the church."

The completion of this film and its use to present the gospel to so many millions is the fulfillment of a dream for me. Since 1947 I had wanted to be involved in the production of a film about the life of our Lord. At that time I was a young Christian and had a great deal of zeal, but not a lot of knowledge. Still, I approached Cecil B. DeMille, the famous filmmaker, about the project. In the silent era he had made a film about our Lord entitled, *King of Kings*, as well as other masterpieces including *The Ten Commandments*. DeMille was a great inspiration to me. On one occasion I met with him after he spoke at a church service.

DeMille told me that his father had been a Broadway actor who had come to Christ and endeavored to take the gospel to that segment of the entertainment industry. DeMille had come to Hollywood to make Christian films and said he would make nothing but Christian films if he had the money.

Neither did I have the funds to begin such a project. This lack of funding continued to thwart my dream for thirty years. For years after the founding of Campus Crusade for Christ, we discussed the need for a film on the life of Christ as an ideal tool for evangelism. We obtained copies of many of the more than thirty films done on the life of our Lord. Most of the films were not biblically correct. We even seriously considered buying the rights to one of these films and doing the work necessary to make it biblically accurate.

Although we felt that such a film would have incredible potential as an evangelistic tool, we never were able to secure sufficient funds for the production costs.

Then in the fall of 1976, I met a man in my office who had an amazing concept. He wanted to put the entire Bible on film. It was an awesome undertaking, but John Heyman seemed like a person with the background to make such a dream come true. Heyman was an outstanding Jewish movie producer who had produced more than twenty feature length films.

I introduced him to Paul Eshleman, who at that tim
was the director of our Campus Ministry in the Unite
States. Paul and John formed a solid friendship.

Over the next few months, I had numerous meetin
with John. Often when I was in Washington, D.C., h
would fly in from his office in New York and we wou
talk until the wee hours of the morning about Jesus beir
the Messiah. Paul had even more frequent conversation
with John.

Finally the day came when John was ready to ma
his commitment to Christ and God touched his life
an encouraging way. It was not long after that whe
John came to Arrowhead Springs for a special meetin
Paul Eshleman was with him, as were Bunker ar
Caroline Hunt, longtime friends and generous suppo
ters of the ministry.

We chatted about the possibility of a film on the li
of Christ which John Heyman would direct. The Hun
volunteered to play a major role in financing the proje
In just a few moments, what I had prayed about for mo
than thirty years became a joyful reality.

Accuracy and authenticity were the watchwords
the film. Painstaking work by a team of researchers pr
duced a 318-page document giving the biblical, theolo
ical, historical and archeological background of eve
scene. The Gospel of Luke provided the foundation
the script. In essence, the film was really a documenta
drama, with the film moving simply from scene to sce
with no embellishments to the Scripture.

Jewish actors were used for most roles, but the sear
for an actor to play the lead role took months. Tw
hundred sixty-three actors were screen tested, and fina
Englishman Brian Deacon was chosen.

Brian memorized whole chapters of Luke and re
the Gospel twenty-two times before filming began. H
was so convincing as Jesus that bystanders often bro

into applause at the end of one of his speeches, and many asked to be healed by him after the healing scenes were filmed.

During the filming, all of which took place in Israel, Heyman demanded excellence, paying meticulous attention to detail. He stopped the filming once when he noticed a ripple-soled tennis shoe print in the dust.

Movies are notoriously difficult to make, and this one was no exception.

"This is absolutely the most difficult film I've ever tried to make," Eshleman remembers John saying. "You have no idea the problems we've faced."

When shooting began for Jesus' baptism and for the calming-of-the-storm scenes, the weather and water were freezing. Deacan caught pneumonia, and two days of filming were lost.

During the filming the message of Christ touched the lives of many involved. On one occasion a college dropout showed up looking for work. He had been drifting through Europe trying to find direction for his life. He wound up in Israel with empty pockets and an empty heart.

After carrying props on the set for a couple of days, he picked up a Gideon Bible in a Tel Aviv hotel room and began reading Luke. As he finished he slid to his knees and received Christ as his Savior. Five months later he was studying at Dallas Bible College to become a minister.

Even before *JESUS* was shown in theaters, it changed lives, often in surprising ways. When Eshleman was meeting with Hollywood executives to work out the film's distribution, he met one Warner Brothers executive who asked, "How would I begin, I mean with a faith in Jesus?"

Later, with a tear-choked voice, he bowed his head and asked Christ to come into his life.

"This is what the *JESUS* film is about," Paul says. "Searching people given new life, new hope and a reason to live."

JESUS opened in America in the fall of 1979. By the end of the commercial run a year later, more than four million people had seen the film.

After one film showing a teacher told her students she would be happy to tell them how to know Christ personally if they would come to her after school. Two days later she had led fourteen students to Christ.

In Birmingham and Jacksonville, theater managers gave their lives to Christ. At a special screening for college students in Sacramento, twenty-one indicated their desire to become followers of Jesus.

From its inception, however, *JESUS* was planned for the world. The very format of *JESUS* — with its simple, straight narrative right out of Luke — makes it easily adaptable for foreign translations. More than $10 million has been raised and spent so far on 100 translations — most of them lip-synchronized. Most versions also include an attached evangelistic closing. Campus Crusade plans to finish translations for 271 major languages by 1990, and another 1,000 dialects by 1995.

When the film opened in Europe's theaters, few expected much response. A theater owner in Zurich, Switzerland, reluctantly agreed to show the film, but only for a few days because he felt it would not be profitable. Six weeks later the film had shown to nearly 4,800 people.

A headline in England, where at one theater 10,000 people saw the film in four weeks, read "*JESUS* outdraws *E.T.*" The greatest theater run was in Singapore, where 200,118 people saw the film in four weeks.

We have seen phenomenal response in developing countries, where oftentimes fishermen and farmers still ply their trade the same way people in Jesus' day did. While hundreds responded to the film in America and Europe, thousands responded in Asia, Africa and Latin America. In these Third World countries, film teams equipped with portable screens and projectors take the film to remote villages. After setting up their equipment and passing out fliers, they often draw crowds of more than 1,500 people. For many it is their first opportunity to view a movie.

Team members sometimes operate at great risk to present the film. They have been attacked, robbed, imprisoned, stoned, poisoned and burned with firebrands.

"Every film team in India has been stoned and beaten," says Charlie Abro, coordinator of the film there. "We don't even think about it anymore. We just expect to have difficulties, and this is one of them."

The sacrifice and persecution is worth the effort. In several villages of Maharashtra, India, people often waited until 3 A.M. for the electricity to come on — and the program didn't conclude until 5:30 A.M. In other areas the people asked the team to show the film again as soon as it ended the first time. In one location it was shown three consecutive times.

The stories seemingly never end. During one week of some of the fiercest fighting in El Salvador, *JESUS* was shown in Santa Telca. Half of the city of 52,000 saw the film with 5,600 indicating salvation decisions. By the end of 1984, the film had been shown to more than 250,000 people in El Salvador.

In Burma the remote people of Hsanguang sent word to a Campus Crusade film team that they wanted to see *JESUS* during their harvest festival. The only way to get there was by helicopter, and the expense of that was prohibitive.

But the villagers did not give up easily. Soon projectors, generator, petrol, screen, cords, follow-up materials and team members were loaded onto elephants to carry them over the mountains to Hsanguang. During the harvest festival on two successive nights, 6,500 saw the film, and of those, 141 professed faith in Christ.

In many cases, some of the best news about the film takes place after it leaves. The village of Pamongan lies in the heart of Indonesia's Muslim stronghold. Still, about 200 villagers gathered in an open area one balmy evening to view *JESUS*. Just as the projector had started, the amplifier blew out. There seemed no choice but to cancel the show. A mullah (Muslim teacher) quickly offered to lend an amplifier from the local mosque.

At the end of the film, a villager named Subawi, his mother, Sunarti, and a brother named Swandini were the first to take a public stand for Christ. Two others, including a 50-year-old laborer named Parti, followed. The other was a mullah.

Campus Crusade staff members came to conduct follow-up sessions with the new believers. The first meeting had eight people present. But by the end of one year, nearly 200 people from the village gathered at Sunarti's house. This young church was then transferred to the care of a Southern Baptist church in Semarang.

"Jesus Christ is amazing," said Parti, the laborer who trusted Christ that first night at the film showing. "In the eyes of people, I am nothing. But because I am a Christian now, I am a son of God. It is a great privilege."

It is my prayer that in the coming years, literally billions of people — many in the Third World — will have the same opportunity Parti had to hear the life-changing message of Jesus Christ through the film, *JESUS*.

CHAPTER NINETEEN

Life at the Nerve Center

For many years, I have spent much of my time living out of a suitcase. Because of this, whenever Vonette and I return to Arrowhead Springs, every day there is almost like Christmas. No place in the world is more attractive to Vonette and me than Arrowhead.

I am not the only one who looks forward to coming to Arrowhead Springs. Often guests visiting Arrowhead comment on the radiant countenances, the cheerful attitude, the overflowing life and the beautiful spirit they see in our staff at Arrowhead Springs. It is the staff at our international headquarters who provide a vital supportive ministry for the worldwide work of Campus Crusade.

Oftentimes I am given credit for the phenomenal ministry of Campus Crusade — credit which I do not deserve or seek. The real credit must go to the Lord. But in His sovereign wisdom and grace, He has called a most unusually gifted and dedicated group of men and women to assist me in the direction and leadership of this ministry. These individuals with whom I am privileged to work are mature, Spirit-filled, able people who for the most part average 10 years of more with the ministry. Together we pray, plan, strategize and work to help fulfill the Great Commission.

Steve Douglass, vice president for administration, gives leadership to all the headquarters ministries which support the worldwide outreach. Steve graduated with honors from MIT and in the upper two percent of his class from Harvard Business School. Loren Lillestrand, our field director for the U.S. Ministries, is also based at

Arrowhead Springs and gives direction to our staff in various ministries.

Board of Directors

A remarkable group of outstanding businessmen serve as the board of directors for Campus Crusade. Their wise counsel has helped me to avoid many mistakes and make better decisions than I could have on my own. These men are:

S. Elliot Belcher, Jr., Chairman of Southern United Life Insurance Co.; Clarence E. Brenneman, Chairman, C.W. Tozer, Ltd.; Claude T. Brown, Chairman, Brown Transport Corporation; Bruce A. Bunner, Partner, Peat, Marwick, Mitchell & Co.; Leroy O. Eger, President, Decent Devices and IXTUS F.A. Costa Rica; Edward L. Johnson, Chairman and President, Financial Federation, Inc.; L. Allen Morris, President of the Allen Morris Co.; Arlis Priest, President, Priest Enterprises. The final member of the board is my beloved wife, Vonette.

I would like to write an entire chapter on each of these people and the others who report to me because of all that they mean to me and to this ministry, but to do so would require another 200 pages at least. Yet, you cannot understand the reason for the remarkable success of this ministry apart from these and thousands of others whom God has called and anointed to make this ministry possible.

Those who are responsible for the headquarters ministry at Arrowhead Springs belong to a team of qualified and successful businessmen who have dedicated their lives to Christ and to helping fulfill the Great Commission through the Campus Crusade ministry. These men serve under the direction of Steve Douglass and assist me in many important management decisions.

Choosing Campus Crusade Over a Secular Position

Typical of these is Jim Schroeder, who, with his wife,

Marti, left a profitable career in management with a telephone company to join He explains his reason for leaving business to join the staff as follows: "I found I was really desirous of living and sharing my faith constantly. And I felt that God had provided me with the skills in business that could be used in the best possible way for Him in full-time Christian work. I am thrilled with being able to share in the miracles God continuously performs through this ministry."

Says one staff member serving in a secretarial position, "I sincerely believe that every single function at Arrowhead Springs helps to reach thousands of people."

"Just knowing that I'm helping someone get information about what God wants him to do in terms of reaching the world for Christ is exciting for me," adds a secretary who works in personnel. She handles up to 40 letters a day from individuals asking how they might serve in the various ministries of Campus Crusade.

"We're all members of the same body," says one administrator, "and I count it a privilege to be serving in any capacity at headquarters. I love what I'm doing, but more important I love the Person I'm serving. Because God has called me to this ministry, I have a worldwide ministry and an excitement for what He can do."

These people, together with many other qualified, dedicated individuals who are totally committed to Jesus Christ and are bearing fruit in His power, are the force that makes Arrowhead Springs the bustling, productive, exciting, *living* place that it is.

Impact on Others

Arrowhead Springs is alive with impact. The 800 staff members, because of their direct involvement with thousands of programs and materials and millions of lives in a worldwide ministry, are influencing for Christ an unbelievable number of people of other lands and cultures. While field staff man the front lines, execute

programs and use an increasing amount of materials
they depend on the staff at Arrowhead Springs to provide
the supply line — to keep the action going.

Arrowhead Springs is alive with work. The staff a
the international headquarters are constantly planning
organizing, corresponding, creating, reviving, reporting
training, teaching, publicizing, studying, rehearsing
praying, writing, reaching. Although Arrowhead
Springs was formerly a resort and spa for business ty
coons and Hollywood movie stars, it is now definitely a
workspace for the Lord.

Arrowhead Springs is alive with multiplication. A:
an international training center, it is the location for con
tinuous teaching and training of Christians — showing
them how to experience the Spirit-filled life, how to share
their faith, how to teach others to experience and share
the same life of victory and fruitfulness. In other words
they are trained to multiply. This training — whether i
is through a Lay Institute for Evangelism, the Institute
of Biblical Studies, a high school conference, Pastors' o
Executive Seminar, a Church Growth or Managemen
Institute — is also available to all of the headquarter
staff.

Fellowship

The entire Campus Crusade staff, including myself
whether at headquarters or on a campus or in a commu
nity, are daily challenged to be all that Christ wants u
to be — that is, servants living in obedience to His com
mands under the power of the Holy Spirit. Together w
are laboring to help fulfill the Great Commission in thi
generation. Every ministry, every office, every publica
tion, every policy, every activity and every project re
volves around this goal.

A major department within the financial system c
the ministry is accounting. This office reports to the dire
tor of finance and assists me with the responsibility c

caring for God's money; administering all financial policies, bookkeeping, budgeting, payroll, accounts receivable and payable; and administering insurance.

Also under the financial system are computer services, purchasing and the word processing center which handles much of the ministry's typing and correspondence. For greater efficiency and economy of operation and thus greater glory to God, computer services use electronic data processing equipment. Computer operation, key punching, programming and systems analysis are the main responsibilities of this necessary department.

Conference Services

The conference services department seeks to provide warm, efficient Christian hospitality to visiting staff, students, laymen, conferees and dignitaries. This responsibility involves hotel management, guest reception, food services and housekeeping. The Arrowhead Springs campus is considered one of the most beautiful conference centers in America. When not used for our training conferences, the facilities are made available to churches and other Christian organizations.

Technical services is another area vital to the management and upkeep of headquarters. Since the time the Lord first gave Arrowhead Springs to us, we have shown our gratitude and willingness to care for His gifts by assigning a full-time staff to maintain the grounds and buildings and to landscape and plan the development of new facilities. Under the direction of the grounds staff, the Arrowhead Springs campus becomes increasingly more beautiful each year.

With plans and prayerful expectation for 110,000 regular and *Agape* Movement staff, the personnel department is constantly involved in recruiting and placing staff, maintaining personnel files and managing personnel. Its primary aim is to be used of God to place His people in strategic areas of His service.

The Mass Media Ministry serves with the belief that nothing is impossible with God. Through wise use of magazines, newspapers, mail campaigns, radio, films, television programs, evangelistic audiovisual aids and counseling by mail with both Christians and non-Christians, we are helping this generation hear of the love of Jesus Christ and learn how to know Him personally.

Handling the Mail

Within mail systems is the correspondence department. It has the mammoth but rewarding task of corresponding with thousands of new Christians on a regular follow-up schedule, plus maintaining the entire Campus Crusade mailing list.

Separating and making sure that incoming mail gets to the right people is a major function of mail systems. In addition, the department records all contributions made through the mail and relays the information to the accounting department.

Using God-given Skills

Arrowhead Springs is alive. Here is a place where any committed Christian, no matter what his special skill or talent is, can fit in and be used of God in a fruitful and world-changing way. In fact, we are continually praying for more individuals with secretarial, clerical and administrative background and skills — qualifications that one does not normally associate with Christian service but that are actually indispensable to a worldwide evangelistic movement.

The headquarters staff member is in a strategic spot. He is in the heart and nerve center of a movement that is being directed and blessed by God. He is a prayer warrior for missionaries of the whole world; daily he has cause to praise God for specific miracles occurring throughout the world. He is doing the initial, necessary work that results in much more fruit on the field. Every day he is helping to plant and water thousands of seeds of the Word of God and is reaping 30-, 60-, or 100-fold. If you are interested and qualified for one or more openings for headquarters staff, please write for more information.

CHAPTER TWENTY

EXPLO '72

In 1969, I was sitting on the platform of the great City Auditorium in Minneapolis during the U.S. Congress on Evangelism. Together with evangelist Akbar Haqq of India, I was enjoying one of Dr. Billy Graham's messages.

At one point during the message, I leaned over and mentioned briefly to Dr. Haqq that I had felt a strong impression from the Lord that Campus Crusade should sponsor a congress on evangelism — primarily to train young people in how to share their faith.

"Bill," he said, "I think you should do it."

This was the birth of an idea which later became one of the most tremendous events in the history of our movement.

100,000 Delegates

After returning to Arrowhead Springs, I presented the idea to our ministry directors, some of whom were enthusiastic. Others were skeptical that we should undertake such a big task. Finally, after several months, we were in agreement to proceed. So, we began talking and praying about assembling possibly 100,000 students in a major city of America for such a congress. The suggested time was the summer of 1972.

On February 21, 1970, I was speaking at a conference in a Chicago hotel. After my message, I asked Paul Eshleman, then our campus director in Madison, Wis., and his wife, Kathy, if I could meet with them for a few minutes. That was when I told Paul that our regional directors had voted to assign the general management of this gigantic, week-long training session to him. I asked him if he would do it, and after several days of seeking the Lord's guidance, he accepted.

Things started rolling very soon as, in March of that year, Paul visited the two possible locations for EXPLO '72 — Dallas and Chicago. The Texas city turned out to be the one which, we discovered, could best accommodate the number of students and lay people we were going to host.

As Paul met with incredulous officials at the Dallas Convention Bureau and the Chamber of Commerce to discuss our plans, the task became realistically clear: We were going to be moving a city into a city! But the leaders of Dallas gave us the go-ahead.

In May, Paul and Kathy moved to Dallas and then spent the summer at Arrowhead Springs, where we developed the initial plans for EXPLO.

At the end of the summer, 10 "charter staff members" for EXPLO accompanied them back to Dallas to begin the two-year-long preparations.

The responsibilities of the EXPLO staff, which eventually grew to 300 by the time of the Congress arrived, were mammoth: building a national promotional strategy including radio and TV spots, a promotional film, newspaper releases, ads, brochures, church bulletin inserts; inviting Christian leaders from across the U.S. to speak, *and* arranging for rooms, beds, meals, transportation and registration for 100,000.

Prayer Power

They worked long hours, sacrificing personal time and sleep. But even more, they prayed. And around the country, as we prayed with and for them, we saw God supply their needs day by day as they believed Him for big things.

For example, we prayed for 200 promotional film agents who could help build enthusiasm for EXPLO. By the time EXPLO began, there were at least that number, with 1,000 films in circulation — the largest distribution of Christian films ever developed, the producer told us.

Trusting God for office equipment, the staff prayed for an adding machine. A man brought one to them. They prayed for a copier. A man donated the use of his. They asked the Lord for a good entree with hotel sales managers, and before the congress was over we had the largest bookings ever given to any organization for a convention in Dallas.

And, of course, we continued to pray for the delegates who would come. We prayed that the Lord would cause many thousands to see a need in their lives for a closer walk with Him, a desire to share Him with others, and practical, natural ways of doing just that.

85,000 Registered

In February, 1972, only four months before EXPLO was to begin, we had registered only 19 delegations. By opening date, under the dynamic leadership of Mary Banks, a remarkable businesswoman who volunteered her services, we had 1,300 delegations coming from 1,000 cities. The total number of registered delegates grew to approximately 85,000, with representatives from about 70 countries. On June 12 they poured into Dallas by plane, automobile, motorcycle, bus, in campers, on foot and on bicycles. As early as 3 a.m. that morning, buses began arriving at huge Market Hall, just off the Stemmons Freeway, where the delegates would register.

During the long hours of waiting to register that day, amid the heat, the inevitable inconveniences and the transportation complications, many of the conferees sat on suitcases, studied their Bibles, sang or prayed. Their attitude was an inspiration. Most of the delegates adopted the slogan, "You can't make it tough enough for me to complain."

As the staff met for prayer at dawn, Dallas morning papers carried full-page ads with the words: "Something historic is happening here." The same message flashed continuously from an electronic sign on the Blue Shield Building downtown. Mayor Wes Wise repeated the words on TV spot announcements all morning. Dallas gave a warm welcome to EXPLO '72.

The congress became historic because it was the largest week-long Christian training effort in the history of the world (up to that time). Specialized training was held in 63 locations throughout the city for collegians, high school students, lay men and women, pastors, faculty members, military personnel, blacks, business executives and their wives, athletes and 2,000 international delegates.

Basics of the Christian Life

In morning sessions, presented in workshop and lecture format, conferees heard about the basics of the Christian life: how to walk in the power of the Holy Spirit daily, how to experience God's love and forgiveness, how to know His will, and how to communicate His love and plan to someone else. This was the "meat" of EXPLO. Many guest Bible teachers like Dr. J. Edwin Orr, Dr. Harold Ockenga (president of Gordon-Conwell Seminary), and Sam Wolgemuth (president of Youth for Christ International) gave messages that helped clarify the real meaning of discipleship.

Students were also assigned to small action groups of six to eight with a leader. Action groups met several times during the week so that students could discuss what they had been learning and receive personal counseling from their group leaders.

Afternoons offered an array of 49 optional seminars of which delegates could take advantage. Topics ranged from Christian marriage and dating to using the mass media for Christ, black rap sessions, self-acceptance and dealing with the occult.

After hearing a message entitled "How to Live With

Your Parents," one girl, a graduate student at the University of California at Berkeley, said, "I'm going to go home and ask my mother's forgiveness for my rebellion."

Free time in the afternoons found the delegates visiting the Christian Opportunities Exposition, which allowed them to investigate staff possibilities with 206 Christian missionary groups, schools and churches from around the world. We had invited them to come to EXPLO '72 as our guests to promote their ministries. We were told that nothing like this had ever happened before. Many delegates, having come to EXPLO with open hearts, willing to go anywhere for God, found the exposition invaluable.

Intercristo, a Christian computer matching service, provided a personalized computer report on specific job openings in many of the organizations at the fair. For $3, the delegates received lists of five to ten opportunities which matched their own skills and education. With that, they were prepared to investigate the organizations that they knew were looking for someone with their qualifications.

The Wycliffe Bible Translators showed a multimedia presentation of its work in primitive countries. By the end of the week, in addition to 480 requests for more information, four couples had made definite plans to begin training for Wycliffe staff.

We did everything we could to enable the students to spend as much time as they needed at the Exposition, allowing the pavilions to open early and stay open until midnight on some occasions. We were encouraged and overjoyed to hear most of the exhibitors report that the EXPLO exposure was the most profitable they had ever had.

Nightly Meetings in the Cotton Bowl

Each evening of EXPLO week, the Dallas Cotton Bowl literally rang with praise to God as delegates, united in

what seemed to be a gigantic family reunion, filled nearly
every seat in the stadium. An overflow crowd, made up
primarily of enthusiastic high schoolers, settled on the
plastic-covered astroturf of the playing field, and still
others watched by closed circuit TV in nearby Memorial
Auditorium.

The evenings were filled with the blessing of God as
Dr. Billy Graham, EXPLO's Honorary Chairman, and Dr.
E. V. Hill of the Mt. Zion Baptist Church in the south
central area of Los Angeles joined me in speaking to that
vast and enthusiastic multitude. Performances by well-
known Christian singing groups, on-stage interviews
with delegates who were eager to share something that
God had done or taught them during the week and
reports from international representatives rounded out
the mass rallies.

Each night the spirit was spontaneous and full of
rejoicing as delegates clapped to the music and sang
along with the performers. The stands resounded with
the words "Praise the Lord!" and often the response
"A-a-a-a-men!" would come from another place in the
stadium. Bob Horner, our area director for Colorado-
Wyoming, emceed these sessions. "I've never been on a
stage where there was so little fear," he said. "It's just
like performing at a family reunion."

Governor Reubin Askew of Florida, an EXPLO delegate himself, agreed. "What stands out the most when
I see this group of young people, black, white and yellow,
in the Cotton Bowl [approximately 60,000 of the delegates were college and high school students] with long
hair and short hair — is that they have found a common
bond in Christ. They accept each other for what they
are — God's children."

Spreading the Good News

But the delegates to EXPLO '72 could not and did
not keep the love of Christ just within the "family circle."

His love caused them to take advantage of every opportunity that week to tell Dallas citizens, policemen, shoppers, bus drivers and news reporters that God had a plan — a wonderful, abundant plan — for their lives, too.

We were praying that EXPLO would serve as an important steppingstone toward the fulfillment of the Great Commission in the entire United States by 1976 and the world by 1980. And as we saw 85,000 delegates, supplied with Four Spiritual Law booklets and Gospels of John, move throughout the Dallas-Ft. Worth area and willingly take the good news of our Lord to tens of thousands on the Tuesday and Wednesday afternoons of witnessing, we were reassured that the Great Commission truly can and will be fulfilled.

Although records were incomplete, estimates indicated that at least 25,000 had received Christ by the end of the week.

Joye Scott, from Rockford, Ill., said the people she talked to were open and receptive. "They welcomed us into their homes and were curious to find out what we really had to say. Most agreed that we did have something to tell the world."

"I've been approached by several [delegates] and they all seem very sincere," noted Dallas public accountant, J. M. McDonnel. "The EXPLO movement is the greatest hope the world has had in decades."

In a spot survey taken by the *Dallas Times Herald* the reporters found that "the mood of an overwhelming majority of businessmen, secretaries and office workers interviewed on downtown streets Thursday was one of frank support for the delegates."

Captain John Squier of the traffic division reminded Dallas citizens of the importance of being patient in the midst of traffic tie-ups during the week. "When you consider that these people are here in the spirit of Christ and brotherhood, I would say that it's a worthwhile traffic jam were are having."

As did many that week, Dr. Graham commended the hospitable Texans. He praised them for the "wonderful spirit in which you have taken EXPLO delegates to your hearts and into your homes."

Final Rally

A final Cotton Bowl rally was held on Friday evening, ending in a moving candlelighting ceremony which symbolized the spreading of God's love from person to person throughout all the world. Then on Saturday the congress was climaxed by an evangelistic Jesus Music Festival attended by 180,000 — many of whom were not Christians when they came. The festival began at 7:25 a.m., since people had already started settling down in front of the 150-foot wide rolling stage, erected on a huge vacant area downtown where the Woodall Rodgers Freeway would later be built. Christian musicians such as Johnny Cash and his family, the Statler Brothers, Andrae Crouch and the Disciples, Connie Smith, Kate Henley (from "Godspell"), Larry Norman and scores of others made the arena reverberate with songs that uplifted the Savior.

By 3 p.m., after Dr. Graham had given his message, everyone at the festival had heard a clear explanation of how he could receive Jesus Christ if he had not already done so. And afterward, across the long stretch of pavement, EXPLO delegates could be seen sharing God's love through the Four Spiritual Laws with individuals hungry for a new life.

That day, 85,000 trained men and women and students left Dallas with a plan and a desire to capture their communities for Jesus Christ. As a result, I believe that a new emphasis on evangelism was introduced into many churches and Christian youth groups. As newscasters interviewed delegates to ask what the week had meant to them, the most common reply was, "This week I learned how to witness for Christ." Trained people can change communities everywhere.

On the last two evenings in the Cotton Bowl, when I challenged delegates to stand if they were willing to invest their time, talent and treasure for the fulfillment of the Great Commission, the majority of the audience stood.

Also, we praise God for the testimony that EXPLO was to the non-Christian world. Approximately 400 media representatives converged on Dallas from the U.S., Holland, Norway, New Zealand, Israel, Germany, France, India and the Philippines. National media — CBS, NBC, UPI and AP — major Christian and secular magazines and even some radical underground papers were also on hand. Around the world, the news media were saying, "These students are different."

The exposure of the congress was increased even more during the two months that followed, as three hour-long EXPLO '72 specials were broadcast over nationwide television on 235 stations across the U.S. Each program had an estimated audience of 35 million.

And finally, EXPLO '72 served to give us all an increased concern for the nations of the world — that millions would have an opportunity to hear the gospel.

The five days in Dallas were ended, but we believe that the spiritual explosion begun there will continue to have results around the world for generations.

CHAPTER TWENTY-ONE

The Great Commission
Prayer Crusade

"There's nothing I can do."

I've heard that statement many times, and yet I am amazed that even Christians believe that to be true of the crises confronting our world.

There is something anyone can do — whether he or she is a business man or woman, a homemaker or a student. Any Christian can pray, and prayer is the greatest power in the world.

One day, when all of the secrets of God are fully understood by the children of men, most Christians will marvel that they never fully appropriated the mighty spiritual resources of God's promises to all who believe in Christ because they never learned how to pray. No privilege known to men compares with the privilege of having fellowship with God — literally talking to Him and experiencing His response.

In 1972, our nation was faced with one of its greatest times of crisis in 200 years. Because of the importance and the urgent need for prayer, my wife, Vonette, felt impressed to launch the Great Commission Prayer Crusade, which was initially designed to organize, mobilize and motivate women to pray. Leading Christian women, including Mrs. Billy Graham; Mrs. Harold Lindsell, wife of the editor of *Christianity Today*; the late Mrs. Howard Davidson, daughter of Abraham Vereide, founder of International Christian Leadership; and Mrs. Fred Dienert, speaker with the Billy Graham Evangelistic Association, joined Vonette in speaking at various citywide prayer rallies. There was a great response, not only on the part of women but also by men. Their concern for the spiritual and moral climate of our nation became a basis for a movement to inform and unite Christians from all denominations and organizations to pray, in groups of two to 20, for a spiritual awakening throughout the world.

Encouraging Christians to Prayer

As the name Great Commission Prayer Crusade suggests, it is the purpose of this ministry to encourage millions of Christians to unite in praying for world revival and the fulfillment of the Great Commission. God has impressed us throughout the years to continue to give the highest priority to prayer. I believe that is one of the major reasons why He has consistently poured out His blessings on Campus Crusade ministries.

The ministry began in 1951 with a 24-hour prayer chain. The 24 hours were divided into 96 15-minute periods, and around the clock people were praying that God would speak to the students on campus. There were dramatic conversions; people who hated God and who were enemies of God had fantastic transformations. There is no way to account for what happened apart from the supernatural intervention of God in answer to prayer.

I think of a young man who was a big man on campus, socially and athletically. He hated God and was very critical of the Christians on campus and in his fraternity. He drank heavily and was on the verge of becoming an alcoholic.

I was invited by some of the men who had received the Lord through our ministry to speak in the fraternity house where he was president. When they approached him to extend to me a formal invitation to speak in their fraternity, he said, "I don't want any of those religious fanatics in this house. If Bill Bright comes, it will be over my dead body." I didn't know about this at the time, but later these men, several of whom were husky athletes, told me that they replied that was all right with them — over his dead body. So, over his objection, I was asked to speak.

As I spoke that night and gave an invitation for those who wanted to receive the Lord to come and talk to me, this fraternity president was one of the first to approach me. I invited him to have lunch with me later in the week.

"I Need God"

As we sat over lunch, he told me that everyone thought he was happy because he was always the life of the party, a big athlete, a big fraternity man and always living it up. "But," he said, "I'm probably the most miserable fellow on this campus, and I need God." In the car as I drove him back to his fraternity, he received Christ into his heart.

That afternoon he began to read his Bible. His roommate inquired, "What did you do, get religion?" He said, "Today I received Christ." The roommate answered, "I know you. You are just boning up for a debate." The next morning he stood before all his fraternity brothers, many of whom were also Christians, and announced, "Yesterday I received Christ. You know what kind of a fellow I've been, and I know I'm going to have a rough time living the Christian life; I want you to pray for me." God used him to make an impact on the entire campus; I believe this was a result of prayer.

Year after year we have witnessed miracle after miracle, I believe, as a result of prayer. In December of 1971, many groups of Christians in neighborhoods, businesses, churches and on campuses began to pray for EXPLO '72. There were many problems, and the registration was very small. The future looked bleak indeed. It was only as thousands of Christians around the country began to pray with a deep sense of urgency and faith, largely because of Vonette's influence through the Great Commission Prayer Crusade, that God met many of the logistical needs of the gathering, and registrations began to pour into Dallas. Through prayer, God brought more than 85,000 people to EXPLO '72.

Around the Clock Prayer

In the wake of the mighty outpouring of God's Spirit at EXPLO '72, we decided to broaden our prayer base even further by establishing an ongoing 24-hour prayer ministry at the Guy F. Atkinson Memorial Chapel at Arrowhead Springs. We have seen some dramatic answers from that prayer chain and the others that have sprung up on campuses and in communities around the United States and the world.

On one occasion, I was to speak to more than 1,350 leaders at a governor's and mayor's prayer breakfast. I had to fly all night to arrive in time for the meeting. In spite of my weariness, 369 people indicated that they received Christ that morning. Certainly one important reason was prayer. While I was speaking, there were 30 staff members on their knees in the chapel at Arrowhead Springs where it was 5:30 a.m. I believe that this was a dramatic demonstration of the power of their prayers, and those of others, including my own.

In an effort to unite individuals and groups to pray, we discovered that people are relatively easy to marshal together for urgent crises or emergency issues. After a few meetings, however, the interest for many people wanes because persistent prayer seems mechanical and repetitious. Even though prayer is the Christian's most powerful weapon against wickedness and the powers of darkness, it is perhaps the most neglected facet of Christian worship — probably because people don't know how to pray. Realizing this, the Great Commission Prayer Crusade developed the Dynamics of Prayer workshop to teach people how to pray. Trained representatives teach these workshops through a concept that is transferable.

Prayer/Care Ministry

Another ministry, the Prayer/Care Ministry, blossomed in 1977 when Vonette posed the question, "If prayer is so important, so vital to any ministry, then why aren't there full-time ministers of prayer?" Senior staff were recruited for this ministry. Assessing the implications of Vonette's question, staff member Paul Utley responded by giving his full time to prayer and encouraging other staff who joined Prayer/Care. "I thought about that over and over again," he said. "Then I found a scriptural precedent in the life of the prophetess Anna. She spent every day in the temple in intercessory prayer."

Contrasting Anna's vibrant example with the prayerlessness of most American Christians, Utley agreed with Vonette that combining a telephone prayer and counseling ministry with round-the-clock intercession for a host of prayer requests could have a significant impact. September 16, 1977, was inauguration day for Prayer/Care.

That day, the first caller was an 18-year-old girl, a victim of leukemia. One of our staff members listened as the girl told how doctors had given her but three months to live. Soon the staff member led her in prayer as she indicated her willingness to trust Christ as her Savior.

Her story, however, doesn't end here. Intercessory prayer will attend her far beyond the first phone call and those infant steps as a new believer. Such follow-up is the goal of Prayer/Care's request monitoring system.

Neighborhood and Church Prayer Groups

A number of cities have adopted the strategy of choosing a prayer coordinator with a steering committee of individual church prayer coordinators who divide the city in areas, encouraging neighborhood churches and church prayer groups. A monthly praise and prayer

bulletin is distributed to inform individuals, churches
and groups about local and national concerns for which
to pray. This effort supports the various Christian out
reaches in the city. The bulletin locally is a supplemen
to the Praise and Prayer Sheet that is mailed monthly
by Campus Crusade to thousands throughout the United
States and other parts of the world. This mailing encour
ages Christians to pray for many different projects and
organizations.

The Great Commission Prayer Crusade is a vital par
of the prayer movement for Here's Life around the world
As a result, city-wide 24-hour prayer chains in man
churches have continued.

"Calling the world to prayer" is the slogan of th
Great Commission Prayer Crusade. It is the goal of thi
ministry that every major city around the world initiat
an established prayer ministry, uniting and informin
Christians of issues for which to pray, with a praye
center similar to that of the present Prayer/Care Ministr
at Arrowhead Springs. This goal can be realized b
churches committing themselves to praying within
specified number of hours one day a month. It is possibl
for as few as 31 churches to support such a ministry
one church is responsible for 24 hours only once a month

To unite and aid individuals in specific prayer, a pe
sonal prayer diary was developed in 1978 encouragin
Christian people to pray for specific concerns Sunda
through Saturday. It also includes a map and listing c
countries of the world, encouraging prayer for worl
concerns. There are also included many prayer help
allowing the individual to adapt the diary to his person
use.

Calling Thousands to Prayer

In recent years, since our sons have gone away t
college, Vonette has called thousands to prayer as sh
has traveled with me. She has helped to launch the Grea

Commission Prayer Crusade in scores of countries.

Prayer has steadily been an integral part of our work in Latin America, too. At the Latin American Training Center in Cuernavaca, Mexico, a beautiful Great Commission Prayer Chapel has been built almost entirely by Latin American Christians. In this center, two 24-hour prayer chains operate. One chain prays for Latin American concerns, while the other concentrates on world needs. At 3 p.m. daily, Latin American Christians are encouraged to pause for prayer for their country. This hour was chosen because of *siesta* time, and also because of the accepted hour that is attributed to Jesus' death on the cross. Many churches which were formerly locked are opening their doors for people also to come to early morning prayer meetings.

Prayer in the Middle East

Iqbal Massey, the wife of our director of affairs for the Middle East, Kundan Massey, has traveled throughout this part of the world speaking to thousands promoting united prayer. In Morocco, where there are only a few more than 150 Christians, there are seven prayer chains in existence — one chain for every day.

There have been many faith-building experiences in regard to specific prayer. In Egypt, where Vonette traveled with a group of staff women, she met with church leaders from around that nation. This meeting took place at the same time as the first summit meetings to agree on peace terms for Israel and Egypt were being held with Sadat, Begin and Carter in Washington. The women went to their knees numbers of times, praying for these leaders. At the same time, they were planning a prayer strategy to help fulfill the Great Commission in Egypt.

In the summer of 1984, Vonette was one of the leaders in gathering together 3,200 people from 68 countries for the International Prayer Assembly in Seoul, Korea.

Christian leaders from all over the world have referred to that week of meetings as a second Pentecost. Most of us who participated would never again be the same because of what happened that week.

One reason for such a blessing was our opportunity to see the commitment of the Korean Christians to prayer. The church in Korea is more like the first-century church than that of any other nation in the world. Each week hundreds of thousands of people spend all night in prayer. The church there has grown from three million to seven million in the last 10 years. I believe the reason for this growth is largely due to prayer. Dr. Joon Gon Kim, our director for Korea and for all of Eastern Asia, has played a large part in this commitment.

I am grateful to God for Vonette's leadership in the prayer assembly and in so many other prayer movements in our country and around the world. We are committed to prayer because we know that no matter how effective the strategies, plans, techniques, materials and leadership, unless the Holy Spirit of God empowers, little spiritual fruit will be harvested for the glory of God.

CHAPTER TWENTY-TWO

To Reach the World

Can you imagine the impact of 100,000 lay men and women going to the cities and villages of the world to practice their vocations and make Christ known? God gave me the vision for such a movement shortly after EXPLO '72. He assured me that if He could bring almost 100,000 to that historic conference, He could certainly raise up 100,000 men and women to invest two years or more of their lives to help take the gospel to the ends of the earth. As I prayed, God confirmed in my heart that this was indeed His will, and the leaders of the movement responded very favorably to the idea.

In the next few months we put together the basic structure of what would soon become The *Agape* Movement. (*Agape* is the Greek New Testament word for God's love.) In January, 1973, we invited the leaders of several missionary organizations to consult with us. Those who came were Dr. Clyde Taylor, general director of the National Association of Evangelicals; Dr. Edward Frizen of the Interdenominational Foreign Missions Association; Dr. Donald McGavran of the Fuller School of World Mission; and Cliff Barrows and Walter Smyth from the Billy Graham Evangelistic Association.

We shared with these men as fully as possible the shape which we wanted the new movement to take. After we had told them everything that we knew at that point, I asked these men, whose judgment I greatly respect, whether they thought we should proceed with the idea. There was a breathless pause for a moment around the table.

Encouragement From Christian Leaders

Dr. Taylor broke the silence: "If you had asked me this a year ago, I would have said, 'No, you have no business attempting anything so large.' But EXPLO '72 changed my answer. When I saw how God used this organization to bring nearly 100,000 people together and solved the unbelievable logistical problems, not only do I think you should do it, I also think you are the only organization in North America which ought to attempt it."

Dr. Frizen spoke next: "I too feel you ought to proceed. My reason is not because of the magnitude of EXPLO '72, but because of the spirit of EXPLO '72. When I saw that you had brought 200 Christian groups together to present opportunities within their organizations, I knew that this is the kind of spirit it is going to take if we are ever going to see the world reached for Christ."

(Campus Crusade had invited these Christian organizations to come to EXPLO as our guests to promote their ministries, as an expression of our love and desire to help create a spirit of unity among different Christian groups.)

Dr. McGavran shared: "Twenty years ago, when I was inaugurated as the dean of the School of World Mission at Fuller, I said in my address, 'If we're really serious about the Great Commission, we've got to ask God to raise up at least 100,000 missionaries to reach the world.' I've sat here today and heard that God has impressed you with the same vision and, not only that, but He has also given you the wherewithal to make it possible."

The next around the table was Cliff Barrows: "You don't have to convince me of the merit of this kind of a program. My father, who is a retired farmer, actually served in this kind of a program, and it changed his life."

All that was left for Walter Smyth to say was, "I want to pledge all the resources and influence of the Billy Graham Evangelistic Association to support the pursuit of this vision."

Seeking a Director

Assured that we were headed in the right direction, we needed to find a director for this new venture. In December, 1972, God had impressed me that Dr. Larry Poland, president of Miami Christian College, was the man for the job. But when I asked him to assume this position, his response was, "No, I'd like to, but I am already committed to an expansion program here." However, he did agree to consult with us as we constructed the basic framework for the movement.

It became almost humorous as I periodically asked Larry if God was yet speaking to him as He was to me. Of course, I made it clear that I would not want Larry to come unless God called him, but in my heart, I had the assurance that he was God's man for the task of helping us achieve the vision that God had given me. God never gave me a peace about any other man for the position, though Larry continued to say "No." Finally, in March, 1973, through a series of remarkable circumstances, God's timing was complete, and He called Larry to come to assist us as director of this new venture.

First of all, The *Agape* Movement is designed for laymen, many of whom have little formal theological background. Bible college and seminary training are important, but there simply are not enough people with this kind of training to do the job. If the Great Commission is going to be fulfilled, we must mobilize masses of laymen to do their part.

Staff From Around the World

Not all of the *Agape* staff are North Americans. Already European *Agape* staff have gone to other countries to meet needs. Training centers are being planned for each continent and in several countries to prepare the nationals to help others on their continent and in other parts of the world. Our Chinese staff are praying specifically that God will raise up 10,000 Chinese to be involved in this way.

Before reporting overseas, the *Agape* staff attend both the regular staff training for Campus Crusade staff and a special three and a half month program called *Agape*-International Training. In addition to the basic Campus Crusade training in how to live a Spirit-filled life and how to share Christ more effectively with others, much attention is given to helping the trainees feed themselves through Bible study and understand scriptural principles. Emphasis is also placed on cross-cultural communication and interpersonal relationships. Practical lessons for living overseas include how to learn the language once you arrive and precautionary health measures.

The *Agape* staff have found that what they learn in their training sessions is invaluable. One young teacher who was on her way to Africa commented, "I've seen my deepest weaknesses become my strengths. I'm a totally different person."

The *Agape* Movement involves strategic placement. Doctors, nurses, teachers, agricultural workers, engineers and financiers can go so many places that missionaries cannot. The need for trained people like this is so great that they are allowed into many countries where missionaries are banned, even though the authorities know that they will be sharing their faith in Christ while doing their assigned tasks.

A good example of strategic placement is the case of an *Agape* staff member sent to a West African nation. Since he is an athlete and coach, he was placed in the national sports commission to help the country develop national competitive teams. Athletes are so highly re-

arded in this country that this man will likely have a
r greater impact for Christ than would almost anyone
a purely missionary capacity.

Another unique aspect of this movement is the com-
ination of the vocational with the spiritual in the staff
member's work. A large portion of the staff member's
me is involved in discipleship and evangelism, and as
e uses his unique skills, he will be communicating some-
ing about the gospel through His Christ-centered lifes-
le.

eam Concepts

The *Agape* Movement utilizes a team concept. Often
issionaries are sent into an area by themselves or with
nly one other person. *Agape* staff, however, are always
laced with their team members nearby and at least one
ther staff person with them. A strong witness is produc-
d as the nationals watch these team members relate to
ne another. As they see Christ at the center of this
iniature community, they begin to grasp what He can
o within their own society.

"We were living in a fishbowl," said one *Agape* staff
ember who taught school in Swaziland. "Every mo-
ent we asked the Lord to help us reflect His character.
think it is understandable that people accept as credible
hat you say if your life shows it. One of the happiest
oments for my roommate and me was when one of
ne students said she had seen Jesus Christ in our re-
tionship."

The *Agape* staff members agree to spend two years
the country to which they are assigned, though they
ften choose to continue on a permanent basis after the
xperience of being used of God in such a wonderful
ay. Since they know their stay may only be temporary,
eir minds can be focused on what they can do to help
repare the nationals to reach their own country for
hrist.

The multiplication of nationals, vocationally and spiritually, is the key to The *Agape* Movement. When the staff member returns home, he expects to leave behind nationals who are trained in his vocation and to leave behind more believers who are trained and discipled to reach their nation for Christ.

Medical Clinic in Korea

A team of *Agape* staff in Korea demonstrated this principle of multiplication vocationally and spiritually when they established a medical clinic in one of the poorer sections of Seoul. Working alongside Korean nationals, the team treated approximately 20,000 patients and saw more than 3,700 decisions for Christ in little more than a year. When they left the clinic to return to the United States, they left behind a Korean doctor and nurses to continue the ministry.

The spirit of The *Agape* Movement is that of having a servant's heart. No matter how skilled the staff may be, it is of no use if they do not go in the fullness of the Holy Spirit, with humble hearts. In many cases they will be serving under national staff members and must be willing to do so with the attitude of a servant.

Aiding National Christians

In addition to the trained lay men and women who travel overseas using their vocational skills as a platform for sharing the good news of Jesus Christ, some 375 North Americans are currently overseas providing training, specialized skills and administrative expertise to help the national Christians in reaching their countries with the gospel.

Dr. Al Rhea is an example of staff who serve in this capacity. A successful dentist in Jacksonville, Fla., Dr. Rhea left his practice to join our staff and subsequently moved his family some 8,000 miles to Nairobi, Kenya where he works closely with individuals from various African nations in the East Africa Great Commission Training Center. Dr. Rhea supervises three to four men during each training period, schooling them in the principles of evangelism and discipleship and aids them as they put what they have learned into practice by developing their own ministries.

"It's very rewarding to build relationships with the trainees, knowing that these leaders will return to their own countries and put the training into their own languages and situations," said Dr. Rhea. "They go places that we never will. If we did go to their area, it would take us years to understand their culture."

In the fall of 1976, The *Agape* Movement convened the first World Thrust conference in Birmingham, Ala. The conference was the first of many such gatherings held for the purpose of showing practical ways for believers to be involved in the world evangelization effort.

Assisting Missions Agencies

During the conferences, delegates were encouraged to talk with representatives from dozens of world missions sending agencies, including denominational and interdenominational missions boards such as OMS International, Gospel Recordings, Mission Aviation Fellowship, Wycliffe Bible Translators, Christian and Missionary Alliance and the Conservative Baptist Foreign Mission Society. In all, 145 agencies exhibited at one or more conferences.

"We have been able to share with people about our ministry and how they can become more involved even if they can't go personally," said Alison Boyer of Language Institute for Evangelism. "Already we have had some people from past World Thrust conferences apply to our mission as missionaries. "These experiences have been shared by many of the missions agencies represented at World Thrust.

The first 18 World Thrust conferences were attended by 18,406 people. Of these, 2,150 made decisions to go to other lands with the gospel, 3,677 committed themselves to pray for a specific group of unreached people, and 979 made decisions to support world evangelization through financial investment.

I personally believe that preaching the gospel of the Lord Jesus Christ involves a concern for the widows, orphans, prisoners, the poor, the sick, the illiterate and the aged. One cannot say "I love God" and not demonstrate love for those in need. Genuine concern results in specific action. But I also believe that the greatest thing one can do to help other people, whether young or old, sick or well, in prison or free, is to tell them about the love and forgiveness of Jesus Christ and help them receive Him as their Savior. As servants of the Lord, we need to emphasize caring for the poor and the downtrodden. But we need even more to give a strong emphasis to preaching the gospel. In that way, every person on the face of the earth will have a chance to say "Yes" to Jesus Christ and to know the liberating joy that comes from following Him in faith and obedience.

Barrio of Thieves

One beautiful example of the combination of social concern coupled with evangelism occurred in the Philippines. A young Filipina doctor together with some American *Agape* staff formed a medical team to work in a village known as "the barrio of thieves." Within one year, more than half of the population of 2,000 had been converted to Christ, and many Bible studies were being held in the village.

When I arrived in Baguio City, I asked that an interview be arranged for members of our team with the mayor of the barrio, who was a teacher. He shared that few if any of the villagers worked; most stole for a living. Then the medical team came into the village and set up the clinic. It was open certain hours of the day with the rest of the day set aside for door-to-door witnessing and Bible studies. As a result of more than 1,000 people receiving Christ, crime was reduced 80%. No longer is the village known as "the barrio of thieves"; the citizens renamed it Easter Village.

This is what can happen when individuals decide to invest at least two years of their lives with The *Agape* Movement, serving others. We are praying that God will use our *Agape* staff, currently under the direction of Paul McKean, to produce similar results in hundreds of thousands of other villages and cities throughout the world.

May I suggest that you pause right now and ask the Lord if He wants you to be a part of this remarkable witness for Him. Write today for more information.

CHAPTER TWENTY-THREE

God's Speciality: The Impossible

Now that we talked about our ministry overseas through The *Agape* Movement, I would like to go back to EXPLO '74 and share with you the tremendous vision for reaching the world that the experience in Seoul gave to tens of thousands who attended.

That week was truly an example of how God's supernatural blessings have been on the life of one man — Dr. Joon Gon Kim, our ministry's national director in Korea. God has brought Dr. Kim along a unique path in making him the great man of God that he is today.

One of the difficult steps along that path took place when he was enjoying one evening with his family. It was springtime, and the rain was falling gently as the family was sharing the events of the day. Suddenly, an angry band of Communist guerillas invaded the village, killing everyone in their path. The family of Dr. Kim was not exempt. In their trail of blood, the guerillas left behind the dead bodies of Dr. Kim's wife and his father; he himself was beaten and left for dead. In the cool rain of the night, Dr. Kim revived and fled to safety in the mountains with his young daughter. They were the sole survivors.

Loving His Enemies

Dr. Kim is a man of God, and he had learned from Scripture to love his enemies and pray for those who persecuted him. What was he to do? What was to be his attitude concerning those who had snatched his dear ones from his side — his beloved wife and honored father? The Spirit of God impressed upon Dr. Kim that he was to return to the village, seek out the Communist chief who led the guerilla attack and tell him that he loved him. then he was to tell the man of God's love in Christ and seek to win him for the Savior. This he did, and God honored his obedience. Dumbfounded, the Communist chief knelt in prayer with Dr. Kim and committed his life to Christ. Within a short time, a number of other Communists were converted to Christ, and Dr. Kim helped to build a church for these and other Communist converts.

The name of Dr. Kim became known throughout South Korea, but this humble servant of God wanted to help evangelize his whole nation for the Savior. Indeed, his vision reached far beyond Korea to the whole of Asia, and he believed that his people, the Koreans, could help evangelize the Orient. Though he was a pastor of a large church, one of the largest in Korea, and had finished his theological studies in Korea, he came to the United States for further graduate study, working toward an advanced degree at Fuller Theological Seminary.

Campus Crusade in Korea

Upon meeting Dr. Kim at Fuller in 1958, I was challenged by his dedication to Christ, his humility and his vision. Together we covenented with God that we would seek to help evangelize Korea. This was in keeping with the original vision that God had given me for Campus Crusade. When I laid before Dr. Kim my strategy for the world, he responded by agreeing to launch the ministry of Campus Crusade in Korea and to be our first national director overseas.

From the beginning, Campus Crusade has believed that the national can do a better job of reaching his own people than can the missionary. The national does not have the problems of language and culture that confront the missionary. However, we strongly believe in the importance of the missionary, so long as he is willing to serve the national. Dr. Kim and all overseas directors who have joined us since 1958 have been indigenous leaders. They have been trained and instructed in the philosophy, techniques and strategy of Campus Crusade, and we stand ready at all times to assist them in reaching their own people. Therefore, it was with joy that we saw Dr. Kim become a staff member.

Within a relatively short period of time, he was established in the ministry and was recruiting and training other nationals to join with him to help reach students of Korea for Christ. His has been one of the most remarkable ministries in the history of Korea.

Holy Ground

The culmination of this ministry was EXPLO '74. During that entire week, I felt as if I were on holy ground. Day after day I observed the supernatural, miraculous work of God. Night after night as I stood to speak from the elevated platform and looked out over the sea of faces, I was filled with awe and reverence. I could sense the presence of God in a very real way.

Every time I think about what God did at EXPLO '74, I want to sing praises to Him, for truly all of the honor, praise and glory are due to Him alone.

I have already shared with you some of the "firsts" of that unprecedented gathering. The most meaningful to me was the information Dr. Kim gave me on the phone — that 80% of the first-night audience of 1.3 million people indicated that they had accepted Christ or received assurance of their salvation by faith as a result of my message. The essence of that message is recorded in the appendix of this book.

No number of human beings nor group of organizations could ever have accomplished what happened at EXPLO '74. All the glory, honor and praise must go to God. Nils Becker, coordinator of the international delegations (more than 3,000 came for the week from 78 countries), said that in the early planning fo EXPLO everything was just too big for them to even comprehend, much less accomplish. But miracle after miracle occurred because, as he explained, "People were praying and God answered."

Importance of Prayer

No doubt prayer, more than anything else, prompting the moving of God's Spirit, can explain EXPLO '74 and the spiritual revival that has been going on in Korea for many years. The road has not been an easy one. Since the gospel first reached that country if 1876, the Korean church has survived difficulties. During a bitter 35-year occupation, the Japanese tried to force Shintoism on the people. Then the land was cut in two by Communism. Indeed, two-thirds of the Christians formerly lived in what is now North Korea. During the Communist takeover, many thousands were slaughtered and many fled south, leaving behind their possessions and, in many cases, their families.

Still the Christians' dedication to prayer and commitment to evangelism have caused the church in South Korea to double in size each decade since 1940 and to grow at a rate presently four times that of the population. For years, believers have gathered in the pre-dawn darkness in churches to pray for their country. At least 30 prayed and fasted for 40 days and nights specifically for EXPLO. The night before EXPLO '74 officially began, an estimated 300,000 Koreans held a spontaneous prayer meeting. And each night after that, hundreds of thousands stayed on the Yoido Plaza to pray until daybreak. "Christians have been praying for three decades for a spiritual awakening in our country," said Dr. Kim. "EXPLO '74 was part of God's answer to their prayers."

Sacrifice

Such commitment to prayer exemplified EXPLO.

Hundreds of families tithed their rice the months before to help provide food for the delegates. Some families sacrificed one meal a day for several months to help provide scholarships. Twenty college students sold their blood to pay for the registration. During the week of EXPLO, some 44,000 Koreans lived in a tent city of Yoido Island, where they endured two days of rain and, later in the week, hot sun and winds. Another 176,000 slept on the floors of 2,944 primary, middle and high school classrooms. Most of the remaining 100,000 delegates stayed at their homes or in the homes of friends and relatives in Seoul.

To feed such a group took 7,000 sacks of rice and 20 mammoth rice steamers designed by Dr. Joon Gon Kim. A staff of 320 men and 60 women worked from 5 o'clock in the morning until late each evening supplying the EXPLO delegates with food. They supplemented the rice diet with *duk kwang*, a yellow radish-type vegetable; *saewoo*, a type of fish; and bread. A total of 600 tons of rice, 150 tons of *duk kwang* and *saewoo*, and 3.6 million pieces of bread were consumed by the Koreans during EXPLO week.

The more than 3,000 "international" delegates lived in more comfortable conditions. Half stayed in 12 Seoul hotels and the other half in dorms of Ewha Women's University (the largest women's university in the world), the 18-story Korean Campus Crusade building and in U.S. military housing for the more than 200 service personnel who came in for the training. A fleet of 50 buses transported these foreign delegates to Yoido Plaza each evening. The rally messages were then translated for them into English, Japanese, Cantonese, Mandarin, Spanish and German which could be picked up by special transistor radios provided for each international delegate.

The delegates came to Seoul by almost every means possible. Approximately 1,000 young Koreans came in a bicycle caravan. Each night most of the Koreans walked many miles to attend the mass rallies. Some even jogged, chanting "Jesus Revolution! Explosion of the Holy Spirit" as they ran.

High school students in Hartford, Conn., raised $3,750 in four weeks through bake sales, car washes and church donations to send five representatives. One American girl was so determined to go that she joined the U.S. Air Force a year before in order to attend as part of the military delegation. Gideon Umandap missed the Philippines charter flight when he was denied an exit permit due to his record of communist activity before becoming a Christian. Meeting the next day with an army general, Gideon explained his "new life in Christ." The general not only gave him the exit permit but also had him driven to the airport in time to catch a plane.

Vital Training

Each morning the various conferences met at locations throughout Seoul. But regardless of whether the delegates met in a tent, classroom, or hotel, each received training in how to live a meaningful Christian life, how to appropriate the fullness of the Holy Spirit and how to communicate his faith in Christ with others through the Four Spiritual Laws. Special Four Laws booklets for EXPLO were printed with one side in Korean and the other side in English, Japanese or Chinese.

The afternoons were free for delegates to attend optional seminars which made up what was called the Institute of World Missions. These featured such men as Dr. Peter Beyerhaus, professor of missions at the University of Tubingen in West Germany; and Dr. Samuel Moffett, president of the Presbyterian Theological Seminary in Seoul.

On Saturday afternoon, August 17, the delegates spread out through the streets of Seoul, the world's ninth largest city with 6.5 million people. They talked to

420,000 people and saw 272,000 indicate decisions for Christ with another 120,000 expressing a desire to know more about how they could become Christians.

One American serviceman, who had been stationed in Korea for two months, witnessed to a wealthy contractor that afternoon. Not only did the man receive Christ, but he also eagerly asked God to control every area of his life with the power of the Holy Spirit. The soldier commented, "This man was hungry for all the material I gave him. I gave him everything I could, and he would have wanted more if I had had it."

A Canadian businessman and Campus Crusade board member, Peter Dueck, stated, "I had heard of the openness of the Korean people to the gospel but didn't think we would be able to share with people who didn't know the language." He proved himself wrong. During dinner one evening, Peter shared Christ with a couple from the university and then invited them to the meeting on Yoido Island. They were there at 7 p.m. sharp, and the young man received Christ.

Counting the Crowds

As you have been reading about the large crowds who attended EXPLO '74, you may be asking, "How can one determine to any degree of accuracy the number of people attending such a large gathering?" The Rev. David J. Cho, one of Korea's most prominent Christian leaders, who served as arrangement chairman for EXPLO as well as for the 1973 Billy Graham Crusade in Seoul, explained the process: "According to official measurements, Yoido Plaza is 1,400 meters or 4,714 feet long and 480 meters or 1,901 feet wide. If 3,000 people are seated at 50-centimeter or 20-inch intervals along the width, a total of 2,100,000 can be accommodated at one time. At each meeting, under my direction, the planning coordinator with six assistants used a map and the above figures to estimate the crowd. This estimate was then given to Dr.

Kim who examined the figures so that they were as conservative as possible and that they were consistent with police estimates. The official estimate was then released to the public."

One amazing fact of EXPLO was that 600,000 people (by police estimate) turned out for the Thursday night meeting despite all-day rains and the tragic death of President Chung Hee Park's wife in the assassination attempt on the President's life. Even with the rain that night and the fact that a Japanese citizen had been arrested in connection with the assassination, Dr. Akira Hatori, noted Japanese evangelist, spoke as scheduled.

Asking Forgiveness

Everyone was visibly moved as Dr. Hatori asked the many Japanese delegates to stand and then told the Koreans, "We stand here with broken hearts for the sins we Japanese have committed against you. We ask for your forgiveness in Jesus Christ, and we long to be like you Christians in Korea, sacrificing ourselves."

Mrs. Georgalyn Wilkinson, who heads the Far East Broadcasting Company in Japan, well remembers that night. "I opened the door to the booth where the Japanese men were translating the invitation to receive Christ," she said. "Tears were streaming down their faces as they spoke, and they prayed silently that their own people would respond to the invitation."

Though Dr. Kim asked me to bring the major messages during the week of meetings, a number of internationally-known Christian leaders also addressed the evening meeting. Other speakers in the evening rallies were Dr. Kyung Chik Han, pastor emeritus of the Young Nak Presbyterian Church, the world's largest Presbyterian church; Dr. Chandu Ray, executive director of the Coordinating Office for Asian Evangelism; and Dr. Philip Teng, pastor of the North Point Alliance Church and professor at Alliance Bible Seminary in Hong Kong.

Worldwide Broadcast

Each mass rally was aired worldwide by the Far East Broadcasting Company. One station beamed the address across Latin America while another reached the Philippines, Southeast Asia, Australia, New Zealand and Indonesia. FEBC's Carl Lawrence and Dave Hudson worked with the taping and editing of all major talks. Mrs. Wilkinson, who had the difficult task of arranging all the interpreters for us, remarked, "The Lord gave us the best people we could have found." How grateful we were for the invaluable help of the Far East Broadcasting Company.

EXPLO '74 was a time most of all for discipleship and training. As Dr. Kim told the crowd, "Each of you must become a spiritual fireseed — a spark that will in turn set fire to your local church." No doubt most of the delegates became such "fireseeds."

Dr. Hatori told me, "We have had some big spiritual conventions in the past where people received blessings, but nothing like EXPLO '74. This convention was characterized by training and by total dependence upon the Holy Spirit and a holy, biblical strategy."

Dr. Chandu Ray said, "I am excited about the training of more than 300,000 lay people. I believe this is a new phase that will revolutionize and explode all over Asia. This brings tremendous encouragement to me."

Chinese Delegation

When one considers that two-thirds of the world lives in Asia, the importance of such training becomes even more obvious and urgent. I was thrilled about the more than 450 Chinese delegates who came to EXPLO from Hong Kong, the Republic of China and other Asian countries. One afternoon many of them met together to discuss strategies to help reach the then 800 million people in mainland China. These delegates were excited about the EXPLO training and wanted more training. On the day of witnessing, they saw 419 of the 963 people with whom they had shared the Four Spiritual Laws indicate that they received Christ.

Chi Young Min, one of the 1,200 delegates from Cheju, a small island off South Korea, said, "After EXPLO '74, we want to go back and begin evangelizing the whole island."

Pastors Participate

Campus Crusade has always sought to serve the local church, and this was another key goal of EXPLO. Some 13,000 Korean pastors, assistant pastors and evangelists, representing nearly all of Korea's 12,000 protestant churches, attended the pastors' conference. For five days they crossed denominational and doctrinal lines to study, pray and spend time together. Including personal devotions, lectures, optional afternoon seminars and the nightly mass rallies, their schedule ran from 5:30 a.m. to 11 each night. Then the schedule read "all night prayer." Sleep was optional! But as one pastor put it, "When these pastors return to their rural or city churches, we'll begin to see throughout Korea a preaching of the gospel like that in the book of Acts."

Many other pastors and laymen attended the Ministry of Management course, designed to teach Christians to be the best stewards of their time and talents. One of the speakers, Dr. Howard Hendricks of Dallas Theological Seminary, pointed out, "If you don't plan your time, other people will plan it for you. And they will be the ones who do not have your interests or your commitment to Jesus." Korean evangelist Joseph Toh and Chinese theological student Chiu Pei-Chi said they increased their understanding of how leadership principles and goal-setting related to their full-time ministries. Hexel Hernando, one of the 80 students from the University of the

Philippines, spoke for his classmates, many of whom attended management seminars: "There is a real excitement in us about going back to school this fall and applying the things we're learning about management." Dr. Hendricks concluded his last message with, "The effect of EXPLO '74 will not be determined by what happens this week here in Seoul. . .but by what you do as a result."

And the results have truly been miraculous! Eisuke Kanda, our director in Japan, stated, "As a result of this week, most of the 1,000 Japanese delegates are now convinced that the saturation of our country with the gospel is a real possibility." A woman from Idaho said, "God really opened my life to believe Him for things I never could believe Him for before. This has resulted as I've seen the people in Korea and have been impressed by their hard work and singlemindedness." A Korean layman stated convincingly, "Our nation will be altered, changed, transformed because we now know how to take evangelism home. By taking these skills home, we can Christianize the whole nation. In that way, Korea will be changed." A government report published in 1978 showed one of the long-lasting effects EXPLO '74 helped to contribute to Korea. The report revealed that the Korean church grew from three million in 1974 to seven million in 1978. In the four short years following EXPLO, the church of Korea more than doubled, and the miracle continues. To God be all of the praise!

CHAPTER TWENTY-FOUR

Here's Life, America:
Saturating the Nation City by City

I remember sitting with several of my fellow staff leaders one day in 1973, discussing the challenge of reaching our nation for Christ. As we discussed the problems of our society — crime, poverty, divorce, alcoholism, drugs, etc. — we were all increasingly aware of the only solution: a spiritual and moral rebirth in our land. And yet, we realized that this solution in Jesus Christ would come about only as every person in the United States had the opportunity to respond to His invitation, "Come to Me, all who are weary and heavy-laden, and I will give you rest" (Matthew 11:28). Then, as these people were trained and discipled, change would occur in the moral fiber of our country. We discussed and prayed about the answers to this question for several months. During this planning period, eight principles emerged that seemed to provide the foundation for a plan which could actually help us achieve our goal.

First, we recognized that if we were talking about reaching our entire nation, we must go where most of the people are — in the cities.

Second, we recognized that the resources for accomplishing what we had talked about were already available in and through the local churches.

Third, we determined that local leaders were needed in each metropolitan area — pastors and laymen who would be willing to commit their time and resources toward accomplishing the task.

Fourth, we realized that Christians must pray and believe God for a plan to reach their cities for Christ.

Fifth, we anticipated that Christians would need to be trained in order to release their full potential for our Lord.

Sixth, we determined that at some point we needed to get the attention of an entire city. That can be done only through mass media — TV, radio, newspapers, etc.

Seventh, we reasoned that the city must be broken down into small, "bite-size" pieces so that each trained Christian could have his personal part in reaching the city for Christ.

Eighth, we felt that churches should be assisted in developing ongoing discipleship and evangelism programs within their own congregations.

Considering these eight points and praying much, we launched a movement which was ultimately to be called Here's Life, America and later, Here's Life, World — a movement which would help to introduce many millions of people to Christ.

We were convinced that the principles were sound. But in the fall of 1973, the real question had to be answered — would it work?

To verify the principles in a real life situation, I asked three men to launch this plan in three cities. Bruce Cook, my special assistant at the time, was asked to go to Atlanta, Ga., to try out the plan. I sent an outstanding businessman who had joined our lay staff, Bob George, to Dallas, Tex., and Sid Bruce, our Military Ministry director, to Nashville, Tenn.

For the following year, we learned lessons in each city which began to point toward a workable "city saturation" strategy. From Bob George, the Dallas coordinator and his work at the First Baptist Church, emerged the concept of neighborhood church outreach groups. From Sid Bruce, the Nashville coordinator, and Tom Cummings, a Nashville businessman, came the idea of using a computer to divide the city into workable units and track the progress in calling every household.

Initial Testing Ground

It was in Atlanta that our staff team first had an opportunity to bring all the pieces of the plan together to see a city begin to be saturated with the gospel message. Every step of the way was marked by a pattern of prayer, plan, work, problem, more prayer and miracle!

Bruce Cook, whom I later asked to co-coordinate the nationwide Here's Life movement with Paul Eshleman, shared some of the highlights of what happened in Atlanta: "The first step in the plan was to organize a local committee of pastors and laymen who would provide leadership for the effort. Then, as a result, we in Campus Crusade felt that we would be in a position to do what we do best — assist, train and serve in a resource role.

"But after three months of meeting with various laymen and pastors, no leadership seemed to surface. Then as Cobby Ware, the Atlanta city director for Campus Crusade, and our staff prayed, a man came to our minds — Jerry Nims, president of a newly-formed business in Atlanta. On presenting to Jerry our vision and challenge for the movement, we witnessed our first miracle in his response, "I've been praying that God would give me something in which I would really be involved in serving Him," he said. "This is it. Tell me what to do.'"

Nims, chairman of the board of Dimensional Development, Inc., crowded an already overloaded schedule with countless meetings and telephone calls for the movement, often beginning the day with pre-dawn breakfast sessions.

"I'd been praying for a long time for a chance to really get involved for the Lord — to climb right into the trenches," Nims later told us. "When this opportunity came along, I have to admit that it was more than I expected. But God reassured me that He would enable me to do a good job."

Prayer Coordinator Chosen

One month later, in February of 1974, we saw our second miracle. Mrs. Joyce Hopping, when approached to lead a city-wide prayer effort, replied, "Now I know why God has been teaching me about prayer in my own life over these last two years." Within one month, more than 1,000 women had committed themselves to a 24-hour prayer chain to undergird *Agape* Atlanta, as the movement was then called in Atlanta. What an answer to our prayers!

That spring we saw various lay people and staff begin ministries in various areas of the city. Bob Reinhart, a stock broker, organized an outreach in the "singles" community; Rusty Wright, one of our staff, organized classroom speaking teams to present Christ in relevant terms in the 23 colleges in the Atlanta area; Martha Ozmit, an Atlanta homemaker, began training women in how to conduct evangelistic coffees and teas in their neighborhoods; Harold Thompson, an ex-convict, spearheaded a prison ministry, not only in Atlanta but also throughout Georgia — with the approval and endorsement of then Governor Jimmy Carter.

With so much to be excited about, we still had to recognize that the key to reaching Atlanta was church members. Unless a significant number of churches came together for a concentrated campaign in the city, Atlanta would not really feel the impact.

The spring of 1975 seemed to be the obvious time for such a campaign, so Bruce and his staff began to plan. Throughout the summer and fall of 1974, a saturation campaign strategy began to take shape.

In this strategy, the city would be divided into various neighborhoods. A single participating church would be responsible for each neighborhood. Each neighborhood would then be subdivided by a computer into street blocks of 50 homes each. So, only 8,000 trained workers from the churches would be needed — each to reach one block. With this plan, a pastor could show people how they could have a specific part in reaching an entire city for Christ.

At the same time, a city-wide media campaign would be launched using every form of media — TV, radio, newspaper, billboards, lapel buttons and bumper stickers — to make Jesus Christ a relevant issue in the lives of all the people in the city.

Problems Encountered

After developing this plan and beginning to work toward its implementation, the inevitable happened. We ran into problems. On November 15, 1974, the Atlanta staff found themselves with no money, no computer system, no media plan and worst of all, no committed pastors to lead the campaign which was scheduled to begin in just five months!

Bruce, Cobby and the rest of the staff went back to their knees, and God began to work miracles. First, He provided leaders. Dr. Charles Stanley, pastor of the First Baptist Church, agreed to head up a pastors steering committee to direct the campaign. Second, I invited Bob Screen, an advertising consultant, to meet with us for a number of creative sessions that gave birth to a campaign theme — "I found it! New life in Christ." Third, a computer system took shape that divided the city into blocks with names and phone numbers for each block assignment. But the money was a little slower in coming.

By March 30, 90 churches were involved with 4,000 trained workers. Enough money had come in to pay the early expenses for the campaign, including 122 billboards strategically located in various parts of the city.

But April 1 was the deadline for the money needed for the television and newspaper advertising — $50,000. On April 1, at 2 p.m., the staff received a phone call. King Grant, one of Atlanta's leading businessmen, agreed to take the responsibility of raising the $50,000 over the next few months and arranged for a personal note which he signed for the money to enable them to go ahead with the campaign.

10,000 Decisions

During the three-week saturation campaign, more than 140,000 households were contacted, and 25,000 phone calls were received from interested people, with more than 10,000 decisions for Jesus Christ. That was just the beginning of a week-by-week continuous effort by church members to reach the city.

How would I describe what happened in Atlanta? Only in miraculous terms. It reminds me of what Nehemiah said in the Old Testament when the Jerusalem wall was rebuilt in 52 days: "They recognized that this work had been accomplished with the help of God" (Nehemiah 6:16).

Those few weeks were exciting beyond words to express. The phenomenal success of the campaign in Atlanta and the launching of Here's Life, America in other cities, with its potential for introducing millions to Christ, were all added blessings to the reports of what God was doing through the lives of our staff.

What started in Atlanta was only a beginning. In the next two years, Here's Life, America reached 246 major cities and thousands of smaller communities. Through the media campaign, our marketing consultants assured us that at least 179 million Americans were exposed to the "I found it!" campaign. A total of some 7.7 million people were contacted personally and exposed to the claims of Christ through the witness of 325,000 trained workers from 15,000 cooperating churches. More than 532,000 people indicated salvation decisions during the campaigns.

Impact on Millions

I believe that these figures represent only the tip of the iceberg because it is completely impossible to record all that God has done and is doing through so many trained workers and cooperating churches. It is my conviction that millions of people made decisions to invite Christ into their lives during the Here's Life movement and many thousands of trained Christians have continued to live Spirit-controlled lives and to witness for Christ.

During those two years that the Here's Life movement was being planned and implemented, I lived out of a suitcase. When I was traveling, which was most of the time, I spoke in a different city almost every day, sometimes three cities a day — working with students, laymen and pastors, trying to encourage Christians to pray and work for a worldwide spiritual revival. I wouldn't have done that for a million dollars, but I was glad to do it for my Lord.

I attempted to devote every waking moment of that time to helping to accelerate Here's Life, America and to raising the necessary funds to help saturate the United States with the gospel by the end of 1976. I said "No" to everything that did not directly contribute to the total saturation of this country and to help bring the United States back to God.

That was an exciting time in the history of our nation as we saw God work miracles across the land through the Here's Life, America campaigns.

"One of the highlights of the campaign was the unity of the churches from different denominations all working together," said Tim Calahan, a lawyer who worked with the movement in the Washington, D.C., area. "People from different racial groups and different economic levels were all working together."

Two high school students in the Washington area, Pam and Scott Cox, decided, as part of the campaign, to phone the members of the school band in which they played. Twelve of the 17 students Scott called and 18 of the 23 his sister called accepted Christ as their Savior. All 30 of the new Christians began meeting with more mature Christians to learn about their new life in Christ. More than 9,000 people in the area made decisions to receive Christ.

Warm Response in Inner-city

In Philadelphia, a total of 430 churches cooperated in reaching that city of nearly five million people for Christ. Approximately 100 black churches were involved in the campaign, and some of the most outstanding results occurred in predominantly black areas.

The Rev. Nathaniel Winslow's church, New Testament Baptist, is one of many black churches that participated. In addition to his 30 members, Rev. Winslow found 10 more people to take the Here's Life training. These trained workers then contacted people in their neighborhoods. Some 130 individuals received Christ with the workers, and 206 enrolled in follow-up Bible studies.

"In the inner-city, it's unusual for people, for any reason, to let a stranger into their house at night," said Woody Parker, pastor of another small black church involved in the campaign. "Usually they think that you're going to try to mug them. But they've been open to the members of our church, and 50% of the people we contacted received Christ."

In the western United States, the Lord also brought about great results. "One of the highlights was the cooperation of the churches," said Jim Burke, city coordinator in Portland, where 230 churches worked together during the campaign. "Many pastors and laymen commented about how so many churches of all denominations were working together to reach the city."

A crisis occurred during the Portland campaign when 80% of the "I found it!" TV schedule was canceled and the TV station personnel made it clear that nothing would change their minds. The people in Portland and several other cities began to pray. Later on that day, the man who had flatly refused to allow any broadcast time to be purchased asked them to hurry over so they could figure out a new schedule to air the spots.

In the greater Los Angeles area, 950 churches cooperated in the campaign, including 35 Oriental, 67 Hispanic and 73 black churches. A total of 27,600 people received Christ as their Savior during the campaign.

Chain Reaction

Two of the workers in the campaign saw some unexpected results when they went to follow up a man they had made an appointment to see. When they arrived at his house, they found that the man had been called to work, but his teenage son was at home, so they asked if they could talk with him.

As the two workers presented the gospel, the boy received Christ and asked Him to take control of his life. He asked the workers to wait while he called some of his friends to come over.

Soon five more boys arrived. Again the workers went through the Four Spiritual Laws, and all five boys received Christ. One of the boys called his parents, and they said, "We want to see what is happening over there. We'll be right over."

When that boy's parents arrived, the two workers again shared the claims of Christ and the parents chose to receive Christ.

Seeing what had happened, three of the other boys contacted their parents. Soon after arriving, the parents of these boys received Christ. The final outcome of the one follow-up appointment was 14 people coming to Christ.

In the Phoenix area, some 5,800 people indicated that they invited Christ into their lives. A crippled woman who lived in the area and was confined to a wheelchair took advantage of her C.B. radio during the campaign. As truck drivers came through town, she told them to come by and see her if they wanted to know what "I found it!" meant. Five truckers responded to her invitation and asked Christ to come into their hearts through her witness.

The same type of miraculous results that occurred in the East and West also happened in the South and Midwest. "I resolved doubts about assurance of my salvation," said one Here's Life worker in the Chicago area. "And for the first time I shared my faith and that person received Christ." This worker's story was multiplied innumerable times across the country as thousands of those who were trained were assured of their salvation and thousands more were used of God to lead their first person to Christ.

Negative Story Brings Positive Results

"I believe our greatest strength has been our weakness," said Col. Nimrod McNair, one of the leaders of the Chicago campaign. "Our media effort was weak due to lack of funds, plus the fact we could not get on the major TV networks. However, on November 19, the Chicago Tribune hit the streets with a critical story on the Chicago Here's Life campaign. Negative, yes; but the results were positive." In the wake of the Tribune article came more objective interviews with NBC, ABC and CBS TV news and an article in Chicago's Sun-Times. As a result of the publicity from these sources, the awareness of Chicagoans about the campaign leaped from 20% of the population to 70%. Thousands recorded decisions for Christ.

The South, where the Here's Life campaigns began, had similar experiences to those in the other sections of the country. "Here's Life, Dallas, has revolutionized our church," said the Rev. Joe Masterson of Kenwood Baptist Church. In another Dallas church, 17 of its members introduced someone to Christ for the first time in their lives during the first week of the campaign.

Roger Vann, Houston city coordinator, pointed to God's dealing with the media as an interesting development in their campaign. "One network station had a policy against paid religious advertising," he said. "God changed their hearts and gave us $20,000 of prime-time TV spots. It was better coverage than both of the other stations which were paid for."

"We placed quite a bit of emphasis on follow-up," said Dick Burr, who coordinated the outreach in Miami. As a result, 34% of those who invited Christ into their lives enrolled in follow-up Bible studies. This total of 2,240 people signing up for the Bible studies was one of the highest in the nation.

Praise Rallies

At the conclusion of the campaigns in most of the 246 cities, praise rallies were held to give glory to God for what He had accomplished. As I visited city after city to participate in these rallies, I was intoxicated with joy and gratitude to God for the thousands who were introduced to Christ in each city.

In Chicago, Vonette and I attended the National Association of Evangelicals convention. Scores of pastors stopped us every few feet in the halls between sessions and in display areas to tell us how God had used Here's Life, America and a particular staff member or members to bless them and their church.

I would say that the Here's Life movement was phenomenally successful. So far as I have any knowledge, it was the most remarkable movement of its kind in history. During a single time span, more people in our country heard the gospel of Jesus Christ and made commitments to Him as Savior and Lord than at any time since the birth of our nation, and more people became involved in discipleship and evangelism training than ever before in the history of this country.

Also, one of the most important aspects of the movement, according to the pastors and laymen whom I meet, is the feeling of brotherhood that exists between denominations and in other local churches. They worked together, witnessed together, prayed together and demonstrated the love of Christ together.

Dr. Billy Graham frequently states that the real success of his city-wide crusades cannot be determined for at least five years; authorities say that same principle applies to Here's Life America. Only God knows what the results will be as thousands of laymen have learned to share their faith, as tens of millions have heard the gospel and as churches have learned to work together toward the common goal of reaching the world for the Lord Jesus Christ.

CHAPTER TWENTY-FIVE

Here's Life, World

God has truly accomplished miracles in bringing people to Himself through our staff and volunteers in the 150 countries where we have ministries. But there are still so many people who do not yet know Him. Authorities tell us that in 1984 the world's population was 4.7 billion people, with the total expected to reach 6.25 billion by the turn of the century. From the human perspective, our goal of helping to reach every one of these people with the gospel seems ludicrous and impossible. But so was the parting of the Red Sea and the feeding of the five thousand with a few loaves and fishes.

When Jesus commanded us to go into all the world and preach the gospel, making disciples of all nations, He promised to go with us. Because all authority in heaven and earth is His, we can go to each of the 210 countries and protectorates of the world with the absolute confidence that the One in whom dwelleth all the fullness of the Godhead will go with us and supply our needs. Thus, the very thing He came into the world to accomplish — to seek and to save the lost and to communicate His love and forgiveness to all men — will be fulfilled.

Proven Strategy

God has been enabling us to take great strides toward helping to fulfill His Great Commission through Here's Life, World. This movement incorporates much of the same strategy and many of the concepts that proved so successful in the Here's Life, America campaigns. These strategies are received by other nations with even more enthusiasm and success than they were in the United States, if that is possible.

During 1977, Bailey Marks, then our director for Asia, invited me to help launch Here's Life in a number of countries throughout the continent. Again and again I heard the expression, "Nothing like this has ever happened in the history of our country." There seemed to be an unprecedented moving of God's Spirit, calling Christians from various organizations and denominations which did not normally cooperate to work in harmony and love.

When I arrived in Pakistan to help initiate the Here's Life movement in that country, Pakistan was in a state of political turmoil. Even though riots were raging all around us, with buses and trains being burned and people being killed, the Christians still came to the meetings. Sessions were held each morning and afternoon with as many as 1,200 present in a single meeting. Many of the Christian leaders of Lahore and Karachi, Pakistan's two largest cities, met together for prayer, fellowship and strategy sessions, with a view toward launching Here's Life in those key cities.

The media campaigns in Manila and Baguio City in the Philippines started in March that same year, and God blessed in a mighty way with many thousands receiving Christ. Early returns on the campaign encouraged me and the other staff greatly as we heard what God was doing. Statistics showed that 1,971 workers and 102 churches participated in the outreach; and 209,830 responses were received from the various forms of media advertisements. In the first 13,000 times the gospel was presented as a part of the campaign, 9,242 persons indicated decisions to trust Christ, an incredible 70% positive response. More than half of these individuals who accepted Christ as their Savior enrolled in Bible studies to be trained in the basics of the Christian faith.

Cultural Adaptations

Although many of the strategies were the same as those used in Here's Life, America, cultural differences made alterations in the Asian campaigns a necessity. For example, the outdoor "I found it!" advertising was more prevalent in Manila and Baguio City than in American cities. Shop owners were much more willing to have banners and posters displayed in their windows. Thousands of taxis — which dominate the streets in both cities — carried bumper stickers. "Sometimes you couldn't look anywhere without seeing 'I found it!'" noted Bailey Marks.

Also, in Manila and Baguio City, there was only a small systematic telephone calling campaign, which was the main thrust in America. This was true in many of our subsequent campaigns conducted in areas where only a few people have telephones. So the main emphasis of the media campaign was to urge people who wanted more information about Christ to respond either by telephone or by filling out a coupon and dropping it into one of the 800 "I found it!" boxes located throughout the two cities. The strategy worked: more than 180,000 of the 210,000 responses were retrieved from the boxes.

One couple in Manila spent 40% of their time contacting people who had responded during the media campaign. All of the employees in the five offices this couple own found new life in Christ.

Eager to Hear

The campaign held in Tijuana, Mexico, in November of that same year was also highly successful. On the first day of the "message revealed" phase of the campaign, when people could respond by calling the Here's Life number or returning a coupon, residents of a village suburb of Tijuana were so eager to find out how they

could find new life in Christ that they waited in line
to deposit their coupons in a box outside a local super-
market.

One woman in another part of the city not only listed
her name and address on the coupon, but on the back
she also explained exactly how to arrive at her house,
which bus to take, where to get off and how to go from
there. "She was so anxious for someone to visit her home
that she did everything but enclose bus fare," commented one worker.

Many of the people who came to Christ during the
campaign showed an intense desire to grow in their faith.
Of those who made decisions for Christ, 89% enrolled
in the follow-up Bible studies.

Another Latin American campaign occurred in the
Caribbean city of San Cristobal, the Dominican Republic.
Located near the country's capital, Santo Domingo, San
Cristobal is a city of about 44,000 of whom 2,000 are
evangelical Christians. There are 18 Protestant churches,
17 of which took part in the campaign, creating a corps
of 640 trained workers. That many volunteers were definitely needed, because more than one-third of the city's
total population requested the "You Can Find It, Too,"
booklet, an explanation of the gospel.

90% Response

As workers began to follow up the requests, they
encountered a level of receptiveness unprecedented even
for campaigns in gospel-responsive Latin America,
where an overall average of 50% of the people who hear
a personal presentation of how to receive Christ ask
Him into their lives. Yet in San Cristobal, the average
was an incredible 90% — 10,260 recorded decisions
from among the 11,400 people who personally heard the
gospel.

The campaign in Singapore faced special problems.
This tiny island republic of about two million people is

omposed of large international populations including Chinese, Malays, Indians and westerners. Not only is it multi-racial, but it is also multi-lingual and multi-religious, and many people wanted it to stay that way. Because the task of reaching this city seemed so overwhelming, leaders of the Here's Life movement there asked God to raise up enough prayer warriors to have at least 10 Christians praying at all times for the saturation strategy. By February, 1977, five 24-hour prayer chains had been formed. By the beginning of the media campaign, the remaining five chains had been formed. Almost 8,000 Christians were involved in these two prayer chains.

Churches Working Together

The campaign was well supported by the churches as 100 of the approximately 180 churches in Singapore were represented by campaign workers. "The training I received has turned me from a convert into a disciple with fire and zeal in my heart," said one young man from Jurong Christian Church.

Nine of the individuals in the city's main telephone center were blind. As they telephoned people, they used braille copies of the Four Spiritual Laws in their sharing with people. Reports indicated that they were leading people to Christ with the same effectiveness as other campaign workers.

The Here's Life campaign in Malaysia was the first effort of its kind to be launched in a Muslim nation. The law in Malaysia is clear: Christians are not allowed to approach Malays with the gospel. Therefore, Here's Life, Malaysia represented a united effort to reach the 48% of the population which is Chinese.

Although threatening telephone calls were received every day, and vehicles bearing "I found it!" bumper stickers were maliciously damaged, campaign workers remained undaunted. George Lee, a member of the Here's Life, Malaysia executive committee, returned to his car one afternoon to find that the "I found it!" stickers had been scraped off with a knife, along with much of the car's paint. He responded to the situation by saying, "Automobile paint is still being manufactured. When Here's Life, Malaysia is over, we will repaint the car. In the meantime, we will simply cover the scratches with more 'I found it!' stickers."

Hong Kong Campaign

Another remarkable campaign was held in Hong Kong, a city of some 4.5 million people. I remember how thrilled I was to receive the initial report from Andrew Ho, the director of the outreach there. A total of 359 churches were involved in the campaign, and 300 of these churches held evangelistic, revival campaigns simultaneously with the Here's Life media campaign. Trained campaign workers numbered 15,000 while another 85,000 people participated in other ways. These 100,000 believers represented about half of the colony's Protestant population.

By the close of the campaign, 28,174 people had indicated decisions for Christ. One exciting aspect of the campaign was the number of new believers who became involved in local churches. One month after the campaign, 200 churches reported growth in attendance of between 30 and 150 persons each. Several congregations started branch churches.

Prior to the media campaign, a missionary guest speaker in a church began by endorsing Here's Life, Hong Kong. He explained that he wasn't sure what the church was doing with the movement but encouraged them to participate. In response, the pastor tapped the guest on the shoulder and explained that, as a result of the Here's Life training, 70 new members had been added to the church. The pastor asked everyone who was present as a result of the campaign to raise his hand. "Hands were up all over the congregation," recalls the astonished missionary.

The campaign in Nairobi, Kenya, was another one that saw churches benefit immensely. Following the campaign which recorded some 15,000 decisions for Christ, six Baptist churches baptized a total of 2,600 new members as a direct result of the outreach.

Cities on the European continent also successfully implemented Here's Life campaigns. In Barcelona, Spain, 35 churches took part in the campaign, representing 75% of the city's evangelical population. The Tolra Church is an example of those who participated. Although it became involved late, Tolra's members were still able to participate in all aspects of the training. They made 119 home visits and shared their faith in 109. Twenty-four people accepted Christ, and 31 signed up to be in Bible studies.

Tripled Attendance

Tampere, Finland, saw church attendance triple in the first three Sundays following the start of its campaign. One church in the suburbs, with a seating capacity of 350, had a regular attendance of 150. But during these three weeks, there were more than 600 trying to sit in the 350 seats. Our director of affairs for Europe, Kalevi Lehtinen, who is a native of Finland, has expressed great enthusiasm about these two campaigns and others that are scheduled. He feels, as I do, that the campaigns in Europe can help spark a great revival that could very well sweep the continent.

Lahore, Pakistan, was the site of our first campaign conducted in the Middle East. Our national director for Pakistan, professor Daniel Bakhsh, said that Jesus Christ was the talk of the town for probably the first time in history.

With such a large majority of the population being Muslims, the campaign faced opposition on every side.

Yet, through it all, God blessed in a unique way. Professor Bakhsh reports that the 1,000 decisions for Christ are unprecedented in Pakistan.

A campaign volunteer working among non-Christians where he was employed said that for the first time his fellow workers were coming to him to learn more about Christ. He said hundreds of students were asking him what "I found it!" meant.

The success of these campaigns in reaching cities around the world filled me with praise and gratitude to our wonderful Lord. But, it has been a sobering thought to realize that an estimated 62% of the world's population doesn't live in cities at all, but in villages and rural areas. That's why I became so excited about what happened in the Kilungu hills, a rural area of Kenya.

Like much of the world's rural areas, the majority of the people in Kilungu (75%) were non-literate. Therefore, a tape recording was used to train pastors and laymen in evangelizing the area. A booklet of photographs illustrating how to receive Christ was used in conjunction with the tape training.

Material Memorized

Since learning through hearing is the norm in most African countries, and memorization often replaces written notes, the training tool proved very effective. Thus, trained pastors and laymen could equip their own churches, using the same tape packages they had learned from. The successful development of this vital training is a tribute to the prayer and hard work of our African staff and the outstanding leadership of our director of affairs in Africa, Don Myers.

Once the training was completed, four cars and a motorcycle — equipped with loud speakers — began sounding the local language's equivalent of "I found it!" — "*Niniwonete*" — through the 100-square mile section of the Kamba tribal lands. Soon the cars couldn't go anywhere in the area without being met by children singing the *Niniwonete* jingle.

During those first days, the drivers helped churches set up bright yellow banners to aid interested people in locating the places where they could find the new life in Jesus Christ that the cars "sang" of. These same banners also showed where follow-up Bible studies were being held.

People frequently walked miles — often up steep hills — to find out about the new life that Jesus Christ offers. An average of 50 % of those who came to the information centers indicated decisions to accept Christ. In some places, where the climb was most difficult, 75% of those who came accepted Christ as their Savior.

Other types of rural campaigns have been used in Mexico and the Philippines to circulate the life-changing message of Jesus Christ. The potential of these campaigns thrills me as I think of the hundreds of millions of people living in villages that can be reached in this manner.

Saturation Campaign in India

One of the most spectacular results of the saturation strategies occurred in the Indian state of Kerala. Our national director in India, Thomas Abraham, chose to believe God for the total saturation of this state of 22 million people by the end of 1976. From the busiest streets of sprawling coastal cities to remote mountainous tea plantations, trained workers went house to house communicating the good news of Jesus Christ. At the end of the campaign, 99% of the homes had been contacted.

During the last three months of the campaign, large evangelistic meetings were held in all 11 districts of Kerala. This was done to insure that those people who were at work or school during the day and had missed the visits of the workers going house to house would still have a chance to hear the gospel.

The program at these public meetings was structured so that individuals had three opportunities to receive Christ: through a short, evangelistic message given by a Campus Crusade staff member; in Andre Kole's film, "World of Illusion"; and through another film, "Life Is Where I'm Going."

On one occasion, a church which had given permission to use its property for a public meeting withdrew permission. "As we were praying about what to do, someone suggested we use the compound in front of a mosque," said Thomas Abraham. "It is inconceivable that Muslims would provide a place with electricity free of charge for a gospel meeting, but that's exactly what happened. It is probably the first time a Christian meeting was held in a temple yard. Many came to know the Lord in a personal way that evening." A total of 380,028 people invited Christ into their lives through meetings such as this one, making a grand total of 1,850,982 individuals who accepted Christ as their Savior during the campaign.

"It began as an impossible dream in 1969," said Thomas. "But by the grace of God, on December 31, 1976, almost every home in Kerala had been contacted. The staff of India Campus Crusade and I are praising God for the completed task of saturating our Jerusalem with the good news."

Reaching Colombia

We saw God do a similar mighty work in Colombia. I had the opportunity of joining Sergio Gargia, director of affairs for Latin America, and Nestor Chamorro, our director in Colombia, for three fantastic days of witnessing firsthand the saturation campaign in this Latin American nation. During 1978, an estimated 65-86% of Colombia's 27 million people heard how they could have a personal relationship with Jesus Christ. Many were approached on a personal basis, others heard through radio announcements, television, newspaper ads and fliers.

During the first half of that year, the emphasis was on house-to-house evangelism. Cities were sectioned off geographically, and thousands of associate staff members of Campus Crusade and volunteers were given the responsibility to saturate specific blocks.

There were also mass outreaches. At least 750,000 people were exposed to the gospel during Easter week alone. By July 1, Nestor estimated that 45% of the population had heard the gospel.

On August 1, nine groups of students and single staff embarked on the "sacrificial mission." These teams traveled throughout Colombia's villages and rural areas, saturating them with the gospel and establishing prayer groups. Another group, the "mission impossible" team, developed a ministry among government officials in Bogota. In December, media campaigns, mass rallies and other projects completed the task of saturating the nation.

Reports indicate that nearly 18 million people were directly contacted through personal presentations or in group meetings. They and millions of others were also touched through the mass media. Only God knows the true extent of their response, but more than 2.6 million decisions to accept Christ as Savior and Lord have been recorded.

Fund-raising Campaign

Undergirding much of the efforts to reach people around the world is a massive fund-raising campaign. Helping to coordinate this project are our Office of Development staff members. These dedicated people are in regular contact with many individuals, ministering to them spiritually as well as informing them how their finances can be used to help fulfill the Great Commission.

The campaign has been designed to supply badly needed funds for the Here's Life movements in various cities overseas. The goal is to raise one billion dollars to help finance these efforts in order to help reach at least one billion people for Christ by 1990.

Wallace E. Johnson, co-founder of Holiday Inns, Inc., is the honorary international chairman of Here's Life, World; Joe Foss, former governor of South Dakota, is the international chairman; Roy Rogers, actor and business-man, is vice-chairman; Nelson Bunker Hunt, oil executive and investor, is the chairman of the international executive committee; and Ed Johnson, chairman and president of Financial Federation, one of America's leading financial institutions, is the campaign chairman for the United States.

Wallace Johnson's words at the initial stages of the campaign to raise the funds set the tone for the entire effort: "We must dedicate ourselves to this program which is so vital, so big, that it will set fire to the minds and imaginations of others for decades to come," he said. He also emphasized that the fund-raising campaign was to be targeted at potential funds not now being channeled into other Christian organizations or churches. "It is not our desire to compete with any other religious group for money or projects," he said.

As God continues to work through the Here's Life, World movement, I have never felt more optimistic or more confident. Never have I felt more assured that God is going to do something incredibly great to demonstrate His love and forgiveness to all men and nations throughout the world by the end of 1980.

CHAPTER TWENTY-SIX

"P.S." Ministries

Campus Crusade's prison outreach, "P.S." Ministries (a **P**ersonal **S**avior is the only solution to a **P**enal **S**ituation), had a unique beginning. It started with a phone call to staff member Larry Benton who was later to become the director of the ministry. "Larry, this is your neighbor, Pat," the voice over the phone said. "A man broke into your home, assaulted your wife and stole your car. Can you make it home?"

Larry Benton quickly hung up the phone and headed for home. He began to pray, "Dear God, I know You are in charge of all things and that You either cause or allow things to happen in our lives. I know You didn't cause this, but You did have to allow it. Why? You have promised to work all things together for good, but how can You do it in a case like this? I know You have commanded us to give thanks in everything, and although I don't feel like it, I thank You by faith. Please, God, use this to Your glory."

When Larry arrived at his driveway, the first thing he noticed was an empty garage. The front door gaped open; knotted belts strung the hallway welcoming him home. The house was teeming with policemen.

Larry's wife, Beverly, was at the neighbors, crying convulsively; her face was badly bruised. Soon, the ambulance came, and she was gone, giving Larry time to study the situation as he traveled from room to room. The evidence was clear — a fight in the kitchen, Beverly dragged to the living room and then to the bedroom. A dirty razor was lying in the sink where her assailant had taken a leisurely shave.

At the hospital Beverly related more. "He said he was going to keep on committing one crime after another 'because the world is in such a mess.' I told him that was not the answer, but Christ in the hearts of men was the answer to peace in the world. Before he left he said, 'I had planned to kill you, but you can thank your God that I didn't.'"

32-year Prison Record

This man was caught and extradited to the county jail; he had a 32-year long record of crime. As a result of Larry and Beverly's letter of forgiveness and personal witness, he came to know Christ. A happy ending to an otherwise traumatic incident!

Instead of an ending, this event was to be the beginning of a whole new chapter in the lives of Larry and Beverly Benton. It became a launching pad for the "P.S." Ministries, an outreach of evangelism and discipleship to inmates in a variety of penal institutions.

A year after the break-in at their home, Beverly began teaching craft classes in the San Bernardino County jail. The classes expanded to Sunday evening services; eventually 150 women prisoners received Christ as a result of her jail ministry.

From the city jail, the ministry moved to the California Institute for Women at Frontera, Calif. There, Beverly began to teach the Ten Basic Steps Toward Christian Maturity and the Transferable Concepts. Also, she began to show a series of films entitled "The Christian Home," featuring Dr. Henry Brandt, a noted Christian psychologist and lecturer.

Because of the success of these films, the Bentons arranged for them to be shown in 18 California prisons and prisons in Texas, Idaho and Pennsylvania. In the process of distributing the film series, the Bentons were able to visit chaplains in each of the major penal institutions in California and hold Lay Institutes for Evangelism at these prisons.

Overworked Chaplains

Most of these chaplains had more work than they could possibly handle. For example, one exhausted chaplain was in charge of 3,000 men. Because of the shortage of staff, the men had to sign up three weeks in advance to attend chapel. Shortly thereafter Larry and Beverly began to lay plans to train "para-chaplains" to help lighten the load of chaplains in ministering to the spiritual needs of the inmates. In the summer of 1975, the training of the first para-chaplains was begun.

Most discipleship takes place as Campus Crusade staff meet together with the inmates one-to-one or in small groups. Antha Avril, formerly an inmate in the California Institute for Women, is one of the many individuals Larry and Beverly have discipled.

"One evening a friend invited me to come to a meeting sponsored by 'P.S.' Ministries," says Antha. "At the meeting, these people didn't condemn me for my mistake in life as so many others had; they were telling me of God's love and plan for my life — my ruined, hopeless life. I knew I had to find out more about this love and plan. So, I invited Christ into my heart. Six people have become Christians through my singing in the shower. 'Why are you singing in prison?' they ask. 'How can anyone be happy here?' Then I share with them about Christ."

"P.S." Ministries' work with inmates once they are out of prison includes special Bible studies led by laymen trained by "P.S." staff. They are set up to help the inmate readjust to society. "We found that one of the hardest things for them is re-entry," says Larry. "I realized one day that there was as much cultural difference between the inside of a prison and the outside as there is between any two countries. The networkd Bible study serves as a bridge between the inmate and his family and the institutional church."

The man who assaulted Beverly was a recipient of the Prison Ministries' follow-up and discipleship program. When he had served his prison term, he left to take his place in society. After some time passed, he wrote to the Bentons, sharing that for the first time since he was a boy he was off parole and supervision by the law. He also expressed his gratitude to the Bentons for their influence in leading him to the new life he had found in a personal relationship with Jesus Christ.

The change in the life-style of inmates working with "P.S." Ministries presents an interesting contrast to crime studies. Robert Martinson, a sociologist from the City College of New York, conducted a major study and concluded that "the prison which makes every effort at rehabilitation succeeds no better than the prison which leaves its inmates to rot." In spite of this, "P.S." Ministries has had success in turning the lives of inmates in a new direction. Larry Benton believes this has happened because the para-chaplains and volunteers in "P.S." Ministries help to deal with the root causes of crime instead of the surface symptoms. "Crime is simply the outward manifestation of sin," he says. "The real problem is with men's hearts. A personal relationship with Jesus Christ and learning to apply the Word of God on a daily basis is the only solution."

CHAPTER TWENTY-SEVEN

Family Ministry

She had lost all hope for her marriage, her family and her life. She had decided to commit suicide. Divorce was the only other option. The pain in her relationship with her husband was unbearable, and her days were filled with total despair. She never dreamed such misery could exist. She felt like a complete failure as a wi`e, mother and businesswoman.

Friday, April 27, was the first day of the Family Life Conference sponsored by Campus Crusade for Christ's Family Ministry. This woman's husband, who was not a Christian, called her to invite her to go to the conference. She told him no and said she would meet him Monday at the courthouse to start divorce proceedings.

But something rare and wonderful began to happen. This woman's husband somehow convinced her to go with him to the conference. During the weekend, the husband committed his life and his future to the Lord. For the first time the couple found hope they could cling to and a plan for their lives.

On the last day of the conference, the wife came up to one of the speakers in tears and hugged him. She then explained how she and her husband were starting afresh with a new life, a new marriage and a new hope. They also agreed to follow up with professional counseling in the weeks and months ahead.

The American family is indeed in a time of great conflict. For the past several years, a million couples each year have been dissolving their marriages. Statistics tell us that 59 percent of America's children under the age of eighteen will spend part of their lives living with just one parent. The single parent family is the fastest growing family unit in America.

Against this backdrop of families in crisis, our Family Ministry has risen to answer the cry of the distressed. During 1984 this ministry experienced another year of incredible growth, with a 60 percent increase in attendance at its conferences. At 19 conferences, 17,000 people attended, as conferences in Denver, San Francisco, Dallas, New York and Minneapolis each drew more than 1,000 people, with the gathering in Chicago attracting 1,550. Without question, people are hungry to find answers to the family problems they are experiencing.

They are finding answers. One couple who attended the conference in New York City had been married for about thirty years. One of the application projects had been to write a love letter to your spouse. As this couple began the project, they both began to cry and continued to cry for more than an hour as they poured out their hearts to one another. The wife said later that it was the first time her husband had really communicated with her in all of their years of marriage. She said that Saturday night was when their honeymoon finally began. A year later she shared that their marriage had grown into an intimate, joyful and fulfilling relationship.

The Family Ministry was initially formed to aid the staff members of the Campus Crusade ministry. At first, the emphasis was to help prepare engaged staff members for marriage, but gradually it shifted to add marriage enrichment. The idea was to help couples be strong in their marriages so they could be more effective in ministering to others and help to fulfill the Great Commission.

"We seek to show in our seminars what has happened to the American marriage today, and how the Bible gives us a plan for action," says Dennis Rainey, the director of the Family Ministry. As Dennis and other conference speakers present God's plan for marriage, they are able to help couples come to grips with the pressures of life by showing why marriages are failing in our society today. Then, from this emphasis the conference goes on to teach practical aspects such as communication, sexuality, handling conflicts, etc.

But the conferences are not all lecture. The subject material is spread out over a three-day period, with evenings free for the conferees to discuss with their mates what they have been learning.

This ministry fits beautifully with the evangelistic and disciple- building emphasis of Campus Crusade. The purpose of the Family Ministry is to help churches equip families so they can be healthy to go to the world with the good news in this and in the next generation.

Healthier Christian families will help produce more missionaries to send to the world. And unless something happens to improve the health of American families during the next two decades, we're going to be needing missionaries ourselves.

The great need in American families for a biblical perspective on marriage has caused explosive growth in the Family Ministry. A cassette tape series, "Foundations for Family Living," and a conference notebook enables conferees to take the material home for personal study and use in churches, as well as for small group studies.

In 1983 Here's Life America staff members organized a New York City conference and saw 700 people attend — more than twice what they expected. The next year saw even more astonishing results. About 1,325 people attended, which at that time was the largest conference in the Family Ministry's history. It was so large, in fact, that 200 people had to watch the speakers on a video screen in an overflow room. As a result of the conference's success, gatherings were later scheduled in Philadelphia, attended by 900 people, and Boston, attended by 800. This draws a striking picture of spiritual warmth in an area that is usually thought of as cold to spiritual matters, Dennis says.

A pastor who attended the New York City meeting approached one of the speakers. Though he and his attractive wife looked like they had a good marriage, such was not the case. As he held his wife's hand, he told the speaker that his marriage was near divorce. The following Monday he was prepared to tell his congregation that he and his wife were going to divorce. But God had dealt with this couple that weekend and had healed many of their wounds. The conference had given them a sound biblical blueprint for their marriage and family. He said that they were not going to get a divorce, but that their marriage had new hope.

Changing lives for the glory of God is what the Family Ministry's 61 full-time staff and team of 20 speakers are trusting God to do. And it continues to happen at conference after conference.

"We came to this conference with some serious marital difficulties, discouraged and questioning our commitment to working on our relationship," said a Kansas City housewife who had been married for fourteen years. "But the practical methods and application of biblical principles has helped us to renew our commitment to each other and to our family. I praise the Lord for this weekend as it took us from despair to delight with our marriage and each other."

"This has revolutionized me as a Christian, a husband and as a father," said a Dallas insurance agent and real estate broker. "Setting aside two and a half days with my wife alone and *working through* the projects, has helped me get my role and priorities together as a Christian, husband and father. This is the most practical experience for marriage and guidance I have had."

CHAPTER TWENTY-EIGHT

Reaching the Nation's Leaders

Through the centuries, world history has been shaped by men of vision, faith and dedication. For example, those who gave birth to America were men who possessed these qualities. They were willing to pay a great price for their freedom and ours. Consider the bitter winter of 1777-1778 when Gen. George Washington knelt in the snows of Vally Forge. It seemed that the battle for independence was lost. He cried out to God for help and that battle for freedom was won.

Consider that critical meeting of the Continental Congress when the representatives from various colonies had reached an impasse. When there seemed to be no hope for reaching an agreement, Benjamin Franklin stood to his feet. "Gentlemen," he said, "I have lived long enough to know that God rules in the affairs of men and nations, and if a sparrow cannot fall to the ground without His knowledge, neither can a nation rise without His benediction. I move that we adjourn for prayer." History records that following that prayer meeting, the representatives came to a happy and immediate solution of their differences.

In a very real sense, we are a free people today, living in the most spiritually blessed country of history because God answered the prayers of multitudes of Christians.

Righteousness Important

It is vitally important that our nation have righteous leaders making the decisions that guide our country. The Bible tells us, "With good men in authority, the people rejoice; but with the wicked in power, they groan"

(Proverbs 29:2, Living), and "Righteousness exalts a n
tion" (Proverbs 14:34a). Because of this great need f
righteous people in positions of authority, we began tl
Christian Embassy to minister to leaders in the variou
branches of government in Washington, D.C. By sharir
the good news of Jesus Christ with these individual
they could have the opportunity to know Him and le
on His wisdom and strength for the great responsibiliti
of their jobs.

Though Campus Crusade staff had worked
Washington for a couple of years before, and st
member Eleanor Page had had a fruitful ministry wi
several congressional wives, the Christian Embas
ministry was officially launched on February 23, 197
in a gathering that included a number of leaders
Washington as well as Swede Anderson, the director
our ministry there, and our Embassy staff. From tl
beginning of this work, God has repeatedly shown
the spiritual hunger of the men and women in positio
of leadership.

I saw this hunger demonstrated one day when
walked into the office of a senator whom I had nev
met. A mutual friend had said, "Drop by to see him
Within a few moments it seemed as if we had know
each other for a lifetime. I asked him if he was a Christi
and shared the gospel with him through the Fo
Spiritual Laws. Within 10 to 15 minutes after I had enter
his office, he said he would like to receive Christ.

On another occasion, I spoke at a congressmar
home to several congressmen and their wives. After tl
meeting, several individuals came up to me and ask
me to come see them.

I went by the office of the first man the next day ar
asked him, "Did what I said last night make sense
you?" "It sure did," he replied. "Would you like to recei
Christ?" I asked. He said that he would and knelt besi
his couch to pray.

Down the hall I shared Christ with another congressman who had been present the night before. He too, said he would like to receive Christ.

Interested in Training

Not only are these individuals interested in receiving Christ, but they also are interested in being trained in how to live a more effective Christian life. At one meeting, I asked a leading senator to attend a 14-hour mediated Christian training session. I told him that I recognized that his busy schedule might not permit him to attend all of the training. He responded by saying, "Bill, if I'm too busy to take this training, I'm too busy. There is nothing more important. When can I begin?"

The Christian Embassy staff involve leadership of all branches of our government and the military in dinner meetings and luncheons, both large and small, to share Christ with them. Those who respond are invited to study the Bible with their colleagues (over 20 such groups are in action now) and to attend special seminars designed to equip them to grow in their Christian life and introduce others to the Lord.

Washington for Jesus

The highlight of our ministry in Washington, D.C., was a huge rally of an estimated 500,000 people. They came to spend April 29, 1980, in prayer for our nation. I believe this event, entitled "Washington for Jesus," was a great turning point in our nation's history.

Emotions welled up within me as I sat on the platform on the mall a couple of hundred yards from the Capitol Building. Indescribable feelings of worship, praise and joy vibrated through my heart as I looked out on the vast crowd of men and women who had come from across our country.

I had joined Pat Robertson of the Christian Broad casting Network as the co-progam chairman of the event. In that capacity it was one of my responsibilities to encourage evangelical leaders to participate in the event and lend their efforts to making it a success. The group which attended represented a broad spec trum of the body of Christ. Greek Orthodox, Roman Catholics, Protestants, charismatics and non-charisma tics all came together for one purpose: to repent, to turn back to God on behalf of our nation, and to express sorrow for our sins.

The day was filled not only with powerful, anointed preaching, but also with prayer and musical reminders of our dependence on God. I joined in prayer with my brothers and sisters in Christ, together claiming the promise of 2 Chronicles 7:14: "[If] My people who are called by My name humble themselves and pray, and seek My face and turn from their wicked ways, then I will hear from heaven, will forgive their sin, and will heal their land."

It occurred to me that surely this great host of men and women — and our sincerity — had touched the heart of God. Following the rally, Adrian Rogers, Ben Haden, Pat Robertson and many other Christian leaders agreed that this was one of the most important days in our nation's history.

U.N. Outreach

About half of the Christian Embassy staff come from fruitful ministry experience on other continents and con centrate their ministry efforts among the diplomats who people the embassies in Washington and the United Na tions in New York. This ministry was begun in 1978.

Most nations send their most outstanding leaders to represent them in Washington and New York. Few of these people develop close relationships with American Christians. Christian Embassy staff spend time with them personally, entertain them in their homes and hold special dinners and receptions for them.

A Latin American couple who received Christ antici-
pate sharing their new- found faith with their friends in
the leadership of their nation when they return home,
and the same is happening among Africans, Europeans,
Asians and Middle Eastern diplomats.

Twelve staff led by Frank Obien and Glen Kleinknecht
talked with delegates and U.N. staff about a personal
relationship with Christ and invited them to a reception.
Included among the 70 who attended the reception heard
a short gospel presentation were a minister of foreign
affairs, more than six ambassadors, vice consuls, under-
secretaries, U.N. delegates and their staff.

Influential Contacts

Swede Anderson feels that this work in the U.N. and
embassies in Washington can help expand our
worldwide movement. "One of the most important facets
of the Christian Embassy, we believe, is that through
leadership persons introduced to Christ (those who work
at the U.N., World Bank or in embassies), the lives of
leaders on each continent will be changed and doors of
opportunity for spreading the gospel in many nations
will open."

We find that, when these people recognize their need
for Christ and as He enters their lives, He begins to
satisfy the deepest concerns of the person and of his
family life. Christ also gives him confidence that He can
guide him in the midst of the pressures of his professional
responsibilities. Restored families and new hope are
among the results seen in this vital international outreach.

With the Christian Embassy ministry established in
these two cities, a foundation is now laid for launching
embassies in all the major capitol cities of the world.

Another vital outreach that is designed to work w
the leaders of the world is the Executive Ministr

Campus Crusade. Reaching business and professional leaders, the Executive Ministries is making a powerful impact on these influential people.

Executive Seminars

One of the key elements of the strategy is the Executive Seminars, held several times each year at Arrowhead Springs and other locations across the country and around the world. Through large meetings, small group seminars and one-to-one interaction, the executives and their wives learn how to maximize their talents and resources for Jesus Christ. They learn that they are important in helping to fulfill the Great Commission. And, just as important, they discover that they have personal needs that only God can meet.

Throughout the week of a seminar, men and women respond personally to God's love and to the challenge of beginning or renewing their relationship with Him. When executives who have reached the top of the financial, business and professional ladder come to Christ, they frequently become as excited as any other group, including students.

Joyful Experience

On one occasion, one of the executives with whom I had prayed the second day of the seminar (his wife had received Christ only the day before) spoke across the table during lunch to another businessman with whom I had prayed only 20 minutes before. The first man, although very dignified and reserved normally, was bubbling over with great joy. "My wife is four days old," he said, "and I am three days old." (He was referring, of course, to his age as a Christian.) "How old are

ond man paused for a few moments and then am 20 minutes old." Many others scattered dining room at Arrowhead Springs were only a few minutes, hours or days old. Great rejoicing was taking place among us and in heaven as well!

The desire to lead a changed life ultimately infects nearly everyone who attends the seminar, and the contrast between the arrival and departure atmospheres is evident in the radiant faces, warm interaction and joyful singing at the close of each seminar. But the difference is most evident when they return to the "old routine" with new perspectives and priorities.

One woman wrote, "The seminar was so organized and so exciting! I really desire to go back to Oklahoma and come alive with what I've heard and felt. I am asking God to show me exactly what He wants me to do in my community for Him. I want to be totally His woman!"

Another executive commented this way: "My wife and I wish to thank you for the many God-given benefits we have received from the recent Executive Seminar. We have both rededicated ourselves to a Christ-centered life — to seek God's will for us!"

"I liked the evident love and friendliness of everyone," wrote another executive. "The program was worthwhile and most influencing. All of this has made for a week that has changed both my wife's life and mine."

Similar seminars have been conducted with great success overseas, as executives and professionals in Asia, Latin America, Africa and Europe have responded warmly to the invitations to make their lives count for the cause of Christ.

American executives frequently participate in these seminars in other countries as a part of a vision tour. These tours take them overseas where they observe the Campus Crusade international ministry in action. In addition to having their vision stretched as they see what God is accomplishing, they also have the opportunity to minister to executives from other nations.

Ministering Through Dinner Parties

Another aspect of the Executive Ministries outreach is that of evangelistic dinner parties. For 13 years, Art De Moss, who was a member of our board of directors, and his wife, Nancy, hosted dinner parties where the guests had the opportunity to hear the claims of Christ. Art has gone to be with the Lord, but Nancy has continued the ministry.

About every six weeks, the couple hosted a dinner party for 150-700 people at their home. After dinner, the guests heard from such nationally-known figures as Charles Colson, Pat Boone, author Joni Eareckson, Senator Bill Armstrong, Roy Rogers and Dale Evans, and several professional athletes, all of whom shared their faith in Christ.

Those who trusted in Christ during the presentation were invited back for a smaller dinner party which could lead to their involvement in Bible studies to foster their spiritual growth. Approximately 600 men and women participated in these studies led by Campus Crusade staff.

An individual who became involved in one of the Bible study groups said, "My decision to join the group was only part of a larger decision to let the Lord guide me practically instead of just in theory. Life is suddenly more meaningful when I ask Christ what I should do and let Him guide me in doing it."

Many Christian couples from around the country attend dinner parties now given by Nancy, and then they participate in two-day seminars on how they can hold their own evangelistic parties. Using these principles in their own communities, these individuals also see gratifying results, and have had as many as 54 people indicate decisions to receive Christ at a single dinner.

Art saw the spiritual hunger of the socially prominent as one cause for the success of this ministry. "But the ost significant factor," he emphasized, "is that God is this, and people who seemed unreachable are being ached for Christ."

Reaching people who can have a wide influence for hrist not only in their community but also throughout he world is what the Executive Ministries is all about. nd it is a ministry that God is using greatly. To Him be ll the honor, glory and praise!

CHAPTER TWENTY-NINE

Training Centers

Several years ago I had the privilege of addressing unique group of people. It was another hot, humid da in Manila, the capital city of the Philippines, when stood in a simple classroom, bare of all but the mo necessary essentials. The students had a plain desk wit hard wooden chairs. A blackboard was the only oth adornment in the room.

Gathered from many countries across Asia, these st dents had come to be trained to be more effective in the service to our Lord. I spoke to them that day on t qualifications for spiritual revolution. My message w a simple one. I challenged them to crown Christ as Lo of their lives, be filled with the Holy Spirit, mainta their first love for Christ and keep fresh their vision f the task of reaching the world for Christ. Finally, I urg them to be committed to God's Word and to prayer a to tell everyone who would listen about Christ (Col sians 1:28).

I emphasized that they could do this only throu the power of the Holy Spirit and not in the energy the flesh. I reminded them that God does not call us do anything for which He does not supply the pow the wisdom and the grace. After my message the st dents were excited about what I had to say and we had a great time of fellowship together.

In the days and weeks following my visit, the in viduals continued an intensive time of evangelizing a discipling of new believers in preparation for their min try in their home countries. I'm sure some of the studer were somewhat apprehensive at first about their time the training center. They were unsure of how this time was going to benefit them as they prepared for the ministry they felt God wanted them to have back in their home country.

But as the weeks went by, they continued to receive instruction on many of the essentials of the Christian life — how to be filled with the Spirit, how to live a holy life, how to witness, how to help fulfill the Great Commission, and many others. Not only did they hear lectures, but they actually put the instruction into practice by leading Bible studies at local campuses and witnessing for their faith as they went about their daily activities.

The results were that when they returned to their home countries, they had not only knowledge, but experience. They then launched successful ministries that in some cases greatly affected the cause of Christ among their people.

One of the graduates of the training center came to Bailey Marks, who was then the director of affairs for our ministry in Asia, saying, "If I go back to my country and do what I have been taught to do, I will end up in jail or dead, because in my country it is against the law for someone to change his religion."

Bailey assured him, "You just do what God tells you to do. You won't be under any pressure from us."

When the recent graduate of the training center returned to his home country, he began translating Campus Crusade's materials into his native language. At that time only a few hundred believers lived in this isolated nation.

As important as the translation work was, our director became increasingly exasperated at his lack of witnessing experiences. Finally, he told his wife, "I am going out to witness, no matter what happens."

That afternoon the first three people he spoke to about Christ trusted Him as their Savior. The next day they all came for Bible study and our director began passing on to them what he had learned at our training center in Manila.

Today it is a matter of history that a great explosion of ministry has taken place. More than 25,000 people have been baptized and at least that many people have embraced Christ, but not yet been baptized. And our director, with the emphasis on evangelism and discipleship that he learned at the training center, provided the spark for this revival.

But these great advances have not come without significant cost. Our director has been imprisoned, along with other believers, on a number of occasions. And yet he and his family have maintained a joyful, radiant spirit in spite of this roadblock. I asked his wife how she felt about her husband being imprisoned. She replied, "I'm jealous. I wanted to be in prison for our Lord."

Their teenage daughter responded in like manner. When she learned that her father had been imprisoned for his witness, she said with tears, "Mother, why does Daddy get all the privileges?" Certainly it was a reminder of how the early Christians responded to suffering.

It is my prayer that people like our director and his wife will be raised up in every country and trained through our training centers so they can be as effective as possible in helping to change their communities and nations.

Training centers like the one in Manila have been extremely effective in training staff members around the world. Lasting from nine months to one year, these vital centers provide the foundation our staff need upon which to build dynamic evangelistic and disciple-building ministries.

Similar training centers have been established for laymen. Varying in duration from several weeks to three months, these training centers are an abbreviated version of the instruction which has enabled our staff to plant dynamic ministries in various parts of the world. It has been my prayer for years that we would be able to plant a training center of this type in every city in the free world with a population of more than 50,000. Our present plans call for 5,000 such training centers before 1995.

In this manner, those who come to Christ through showings of the film *JESUS* and evangelistic radio programming will have a place nurturing their faith.

Some of the training centers have been positioned in remote rural areas because of the critical needs there. Dale Robertson, a veteran Campus Crusade staff member from Vista, California, coordinated the training center near Davao, Philippines. He and his staff team regularly made trips to a training center located far from urban life.

The trip began by taking a ride to the end of the bus route. Dale and his co-workers then boarded a jeepney, a small, open mini-bus, for a two- hour ride on which they forded a river and trundled over mountains into the Arkann Valley. The trip was tiring and frequently left their boots and clothes splattered with mud. Once they arrived, however, they found trainees with hungry hearts.

One group of 16 trainees included 12 pastors, representing virtually every church in the valley. "Basically these people are untrained, uneducated farmers who are serving as pastors," Dale said. "It's so exciting to see how teachable they are."

Isobello Bamunya put his training at the Davao training center to good use by leading 50 people to Christ during one two-week period the center was in session. Many of these people responded to the gospel after he showed the *JESUS* film in his home village. On another occasion Bamunya walked nearly 25 miles to another village where he preached and shared the Four Spiritual Laws with local residents. As a result of the trip, the people in that area decided to build their own church.

The Here's Life Training Centers work with local

churches, which benefit from the training and from increased attendance. In some cases, when there are no churches for new believers to join, home Bible fellowships are started so Christians can meet on a regular basis.

In northern Thailand, as a result of the Here's Life Training Centers evangelism strategies, which include showing the *JESUS* film in rural villages, there are thousands of new Christians. Many of them are from villages where there is no church.

Now there are more than 520 home Bible fellowships with at least 15 members each in that part of Thailand. Of those fellowships, 400 are in areas where there were no known Christians before.

The same results are being seen elsewhere:

— During 1984, 280 village evangelists, lay leaders and pastors were trained at the Madhya Pradesh HLTC in India. From that group 60 home Bible fellowships were started and many new believers were baptized.

— In Pakistan, the Lahore training center has trained 1,500 students, 150 pastors and 1,200 laymen since its inception. The *JESUS* film has been shown to 930,000 people by the trainees and trainers, with 139,000 of those people indicating their desire to receive Christ.

— In Indonesia, two training centers were held in 1984 in Kelet, training 95 individuals. Using various methods, trainees shared the gospel with 7,920 individuals, with more than one-fourth indicating their desire to receive Christ. A total of 70 home Bible fellowships were started, and nine branch churches have been formed out of the Kelet church. Most of the training is done by the church leaders.

Under the leadership of Curt Mackey, the director of the Here's Life Training Centers around the world, this strategy is providing a growing base of trained lay people who are equipped to be spiritual leaders. And they are even improving on their own training as graduates of the program return to staff future training center sessions. These lay volunteers often prove extremely effective in discipling their peers.

But what of the countries which cannot be reached through the *JESUS* film, and where converts cannot enroll in training centers or home Bible fellowships? Although at first glance many counties would seem to fall into this category, it is my belief that one day every country will have home Bible fellowships. I am praying for 25 million home Bible fellowships to be operating worldwide.

I believe many of these fellowships will come into being as a result of a worldwide network of radio which will leapfrog the seemingly impregnable barriers which exist in our world today. In the People's Republic of China those barriers are political; in the Middle East, religious; and in India, logistical.

Since 1979, Campus Crusade for Christ has attempted to hurdle these barriers through Christian radio broadcasting. With the help of Christian radio broadcasting facilities such as Trans World Radio and Far Eastern Broadcasting Company, programs of Christian teaching and discipleship have been broadcast into China, India, the Middle East and Indonesia.

Our ministry has received 1,200 letters each month from India, 500 per month from the Arab world and 200 letters per month from China as a result of the broadcasts.

The broadcasts continue to leave their mark on listeners. One listener wrote: "I am an old-time Trans World Radio listener in China. I have been using your programs in encouraging other brothers and sisters. It has also been very helpful to me in my own spiritual growth. Your program is like a rich, spiritual feast to me."

In many parts of Asia programs are used as follow-up for the *JESUS* film. People attending showings of the movie are encouraged to tune in their radios to a Christian station which carries the Campus Crusade training.

By listening to the station they can begin to grow in their faith by hearing the basics of the Christian faith clearly explained.

In India's Quilon district, many people had been listening regularly to Campus Crusade's series of 90 training programs which were being broadcast over the radio. Listeners to the programs were invited to attend a one-day conference at Quilon Mar Thoma Student Center. A total of 107 listeners attended, and 45 invited Christ into their lives. Individuals from 29 localities expressed an interest in establishing New Life Radio Clubs in their area.

Similar conferences have been held in other parts of the country, and now 63 Bible clubs are meeting weekly, with 919 people attending.

By beaming these programs from transmitters located in Guam, Sri Lanka and Cyprus, our ministry has a potential listening audience of one billion people. We're praying that we will continue to receive responses like the letter one Turkish listener sent us.

"I am following your radio lessons, and I will continue," he wrote. "I know very little about Christianity. I will go to the city and search on this subject. I know I will have to seek and struggle hard, but whatever it may cost, I am determined to do this."

Without question, Jesus' observation to His disciples is still true today: "Behold, I say to you, lift up your eyes, and look on the fields, that they are white for harvest" (John 4:35). Through the use of the *JESUS* film, training centers, home Bible fellowships and a worldwide radio ministry, we are seeking to help those who are the results of this harvest become established in a joyful, dynamic walk with Christ.

It is our prayerful objective to establish 5,000 training centers, one in every major community in every country of the free world by 1995. We hope to train millions of Christians of every denomination to help evangelize their

vn communities and countries. These trained Christ-
ns will help to show the *JESUS* film to more than 5
lion people by 2000 A.D., at which time experts esti-
ate there will be approximately 6.5 billion people in
e world. From these film showings and other means
e hope to see one billion people come to Christ. The
ined Christians will also help to lead the 25 million
me Bible fellowships designed to teach and disciple
e billion or more new believers in their Christian faith.

You and your church can be a part of this magnificent
plan to help fulfill the Great Commission by financing
Here's Life Training Center for $25,000 and supporting
for a couple of years until it becomes self- supporting.
u can also help support a *JESUS* film team of approx-
ately six people for an entire year for $25,000, which
cludes their salary, travel, films, projector, etc.

Through your involvement in the Here's Life Training
enters and the *JESUS* film, you can help change the
orld.

CHAPTER THIRTY

International Christian Graduate University

Looking at today's university community, the fou tainhead of secular humanism and a cauldron of confli ing moralities, it is intriguing to note that more than 1 of the first and foremost institutions of learning in tl country were founded on Christian principles.

Consider the example of Harvard University, found in 1636. The school seal reads, "In Cristi Gloriam," whi is Latin for "In Christ we glory." Although the Purita who founded Harvard did not intend it as a theologi institution, one of the college's 19 laws did state tl every student should consider "the mayne end of l life studyes to know God and Jesus Christ. . .and the fore to lay Christ in the bottome, as the only foundati of all sound knowledge and learning." One early auth ity estimated that 52 percent of the school's 17th centu graduates went into Christian service.

Columbia University was originally known as Kin College and its charter was specific in its emphasis spiritual pursuits. Advertisements at the time stated much: "The chief thing that is aimed at in this college to teach and engage [students] to know God in Jes Christ, and to love and serve Him, in all sobriety, goc ness, and righteousness of life, with a perfect heart a a willing mind. . . to lead them from the study of natu to the knowledge of themselves and of the God of natu and their duty to Him, themselves, and one anoth and everything that can contribute to their happine: both here and hereafter."

Scores of other universities like Princetc Dartmouth, William and Mary and others were esta lished as Christian schools.

Obviously, the university community has strayed far from its moorings. Leading educators are expressing their concern, even alarm, over the growing bankruptcy of instruction in the classrooms of our country. Even high school graduates in some areas are functionally illiterate.

What is the problem? For the most part, higher education has abandoned the true and living God to worship the god of secular humanism. Today, humanism has become the dominant emphasis in the classrooms of America. For decades, biblical Christianity has been ridiculed in the classrooms, and outspoken Christians have been frequently intimidated or discouraged from seeking advanced degrees or have even been denied them after years of faithful study.

Since the university influences every facet of society and since Christian ethic is the very basis of our culture, this dramatic trend away from the scriptural basis of our school curriculum has striken our nation with a moral cancer. Is it any wonder that our nation is fast becoming morally and spiritually bankrupt, resulting in all kinds of social, economic and political problems?

It is for this reason that I believe God has led us to start the International Christian Graduate University. This university must be of such high and uncompromising standards, both spiritually and academically, that the finest and most highly-qualified Christian professors and students in the world will seek the opportunity to become associated with it.

This university represents the beginnings of the fulfillment of a dream, a vision which God gave to me many years ago. The dream was to help establish an international graduate university for Christians on the level of Oxford, Harvard or Stanford. I do not minimize the importance of the several very fine Christian schools that presently offer some graduate degrees in selected fields. We strongly support and encourage such schools that honor the Lord and His Word. But at the risk of sounding presumptuous, our graduate university is designed to compare with the very finest graduate schools in the world.

I believe that one of the greatest needs of our time is a university with academic excellence and a biblical world view which honors and exalts God instead of the world view of secular humanism which enthrones man. By training graduate students in the fields of theology, communication, government, education, medicine, law, humanities, athletics, business, and labor, leaders will be developed who can make a great impact on our world for the cause of Christ.

I well remember the day in my office, while in prayer, when the Lord first impressed on me the need to build the International Christian Graduate University.

"Lord, how are we going to build this university?" I asked. "Such a university with extension campuses all over the world will cost hundreds of millions, if not billions of dollars."

During the history of this ministry, since 1951, Campus Crusade has not ended a single day with an extra dollar beyond our immediate needs, so there was no money to build the university. But even if we had the money, I couldn't have ethically used it for the university, because it had not been given for that specific purpose.

One day as I was praying in my office, the Lord gave me a specific plan of action. We were to find 5,000 acres of land, set aside 1,000 acres for the university campus and permit the rest to be subdivided for industrial, commercial and residential use on an endowment basis to provide both short- and long-term financing. This program would provide enough money to build the university and the satellite campuses around the world.

I called some of our key men together and shared the vision with them. "The Lord wants us to build a great world-class university, with satellite campuses in all of the major countries of the world," I said. Anticipating their questions, I explained that the financing of this gargantuan undertaking would come from revenues generated from 5,000 acres of land.

"We don't have any money, but even so, we are to look for 5,000 acres. The Lord will provide the funds to pay for them since this project is His idea, not mine," I explained. I am sure that some of the real estate people with whom we talked about purchasing the 5,000 acres must have laughed and shaken their heads in amazement when they discovered that we had no money. Like Abraham, we didn't know where to go, but we were convinced that we were to trust and obey God.

As we began looking for some of the choicest land in all the world for our purpose, we heard about a large farm in the Washington, D.C., area. It turned out that it wasn't 5,000 acres, and it wasn't what we were seeking.

A friend of the ministry bought approximately 2,500 acres near our headquarters and offered to lease 1,000 acres to build the university at $1 dollar a year for 100 years. This was a most generous offer, but could not generate sufficient funds to build and endow the university. The plan which God gave me called for 5,000 acres. We needed the profit from the 4,000 acres to build and endow the university. So I said, "I appreciate your generosity, but it won't help us. God has impressed us to secure 5,000 acres, so we will keep looking and praying."

Another friend heard about our plans and offered to give us a 5,000-acre ranch.

"It's all yours," he said. "Come and build your university."

That, too, was a very generous offer. Although very valuable, the land was not suited to our needs.

As we continued to look, I heard about 5,045 undeveloped acres within San Diego's city limits. We asked the man who did the land planning for the University of California at Irvine to prepare a special presentation for us to give to the mayor and other city officials in San Diego. I shared with them our vision for the International Christian Graduate University and our desire to build it on this choice property. They were very positive about the idea of the university and the economic benefits to the city that would accompany such a project. They encouraged us to proceed with our plans.

Assured of the support of the city officials, we began to negotiate for the purchase of the land and continued to do so for more than a year. I am sure that there was considerable skepticism and probably some laughter going on behind the scenes when we kept negotiating for the purchase of the property without any money. The asking price was $5,500 an acre, which was very reasonable for that area. Similar land right next to the property we sought to purchase was selling for as much as $45,000 an acre. The Lord had impressed us to find 5,000 acres. He had led us to one of the most desirable pieces of property in the entire country. Now it was His responsibility to enable us to secure the finances to purchase this valuable property.

Since Campus Crusade for Christ could not help financially, I shared the vision of the university with some friends. I also outlined the need for funds to buy three 30-day options on the property at $50,000 each. The money for the first option was made available by a friend to whom we explained that he could lose his investment, but if we purchased the property, he would make a profit of $50,000. The same offer was made to a second friend who provided the funds for the second 30-day option. A third friend put up the money for the third 30-day option under similar conditions.

Ninety days passed quickly, and we still did not have the money to buy the property. As it came down to the last day, I had to leave for some very important meetings in Europe, including our European staff conference.

The owners refused to extend our option, so I told our men to place the property in escrow, even though we didn't have the money to close the purchase. We stood to lose the entire $150,000 we had put down for options as well as $20,000 or so in expenses. But God had obviously brought us this far. I knew of no other place in the entire world where we could find 5,000 acres so perfectly fitted for our needs. Furthermore, it seemed the Lord was saying, "Trust Me. I will supply the finances."

Our flight was late in arriving in London, and we were unable to catch the flight to Vienna, so the airline put us up for the night in a London hotel. For the next eight hours I was in touch by phone with different potential investors in America and was much in prayer. At 4:30 in the morning (London time) the final call was made, and we were able to purchase the property. Truly this was a gift from God, a miracle of miracles! We were able to purchase the property on a joint venture arrangement because of a bank loan guaranteed by two friends. But because the property is worth so much more than we paid for it, another bank refinanced the purchase without any signatures of guarantee.

Many characteristics made this property valuable including the cultural and academic atmosphere and an ideal climate within the city limits of one of the larger cities in the United States.

In the ensuing months, we faced many financial cliffhangers as we sought to retain and develop this valuable property, some of the most valuable in the world, according to knowledgeable land developers. It was ideal for our purposes. We were convinced that thousands of couples would move to our La Jolla Valley property on a lease or life-estate arrangement to help us build and endow this great University for the glory of God.

One of the most critical barriers to us retaining the property occurred September 11, 1984, when San Diego's

City Council met to consider our request to develop part of the LaJolla Valley Property which we had purchased. Under the proposal which we submitted, we would be allowed to develop the 1,000 acres for the university itself and 750 acres for a university high tech industrial park. The remaining 3,300 acres, designated for residential, commercial and recreational uses, would not be developed until later.

From a human perspective, there seemed to be little hope that the university project would be approved. And if our request had been denied, the future of the university itself would have been in jeopardy. For without the income we would receive from the development of the high tech industrial park, we would not have sufficient funds to take the steps necessary to build the university.

The project was strongly supported by many top San Diego businessmen and professional leaders, the San Diego Evangelical Association, and others. But intense opposition had come from a new mayor who had taken office and was supported by the homosexuals and some environmental groups.

After four hours of pro and con presentation among the members of council, they voted — a half hour before midnight. The 5-4 vote in our favor was greeted with an instant of what seemed to be stunned silence, followed quickly by an exuberant, sustained burst of applause from the supporters of the project.

After the council gave us its decision, I was so intoxicated with joy and praise that I went back to my hotel room and spent much of the night praising the Lord. I could hardly sleep at all. In fact, even when I did get to sleep, it was but for a brief time and I soon awakened to praise the Lord again.

Finally, about 5 A.M. I felt it was time to get up and prepare for an early-morning breakfast, where I met with a group of pastors and laymen who had joined with us in this effort to give thanks and praise to our Lord together.

Many times I have been asked, "Why is Campus Crusade establishing a university?" I answer these queries by giving a number of reasons. First, the university's philosophy is compatible with the original vision which God gave in 1951 to help reach the world for Christ in our generation through a continuing process of discipleship and evangelism.

Second, Campus Crusade's more than 30 years of experience in developing educational and training programs provides us with a rich background in educational development.

Third, since our ministry originated on the college campus, we have worked with millions of students on campuses throughout the nation and the world. The *Agape* Movement, in which people with vocational skills use their occupations as a platform to present the gospel, provides a unique vocation-missions outlet for graduates. Leaders trained in the university will be able, through their professions, to disciple influential people in many nations of the world.

In addition, Campus Crusade has had broad experience in seminar development which will be used in organizing business, communications, law and other seminar courses. We are committed to the principle of transferability in all teaching methods; therefore, the university's graduates will be equipped to teach the same principles to others in their field.

We believe that God is leading us to fill the gap of badly-needed graduate level Christian education in major academic disciplines, with the School of Theology, established in 1979, providing the unifying principles and ethical foundation for the entire university.

Since its inception, the goal of Campus Crusade has been to help change the world. In order to do this, men and women are needed who are highly- qualified leaders in their professions and whose ethical base is the Word of God. The International Christian Graduate University will provide leaders who will be trained with a biblical world view to share God's love with others, disciple those who respond and demonstrate the validity of a biblically based lifestyle.

One of the university's key areas is its curriculum. To prepare the curriculum, the graduate university task force, in conjunction with leading educators, is drawing upon the best of 200 years of American educational development in addition to formulating fresh educational concepts. This combination of proven methods with new thought will provide high-quality education from the beginning of the university. The curriculum is planned to exceed the usual academic standards without being bound by traditionally designed systems of training. Since the University will reach out around the world from the mother campus in San Diego, we will employ the finest technology available, including satellites worldwide radio, TV and computers.

Strong, godly and academically qualified leaders are vital in order to make this program a success. We are especially fortunate to have such leaders in the School of Theology in Dr. Ron Jenson and Dr. Ted Cole.

Before accepting his position as president, Dr. Jenson was on the staff of Philadelphia Church of the Savior where in seven years he and the church staff saw it grow from 14 couples to an average Sunday attendance of 1,300. He also served as the dean of the Christian Leadership Training Center — a School of Theology extension in Philadelphia — where he directed the weekly training of 75 pastors from 22 denominations in evangelism, discipleship, management and church growth.

Dr. Jenson received his doctorate at Western Conservative Baptist Seminary where he initiated, taught and directed a discipleship and evangelism program. He first became active in Campus Crusade as a college freshman in Oregon.

"We want to be known as a school that knows the most about, and can, in fact, develop a healthy pastor and church, and trained Christian leaders for inter-denominational and para-church organizations," Ron says. "For this reason we are developing a new model among schools for training students."

The new model to which Ron referred is a method of apportioning half of the student's education to academics and half to on-the-field application. For the School of Theology students, this means they are directly involved in a local church body, putting to use what they have learned in the classroom. By the time the student graduates, he has experience in many phases of church work and is prepared to step into a leadership role in the church. This same pattern of half classroom training and half application will hold true in the other academic disciplines as well.

Dr. Ted Cole, the executive vice-president of the school, was one of America's leading pastors for twenty-eight years with a church of 6,500 members. He has several earned degrees, including his doctorate from Eastern Baptist Seminary. He is a model of eloquent preaching, dedicated soul-winning and a loving, compassionate heart. He gives leadership to the School of Theology on a day-to-day basis, aided by several godly, scholarly professors and staff.

I believe that the real battle for the minds and wills of men is being fought in our schools, where we have lost every major engagement for more than fifty years. This is largely because of our lethargy and lack of awareness of what is happening. As the famous British political philosopher and statesman Edmund Burke once said, "All that is needed for evil to triumph is that good men do nothing!"

Many good people have done nothing, and as a result we have lost our universities. Dr. Charles Malik, one of the great statesmen of our day and a former president of the United Nations General Assembly, feels we must recapture this vital institution.

"Nothing compares with the urgency of seeking to recapture universities for Jesus Christ," he says. "Christ is not welcome in the university. In fact, He is ignored, if not declared the enemy. To reach the world in which we live, this secularizing of the universities, this estrangement, if not downright enmity, between Christ and the great universities cannot continue without disastrous results upon the whole of western civilization."

We are trusting God that the International Christian Graduate University will produce the kind of leaders who will help turn this situation around. We believe this university will produce men and women with a global vision for the honor and glory of Christ that will have far-reaching results.

CHAPTER THIRTY-ONE

EXPLO '85

In the summer of 1984 I met with about 30 directors of the worldwide movement of Campus Crusade for Christ at a beautiful mountainside retreat in Austria. Outside, the sunlight filtered through the clouds and glinted off the rocky mountainside. But we were not there to admire the scenery, as beautiful as it was. Instead we were discussing a project which would accelerate this worldwide movement more than anything we had undertaken since this ministry began in 1951.

Today the details of this project — now known as EXPLO '85 — are falling into place. But at that time it was only an idea.

Our idea was to hold a worldwide congress that would light a spark of spiritual revolution on every continent. In years past we had seen the value of such conferences.

In 1972, EXPLO '72 had drawn 85,000 students and laymen for the largest conference of its kind. These individuals returned to their homes with a determination to make an impact for Christ. They did, and many still are.

Two years later a similar conference was held. This time the site was Seoul, South Korea. More than 323,000 attended the daily training sessions in effective Christian living, and crowds in excess of one million participated in a single evening inspirational session.

In 1976 this life-changing training was made available to 325,000 Christians, representing 15,000 churches of nearly every denomination, as part of a coordinated effort to take the message of Christ to the maximum number of people in the United States. Known as Here's

Life, America, this campaign resulted in 532,000 people registering decisions for Christ. I am convinced that this number represented just the tip of the iceberg as literally millions of lives were changed across the country as a result of Here's Life, America.

Here's Life campaigns similar to the ones held in the United States began to take place in other countries. Christians in many cities across the world banded together to reach their communities. And God blessed in phenomenal ways. One of the most spectacular examples occurred in Seoul when the campaign culminated in a one-week gathering called Here's Life, Korea/World Evangelization Crusade. Crowds in excess of 2 million people attended some of the nightly sessions, with a total of more than 10.5 million participating in the five nightly gatherings.

Truly God had greatly blessed our efforts as we sought to trust and obey Him in His leading to help fulfill the Great Commission. But we were not satisfied. I felt that if we were committed to reaching the world, in obedience to our Lord's command, we needed to organize a gigantic worldwide congress to bring together approximately 40,000-50,000 people who are student and lay Christian leaders in their countries. In this way we could equip, encourage and motivate these people for dynamic ministry in their home countries.

I discussed the idea of the conference at great length with Bailey Marks, who for years had been the director of affairs for our ministry in Asia. Now he was serving as the vice-president for international ministries. As Bailey began to research the feasibility of holding such a conference, he made a startling discovery. The cost of holding such a conference and transporting delegates from around the world to a single location would be astronomical — far more than we could hope to afford.

"For a few days, I lost my enthusiasm for the conference," Bailey said. "However, the Lord would not let me forget about it, and I continued to pray."

One morning after a time of prayer about the situation, Bailey went to his bathroom sink and began to shave. As he was performing this daily ritual, the Lord gave him some remarkable solutions to the apparently impassable barriers we faced.

It was these solutions that he stood to share with our group that day. As I looked around the room before Bailey began to speak to the group, I saw men representing every continent — men of all sizes and colors, from rangy light-haired Europeans to slender, dark-haired Orientals. Americans, Africans, Asians and Latin Americans all gathered around the tables, all one in Christ, all filled with the urgency of taking the good news of God's love and forgiveness around the globe.

As Bailey spoke, God gave us a unity of spirit. Several times we paused to pray for wisdom in dealing with the problems we faced. The difficulty of bringing so many people together did not overwhelm us, because the One who created the heavens and the earth was working through us, as He had so many times in the past.

As we listened, Bailey outlined some ideas that God had given him for making EXPLO '85 a reality. Instead of bringing people from all over the world to a central location, why not hold separate meetings and link them by satellite broadcasts? In this manner as many as 100 conferences could be conducted, and inspiration and training could be beamed to each location. Hundreds of thousands of people could be trained without leaving their own countries.

At first, not every director was enthusiastic about the concept. It was so radically new, and many wondered if it could take place in various parts of the developing world. Yet as these men of God began to pray, think and plan, they began to see how this conference could help them realize their own dreams for their areas of responsibility. They began to see how EXPLO '85 could accelerate their ministry in reaching their countrymen with the message of Jesus Christ. After a few hours of discussion, each of our directors agreed that the plan was God's will and felt we should proceed.

Soon the plans began to gather momentum. Bailey and his assistant, Jerry Sharpless, began to tackle the mammoth tasks of confirming conference locations, preparing satellite broadcasts and trusting God for the finances for the massive conference. A sizable portion of the funds was reserved for scholarships, so that people from the Third World nations would be able to attend who would otherwise be prevented because of a lack of finances.

I continue to be excited by the potential of EXPLO '85. I believe it will be an event of unprecedented significance. At each conference site delegates will be trained in the basics of the Christian life and will be motivated and inspired as they learn through the satellite reports about what God is doing around the world. It will be a worldwide call to spiritual revolution, equipping and motivating people to take the love and forgiveness of God through Jesus Christ to every person in every community in every country of the world.

Satellite broadcasts will be transmitted simultaneously for two hours each day for four days from one of six sites around the world — New York City, Mexico City, Seoul, Berlin, West Germany; and Nairobi, Kenya. These broadcasts will give an international flavor to the event.

Imagine the effect of such a conference on a group of believers in Sri Lanka, where less than one percent of the people are Christians, or in a predominantly Muslim nation. Instead of feeling like a tiny minority, they will see the satellite reports of what God is doing and recognize that they are part of the worldwide body of Christ. They will learn that they too can witness the great and mighty things God has promised to accomplish on their behalf in their own country. Not only will they be inspired, but they will receive the training they need to enable them, through the power of the Holy Spirit, to trust God for great things in their part of the world as well.

My heart leaps with praise to God as I think of what can be accomplished for His glory through such a worldwide gathering as EXPLO '85. I believe the days of December 27-31, 1985, will be remembered in history as this conference sparks explosions of revival across the globe. With conference sites in a hundred locations around the world and hundreds of thousands attending, it is truly an event that can help change the world. It can help change the world as millions of lives are directly and indirectly revolutionized through the living Christ working through this great conference.

CONCLUSION

The greatest challenge ever given to man was given by the greatest person who ever lived — Jesus Christ. This challenge, the Great Commission, was given when our Lord said, "All authority has been given to Me in heaven and on earth. Go therefore and make disciples of all the nations, baptizing them in the name of the Father and the Son and the Holy Spirit, teaching them to observe all that I commanded you; and lo, I am with you always, even to the end of the age" (Matthew 28:18-20).

In Romans, the tenth chapter we read: "Anyone who calls upon the name of the Lord will be saved. But how shall they ask Him to save them unless they believe in Him? And how can they believe in Him if they have never heard about Him? And how can they hear about Him unless someone tells them? And how will anyone go and tell them unless someone sends him?" (Living Bible).

There are 4.7 billion people in 210 countries and protectorates around the world who are waiting to hear the good news of our wonderful Savior. The greatest challenge man can ever begin to comprehend is the privilege of taking the message of God's love, forgiveness, peace and grace through our Lord Jesus Christ to each one of these people.

Continual Challenge

This challenge captivates me day and night. I try to weigh everything I do in the light of the Great Commission. I evaluate and prioritize each hour of every day and try to eliminate those things which have no real significance to the accomplishment of this goal. It consumes me day and night.

I do this not because I am interested in a strategy just for strategy's sake, but because I love my Lord and want to obey Him. He is more important to me than my life. I travel the world day and night making disciples and sharing the "most joyful news" with everyone who will listen because I love Him. We are not to go to the world just to be a part of a strategy, but we go because the Lord commissioned us. This commission is not just for the missionaries or the evangelists or pastors. It is for each one of us in whom Jesus Christ has come to dwell. If we love our Lord, we will take seriously His command.

We must not quietly fold our hands, shake our heads at the evil that surrounds us in our world and do nothing but await Christ's return. It is true that our Lord could return tomorrow, If so, I am ready and would greatly rejoice to see Him whom I have loved and served so long. But, the Scripture tells us that no man knows the day or the hour of His return and that when He does come, it will be when people least expect it, like "a thief in the night."

I applaud every effort to warn Christians and non-believers to be ready for our Lord's return. However, we dare not wrongly interpret the Scriptures as so many in previous generations have done, resulting in a lack of concern for the souls of men and a failure to correct the evil of society. God expects us as His children to be His representatives here on earth. We are to love with His love and meet the needs of widows, orphans and prisoners in His name.

Social Reforms

True believers in previous generations have always been at the forefront of moral and social reforms. For example, child labor laws, women's suffrage, abolition of slavery and other social reforms grew out of a mighty spiritual awakening that swept England through the ministry of John Wesley, George Whitefield and their

colleagues. We in our generation must be no less con
cerned about injustice wherever we find it.

However, the most important way to solve our social
ills is to change the hearts of men by introducing them
to our Lord Jesus Christ. Our priority commitment as
Christians must be to disciple and evangelize in obedi
ence to our Lord's command and then instruct the new
believer that "loving our neighbors as ourselves" in
cludes helping them where they hurt. But remember
the Lord cares more about the soul than the body. The
sick body when healed will become sick again and die
The soul lives for eternity.

In II Peter 3:9 we read, "The Lord is not willing tha
any should perish, but that all should come to repen
tance" (King James). He is giving more time for sinner:
to repent. In fact, He has even delayed His return ir
order to give us more time to get His message of salvatior
to others.

We have this further motivation from Matthew 24:14
"And the Good News about the Kingdom will be
preached throughout the whole world, so that all nations
will hear it, and then, finally, the end will come" (LB).

As servants of our living God and Savior, let us con
tinue to give ourselves in all diligence, as an expression
of our love for Him, to hasten the day of His return
Because "Night cometh, when no man can work" (Johr
9:4, KJ).

Miracles must happen for the Great Commission to
be fulfilled. Nothing short of a supernatural visit of God's
power will be enough. But we need to fulfill certair
responsibilities, too. I believe we need to do at least fou
things to see the Great Commission fulfilled.

Supernatural Thoughts

First, we must think supernaturally. Do you re
member the spies who went into the promised land?
After 40 days they came back with two reports —major
ity and minority. The 10 spies reported. "It is indeed

a magnificent country, but there are giants in the land. They will crush us. We felt like grasshoppers in our own sight. We dare not go."

But Joshua and Caleb said, "God is with us. God will fight for us. He has given us the land." The Israelites cried and said, "Don't lead us into the promised land. We would rather go back to Egypt." So all those above the age of 20 died in the wilderness. Later God gave Caleb and Joshua the opportunity to go into the promised land because they had obeyed Him. The 10 spies were destroyed because they were disobedient. They had a grasshopper mentality. And most Christians of today do also.

The thinking of people with tremendous executive ability is often an amazing thing to me. They think of empires, building great estates, but when it comes to the kingdom of God, they don't even think beyond their little church. They may usher, sing in the choir, go once or twice a week to church and feel that their religious duty is fulfilled. Then when problems arise in their community they say, "Why doesn't somebody do something about that?" Some 125 million Americans profess to be followers of Christ. And yet we have allowed this great nation to disintegrate morally and spiritually.

We need to begin to think with the mind of God. "For as he thinketh in his heart, so is he" (Proverbs 23:7, KJ). We become like we think. If we think of ourselves as weak and insignificant, we become that. Instead, we need to see ourselves as able to accomplish great things for our Lord. We become the kind of person who says, "I can do all things through Christ which strengtheneth me" (Philippians 4:13, KJ).

Supernatural Prayers

Second, we must begin to pray supernatural prayers and believe God for mighty things. Soon after the Supreme Court decision in 1963, which most interpreted as meaning that prayer and Bible study in the schools was illegal, God began to chasten us. It was as though the plug was pulled, and evil came upon us like a plague of locusts. Within a brief period of time, President John F. Kennedy was assassinated in Dallas, the drug culture swept up millions of our choice young people, the black and white racial controversy bordered on civil was in city after city, the campuses were aflame with riots, violence and revolution and the war in Vietnam divided our country.

But something wonderful happened in 1968. God's children began to pray for a great spiritual awakening to come to our land. They claimed God's promises. They interceded, they cried out in obedience to II Chronicles 7:14. And across the nation there were prayer rallies, pastors began to give more attention to prayer, prayer chains became a common thing across the nation until millions of Americans were praying. The tide began to turn.

God raised up an army of people like Rex Humbard, Jerry Falwell, Pat Robertson, Kathryn Kuhlman, Robert Schuller and many others on radio and television, until 125 million people were hearing the gospel every week. Some 85 million people were attending church. The Gallup poll did a survey and discovered that more than 50 million people over the age of 18 said that they were born again. God honored supernatural praying.

Supernatural Plans

The third thing that we must do if we are to see the Great Commission fulfilled is that we must plan supernatural plans. I have shared with you earlier about Dr. Joon Gon Kim and EXPLO '74, but you can imagine his presumption when he stood before 85,000 people assembled in Dallas for EXPLO '72 and said, "In 1974, we're going to have 300,000 people come to EXPLO '74 in Seoul,

Korea, and we want you to come." Never in history had 300,000 Christians been trained at one time.

Dr. Kim, a humble servant of God, predicted something that was impossible. As a matter of fact, his staff gave him more than 70 reasons why it couldn't happen. He cancelled them all by saying, "Jesus said, 'The things that I do shall you do also, and greater than these shall you do because I go to My Father. If you ask anything in My name I will do it.'"

A total of 323,419 people from 78 countries came for training. In the four years following EXPLO '74, the church in South Korea grew from three million to seven million. This man of God, Dr. Kim, had planned supernaturally and God had used him to touch the entire nation.

Expect Great Things

Finally, we must expect God to do something great. "According to your faith be it unto you" (Matthew 9:29, KJ). Some time ago I was in Nazareth and had the opportunity to pray with a man who was one of the leading officials of the city. We were sitting in the hotel in the dining room, and after we prayed together, he was radiantly happy. He turned to me and said, "Mr. Bright, will you send someone back to Nazareth to help us share this new truth with others?" Jesus spent 30 years in Nazareth, and this man was saying, "Send someone to help us share this new truth."

Suddenly, it occurred to me that it was said of our Lord when He walked those dusty, winding streets of Nazareth, "And He did not do many miracles there because of their unbelief" (Matthew 13:58). Then it struck me, this is the tragedy of the whole Christian world — our Lord is hindered because of the spirit of Nazareth — the spirit of unbelief — which has placed much of the Body of Christ in bondage. God honors faith, and apart from faith it is impossible to please Him.

Committed to Christ

Before you can genuinely be involved in helping to fulfill the Great Commission and help change our world, you must first turn over your life completely to God. Jesus said, "But seek first His kingdom, and His righteousness; and all these things shall be added to you" (Matthew 6:33).

Our finances also must be turned over to the Lord. There is nothing wrong with making money. Thank God for people who have the ability to make money, who acknowledge that it all belongs to the Lord and it is not theirs to hoard, but it is theirs to pass on for the kingdom's sake.

Some time ago it occurred to me that there are many Christians who are building estates and putting their money into foundations. When they die, those foundations will be under the control of other people, who ultimately will no longer be faithful to the Christian convictions of the one who built the estate.

If I understand Scripture correctly, God expects us to care for our families. But beyond that, Christians are never to hoard. They are to invest in the kingdom. The very process of hoarding causes souring, just like the manna in the wilderness. God gave the manna for one day, and if it was kept for another day, it soured. As you study the lives of Christians who hoard, you find that their money has cursed them, and it has cursed their children because they have disobeyed God. The money did not belong to them. They were only stewards of it.

Reaching People Around You

Once we have turned our lives and finances over to the Lord, we need to go forth with the gospel. Go to the people in your community where you live. Reach your loved ones, your neighbors, your friends, the people in your peer group.

This is the only way that the entire world can be saturated with the good news of Jesus Christ — if Christians take seriously our Lord's command to proclaim the "most joyful news ever announced" to people everywhere.

Are you willing to turn your life over completely to Jesus Christ right now? Are you willing to give over your time, talent and treasure to be used by Him to help fulfill the Great Commission? If you are, please join me in this prayer:

> O Lord, my God, I bow to acknowledge Your Lordship over my life. I will follow You wherever You want me to go. With Your help, Lord, I'll do anything You want me to do, whatever it costs me. Now, I give You my time, talents and treasures — all that I am and possess — that I may be used by Your Spirit to help change our world and help fulfill the Great Commission in this generation. In Jesus' name, Amen.

If you offered this prayer sincerely, God has heard you and promises to direct your steps. May I encourage you to give special time to fellowship with the Lord in prayer, Bible study and witnessing and to become active in a local church fellowship if you are not already involved. If I or the staff of Campus Crusade can be of any help to you, please grant us this privilege. We shall also be happy to send you additional materials for study designed to assist you in your spiritual growth.

If you feel that God would have you serve Him through the ministry of Campus Crusade, opportunities are many and varied. Please contact our Personnel Department for more information. You can write them at Arrowhead Springs, San Bernardino, CA 92414. They will be glad to assist you.

One final thought to take with you. The life of a true disciple of Christ is not an easy one, though it is a life filled with adventure and excitement. Actually, I have thought of life like this: whether Christian or not, we

are going to have problems in this life. Christian or not
we will die one day. If I am to suffer at all and one day
die, why not suffer and die for the highest and best — for
the Lord Jesus Christ and His most worthy cause! I invite
you to join with us:

COME HELP CHANGE THE WORLD!

APPENDIX

How to Be Sure You Are a Christian

My experience in counseling students and laymen through the years since I met Christ personally has convinced me that there are millions of good, faithful churchgoers who have "received" Christ but who are not sure of their salvation. Regardless of how hard they try and how disciplined are their efforts to please God, they are still uncertain of their relationship with Him.

Misinformation

Why does this heartbreaking uncertainty exist among so many who genuinely want to know God and have sought Him for years? I am persuaded personally that for many people this lack of assurance is due simply to misinformation regarding who God is, the true meaning of the crucifixion and the resurrection and what is involved in receiving Jesus Christ as Savior.

Could it be that you are still unsure of your relationship with God even though you may have been reared in a Christian environment and have "believed" in Him and in His Son for years?

If you were to die this very moment, do you *know* for sure where you would spend eternity?

Do you have the assurance right now that the Lord Jesus is in your life, that you are a child of God, your sins have been forgiven, and that you have eternal life?

Or perhaps you have only recently received Christ and are still not sure that anything has really happened — you have no assurance of your salvation and have serious misgivings about where you will go when you die.

If you are among the vast multitude who are still looking for God, I am praying that your quest will be realized this very day as you continue to read.

The Greatest Gift

Becoming a Christian involves receiving by faith the greatest gift ever offered to man — God's gift of His only begotten Son — through whom we can experience God's love and forgiveness. Receiving Jesus Christ as Savior and following Him as Lord involves one's *intellect, emotions* and *will*.

In order to become a Christian, or to be sure that you are a Christian, you must have a clear intellectual understanding of what is involved. Christianity is not "a blind leap of faith." It is built upon historical fact, documented by centuries of scholarship and research. Many leading scholars have dedicated their lives to investigating the life, teachings, death, resurrection and influence of Jesus of Nazareth.

Jesus Christ claimed to be God. He said, "I and the Father are one" (John 10:30). "He who has seen Me has seen the Father" (John 14:9). "I am the way, the truth, and the life; no one comes to the Father, but through Me" (John 14:6). To become a Christian, you must honestly face these claims and believe intellectually that Jesus is God, that He died for your sins and was buried, that He rose again and that He wants to come into your life and be your Savior and Lord.

Emotions

Being sure that you are a Christian also involves the emotions. An emotion is a feeling or reaction to a specific act, event or experience. The failure to distinguish between different types of emotions has caused many people to be confused in their relationship with God. Probably no one thing has caused more people to lack the assurance of a vital relationship with God through Jesus Christ than a wrong emphasis on emotions.

One person may be aggressively extroverted and highly emotional, while another may be calm, reserved and introspective. Viewing the same act or participating in the same experience, these two may respond quite differently — one with great joy and the other calmly.

Each person who receives Jesus Christ as his Savior and Lord will have a different kind of emotional experience. Paul met Christ through a dramatic encounter on the road to Damascus. Timothy, on the other hand, was raised in a Christian home where he came to know Christ at an early age and gradually grew in his faith. The fact that your experience with God may not be as highly emotional as that of someone else does not make it any less real. We must not depend on our emotions, for they can be deceiving.

How, then, can one be sure that he is a Christian? Is there not some confirmation that God gives to the man who sincerely receives Christ? Scripture assures us of a three-fold confirmation that Jesus Christ is in our lives, that we are children of God and have eternal life.

God's Word

First, we have the external witness of the Word of God. Assurance is based on the authority of God's Word. When you meet God's conditions, as revealed in His Word, you can be assured that you are a child of God. Second, there is the internal witness of the Holy Spirit who "speaks to us deep in our hearts, and tells us that we really are God's children" (Romans 8:16, LB). Our changed lives are a third witness to the fact that we are Christians. "When someone becomes a Christian he becomes a brand new person inside. He is not the same anymore. A new life has begun!" (2 Corinthians 5:17, LB). This change may be sudden or gradual, according to the personality of the individual.

There is a place for emotions in the Christian experience, though we should not seek them nor attempt to recapture them from the past.

We are not to ignore the value of legitimate emotions. It is more important, however, to remember that we are to live by faith — in God and in His promises — and not be seeking an emotional experience. The very act of seeking an emotional experience contradicts the concept of faith, which is the only way to please God.

Will

In addition to the intellect and the emotions, becoming a Christian involves the will. Our relationship with Christ can well be illustrated by the requirements for a marriage relationship, which ideally must contain these same three ingredients — intellect, emotions and will.

For example, a man may be convinced intellectually that the woman who is his intended bride is the "right" one for him. He may be involved emotionally and love her with all his heart, but marriage requires more than the intellect and the emotions. It also involves the will.

It is not until the man and woman, as an act of the will, commit themselves to each other before a minister or another person of authority that they become husband and wife. The two words "I do" make the difference. So it is in our relationship with Jesus Christ. It is not enough to believe intellectually that Jesus Christ is the Son of God and Savior of men, nor is it enough to have an emotional, spiritual experience. Though both are valid, one does not become a Christian until, as an act of the will, he receives Christ into his life as Savior and Lord.

There may be a difference, however, between the marriage relationship and the Christian experience. In marriage the sequence of commitment is often intellect, then emotion and, finally, will. But in commitment to Christ, the sequence is usually: first, intellect; then will; and, finally, as a by-product or result, emotions or feelings.

Basic Truths

To be sure that you are a Christian, you must be aware intellectually of certain basic scriptural truths.

First, God loves you and offers a wonderful plan for your life.

Second, man is sinful and separated from God; thus he cannot know and experience God's love and plan.

Third, Jesus Christ is God's only provision for man's sin. Through Him you can know and experience God's love and plan.

And fourth, we must individually receive Jesus Christ as Savior and Lord; then we can know and experience God's love and plan.

Does this make sense to you? Have you ever personally received the Lord Jesus Christ as your Savior? If you have received Him, do you have the assurance of your salvation? Are you sure that, if you died right now, you would spend eternity with God in heaven?

If you cannot answer "Yes" to these questions, may I suggest that you find a quiet place where you can be alone and receive the Lord Jesus as your Savior right now.

If you have never received Christ by a definite, deliberate act of your will, you can do so now in prayer. And if you are not sure you are a Christian, you can make sure now. In either case, may I suggest that you pray this prayer, making it your very own:

> "Lord Jesus, I need You. I thank You for dying for my sins. I open the door of my life and receive You as my Lord and Savior. Thank You for forgiving my sins. Take control of the throne of my life. Change my life and make me the kind of person You want me to be. Amen."

Recently a businessman approached me at one of our Executive Seminars. He had been active in his church for more than 50 years. He had always assumed that he was a Christian though he had never "received" Christ as a deliberate act of his will by faith.

He had for the first time heard testimonies of other businessmen who had received Christ and had heard an explanation of how one became a Christian as recorded in this chapter. Now, he had some doubts concerning his relationship with God. "I am 90 to 95% sure that I am a Christian — that Christ is in my life — but I am not absolutely sure."

It occurs to me that you, dear reader, may also be unsure. If so, I would like to encourage you, as I did this man, to offer the following prayer:

> "Lord Jesus, I am not absolutely sure that You are in my life and that I am a Christian. If You are not already dwelling within me, I invite You today to come into my life, forgive my sins, change me and make me the kind of person You want me to be. By faith, I thank You that You have now come into my life according to Your promise in Revelation 3:20 and will never leave me. I now know according to Your Word that I have eternal life and if I were to die today I would spend eternity with You in heaven. Amen."

This simple suggestion was all that my new friend needed. Immediately he responded and received the assurance of his salvation. I pray that if you, too, have doubts about your salvation, you will take this step.

RESPONSE PAGE

You are invited to write to Dr. Bill Bright.
Your comments are most welcome.

Dear Dr. Bright:

After reading *Come Help Change The World*, I want to be involved in changing our world by helping to fulfill the Great Commission in this generation.

Please inform me how I can:
Become a part of the Great Commission Prayer Crusade (SL 8294).
Participate financially in this great movement of God's Spirit (WIM).
Become a part of the staff of Campus Crusade for Christ.
Receive more information on other Campus Crusade materials (CCM).
Mr.   ☐ Mrs.   ☐ Mr. & Mrs.   ☐ Miss

COMMENTS:

Name _____
Address _____
City, State, Zip _____
Phone (   ) _____

(Though not actually written to Paul Brown, this letter contains the basic counsel which Dr. Bright gives students and adults concerning. "How to know the will of God for your life.")

Mr. Paul V. Brown
The Graduate House
University of California
Los Angeles, California 90024

Re: How to Know the Will of God for you
Life according to the "Sound-Mind Principle
of Scripture

Dear Paul:

Thank you for your recent letter sharing some of the exciting experiences which you are having in your new and adventuresome life with Christ.

When I read that part of your letter in which you expressed the desire to invest your life fully for Christ I paused to give thanks to the Lord, first, for His great love and faithful direction of the lives of all who will trust Him, and second, for your response to His love and your willingness to trust Him with every detail of your life.

It is at this crucial point that many Christians deprive themselves of the full, abundant and purposeful life which the Lord Jesus promised in John 10:10. Failing to comprehend the true character and nature of God, His absolute love, grace, wisdom, power and holiness, many Christians have foolishly chosen to live according to their own plans rather than consider and do the will of God. Some have such a distorted view of God that they think of Him as a tyrant whom one must either appease or experience His wrath, as those who worship a pagan god. Since they are afraid of Him, they cannot love and

266

trust Him. This is sometimes true of individuals who have transferred to God their fear of an earthly father who may have been overly strict, unduly demanding, or even tyrannical.

In all fairness I should say that there are many sincere Christians who want to do the will of God but do not know how to go about discovering His will for their lives.

A choice young college graduate came recently for counsel concerning God's will for his life. "How can I know what God wants me to do?" he asked. Briefly I explained the safest approach to knowing the will of God — to follow what I have chosen to call the "sound-mind principle" of Scripture. In less than an hour, by following the suggestions contained in this letter, this young man discovered what he had been seeking for years. He knew not only the work which God wanted him to do, but the very organization with which he was to be affiliated.

Now you may ask, "What is the 'sound mind principle' of Scripture?" In 2 Timothy 1:7 we are told that "God has not given us the spirit of fear; but of power, and of love and of a sound mind." The sound mind referred to in this verse means a well-balanced mind, a mind that is under the control of the Holy Spirit, "remade" according to Romans 12:1, 2: "Therefore, my brothers, I implore you by God's mercies to offer your very selves to Him, a living sacrifice dedicated and fit for His acceptance, the worship offered by mind and heart. Adapt yourselves no longer to the pattern of the present world, but let your minds be remade and your whole nature thus transformed. Then you will be able to discern the will of God and to know it is good, acceptable, and perfect" (NEB).

There is a vast difference between the inclination of the natural or carnal man to use "common sense" and that of the spiritual man to follow the sound mind principle. One, for understanding, depends upon the wisdom of man without benefit of God's wisdom and power;

the other, having the mind of Christ, receives wisdom and guidance from God moment by moment through faith.

Are your decisions as a Christian based upon unpredictable emotions and chance circumstances, the common sense of the natural man? Or do you make your decisions according to the sound mind principle of Scripture?

Through the years, as I have counseled with many Christians, the question most frequently asked has been, "How can I know the will of God for my life?" Inevitably, the majority of Christians who come for counsel are looking for some dramatic or cataclysmic revelation from God by which they will know God's plan. Without minimizing the importance of feelings, which Jesus promised in John 14:21 as a result of obedience, more emphasis needs to be placed upon the importance of the sound mind which God has given. Multitudes of sincere Christians are wasting their lives, immobile and impotent, as they wait for some unusual or dramatic word from God.

The Scripture assures us that "God has not given us a spirit of fear, but of power, and of love, and of a sound mind." Thus, a Christian who has yielded his life fully to Christ can be assured of sanctified reasoning, and a balanced, disciplined mind. Also, God has promised to give His children wisdom according to James 1:5-7. Further, we can know with settled and absolute assurance that when we pray according to the will of God, He will always hear and grant our petitions (John 5:14, 15). Since the Christian is to live by faith, and faith comes through an understanding of the Word of God, it is impossible to over-emphasize the importance of the Scripture in the lives of those who would know and do the will of God.

If you would like to know the will of God for your life according to the sound mind principle of Scripture, may I suggest that you follow this bit of logic: Consider these questions. First, "Why did Jesus come?" He came "to seek and save the lost" (Luke 19:10). Then, "What is the greatest experience of your life?" If you are a Christian, your answer quite obviously will be, "Coming to know Christ personally as my Savior and Lord." Finally, "What is the greatest thing that you can do to help others?" The answer is again obvious, "Introducing them to Christ."

Jesus came to seek and to save the lost, and every Christian is under divine orders to be a faithful witness for Christ. Jesus said, "Herein is my Father glorified, that ye bear much fruit; so shall ye prove that ye are my disciples" (John 15:8, KJ). It logically follows that the most important thing I can possibly do as a Christian is to allow the Lord Jesus Christ in all of His resurrection power to have complete, unhindered control of my life. Otherwise He cannot continue seeking and saving the lost through me.

Thus, every sincere Christian will want to make his God-given time, talents and treasure available to Christ so that his fullest potential will be realized for Him. For one Christian, this talent which God has given him may be prophetic preaching, evangelism or teaching; for another, it may be business; for another, the ministry or missions; for another, homemaking, as expressed in Romans 12:5; 1 Corinthians 12; 1 Corinthians 14; Ephesians 4; and other Scriptures.

Campus Crusade		Teaching		Church Ministry		Business or Profession	
Pro	Con	Pro	Con	Pro	Con	Pro	Con

As you evaluate the talents that God has given you in relation to your training, personality, and other qualities, may I suggest that you take a sheet of paper and make a list of the most logical ways through which your life can be used to accomplish the most for the glory of God. With the desire to put His will above all else, list the pros and cons of each opportunity. Where or how, according to the sound mind principle, can the Lord Jesus Christ through your yielded life accomplish the most in continuing His great ministry of "seeking and saving the lost"? Like my young friend, you will find that such a procedure will inevitably result in positive actions leading to God's perfect will for your life. But note a word of caution. The sound mind principle is not valid unless certain factors exist:

1. There must be no unconfessed sin in your life; following 1 John 1:9 takes care of that: "If we confess our sins, God is faithful and just to forgive us our sins and to cleanse us from all unrighteousness."

2. Your life must be fully dedicated to Christ according to Romans 12:1, 2, and you must be filled with the Holy Spirit in obedience to the command of Ephesians 5:18. As in the case of our salvation, we are filled and controlled by the Spirit through faith.

3. In order to know the will of God, you must walk in the Spirit (abide in Christ) moment by moment. You place your faith in the trustworthiness of God with the confidence that the Lord is directing and will continue to direct your life according to His promise that the "steps of a righteous man are ordered of the Lord." For, "As you have therefore received Christ Jesus the Lord, so walk in Him." How? By faith, by placing your complete trust in Him. Now, you must go on walking by faith. Remember, "that which is not of faith is sin," and "the just shall live by faith," and "without faith it is impossible to please God." Faith is the catalyst for all our Christian relationships.

The counsel of others should be prayerfully considered, especially that of mature, dedicated Christians who know the Word of God and are able to relate the proper use of Scripture to your need. However, care should be taken not to make the counsel of others a "crutch." Although God often speaks to us through other Christians, we are admonished to place our trust in Him. In Psalm 37 we are told to delight ourselves in the Lord and He will give us the desires of our hearts, to commit our ways unto the Lord, to trust Him and He will bring it to pass. Also, in Proverbs 3 we are told, "Trust in the Lord with all thine heart; and lean not unto thine own understanding. In all thy ways acknowledge Him, and He shall direct thy paths."

God never contradicts Himself. He never leads us to do anything contrary to the commands of His Word; for according to Philippians 2:13, "It is God who is at work within you, giving you the will and the power to achieve His purpose" (Phillips).

Through the centuries sincere religious men have suggested spiritual formulas for discovering the will of God. Some are valid; others are unscriptural and misleading. For example, a young seminary graduate came to see me. He was investigating various possibilities of Christian service and had come to discuss the ministry of Campus Crusade for Christ. Applying the sound mind principle approach to his quest, I asked him, "In what way do you expect God to reveal His place of service for you?"

He replied, "I am following the 'closed door' policy. A few months ago I began to investigate several opportunities for Christian service. The Lord has now closed the door on all but two, one of which is Campus Crusade for Christ. If the door to accept a call to a particular church closes, I shall know that God wants me in Campus Crusade."

Many sincere Christians follow this illogical and unscriptural method, often with most unsatisfactory and frustrating consequences. Don't misunderstand. God may and often does close doors in the life of an active, Spirit-controlled Christian. This was true in the experience of the apostle Paul. As recorded in Acts 16:6-11, he was forbidden by the Spirit to go into Bithynia because God wanted him in Macedonia. My reference to closed door policies does not preclude such experiences, but refers to a careless hit-or-miss attitude without the careful evaluation of all the issues.

This approach is illogical because it allows elements of chance to influence a decision rather than a careful intelligent evaluation of all the factors involved. It is unscriptural in that it fails to employ the God-given faculties of reason that are controlled by the Holy Spirit.

Further, the closed door policy is in error because it seeks God's will through the process of elimination rather than seeking God's best first. It should be understood that true faith is established on the basis of fact. Therefore, vital faith in God is emphasized rather than minimized through employing Spirit-controlled reason. In making decisions some sincere Christians rely almost entirely upon impressions, or hunches, fearful that if they use their mental faculties they will not exercise adequate faith and thus will grieve the Holy Spirit.

There are those who assume that a door has been closed simply because of difficulties that have been encountered. Yet, experience has taught and Scripture confirms that God's richest blessings often follow periods of greatest testing. This might include financial needs, loss of health, objection of loved ones and criticism of fellow Christians. God's blessing is promised, however, only to those who are obedient, who keep on trying, who demonstrate their faith in God's faithfulness. The apparent defeat of the cross was followed by the victory of the resurrection.

An acceptable consideration for discussing God's will

contains four basic factors somewhat similar to the sound mind principle. God's will is revealed in (1) the authority of Scripture, (2) providential circumstances, (3) conviction based upon reason, and (4) impressions of the Holy Spirit upon our minds. However, such an appraisal is safer with a mature Christian than with a new or carnal Christian, and there is always danger of misunderstanding impressions.

You must know the source of leading before responding to it. To the inexperienced, what appears to be the leading of God may not be from Him at all but from "the rulers of darkness of this world." Satan and his helpers often disguise themselves as "angels of light" by performing "miracles, signs," by "foretelling events," etc. The enemy of our souls is a master counterfeiter.

Remember, just as the turning of the steering wheel of an automobile does not alter its direction unless it is moving, so God cannot direct our lives unless we are moving for Him. I challenge you to begin employing the sound mind principle today in all your relationships. Apply it to the investment of your time, your talents and your treasure; for this principle applies to everything you do in this life. Every Christian should take spiritual inventory regularly by asking himself these questions: Is my time being invested in such a way that the largest possible number of people are being introduced to Christ? Are my talents being invested to the full to the end that the largest possible number of people are being introduced to Christ? Is my money, my treasure, being invested in such a way as to introduce the greatest number of people to Christ?

Every Christian is admonished to be a good steward of his God-given time, talents and treasure. Therefore, these investments must not be dictated by tradition, habit or by emotions. Every investment of time, talent, and treasure, unless otherwise directed by the Holy Spirit, should be determined by the sound mind principle of

Scripture according to 2 Timothy 1:7.

Regarding the questions asked by your girl friend, the same principle applies to her. How does this sound mind principle apply in the case of a secretary, a home-maker, an invalid, or one who, because of circumstances beyond her control, does not have direct contact with men and women who are in need of Christ?

First, each Christian must be a witness for Christ. This is simply an act of obedience for which one need not possess the gift of evangelism. If normal day-to-day contacts do not provide opportunities to witness for Christ, an obedient Christian will make opportunities through personal contacts, church calling, letter writing, etc. Two of the most radiant, effective and fruitful Christians whom I have known were bed-ridden invalids who, though in constant pain, bore a powerful witness for Christ to all — stranger and friend alike. "That which is most in our hearts will be most on our lips" was demonstrated in their lives.

Second, a careful evaluation should be given to determine if God may not have a better position for one. Again, the sound mind principle applies. For example, a secretary in a secular organization may have less opportunity to make her life count for the Lord. It may be that God wants to use one's talents in a Christian organization. (I happen to know that there is a great scarcity of qualified secretarial help in many Christian organizations, including Campus Crusade for Christ.) One should be very careful, however, not to run from what appears to be a difficult assignment. A careful appraisal of one's present responsibilities, with this new understanding of God's leading, may well reveal a great potential for Christ.

Quite obviously, members of an office staff do not have as much contact with men and women who are in need of our Savior as those who are actually working on the campus or conducting evangelistic meetings.

However, according to the sound mind principle, if these staff members' lives are fully dedicated to Christ, they can make a vital contribution to the effectiveness of any Christian ministry. By relieving others who have the gift of evangelism without the talent for business or secretarial responsibilities, the overall ministry for Christ in such an organization is strengthened greatly. In this way, they can more fully utilize their talents in helping to seek and save the lost.

For example, a dedicated member of the secretarial staff of the world- wide ministry of Campus Crusade for Christ is just as vital to the success of this campus strategy as those who are working on the campus. My own personal ministry has been greatly increased by the dedicated efforts of several secretaries who are more concerned about winning students to Christ than their own personal pleasure.

One further word of explanation must be given. It is true that God still reveals His will to some men and women in dramatic ways, but this should be considered the exception rather than the rule. God still leads men today as He has through the centuries. Philip, the deacon, was holding a successful campaign in Samaria. The sound mind principle would have directed him to continue his campaign. However, God overruled by a special revelation, and Philip was led by the Holy Spirit to preach for Christ to the Ethiopian eunuch. According to tradition, God used the Ethiopian eunuch to communicate the message of our living Lord to his own country.

Living according to the sound mind principle allows for such dramatic leadings of God, but we are not to wait for such revelations before we start moving for Christ. Faith must have an object. A Christian's faith is built upon the authority of God's Word supported by historical fact and not upon any shallow emotional experience. However, a Christian's trust in God's will revealed in His Word will result in the decisions which are made by following the sound mind principle. The confirmation may come in various ways according to many factors, including the personality of the individual involved. Usually, the confirmation is a quiet, peaceful assurance that you are doing what God wants you to do, with expectancy that God will use you to bear "much fruit."

As any sincere Christian gives himself to a diligent study of the Scripture and allows a loving, all-wise, sovereign God and Father to control his life, feelings will inevitably result. Thus, the end result of a life that is lived according to the sound mind principle is the most joyful, abundant, and fruitful life of all. Expect the Lord Jesus Christ to draw men to Himself through you. As you begin each day, acknowledge the fact that you belong to Him. Thank Him for the fact that He lives within you. Invite Him to use your mind to think His thoughts, your heart to express His love, your lips to speak His truth. Ask Jesus to be at home in your life and to walk around in your body in order that He may continue seeking and saving souls through you.

It is my sincere prayer, Paul, that you may know this kind of life, that you may fully appropriate all that God has given to you as your rightful heritage in Christ. I shall look forward to hearing more from you concerning your personal application of the sound mind principle.

Warmly in Christ,

(Bill Bright)

"Susan Wiggs has one of the freshest imaginations in romance. *Dancing On Air* features two irresistible characters in a swift and joyous tale of passion, adventure, and healing love."
—Mary Jo Putney

© ENNIS '96

Dedicated with love to my dear friend, mentor, and fellow writer, Betty Traylor Gyenes.

FOOL FOR LOVE

"I want to make love to you," Aidan said. "You know that, don't you?"

"I guessed it as soon as you threw me on the ground and started ravishing me."

He tried to smile at her cocky tone of voice.

Pippa sat up and hugged her knees to her chest. "I have one question, my lord."

"Aye?"

"Why did you stop?"

Books by Susan Wiggs

Dancing On Air
Vows Made in Wine
Circle in the Water
Lord of the Night
The Mist and the Magic
The Raven and the Rose
The Lily and the Leopard
Embrace the Day
Briar Rose
Winds of Glory
"Belling the Cat"
(novella) in the anthology *A Purrfect Romance*

Published by HarperPaperbacks

Dancing On Air

⤬ SUSAN WIGGS ⤬

HarperPaperbacks
A Division of HarperCollins Publishers

HarperPaperbacks *A Division of* HarperCollins*Publishers*
10 East 53rd Street, New York, N.Y. 10022

Copyright © 1996 by Susan Wiggs
All rights reserved. No part of this book may be used or reproduced in any manner whatsoever without written permission of the publisher, except in the case of brief quotations embodied in critical articles and reviews. For information address HarperCollins*Publishers,*
10 East 53rd Street, New York, N.Y. 10022.

Cover and stepback illustrations by John Ennis

First printing: January 1996

Printed in the United States of America

HarperPaperbacks, HarperMonogram, and colophon are trademarks of HarperCollins*Publishers*

❖ 10 9 8 7 6 5 4 3 2 1

Special thanks to:
Barbara Dawson Smith, Betty Traylor Gyenes,
and Joyce Bell, for providing all the generous hours
of critique and support.

The many members of the GEnie® Romance
Exchange, an electronic bulletin board of scholars,
fools, dreamers, and wisewomen.

The Bord Failte of County Kerry, Ireland.

The sublime Jay Wiggs for his eagle-eyed
proofreading skills.

PART ONE

Now is this golden crown like a deep well
That owes two buckets filling one another;
The emptier ever dancing in the air,
The other down, unseen and full of water;
That bucket down and full of tears am I,
Drinking my griefs, whilst you mount up on high.

–William Shakespeare
Richard II, IV, i, 184

FROM THE ANNALS OF INNISFALLEN

*I*n accordance with ancient and honorable tradition, I, Revelin of Innisfallen, take pen in hand to relate the noble and right valiant histories of the clan O Donoghue. This task has been done by my uncle and his uncle before him, since time no man can remember.

Canons we are, of the most holy Order of St. Augustine, and by the grace of God our home is the beech-wooded lake isle called Innisfallen.

Those before me filled these pages with tales of fabled heroes, mighty battles, cattle raids, and perilous adventures. Now the role of the O Donoghue Mór has fallen to Aidan, and my work is to chronicle his exploits.

But—may the high King of Heaven forgive my clumsy pen—I know not where to begin. For Aidan O Donoghue is like no man I have ever known, and never has a chieftain been faced with such a challenge.

The O Donoghue Mór, known to the English as Lord of Castleross, has been summoned to London by the she-king who claims the right to rule us. I wonder, with shameful, un-Christian relish, after clapping eyes on Aidan O Donoghue and his entourage, if Her Sassenach Majesty will come to regret the summons.

—Revlin of Innisfallen

"How many noblemen does it take to light a candle?" asked a laughing voice.

Aidan O Donoghue lifted a hand to halt his escort. The English voice intrigued him. In the crowded London street behind him, his personal guard of a hundred gallowglass instantly stopped their purposeful march.

"How many?" someone yelled.

"Three!" came the shout from the center of St. Paul's churchyard.

Aidan nudged his horse forward into the area around the great church. A sea of booksellers, paupers, tricksters, merchants, and rogues seethed around him. He could see the speaker now, just barely, a little lightning bolt of mad energy on the church steps.

"One to call a servant to pour the sack"—she reeled in mock drunkenness—"one to beat the servant senseless, one to botch the job, and one to blame it on the French."

Her listeners hooted in derision. Then a man yelled, "That's four, wench!"

Aidan flexed his legs to stand in the stirrups. *Stirrups.* Until a fortnight ago, he had never even used such a device, or a curbed bit, either. Perhaps, after all, there was some use in this visit to England. He could do without all the fancy draping Lord Lumley had insisted upon, though. Horses were horses in Ireland, not poppet dolls dressed in satin and plumes.

Elevated in the stirrups, he caught another glimpse of the girl: battered hat crammed down on matted hair, dirty, laughing face, ragged clothes.

"Well," she said to the heckler, "that just means noblemen are even more stupid than we thought. Besides, I never said I could count, unless it be the coppers you toss me."

A sly-looking man in tight hose joined her on the steps. "I saves me coppers for them what entertains me." Boldly he snaked an arm around the girl and drew her snugly against him.

She slapped her hands against her cheeks in mock surprise. "Sir! Your codpiece flatters my vanity!"

The clink of coins punctuated a spate of laughter. A fat man near the girl held three flaming torches aloft. "Sixpence says you can't juggle them."

"Ninepence says I can, sure as Queen Elizabeth's white arse sits upon the throne," hollered the girl, deftly catching the torches and tossing them into motion.

Aidan guided his horse closer still. The huge Florentine mare he'd christened Grania earned a few dirty looks and muttered curses from people she nudged out of the way, but none challenged Aidan. Although the Londoners could not know he was the O Donoghue Mór of Ross Castle, they seemed to sense that he and his horse were not a pair to be trifled with. Perhaps it was the prodigious size of the horse; perhaps it was the dangerous, wintry blue of the rider's eyes; but most likely it was the naked blade of the shortsword strapped to his thigh.

He left his massive escort milling outside the churchyard and passing the time by intimidating the Londoners. When he drew close to the street urchin, she was juggling the torches. The flaming brands formed a whirling frame for her grinning, sooty face.

She was an odd colleen, looking as if she had been stitched together from leftovers: wide eyes and wider mouth, button nose, and spiky hair better suited to a boy. She wore a chemise without a bodice, drooping canion trews, and boots so old they might have been relics of the last century.

Yet her Maker had, by some foible, gifted her with the most dainty and deft pair of hands Aidan had ever seen. Round and round went the torches, and when she called for another, it joined the spinning circle with ease. Hand to hand she passed them, faster and faster. The big-bellied man then tossed her a shiny red apple.

She laughed and said, "Eh, Dove, you don't fear I'll tempt a man to sin?"

Her companion guffawed. "I like me wenches made of more than gristle and bad jests, Pippa girl."

She took no offense, and while Aidan silently mouthed the strange name, someone tossed a dead fish into the spinning mix.

Aidan cringed, but the girl called Pippa took the

new challenge in stride. "Seems I've caught one of your relatives, Mort," she said to the man who had procured the fish.

The crowd roared its approval. A few red-heeled gentlemen dropped coins upon the steps. Even after a fortnight in London Aidan could ill understand the Sassenach. They would as lief toss coins to a street performer as see her hanged for vagrancy.

He felt something rub his leg and looked down. A sleepy-looking whore curved her hand around his thigh, fingers inching toward the horn-handled dagger tucked into the top of his boot.

With a dismissive smile, Aidan removed the whore's hand. "You'll find naught but ill fortune there, mistress."

She drew back her lips in a sneer. The French pox had begun to rot her gums. "Irish," she said, backing away. "Chaste as a priest, eh?"

Before he could respond, a high-pitched mew split the air, and the mare's ears pricked up. Aidan spied a half-grown cat flying through the air toward Pippa.

"Juggle *that*," a man shouted, howling with laughter.

"Jesu!" she said. Her hands seemed to be working of their own accord, keeping the objects spinning even as she tried to step out of range of the flying cat. But she caught it and managed to toss it from one hand to the next before the terrified creature leaped onto her head and clung there, claws sinking into the battered hat.

Torches, apple, and fish all clattered to the ground. The skinny man called Mort stomped out the flames. The fat man called Dove tried to help but trod instead upon the slimy fish. He skated forward, sleeves ripping as his pudgy arms cartwheeled. Just as he lost his balance, his flailing fist slammed into a spectator, who immediately threw himself into the brawl. With shouts of glee, others joined the fisticuffs. It was all Aidan could do to keep the mare from rearing.

Blinded by the cat, the girl stumbled forward, hands outstretched. She caught the end of a book-seller's cart. Cat and hat came off as one, and the crazed feline climbed a stack of tomes, toppling them into the mud of the churchyard.

"Imbecile!" the bookseller screeched, lunging at Pippa.

Dove had taken on several opponents by now. With a wet *thwap*, he slapped one across the face with the dead fish.

Pippa grasped the end of the cart and lifted. The remaining books slid down and slammed into the bookseller, knocking him backward to the ground.

"Where's my ninepence?" she demanded, survey-ing the steps. People were too busy brawling to respond. She snatched up a stray copper and shoved it into the voluminous sack tied to her waist with a frayed rope. Then she fled, darting toward St. Paul's Cross, a tall monument surrounded by an open rotunda. The bookseller followed, and now he had an ally—his wife, a formidable lady with arms like large hams.

"Come back here, you evil little monkey," the wife roared. "This day shall be your last!"

Dove was enjoying the fight by now. He had his opponent by the neck and was playing with the man's nose, slapping it back and forth and laughing.

Mort, his companion, was equally gleeful, squaring off with the whore who had approached Aidan earlier.

Pippa led a chase around the cross, the bookseller and his wife in hot pursuit.

More spectators joined in the fray. The horse backed up, eyes rolling in fear. Aidan made a crooning sound and stroked her neck, but he did not leave the square. He simply watched the fight and thought, for the hundredth time since his arrival, what a strange, foul, and fascinating place London was. Just for a moment, he forgot the reason he had come. He turned spectator, giving his full attention to the antics of Pippa and her companions.

So this was St. Paul's, the throbbing heart of the city. It was more meeting place than house of worship to be sure, and this did not surprise Aidan. The Sassenach were a people who clung feebly to an anemic faith; all the passion and pageantry had been bled out of the church by the Rome-hating Reformers.

The steeple, long broken but never yet repaired, shadowed a collection of beggars and merchants, strolling players and thieves, whores and tricksters. At the opposite corner of the square stood a gentleman and a liveried constable. Prodded by the screeched urging of the bookseller's wife, they reluctantly moved in closer. The bookseller had cornered Pippa on the top step.

"Mort!" she cried. "Dove, help me!" Her companions promptly disappeared into the crowd. "Bastards!" she yelled after them. "Geld and splay you both!"

The bookseller barreled toward her. She stooped and picked up the dead fish. She took keen aim at the bookseller and let fly.

The bookseller ducked. The fish struck the approaching gentleman in the face. Leaving slime and scales in its wake, the fish slid down the front of his silk brocade doublet and landed upon his slashed velvet court slippers.

Pippa froze and gawked in horror at the gentleman. "Oops," she said.

"Indeed." He fixed her with a fiery eye of accusation. Without even blinking, he motioned to the liveried constable.

"Sir," he said.

"Aye, my lord?"

"Arrest this, er, *rodent*."

Pippa took a step back, praying the way was clear to make a run for it. Her backside collided with the solid bulk of the bookseller's wife.

"Oops," Pippa said again. Her hopes sank like a weighted corpse in the Thames.

"Let's see you worm your way out of *this* fix, missy," the woman hissed in her ear.

"Thank you," Pippa said cordially enough. "I intend to do just that." She put on her brightest I'm-an-urchin grin and tugged at a forelock. She had recently hacked off her hair to get rid of a particularly stubborn case of lice. "Good morrow, Your Worship."

The nobleman stroked his beard. "Not particularly good for you, scamp," he said. "Are you aware of the laws against strolling players?"

Her gaze burning with indignation, she looked right and left. "Strolling players?" she said with heated outrage. "Who? Where? To God, what is this city coming to that such vermin as strolling players would run loose in the streets?"

As she huffed up her chest, she furtively searched the crowd for Dove and Mortlock. Like the fearless gallants she knew them to be, her companions had vanished.

For a moment, her gaze settled on the man on the horse. She had noticed him earlier, richly garbed and well mounted, with a foreign air about him she could not readily place.

"You mean to say," the constable yelled at her, "that *you* are not a strolling player?"

"Sir, bite your tongue," she fired off. "I'm. . . I am . . ." She took a deep breath and plucked out a ready falsehood. "An evangelist, my lord. Come to preach the Good Word to the unconverted of St. Paul's."

The haughty gentleman lifted one eyebrow high. "The Good Word, eh? And what might that be?"

"You know," she said with an excess of patience. "The gospel according to Saint John." She paused, searching her memory for more tidbits gleaned from days she had spent huddled and hiding in church. An inveterate collector of colorful words and phrases, she took pride in using them. "The pistol of Saint Paul to the fossils."

"Ah." The constable's hands shot out. In a swift movement, he pinned her to the wall beside the *si quis* door. She twisted around to look longingly into the nave where the soaring stone pillars marched along Paul's Walk. Like a well-seasoned rat, she knew every cranny and cubbyhole of the church. If she could get inside, she could find another way out.

"You'd best do better than that," the constable said, "else I'll nail your foolish ears to the stocks."

She winced just thinking about it. "Very well, then." She heaved a dramatic sigh. "Here's the truth."

A small crowd had gathered, probably hoping to see nails driven through her ears. The stranger on horseback dismounted, passed his reins to a stirrup runner, and drew closer.

The lust for blood was universal, Pippa decided. But perhaps not. Despite his savage-looking face and flowing black hair, the man had an air of reckless splendor that fascinated her. She took a deep breath. "Actually, sir, I *am* a strolling player. But I have a nobleman's warrant," she finished triumphantly.

"Have you, then?" His Lordship winked at the constable.

"Oh, aye, sir, upon my word." She hated it when gentlemen got into a playful mood. Their idea of play usually involved mutilating defenseless people or animals.

"And who might this patron be?"

"Why, Robert Dudley himself, the earl of Leicester." Pippa threw back her shoulders proudly. How clever of her to think of the queen's perpetual favorite. She nudged the constable in the ribs, none too gently. "He's the queen's lover, you know, so you'd best not irritate me."

A few of her listeners' mouths dropped open. The nobleman's face drained to a sick gray hue; then hot color surged to his cheeks and jowls.

The constable gripped Pippa by the ear. "You lose, rodent." With a flourish, he indicated the haughty man. "*That* is the earl of Leicester, and I don't believe he's ever seen you before."

"If I had, I would certainly remember," said Leicester.

She swallowed hard. "Can I change my mind?"

"Please do," Leicester invited.

"My patron is actually Lord Shelbourne." She eyed the men dubiously. "Er, he *is* still among the living, is he not?"

"Oh, indeed."

Pippa breathed a sigh of relief. "Well then. He is my patron. Now I had best be go—"

"Not so fast." The grip on her ear tightened. Tears burned her nose and eyes. "He is locked up in the Tower, his lands forfeit and his title attainted."

Pippa gasped. Her mouth formed an **O**.

"I know," said Leicester. "Oops."

For the first time, her aplomb flagged. Usually she was nimble enough of wit and fleet enough of foot to get out of these scrapes. The thought of the stocks loomed large in her mind. This time, she was nailed indeed.

She decided to try a last ditch effort to gain a patron. Who? Lord Burghley? No, he was too old and humorless. Walsingham? No, not with his Puritan leanings. The queen herself, then. By the time Pippa's claim could be verified, she would be long gone.

Then she spied the tall stranger looming at the back of the throng. Though he was most certainly foreign, he watched her with an interest that might even be colored by sympathy. Perhaps he spoke no English.

"Actually," she said, "*he* is my patron." She pointed in the direction of the foreigner. Be Dutch, she prayed silently. Or Swiss. Or drunk. Or stupid. Just play along.

The earl and the constable swung around, craning their necks to see. They did not have far to crane. The stranger stood like an oak tree amid low weeds, head and shoulders taller, oddly placid as the usual St.

Paul's crowd surged and seethed and whispered around him.

Pippa craned too, getting her first close look at him. Their gazes locked. She, who had experienced practically everything in her uncounted years, felt a jolt of something so new and profound that she simply had no name for the feeling.

His eyes were a glittering, sapphire blue, but it was not the color or the startling face from which the eyes stared that mattered. A mysterious force dwelt *behind* the eyes, or in their depths. Awareness flew between Pippa and the stranger; she felt it enter her, dive into her depths like sunlight breaking through shadow.

Old Mab, the woman who had raised Pippa, would have called it magic.

Old Mab would have been right, for once.

The earl cupped his hands around his mouth. "You, sir!"

The foreigner pressed a very large hand to his much larger chest and raised a questioning black brow.

"Aye, sir," called the earl. "This elvish female claims she is performing under your warrant. Is that so, sir?"

The crowd waited. The earl and the constable waited. When they looked away from her, Pippa clasped her hands and looked pleadingly at the stranger. Her ear was going numb in the pinch of the constable.

Pleading looks were her specialty. She had practiced them for years, using her large, pale eyes to prize coppers and crusts from passing strangers.

The foreigner raised a hand. Into the alleyway behind him flooded a troop of—Pippa was not certain *what* they were.

They moved about in a great mob like soldiers, but instead of tunics these men wore horrible gray animal hides, wolfskins by the look of them. They carried battleaxes with long handles. Some had shaved heads; others wore their hair loose and wild, tumbling over their brows.

Everyone moved aside when they entered the yard. Pippa did not blame the Londoners for shrinking in fear. She would have shrunk herself, but for the iron grip of the constable.

"Is that what the colleen said, then?" He strode forward. He spoke English, damn him. He had a very strange accent, but it was English.

He was huge. As a rule, Pippa liked big men. Big men and big dogs. They seemed to have less need to swagger and boast and be cruel than small ones. This man actually had a slight swagger, but she realized it was his way of squeezing a path through the crowd.

His hair was black. It gleamed in the morning light with shards of indigo and violet, flowing over his shoulders. A slim ebony strand was ornamented with a strap of rawhide and beads.

Pippa chided herself for being fascinated by a tall man with sapphire eyes. She should be taking the opportunity to run for cover rather than gawking like a Bedlamite at the foreigner. At the very least, she should be cooking up a lie to explain how, without his knowledge, she had come to be under his protection.

He reached the steps in front of the door, where she stood between the constable and Leicester. His flame blue eyes glared at the constable until the man relinquished his grasp on Pippa's ear.

Sighing with relief, she rubbed the abused, throbbing ear.

"I am Aidan," the stranger said, "the O Donoghue Mór."

A Moor! Immediately Pippa fell to her knees and snatched the hem of his deep blue mantle, bringing the dusty silk to her lips. The fabric felt heavy and rich, smooth as water and as exotic as the man himself.

"Do you not remember, Your Preeminence?" she cried, remembering that important men adored honorary titles. "How you ever so tenderly extended your warrant of protection to my poor, downtrodden self so that I'd not starve?" As she rambled on, she found a most interesting bone-handled knife tucked into the cuff of his tall boot. Unable to resist, she stole it, her movements so fluid and furtive that no one saw her conceal it in her own boot.

Her gaze traveled upward over a strong leg. The sight set off a curious tingling. Strapped to his thigh was a shortsword as sharp and dangerous looking as the man himself.

"You said you did not wish me to suffer the tortures of Clink Prison, nor did you want my pitiful weight forever on your delicate conscience, making you terrified to burn in hell for eternity because you let a defenseless woman fall victim to—"

"Yes," said the Moor.

She dropped his hem and stared up at him. "What?" she asked stupidly.

"Yes indeed, I remember, Mistress . . . er—"

"Trueheart," she supplied helpfully, plucking a favorite name from the arsenal of her imagination. "Pippa Trueheart."

The Moor faced Leicester. The smaller man gaped up at him. "There you are, then," said the black-haired lord. "Mistress Pippa Trueheart is performing under my warrant."

With a huge bear paw of a hand, he took her arm and brought her to her feet. "I do confess the little baggage is unmanageable at times and did slip away for today's performance. From now on I shall keep her in closer tow."

Leicester nodded and stroked his narrow beard. "That would be most appreciated, my lord of Castleross."

The constable looked at the Moor's huge escort. The members of the escort looked menacingly back, and the constable smiled nervously.

The Moor turned and addressed his fierce servants in a tongue so foreign, so unfamiliar, that Pippa did not recognize a single syllable of it. That was odd, for she had a keen and discerning ear for languages.

The skin-clad men marched out of the churchyard and clumped down Paternoster Row. The lad who served as stirrup runner led the big horse away. The Moor took hold of Pippa's arm.

"Let's go, *a storin*," he said.

"Why do you call me *a storin*?"

"It is an endearment meaning 'treasure.'"

"Oh. No one's ever called me a treasure before. A trial, perhaps."

His lilting accent and the scent of the wind that clung in his hair and mantle sent a thrill through her. She had never been rescued in her life, and certainly not by such a specimen as this black-haired lord.

As they walked toward the low gate linking St. Paul's with Cheapside, she looked sideways at him. "You seem rather nice for a Moor." She passed through the gate he held open for her.

"A Moor, you say? Mistress, sure and I am no Moor."

"But you said you were Aidan, the O Donoghue Moor."

He laughed. She stopped in her tracks. She earned her living by making people laugh, so she should be used to the sound of it, but this was different. His laughter was so deep and rich that she imagined she could actually *see* it, flowing like a banner of dark silk on the breeze.

He threw back his great, shaggy head. She saw that he had all of his teeth. The eyes, blazing blue like the hearts of flames, drew her in with that same compelling magic she had felt earlier.

He was beginning to make her nervous.

"Why do you laugh?" she asked.

"*Mór,*" he said. "I am the O Donoghue Mór. It means 'great.'"

"Ah." She nodded sagely, pretending she had known all along. "And are you?" She let her gaze travel the entire length of him, lingering on the more interesting parts.

God was a woman, Pippa thought with sudden certainty. Only a woman would create a man like the O Donoghue, forming such toothsome parts into an even more delectable whole. "Aside from the obvious, I mean."

Mirth still glowed about him, though his laughter had ceased. He touched her cheek, a surprisingly tender gesture, and said, "That, *a stor,* depends on whom you ask."

The light, brief touch shook Pippa to the core, though she refused to show it. When people touched her, it was to box her ears or send her packing, not to caress and comfort.

"And how does one address a man so great as yourself?" she asked in a teasing voice. "Your Worship? Your Excellency?" She winked. "Your Hugeness?"

He laughed again. "For a lowly player, you know some big words. Saucy ones, too."

"I collect them. I'm a very fast learner."

"Not fast enough to stay out of trouble today, it seems." He took her hand and continued walking eastward along Cheapside. They passed the pissing conduit and then the Eleanor Cross decked with gilded statues.

Pippa saw the foreigner frowning up at them. "The Puritans mutilate the figures," she explained, taking charge of his introduction to London. "They mislike graven images. At the Standard yonder, you might see *real* mutilated bodies. Dove said a murderer was executed Tuesday last."

When they reached the square pillar, they saw no corpse, but the usual motley assortment of students and 'prentices, convicts with branded faces, beggars, bawds, and a pair of soldiers tied to a cart and being flogged as they were conveyed to prison. Leavening all the grimness was the backdrop of Goldsmith Row, shiny white houses with black beams and gilt wooden statuary. The O Donoghue took it all in with quiet, thoughtful interest. He made no comment, though he discreetly passed coppers from his cupped hand to the beggars.

From the corner of her eye, Pippa saw Dove and Mortlock standing by an upended barrel near the Old Change. They were running a game with weighted dice and hollow coins. They smiled and waved as if nothing had happened, as if they had not just deserted her in a moment of dire peril.

She poked her nose in the air, haughty as any grande dame, and put her grubby hand on the arm of the great O Donoghue. Let Dove and Mort wonder and squirm with curiosity. *She* belonged to a lofty nobleman now. *She* belonged to the O Donoghue Mór.

Aidan was wondering how to get rid of the girl. She clung like a monkey, trotting at his side and chattering away about riots and rebels and boat races down the Thames. There was precious little for him to do in London while the queen left him cooling his heels, but that did not mean he needed to amuse himself with a pixielike female from St. Paul's.

Still, there was the matter of his knife, which she had stolen while groveling at his hem. Perhaps he ought to let her keep it, though, as the price of a morning's diversion. The lass was nothing if not wildly entertaining.

He shot a glance sideways, and the sight of her clutched unexpectedly at his heart. She bounced along with all the pride of a child wearing her first pair of shoes. Yet beneath the grime on her face, he could see the smudges of sleeplessness under her soft green eyes, the hollows of her cheekbones, the quiet resignation that bespoke a thousand days of tacit, unprotesting hunger.

By the staff of St. Brigid, he did not need this, any more than he had needed the furious royal summons to court in London.

Yet here she was. And his heart was moved by the look of want in her wide eyes.

"Have you eaten today?" he asked.

"Only if you count my own words."

He raised one eyebrow. "Is that so?"

"No food has passed these lips in a fortnight." She pretended to sway with weakness.

"That is a lie," Aidan said mildly.

"A week?"

"Also a lie."

"Since last night?" she said.

"That I am likely to believe. You do not need to lie to win my sympathy."

She blew out her breath. "It's a habit, like spitting. Sorry."

"Where can I get you a hearty meal, colleen?"

Her eyes danced with anticipation. "Oh, there, Your Greatness." She pointed across the way, past the Change, where armed guards flanked a chest of bullion. "The Nag's Head Inn has good pies and they don't water down their ale."

"Done." He strode into the middle of the road. A few market carts jostled past. A herd of laughing, filthy children charged past in pursuit of a runaway pig, and a noisome knacker's wagon, piled high with butchered horse parts, lumbered by. When at last the way seemed clear, Aidan grabbed Pippa's hand and hurried her across.

"Now," he said, ducking beneath the low lintel of the doorway and drawing her inside. "Here we are."

It took a moment for his eyes to adjust to the dimness. The tavern was nearly full despite the early hour. He took Pippa to a scarred table flanked by a pair of three-legged stools.

He called for food and drink. The alewife slumped lazily by the fire as if loath to bestir herself. In high dudgeon, Pippa marched over to her. "Did you not hear His Lordship? He desires to be served now." Puffed up with self-importance, she pointed out his rich mantle and the tunic beneath, decked in cut crystal points. The sight of a well-turned-out patron spurred the woman to bring the ale and pasties quickly.

Pippa picked up her wooden drinking mug and drained nearly half of it, until he rapped on the bottom. "Slowly now. It won't sit well on an empty stomach."

"If I drink enough, my stomach won't care." She set down the mug and dragged her sleeve across her mouth. A certain glazed brightness came over her eyes, and he felt a welling of discomfort, for it had not been his purpose to make her stupid with drink.

"Eat something," he urged her. She gave him a vague smile and picked up one of the pies. She ate methodically and without savor. The Sassenach were terrible cooks, Aidan thought, not for the first time.

A hulking figure filled the doorway and plunged the tavern deeper into darkness. Aidan's hand went for his dagger; then he remembered the girl still had it.

As soon as the newcomer stepped inside, Aidan grinned and relaxed. He would need no weapon against this man.

"Come sit you down, Donal Og," he said in Gaelic, dragging a third stool to the table.

Aidan was known far and wide as a man of prodigious size, but his cousin dwarfed him. Donal Og had massive shoulders, legs like tree trunks, and a broad, prominent brow that gave him the look of a simpleton. Nothing was farther from the truth. Donal Og was brilliant, wry, and unfailingly loyal to Aidan.

Pippa stopped chewing to gape at him.

"This is Donal Og," said Aidan. "The captain of my guard."

"Donal Og," she repeated, her pronunciation perfect.

"It means Donal the Small," Donal Og explained.

Her gaze measured his height. "Where?"

"I was so dubbed at birth."

"Ah. That explains everything." She smiled broadly. "I am honored. My name is Pippa Trueblood."

"The honor is my own, surely," Donal Og said with faint irony in his voice.

Aidan frowned. "I thought you said Trueheart."

She laughed. "Silly me. Perhaps I did." She began licking grease and crumbs from her fingers.

"Where," Donal Og asked in Gaelic, "did you find *that*?"

"St. Paul's churchyard."

"The Sassenach will let *anyone* in their churches, even lunatics." Donal Og held out a hand, and the alewife served him a mug of ale. "Is she as crazy as she looks?"

Aidan kept a bland, pleasant smile on his face so the girl would not guess what they spoke of. "Probably."

"Are you Dutch?" she asked suddenly. "That language you're using to discuss me—is it Dutch? Or Norse, perhaps?"

Aidan laughed. "It is Gaelic. I thought you knew. We're Irish."

Her eyes widened. "*Irish.* I'm told the Irish are wild and fierce and more papist than the pope himself."

Donal Og chuckled. "You're right about the wild and fierce part."

She leaned forward with interest burning in her eyes. Aidan gamely ran a hand through his hair. "You'll see I have no antlers, so you can lay to rest that myth. If you like, I'll show you that I have no tail—"

"I believe you," she said quickly.

"Don't tell her about the blood sacrifices," Donal Og warned.

She gasped. "Blood sacrifices?"

"Not lately," Aidan conceded, his face deadly serious.

"Certainly not on a waning moon," Donal Og added.

But Pippa held herself a bit more stiffly and regarded them with wariness. She seemed to be measuring the distance from table to door with an expert eye. Aidan had the impression that she was quite accustomed to making swift escapes.

The alewife, no doubt drawn by the color of their money, sidled over with more brown ale. "Did ye know we're Irish, ma'am?" Pippa asked in a perfect imitation of Aidan's brogue.

The alewife's brow lifted. "Do tell!"

"I'm a nun, see," Pippa explained, "of the Order of Saint Dorcas of the Sisters of Virtue. We never forget a favor."

Suitably impressed, the alewife curtsied with new respect and withdrew.

"So," Aidan said, sipping his ale and hiding his amusement at her little performance. "We are Irish and you cannot decide on a family name for yourself. How is it that you came to be a strolling player in St. Paul's?"

Donal Og muttered in Gaelic, "Really, my lord,

could we not just leave? Not only is she crazy, she's probably crawling with vermin. I'm sure I just saw a flea on her."

"Ah, that's a sad tale indeed," Pippa said. "My father was a great war hero."

"Which war?" Aidan asked.

"Which war do you suppose, my lord?"

"The Great Rebellion?" he guessed.

She nodded vigorously, her hacked-off hair bobbing. "The very one."

"Ah," said Aidan. "And your father was a hero, you say?"

"You're as giddy as she," grumbled Donal Og, still speaking Irish.

"Indeed he was," Pippa declared. "He saved a whole garrison from slaughter." A faraway look pervaded her eyes like morning mist. She looked past him, out the open door, at a patch of the sky visible between the gabled roofs of London. "He loved me more than life itself, and he wept when he had to leave me. Ah, that was a bleak day for the Truebeard family."

"True*heart*," Aidan corrected, curiously moved. The story was as false as a strumpet's promise, yet the yearning he heard in the girl's voice rang true.

"Trueheart," she agreed easily. "I never saw my father again. My mother was carried off by pirates, and I was left quite alone to fend for myself."

"I've heard enough," said Donal Og. "Let's go."

Aidan ignored him. He found himself fascinated by the girl, watching as she helped herself to more ale and drank greedily, as if she would never get her fill.

Something about her touched him in a deep, hid-

den place he had long kept closed. It was in the very
heart of him, embers of warmth that he guarded like a
windbreak around a herdsman's fire. No one was
allowed to share the inner life of Aidan O Donoghue.
He had permitted that just once—and had been so
thoroughly doused that he had frozen himself to sentiment, to trust, to joy, to hope—to everything that
made life worth living.

Now here was this strange woman, unwashed and
underfed, with naught but her large soft eyes and her
vivid imagination to shield her from the harshness of
the world. True, she was strong and saucy as any rollicking street performer, but not too far beneath the
gamin surface, he saw something that fanned at the
banked embers inside him. She possessed a subtle,
waiflike vulnerability that was, at least on the surface,
at odds with her saucy mouth and nail-hard shell of
insouciance.

And, though her hair and face and ill-fitting garments were smeared with grease and ashes, a charming, guileless appeal shone through.

"That is quite a tale of woe," Aidan commented.

Her smile favored them both like the sun bursting
through stormclouds.

"Too bad it's a pack of lies," Donal Og said.

"I do wish you'd speak English," she said. "It's bad
manners to leave me out." She glared accusingly at
him. "But I suppose, if you're going to say I'm crazy
and a liar and things of that sort, it is probably best to
speak Irish."

Seeing so huge a man squirm was an interesting
spectacle. Donal Og shifted to and fro, causing the
stool to creak. His hamlike face flushed to the ears.
"Aye, well," he said in English, "you need not perform

for Aidan and me. For us, the truth is good
enough."

"I see." She elongated her words as the effects of
the ale flowed through her. "Then I should indeed
confess the truth and tell you exactly who I am."

It is a mother's lot to rejoice and to grieve all at once. So it has always been, but knowing that has never eased my grief nor dimmed my joy.

In the early part of her reign, the queen gave our family a land grant in County Kerry, Munster, but until recently, we kept it in name only, content to leave Ireland to the Irish. Now, quite suddenly, we are expected to do something about it.

Today my son Richard received a royal commission. I wonder, when the queen's advisers empowered my son to lead an army, if they ever, even for an instant, imagined him as I knew him—a laughing small boy with grass stains on his elbows and the pure sweetness of an innocent heart shining from his eyes.

Ah, to me it seems only yesterday that I held that silky, golden head to my breast and scandalized all society by sending away the wet nurse.

Now they want him to lead men into battle for lands he never asked for, a cause he never embraced.

My heart sighs, and I tell myself to cling to the blessings that are mine: a loving husband, five grown children, and a shining faith in God that—only once, long ago—went dim.

—Lark de Lacey,
Countess of Wimberleigh

2

"I can't believe you brought her with us," said Donal Og the next day, pacing in the walled yard of the old Priory of the Crutched Friars.

As a visiting dignitary, Aidan had been given the house and adjacent priory by Lord Lumley, a staunch Catholic and unlikely but longtime royal favorite. The residence was in Aldgate, where all men of conse-quence lived while in London. The huge residence, once home to humble and devout clerks, comprised a veritable village, including a busy glassworks and a large yard and stables. It was oddly situated, bordered by broad Woodroffe Lane and crooked Hart Street and within shouting distance of a grim, skeletal scaf-fold and gallows.

Aidan had given Pippa a room of her own, one of the monks' cells facing a central arcade. The soldiers had strict orders to watch over her, but not to threaten or disturb her.

"I couldn't very well leave her at the Nag's Head." He glanced at the closed door of her cell. "She might've been accosted."

"She probably *has* been, probably makes her living at it." Donal Og cut the air with an impatient gesture of his hand. "You take in strays, my lord, you always have—orphaned lambs, pups rejected by their dams, lame horses. Creatures better left—" He broke off, scowled, and resumed pacing.

"To die," Aidan finished for him.

Donal Og swung around, his expression an odd mix of humanity and cold pragmatism. "It is the very rhythm of nature for some to struggle, some to survive, some to perish. We're Irish, man. Who knows that better than we? Neither you nor I can change the world. Nor were we meant to."

"But isn't that what we came to London to accomplish, cousin?" Aidan asked softly.

"We came because Queen Elizabeth summoned you," Donal Og snapped. "And now that we're here, she refuses to see you." He tilted his great blond head skyward and addressed the clouds. "Why?"

"It amuses her to keep foreign dignitaries cooling their heels, waiting for an audience."

"I think she's insulted because you go all about town with an army of one hundred. Mayhap a little more modesty would be in order."

Iago came out of the barracks, scratching his bare, ritually scarred chest and yawning. "Talk, talk, talk," he said in the lilting tones of his native island. "You never shut up."

Aidan said a perfunctory good morning to his marshal. Through an extraordinary chain of events, Iago had come ten years earlier from the West Indies of the

New World. His mother was of mixed island native and African blood, his father a Spaniard.

Iago and Aidan had grown to full manhood together. Two years younger than Iago and in awe of the Caribbean man's strength and prowess, Aidan had insisted on emulating him. Gloriously drunk one day, he had endured the ritual scarring ceremony in secret, and in a great deal of pain. To the horror of his father, Aidan now bore, like Iago, a series of V-shaped scars down the center of his chest.

"I was just saying," Donal Og explained, "that Aidan is always taking in strays."

Iago laughed deeply, his mahogany face shining through the morning mist. "What a fool, eh?"

Chastened, Donal Og fell silent.

"So what did he drag home this time?" Iago asked.

Pippa lay perfectly still with her eyes closed, playing a familiar game. From earliest memory, she always awoke with the certain conviction that her life had been a nightmare and, upon awakening, she would find matters the way they should be, with her mother smiling like a madonna while her father worshiped her on bended knee and both smiled upon their beloved daughter.

With a snort of self-derision, she beat back the fantasy. There was no place in her life for dreams. She opened her eyes and looked up to see a cracked, lime-washed ceiling. Timber and wattled walls. The scent of slightly stale, crushed straw. The murmur of masculine voices outside a thick timber door.

It took a few moments to remember all that had

happened the day before. While she reflected on the events, she found a crock of water and a basin and cupped her hands for a drink, finally plunging in her face to wash away the last cobwebby vestiges of her fantasies.

Yesterday had started out like any other day—a few antics in St. Paul's; then she and Mortlock and Dove would cut a purse or filch something to eat from a carter. Like London smoke borne on a breeze, they would drift aimlessly through the day, then return to the house in Maiden Lane squished between two crumbling tenements.

Pippa had the attic room all to herself. Almost. She shared it with a rather aggressively inquisitive rat she called, for no reason she could fathom, Pavlo. She also shared quarters with all the private worries and dreamlike memories and unfocused sadness she refused to confess to any other person.

Yesterday, the free-flowing course of her life had altered. For better or worse, she knew not. She felt no ties to Mort and Dove; the three of them used each other, shared what they had to, and jealously guarded the rest. If they missed her at all, it was because she had a knack for drawing a crowd. If she missed them at all—she had not decided whether or not she did—it was because they were familiar, not necessarily beloved.

Pippa knew better than to love anyone.

She had come with the Irish nobleman simply because she had nothing better to do. Perhaps fate had taken a hand in her fortune at last. She had always wanted the patronage of a rich man, but no one had ever taken notice of her. In her more fanciful moments, she thought about winning a place at court. For now, she would settle for the Celtic lord.

After all, he was magnificently handsome, obviously rich, and surprisingly kind.

A girl could do far worse than that.

By the time he had brought her to this place, she had been woozy with ale. She had a vague memory of riding a large horse with the O Donoghue Mór seated in front of her and all his strange, foreign warriors tramping behind.

She made certain her shabby sack of belongings lay in a corner of the room, then dried her face. As she cleaned her teeth with the tail of her shift dipped in the water basin, she saw, wavering in the bottom of the bowl, a coat of arms.

Norman cross and hawk and arrows.

Lumley's device. She knew it well, because she had once stolen a silver badge from him as he had passed through St. Paul's.

She straightened up and combed her fingers through her hacked-off hair. She did not miss having long hair, but once in a while she thought about looking fashionable, like the glorious ladies who went about in barges on the Thames. In the past, when she bothered to wash her hair, it had hung in honey gold waves that glistened in the sun.

A definite liability. Men noticed glistening golden hair. And that was the last sort of attention she wanted.

She jammed on her hat—it was a slouch of brown wool that had seen better days—and wrenched open the door to greet the day.

Morning mist lay like a shroud over a rambling courtyard. Men and dogs and horses slipped in and out of view like wraiths. The fog insulated noise, and the arcade created soft, hollow echoes, so that the Irish voices of the men had an eerie intimacy.

She tucked her thumbs into her palms to ward off evil spirits—just in case.

Several yards from Pippa, three men stood talking in low tones. They made a most interesting picture—the O Donoghue with his blue mantle slung back over one shoulder, his booted foot propped on the tongue of a wagon, and his elbow braced upon his knee.

Donal Og, the rude cousin, leaned against the wagon wheel, gesticulating like a man in the grips of St. Elmo's fire. The third man stood with his back turned, feet planted wide as if he were on the deck of a ship. He was tall—she wondered if prodigious height was a required quality of the Irish lord's retinue—and his long, soft tunic blazed with color in hues more vivid than April flowers.

She strolled out of her chamber to find that it was one of a long line of barracks or cells hunched against an ancient wall and shaded by the arcade. She walked over to the wagon, and in her usual forthright manner, she picked up the hem of the man's color-drenched garment and fingered the fabric.

"Now, colleen," Aidan O Donoghue said in a warning voice.

The man in the bright cloak turned.

Pippa's mouth dropped open. A squeak burst from her throat and she stumbled back. Her heel caught on a broken paving stone. She tripped and landed on her backside in a puddle of morning-chilled mud.

"Jesus Christ on a flaming crutch!" she said.

"Reverent, isn't she?" Donal Og asked wryly. "Faith, but she's a perfect little saint."

Pippa kept staring. *This* was a Moor. She had

heard about them in story and song, but never had she seen one. His face was remarkable, a gleaming sculpture of high cheekbones, a bony jaw, beautiful mouth, eyes the color of the stoutest ale. He had a perfect black cloud of hair, and skin the color of antique, polished leather.

"My name is Iago," he said, stepping back and twitching the hem of his remarkable cloak out of the way of the mud.

"Pippa," she said breathlessly. "Pippa True—True—"

Aidan stuck out his hand and pulled her to her feet. She felt his smooth, easy strength as he did so, and his touch was a wonder to her, in its way, more of a wonder than the Moor's appearance.

Iago looked from Pippa to Aidan. "My lord, you have outdone yourself."

She felt the mud slide down her backside and legs, pooling in the tops of her ancient boots. Last winter, she had stolen them from a corpse lying frozen in an alley.

"Will you eat or bathe first?" the O Donoghue asked, not unkindly.

Her stomach cramped, but she was well used to hunger pangs. The chill mud made her shiver. "A bath, I suppose, Your Reverence."

Donal Og and Iago grinned at each other. "Your Reverence," Iago said in his deep, musical voice.

Donal Og pointed his toe and bowed. "Your Reverence."

Aidan ignored them. "A bath it is, then," he said.

"I've never had one before."

The O Donoghue looked at her for a long moment. His gaze burned over her, searing her face and form until she thought she might sizzle like a chicken on a spit.

"Why am I not surprised?" he asked.

She sang with a perfect, off-key joy. The room, adjoining the kitchen of Lumley House, was small and cramped and windowless, but the open door let in a flood of light. Aidan sat on the opposite side of the folding privy screen and put his hands over his ears, but her exuberant and bawdy song screeched through the barrier.

> *"At Steelyard store of wines there be*
> *Your dulled minds to glad,*
> *And handsome men that must not wed,*
> *Except they leave their trade.*
> *They oft shall seek for proper girls,*
> *And some perhaps shall find—"*

She broke off and called, "Do you like my song, Your Worship?"

"It's grand," he forced himself to say. "Simply grand."

"I could sing you another if you wish," she said eagerly.

"Ah, that would be a high delight indeed, I'm sure," he said.

She took his patronage seriously. Too seriously.

> *"The bed it shook*
> *As pleasure took*
> *The carpet-knight for a ride . . ."*

She belted the words out unblushingly. Aidan had never seen a mere bath have this sort of effect on anyone. How a wooden barrel half filled with lukewarm water could make a woman positively drunk with elation was beyond him.

She splashed and sang and every once in a while he could hear a scrubbing sound. He hoped she was availing herself of the harsh wood ash soap.

Pippa's singing had long since driven the Lumley maids into the yard to gossip. When he had told them to draw a bath, they had shaken their heads and muttered about Lord Lumley's strange Irish guests.

But they had obeyed. Even in London, so many leagues from his kingdom in Kerry, he was still the O Donoghue Mór.

Except to Pippa. Despite her constant attempts to entertain him and seek his approval, she had no respect for his status. She paused in her song to draw breath or perhaps—God forbid—think up another verse.

"Are you quite finished?" Aidan asked.

"Finished? Are we pressed for time?"

"You'll wind up pickled like a herring if you stew in there much longer."

"Oh, very well." He heard the slap of water sloshing against the sides of the barrel. "Where are my clothes?" she asked.

"In the kitchen. Iago will boil them. The maids found you a few things. I hung them on a peg—"

"Oooh." She managed to infuse the exclamation with a wealth of wonder and yearning. "These are truly a gift from heaven."

They were no gift, but the cast-offs of a maid who had run off with a Venetian sailor the week before.

He heard Pippa bumping around behind the screen. A few moments later, she emerged.

Haughty pride radiated from her small, straight figure. Aidan clamped his teeth down on his tongue to keep from laughing.

She had the skirt on backward and the buckram bodice upside down. Her damp hair stuck out in spikes like a crown of thorns. She was barefoot and cradling the leather slippers reverently in her hands.

Then she moved into the strands of sunlight streaming in through the kitchen door, and he saw her face for the first time devoid of soot and ashes.

It was like seeing the visage of a saint or an angel in one's dreams. Never, ever, had Aidan seen such a face. No single feature was remarkable in and of itself, but taken as a whole, the effect was staggering.

She had a wide, clear brow, her eyebrows bold above misty eyes. The sweet curves of nose and chin framed a soft mouth, which she held pursed as if expecting a kiss. Her cheekbones were highlighted by pink-scrubbed skin. Aidan thought of the angel carved in the plaster over the altar of the church at Innisfallen. Somehow, that same lofty, otherworldly magic touched Pippa.

"The clothes," she stated, "are magnificent."

He allowed himself a controlled smile designed to preserve her fervent pride. "And so they are. Let me help you with some of the fastenings."

"Ah, my silly lord, I've done them all up myself."

"Indeed you have. But since you lack a proper lady's maid to help you, I should take her part."

"You're very kind," she said.

"Not always," he replied, but she seemed oblivious of the warning edge in his voice. "Come here."

She crossed the room without hesitation. He could not decide whether that was healthy or not. *Should* a young woman alone be so trusting of a strange man? Her trust was no gift, but a burden.

"First the bodice," he said patiently, untying the haphazard knot she had made in the lacings. "I have never wondered why it mattered, but fashion demands that you wear it with the other end up."

"Truly?" She stared down at the stiff garment in dismay. "It covered more of me upside down. When you turn it the other way, I spill out like loaves from a pan."

His loins burned with the image, and he gritted his teeth. The last thing he had expected was that he might desire her. Pippa lifted her arms and held them steady while he unlaced the bodice.

It proved to be the most excruciating exercise in self-restraint he had ever endured. Somehow, the dust and ashes of her harsh life had masked an uncounted wealth of charms. He had the feeling that he was the first man to see beneath the grime and ill-fitting clothes.

As he pulled the laces through, his knuckles grazed her. The maids had provided neither shift nor corset. All that lay between Pippa's sweet flesh and his busy hands was a chemise of wispy lawn. He could feel the heat of her, could smell the clean, beeswaxy fragrance of her just washed skin and hair.

Setting his jaw with manly restraint, he turned the bodice right side up and brought it around her. As he slowly laced the garment, watching the stiff buckram close around a narrow waist and then widen over the subtle womanly flare of her hips, pushing up her breasts, he could not banish his insistent desire.

True to her earlier observation, her bosom swelled out over the top with frank appeal, barely contained by the sheer fabric of the chemise. He could see the high, rounded shapes, the rosy shadows of the tips, and for a long, agonizing moment all he could think of was touching her there, tenderly, learning the shape and the weight of her breasts, burying his face in them, drowning in the essence of her.

A roaring, like the noise of the sea, started in his ears, swishing with the quickening rhythm of his blood. He bent his head closer, closer, his tongue already anticipating the flavor of her, his lips hungry for the budded texture. His mouth hovered so close that he could feel the warmth emanating from her.

She drew in a deep, shuddering breath, and the movement reminded him to think with his brain—even the small part of it that happened to be working at the moment—not with his loins.

He was the O Donoghue Mór, an Irish chieftain who, a year before, had given up all rights to touch another woman. He had no business dallying with—of all things—a Sassenach vagabond, probably a madwoman at that.

He forced himself to stare not at the bodice, but into her eyes. And what he saw there was more dangerous than the lush curves of her body. What he saw there was not madness, but a painful eagerness.

It struck him like a slap, and he caught his breath, then hissed out air between his teeth.

He wanted to shake her. *Don't show me your yearning,* he wanted to say. *Don't expect me to do anything about it.*

What he said was, "I am in London on official

business. I will return to Ireland as soon as I am able."

"I've never been to Ireland," she said, an ember of unbearable hope glowing in her eyes.

"These days, it is a sad country, especially for those who love it." Sad. What a small, inadequate word to describe the horror and desolation he had seen—burned-out peel towers, scorched fields, empty villages, packs of wolves feeding off the unburied dead.

She tilted her head to one side. Unlike Aidan, she seemed perfectly comfortable with their proximity. A suspicion stung him. Perhaps it was nothing out of the ordinary for her to have a man tugging at her clothing.

The idea stirred him from his lassitude and froze the sympathy he felt for her. He made short, neat work of trussing her up, helped her slide her feet into the little shoes, then stepped back.

She ruined his hard-won indifference when she pointed a slippered toe, curtsied as if to the manner born, and asked, "How do I look?"

From neck to floor, Aidan thought, like his own private dream of paradise.

But her expression disturbed him; she had the face of a cherub, filled with a trust and innocence that seemed all the more miraculous because of the hardships she must have endured living the life of a strolling player.

He studied her hair, because it was safer than looking at her face and drowning in the misty pools of her eyes. She lifted a hand, made a fluttery motion in the honey gold spikes. "It's that awful?" she asked. "After I cut it all off, Mort and Dove said I could use my head to swab out wine casks or clean lamp chimneys."

A reluctant laugh broke from him. "It is not so bad. But tell me, *why* is your hair cropped short? Or do I want to know?"

"Lice," she said simply. "I had the devil of a time with them."

He swallowed in discomfort. "Aye, well. I hope you're no longer troubled by the little pests."

"Not lately. Who dresses your hair, my lord? It is most extraordinary." Brazen as an inquisitive child, she stood on tiptoe and lifted the single thread-woven braid that hung amid his black locks.

"That would be Iago. He does strange things on shipboard to avoid boredom." Like getting me drunk and carving up my chest, Aidan thought grumpily. "I'll ask him to do something about this mop of yours."

He meant to reach out and tousle her hair, a meaningless, playful gesture. Instead, as if with its own mind, his palm cradled her cheek, his thumb brushing up into her sawed-off hair. The soft texture startled him.

"Will that be agreeable to you?" he heard himself ask in a whisper.

"Yes, Your Immensity." Pulling away, she craned her neck to see over his shoulder. "There is something I need." She hurried into the kitchen, where her old, soiled clothes lay in a heap.

Aidan frowned. He had not noticed any buttons worth keeping on her much worn garb. She snatched up the tunic and groped along one of the seams. An audible sigh of relief slipped from her. Aidan saw a flash of metal.

Probably a bauble or copper she had lifted from a passing merchant in St. Paul's. He shrugged and went to the kitchen garden door to call for Iago.

As he turned, he saw Pippa lift the piece and press it to her mouth, closing her eyes and looking for all the world as if the bauble were more precious than gold.

I am old enough now to forgive Aidan's father, yet young enough to remember what a scoundrel Ronan O Donoghue was. Ah, I could roast for eternity in the fires of my unkind thoughts, but there you are, I hated the old jackass and wept no tears at his wake.

He expected more of his only son than any man could possibly give—loyalty, honor, truth, but most of all blind, stupid obedience. It was the one quality Aidan lacked. It was the one thing that could have saved the father, niggardly lout that he was, from dying.

For certain, Aidan thinks on that often, and with a great, seizing pain in his heart.

A pitiful waste if you ask me, Revelin of Innisfallen. For until he lets go of his guilt about what happened that fateful night, Aidan O Donoghue will not truly live.

—Revelin of Innisfallen

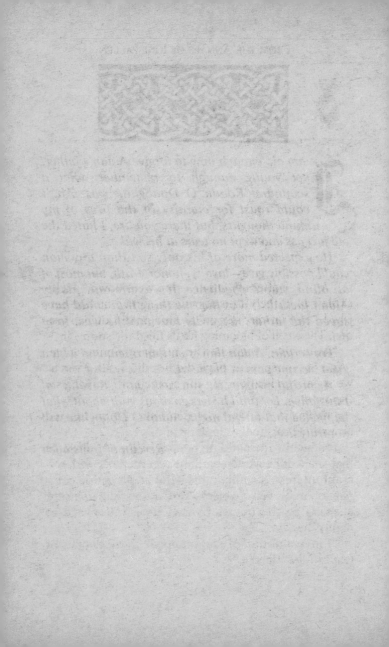

3

"So after my father's ship went down," Pippa explained blithely, "his enemies assumed he had perished." She sat very still on the stool in the kitchen garden. The smell of blooming herbs filled the spring air.

"Naturally," Iago said in his dark honey voice. "And of course, your papa did not die at all. Even as we speak, he is attending the council of Her Majesty the queen."

"How did you know?" Beaming, Pippa twisted around on her stool to look up at him.

Framed by the nodding boughs of the old elm tree that shaded the garden path, he regarded her with tolerant interest, a comb in his hand and a gentle compassion in his velvety black eyes. "I, too, like to invent answers to the questions that keep me awake at night," he said.

"I invent nothing," she snapped. "It all happened just as I described it."

"Except that the story changes each time you encounter someone new." He spoke with mild amusement, but no accusation. "Your father has been pirate, knight, foreign prince, soldier of fortune, and ratcatcher. Oh. And did I not hear you tell O Mahoney you were sired by the pope?"

Pippa blew out a breath, and her shoulders sagged. A raven cackled raucously in the elm tree, then whirred off into the London sky. Of course she invented stories about who she was and where she had come from. To face the truth was unthinkable. And impossible.

Iago's touch was soothing as he combed through her matted hair. He tilted her chin up and stared at her face-on for a long moment, intent as a sculptor. She stared back, rapt as a dreamer. What a remarkable person he was, with his lovely ebony skin and bell-toned voice, the fierce, inborn pride he wore like a mantle of silk.

He closed one eye; then he began to snip with his little crane-handled scissors, the very ones she had been tempted to steal from a side table in the kitchen.

As Iago worked, he said, "You tell the tales so well, *pequeña,* but they are just that—tales. I know this because I used to do the same. Used to lie awake at night trying to put together the face of my mother from fragments of memory. She became every good thing I knew about a mother, and before long she was more real to me than an actual woman. Only bigger. Better. Sweeter, kinder."

"Yes," she whispered past a sudden, unwelcome thickness in her throat. "Yes, I understand."

He twisted a few curls into a soft fringe upon her

brow. The breeze sifted lightly through them. "If you were an Englishman, you would be the very rage of fashion. They call these lovelocks. They look better on you." He winked. "A dream mother. It was something I needed at a very dark time of my life."

"Tell me about the dark time," she said, fascinated by the deftness of his hands and the way they were so brown on one side, while the palms were sensitive and pale.

"Slavery," he said. "Being made to work until I fell on my face from exhaustion, and then being beaten until I dragged myself up to work some more. You have a dream mother too, eh?"

She closed her eyes. A lovely face smiled at her. She had spent a thousand nights and more painting her parents in her mind until they were perfect. Beautiful. All wise. Flawless, save for one minor detail. They had somehow managed to misplace their daughter.

"I have a dream mother," she confessed. "A father, too. The stories might change, but that does not." She opened her eyes to find him studying her critically again.

"What about the O Donoghue?" she asked, pretending only idle curiosity.

"His father is dead, which is why Aidan is the lord. His mother is dead also, but his—" He cut himself off. "I have said too much already."

"Why are you so loyal to the O Donoghue?"

"He gave me my freedom."

"How was it his to give in the first place?"

Iago grinned, his face blossoming like an exotic flower. "It was not. I was put on a ship for transport from San Juan—that is on an island far across the

Ocean Sea—to England. I was to be a gift for a great noblewoman. My master wished to impress her."

"A gift?" Pippa was hard-pressed to sit still on her stool. "You mean like a drinking cup or a salt cellar or a pet ermine?"

"You have a blunt way of putting it, but yes. The ship wrecked off the coast of Ireland. I swam straight away from my master even as he begged me to save him."

Pippa sat forward, amazed. "Did he die?"

Iago nodded. "Drowned. I watched him. Does that shock you?"

"Yes! Was the water very cold?"

His chest-deep chuckle filled the air. "Close to freezing. I dragged myself to an island—I later found out it is called Skellig Michael—and there I met a pilgrim in sackcloth and ashes, climbing the great stairs to the shrine."

"The O Donoghue Mór in sackcloth and ashes?" In Pippa's mind, Aidan would always be swathed in flashing jewel tones, his jet hair gleaming in the sun; he was no drab pilgrim, but a prince from a fairy story.

"He was not the O Donoghue Mór then. He helped me get dry and warm, and he became my first and only true friend." Black fury shadowed Iago's eyes. "When Aidan's father saw me, he declared himself my master, tried to make me a slave again. And Aidan *let* him."

Pippa clutched the sides of the stool. "The jackdog! The bootlicker, the skainsmate—"

"It was a ruse. He claimed me on the grounds that he had found me. His father agreed, thinking it would enhance Aidan's station to be the first Irishman to own a black slave."

"The scullywarden!" she persisted. "The horse's a—"

"And then he set me free," Iago said, laughing at her. "He had a priest called Revelin draw up a paper. That day Aidan promised to help me return to my home when we were both grown. In fact, he promised to come with me across the Ocean Sea."

"Why would you want to go back to a land where you were a slave? And why would Aidan want to go with you?"

"Because I love the islands, and I no longer have a master. There was a girl called Serafina. . . ." His voice trailed off, and he shook his head as if to cast away the thought. "Aidan wanted to come because he loves Ireland too much to stay." Iago fussed with more curls that tickled the nape of her neck.

"If he loves Ireland, why would he want to leave it?"

"When you come to know him better, you will understand. Have you ever been forced to watch a loved one die?"

She swallowed and nodded starkly, thinking of Mab. "I never felt so helpless in all my life."

"So it is with Aidan and Ireland," said Iago.

"Why is he here, in London?"

"Because the queen summoned him. Officially, he is here to sign treaties of surrender and regrant. He is styled lord of Castleross. Unofficially, she is curious, I think, about Ross Castle. She wants to know why, after her interdict forbidding the construction of fortresses, it was completed."

The idea that her patron had the power to decide the fate of nations was almost too large for Pippa to grasp. "Is she very angry with him?" It even felt odd referring to Queen Elizabeth as "she," for Her Majesty had always been, to Pippa and others like her, a remote idea, more of an institution like a cathedral than a flesh-and-blood woman.

"She has kept him waiting here for a fortnight." Iago lifted her from the stool to the ground. "You look as pretty as an okasa blossom."

She touched her hair. Its shape felt different—softer, balanced, light as the breeze. She would have to go out to Hart Street Well and look at her reflection.

"You said when you met Aidan, he was not the O Donoghue Mór," she said, thinking that the queen must enjoy having the power to summon handsome men to her side.

"His father, Ronan, was. Aidan became Lord Castleross after Ronan died."

"And how did his father die?"

Iago went to the half door of the kitchen and held the lower part open. "Ask Aidan. It is not my place to say."

"Iago said you killed your father."

Aidan shot to his feet as if Pippa had touched a brand to his backside. "He said *what*?"

Hiding her apprehension, she strolled into the great hall of Lumley House and moved through gloomy evening shadows on the flagged floor. An ominous rumbling of thunder sounded in the distance. Aidan's fists were clenched, his face stark and taut. Instinct told her to flee, but she forced herself to stay.

"You heard me, my lord. If you're going to keep me, I want to make sure. Is it true? *Did* you kill your father?"

He grabbed an iron poker. A single Gaelic word burst from him as he stabbed at the fat log smoldering in the grate.

Pippa took a deep breath for courage. "It was Iago who—"

"Iago said nothing of the sort."

She emerged from the shadows and joined him by the hearth, praying he would deny her suggestion. "Did you, my lord?" she whispered.

He moved so swiftly, it took her breath away. One moment the iron poker clattered to the floor; the next he had his great hands clamped around her shoulders, her back against a stone pillar, and his furious face pushed close to hers. Though she still stood cloaked in shadow, she could see the flames from the hearth fire reflected in his eyes.

"*Yes,* damn your meddling self. I killed my father."

"*What?*" She trembled in his grip.

Filled with disgust at himself, Aidan thrust away from her, turning back to face the fire. "Isn't that what you expected to hear?" He clenched his eyes shut and pinched the bridge of his nose. Sharp fragments of that last, explosive argument came back to slice fresh wounds into his soul.

Furious, he spun around to face Pippa, intending to carry her bodily out of the hall, out of Lumley House, out of his life. She stepped from the gloom and into the light. Aidan stopped dead in his tracks.

"What in God's name did Iago do to you?" he asked. As if to echo his words, thunder muttered outside the hall.

Her hand wavered a little as she brought it up to

touch her hair, which now curled softly around her glowing face. "The best he could?" she attempted. Then she dropped her air of trembling uncertainty. "You are trying to change the subject. Are you or are you not a father-murderer?"

He planted his hands on his hips. "That depends on whom you ask."

She mimicked his aggressive stance, looking for all the world like a fierce pixie. "I'm asking you."

"And I've answered you."

"But it was the wrong answer," she said, so vehemently that he expected her to stomp her foot. Something—the washing, the grooming—had made her glow as if a host of fairies had showered her with a magical mist. "I demand an explanation."

"I feel no need to explain myself to a stranger," he said, dismayed by the intensity of his attraction to her.

"We are not strangers, Your Loftiness," she said with heavy irony. "Wasn't it just this morning that you undressed me and then dressed me like the most intimate of handmaids?"

He winced at the reminder. Beneath her elfin daintiness lay a soft, womanly body that he craved with a power that was both undeniable and inappropriate. Shed of her beggar's garb, she had become the sort of woman for whom men swore to win honors, slay dragons, cheerfully lay down their lives. And he was in no position to do any of those things.

"Some would say," he admitted darkly, "that the death of Ronan O Donoghue was an accident." From the corner of his eye, he saw a flicker of lightning through the mullioned windows on the east side of the hall.

"What do *you* say?" Pippa asked.

"I say it is none of your affair. And if you persist in talking about it, I might have to do something permanent to you."

She sniffed, clearly recognizing the idleness of his threat. He was not accustomed to females who were unafraid of him. "If *I* had a father, I'd cherish him."

"You do have a father. The war hero, remember?"

She blinked. "Oh. Him. Yes, of course."

Aidan blew out his breath. He slammed a fist on the stone mantel and regarded the Lumley shield hanging above as if it were a higher authority. "What am I going to do with you?"

The wind hurled gusts against the windows, and he swung around to glower at Pippa.

"'Do' with me?" She glanced back over her shoulder at the door. He didn't blame her for not wanting to be alone with him. She wouldn't be the first.

"You can't stay here forever," he stated. "I didn't ask to be your protector." The twist of guilt in his gut startled him. He was not used to making cruel statements to defenseless women.

She did not look surprised. Instead, she dropped one shoulder and regarded him warily. She resembled a dog so used to being kicked that it came as a surprise when it was *not* kicked.

Her rounded chin came up. "I never asked to stay forever. I can go back to Dove and Mortlock. We have plans to gain the patronage of . . . of the Holy Roman Emperor."

He remembered her disreputable companions from St. Paul's—the portly and greasy Dove and the cadaverous Mortlock. "They must be mad with worry over you."

"Those two?" She snorted and idly picked up the

iron poker, stabbing at the log in the hearth. Sparks flew upward on a sweep of air, then disappeared. "They only worry about losing me because they need me to cry up a crowd. Their specialty is cutting purses."

"I won't let you go back to them," Aidan heard himself say. "I'll find you a"—he thought for a moment—"a situation with a gentlewoman—"

That made her snort again, this time with bitter laughter. "Oh, for that I should be well and truly suited." She slammed the poker back into its stand. "It has long been my aim in life to empty some lady's slops and pour wine for her." The hem of her skirts twitched in agitation as she pantomimed the menial work.

"It's a damned sight better than wandering the streets." Irritated, he walked to the table and sloshed wine into a cup. The lightning flashed again, stark and cold in the April night.

"Oh, do tell, my lord." She stalked across the room, slapped her palms on the table, leaned over, and glared into his face. "Listen. I am an entertainer. I am good at it."

So he had noticed. She could mimic any accent, highborn or low, copy any movement with fluid grace, change character from one moment to the next like an actor trying on different masks.

"I didn't ask you to drag me out of St. Paul's and into your life," she stated.

"I don't remember any objections from you when I saved you from having your ears nailed to the stocks." He tasted the wine, a sweet sack favored by the English nobility. He missed his nightly draft of poteen. Pippa was enough to make him crave *two* drafts of the powerful liquor.

"I was hungry. But that doesn't mean I've surrendered my life to you. I can get another position in a nobleman's household just like that." She snapped her fingers.

She was so close, he could see the dimple that winked in her left cheek. She smelled of soap and sun-dried laundry, and now that her hair was fixed, it shone like spun gold in the glow from the hearth.

He took another sip of wine. Then, very gently, he set down the cup and reached across to touch a wispy curl that drifted across her cheek. "How can it be enough to simply survive?" he asked softly. "Do you never dream of doing more than that?"

"Damn *you*," she said, echoing his words to her. She shoved away from the table and turned her back on him. There was a heartbreaking pride in the stiff way she held herself, the set of her shoulders and the haughty tilt of her head. "Good-bye, Your Worship. Thank you for our brief association. We shan't be seeing each other again."

"Pippa, wait—"

In a sweep of skirts and injured dignity, she strode out of the hall, disappearing into the gloom of the cloister that bordered the herbiary. Aidan could not explain it, but the sight of her walking away from him caused a painful squeeze of guilt and regret in his chest.

He swore under his breath and finished his wine, then paced the room. He had more pressing matters to ponder than the fate of a saucy street performer. Clan wars and English aggression were tearing his district apart. The settlement he had negotiated last year was shaky at best. A sad matter, that, since he had paid such a dear price for the settlement. He had bought peace at the cost of his heart.

The thought caused his mind to jolt back to Pippa. The ungrateful little female. Let her storm off to her chamber and sulk until she came to her senses.

It occurred to him then that she was the sort not to sulk, but to act. She had survived—and thrived—by doing just that.

A jagged spear of lightning split the sky just as a terrible thought occurred to him. Hurling the pewter wine cup to the floor, he dashed out of the house and into the cloister of Crutched Friars, running down the arcade to her door, jerking it open.

Empty. He passed through the refectory and emerged onto the street. He had been right. He saw Pippa in the distance, hurrying down the broad, tree-lined road leading to Woodroffe Lane and the eerie, lawless area around Tower Hill. A gathering wind stirred the bobbing heads of chestnut trees. Clouds rolled and tumbled, blackening the sky, and when he breathed in, he caught the heavy taste and scent of rain and the faint, sizzling tang of close lightning.

She walked faster still, half running.

Turn back, he called to her silently, trying to will her to do his bidding. *Turn back and look at me.*

Instead, she lifted her skirts and began to run. As she passed the communal well of Hart Street, lightning struck.

From where Aidan stood, it looked as if the very hand of God had cleaved the heavens and sent a bolt of fire down to bury itself in the breast of London. A crash of thunder seemed to shake the ground. The clouds burst open like a ripe fruit, and it began to rain.

For an Irishman, Aidan was not very superstitious,

but thunder and lightning were a clear sign from a powerful source. He should not have let her go.

Without a second thought, he plunged into the howling storm, racing between the rows of wildly bending chestnut trees. The rain pelted him in huge, cold drops, and lightning speared down through the clouds once more.

He dragged a hand across his rain-stung eyes and squinted through the sodden twilight. Already the ditch down the middle of the street ran like a small, flooding river, carrying off the effluvia of London households.

People scurried for cover here and there, but the darkness had swallowed Pippa. He shouted her name. The storm drowned his voice. With a curse, he began a methodical search of each side alley and path he encountered, working south toward the river, turning westward toward St. Paul's each time he saw a way through.

The storm gathered force, belting him in the face, tearing at his clothes. Mud spattered him to the thighs, but he ignored it.

He went farther west, turning into each alley, calling her name. The rain blinded him, the wind buffeted him, the mud sucked at his feet.

At a particularly grim-looking street, the wind tore down a painted sign of a blue devil and hurled it to the ground. It struck a slanting cellar door, then fell sideways onto a pile of wood chippings.

He heard a faint, muffled cry. With a surge of hope, he flung away the sign and the sawdust.

There she sat, knees drawn up to her chest, face tucked into the hollow between her hugging arms. Thunder crashed again, and she flinched as if struck by a whip.

"Pippa!" He touched her quaking shoulder.

She screamed and looked up at him.

Aidan's heart lurched. Her face, battered by rain and tears, shone stark white in the storm-dulled twilight. The panic in her eyes blinded her; she showed no recognition of him. That look of mindless terror was one he had seen only once before—in the face of his father just before Ronan had died.

"Faith, Pippa, are you hurt?"

She did not respond to her name, but blurted out something he could not comprehend. A nonsense word or a phrase in a foreign tongue?

Shaken, he bent and scooped her up, holding her against his chest and bending his head to shield her from the rain as best he could. She did not resist, but clung to him as if he were a raft in a raging sea. He felt a surge of fierce protectiveness. Never had he felt so painfully alive, so determined to safeguard the small stranger in his arms.

Still she showed no sign of recognition, and did not do so while he dashed back to Lumley House. A host of demons haunted the girl who called herself Pippa Trueheart.

And Aidan O Donoghue was seized by the need to slay each and every one of them.

"Batten the hatches! Secure the helm! There's naught to do now but run before the wind!"

The man in the striped jacket had a funny, rusty voice. He sounded cross, or maybe afraid, like Papa had been when his forehead got hot and he had to go to bed and not have any visitors.

She clung to her dog's furry neck and looked across

the smelly, dark enclosure at Nurse. But Nurse had her hands all twisted up in a string of rosy beads—the ones she hid from Mama, who was Reformed—and all Nurse could say was Hail Mary Hail Mary Hail Mary.

Something scooped the ship up and up and up. She could feel the lifting in her belly. And then, much faster, a stronger force slapped them down.

Nurse screamed Hail Mary Hail Mary Hail Mary . . .

The hound whined. His fur smelled of dog and ocean.

A cracking noise hurt her ears. She heard the whine of ropes running through pulleys and a shriek from the man in the funny coat, and suddenly she had to get out of there, out of that close, wet place where the water was filling up the floor, where her chest wouldn't let her breathe.

She pushed the door open. The dog scrambled out first, and then she followed him up a slanting wooden stair. Loose barrels skittered all through the passageways and decks. She heard a great roar of water. She looked back to find Nurse, but all she saw was a hand waving, the rosy beads braided through the pale fingers. Water covered Nurse all the way to the top of her head. . . .

"*No!*" Pippa sat straight up in the bed. For a moment, the room was all a pulsating blur. Slowly, it came into focus. Low-burning hearth fire. Candle flickering on the table. High, thick testers holding up the draperies.

The O Donoghue Mór sitting at the end of the bed.

She pressed her hand to her chest, hating the twitchy, air-starved feeling that sometimes seized her lungs when she took fright or breathed noxious or frozen air. Her heart was racing. Sweat bathed her face and neck.

"Bad dream?" he asked.

She shut her eyes. Like a mist driven by the wind, the images flew away, unremembered, but her sense of terror lingered. "It happens. Where am I?"

"I've given you a private chamber in Lumley House."

Her eyes widened in amazement, then narrowed in suspicion. "Why?"

"I am your patron. You'll lodge where I put you."

She thrust up her chin. "And what do you require of me in exchange for living in the lap of luxury?"

"Why must I expect anything at all from you?"

She regarded him for a long, measuring moment. No, the O Donoghue Mór was certainly not the sort of man who had to keep unwilling females at his beck and call. Any woman in her right mind would want him. Except, of course, Pippa herself. But that did not stop her from enjoying his strikingly splendid face and form, nor did it keep her from craving—against all good sense—his warmth and closeness.

"I take it you don't like storms," he said.

"No, I . . ." It all seemed so silly now. London offered far greater perils than storms, and she had survived London for years. "Thank you, my lord. Thank you for coming after me. I should not have left in such haste."

"True," he said gently.

"It is not every day a man makes me question my very reason for existing."

"Pippa, I didn't mean it that way. I should not have questioned the choices you've made."

She nodded. "People love to *manage* other people." Frowning, she looked around the room, noting
the wonderful bed, the crackling fire in the grate, the
clear, rain-washed night air wafting through a small,
open window. "I don't remember much about the
storm. Was it very bad?"

He smiled. It was a soft, unguarded smile, as if he
truly meant it. "You were in a bit of a state when I
found you."

She blushed and dropped her gaze, then blushed
even deeper when she discovered she wore only a
shift. She clutched the bedclothes to her chest.

"I hung your things to dry by the fire," Aidan said.
"I got the shift from Lady Lumley's clothes press."

Pippa touched the sheer fabric of the sleeve. "I'll
hang for certain."

"Nay. Lord and Lady Lumley are at their country
estate in Wycherly. I'm to have full use of the house
and all its contents."

She sighed dreamily. "How wonderful to be treated
like such an important guest."

"Often I find it a burden, not a wonder."

She began to remember snatches of the storm, the
lightning and thunder chasing her through the streets,
the rain lashing her face. And then Aidan's strong
arms and broad chest, and the sensation of speed as
he rushed her back to the house. His hands had tenderly divested her of clothes and placed her in the
only real bed she had ever slept in.

She had tucked her face into his strong shoulder
and sobbed. Hard. He had stroked her hair, kissed it,
and finally she had slept.

She looked up at him. "You're awfully kind for a
father-murderer."

His smile wavered. "Sometimes I surprise myself." Leaning across the bed, he touched her cheek, his finger skimming over her blush-heated skin. "You make it easy, colleen. You make me better than I am."

She felt such a profusion of warmth that she wondered if she had a fever. "Now what?" she whispered.

"Now, for once in your life, you'll tell the truth, Pippa. Who are you, where did you come from, and what in God's name am I going to do with you?"

My son Richard's namesake is coming to London! The Reverend Richard Speed, of famous reputation, now the Bishop of Bath, will attend his nephew's military commission. Naturally Speed will bring his wife, Natalya, who is Oliver's dear sister and as beloved to me as blood kin.

Oliver's other siblings will come with husbands and wives. Belinda and Kit, Simon and Rosamund, whom I have not seen in two winters. Sebastian will come with one special friend or other; these days it is a gifted but disreputable young poet called Marlowe.

Dear Belinda still clings to her scandalous pastime of incendiary displays. She has lit her fireworks for members of the noble houses of Hapsburg and Valois, and of course for Her Majesty the Queen. She has promised a special program of Italian colored fire in honor of Richard.

But I wonder, amidst all the revelry, if anyone save Oliver will mark the event that tonight's storm reminds me of so poignantly. For many years I have struggled to survive our loss, and daily I thank God for my family. Still, the storm hurled me back to that dark, rain-drenched night.

It is a time that lives in my heart as its most piercing memory.

—Lark de Lacey,
Countess of Wimberleigh

4

Aidan was watching her with those penetrating, flame blue eyes. Pippa could tell from his fierce chieftain's glare that he would tolerate no more jests or sidestepping.

She combed her hair with both hands, raking her fingers through the damp, yellow tangles. She felt shaky, much as she did after being stricken with a fever and then getting up for the first time in days. The storm had slammed through her with terrifying force, leaving her limp.

"The problem is," she said with bleak, quiet honesty, "I have the same answer to all of your questions."

"And what is that?"

"I don't know." She watched him closely for a reaction, but he merely sat there at the end of the bed, waiting and watching. Firelight flared behind him, outlining his massive shoulders and the gleaming fall of his black hair.

His eyes never left her, and she wondered just what he saw. Why in heaven's name would a grand Irish lord take an interest in her? What did he hope to gain by befriending her? She had so little to offer—a handful of tricks, a few sorry jests, a chuckle or two. Yet he seemed enraptured, infinitely patient, as he awaited her explanation.

The rush of tenderness she felt for him was frightening. Ah, she could love this man, she could draw him into her heart. But she would not. In his way, he was as remote as the moon, beautiful and unreachable. Before long he would go back to Ireland, and she would resume her existence in London.

"I don't know who I am," she explained, "nor where I come from, nor even where I am going. And I certainly don't know what you're going to do with me." With an effort, she squared her shoulders. "Not that it's any of your concern. I am mistress of my own fate. If and when I decide to delve into my past, it will be to find the answers for me, not you."

"Ah, Pippa." He got up, took a dipper of wine from a cauldron near the hearth, and poured the steaming, spice-scented liquid in a cup. "Sip it slowly," he said, handing her the drink, "and we'll see if we can sort this out."

Feeling cosseted, she accepted the wine and let a soothing swallow slide down her throat. Mab had been her teacher, her adviser in herbal arts and foraging, but the old woman had seen only to her most basic needs, keeping her dry and fed as if she were livestock. From Mab, Pippa had learned how to survive. And how to protect herself from being hurt.

"You do not know who you are?" he inquired, sitting again at the foot of the bed.

She hesitated, caught her lower lip with her teeth. Turmoil boiled up inside her, and her immediate reaction was to erupt with laughter and make yet another joke about being a sultan's daughter or a Hapsburg orphan. Then, cradling the cup in her hands, she lifted her gaze to his.

She saw concern burning like a flame in his eyes, and its appeal had a magical effect on her, warming her like the wine, unfurling the secrets inside her, plunging down through her to find the words she had never before spoken to another living soul.

Slowly, she set the cup on a stool beside the bed and began to talk to him. "For as long as I can remember, I have been Pippa. Just Pippa." The admission caught unpleasantly in her throat. She cleared it with a merry, practiced laugh. "It is a very liberating thing, my lord. Not knowing who I am frees me to be whoever I want to be. One day my parents are a duke and duchess, the next they are poor but proud crofters, the next, heroes of the Dutch revolt."

"But all you really want," he said softly, "is to belong somewhere. To someone."

She blinked at him and could summon no tart remark or laughter to answer the charge. And for the first time in her life, she admitted the stark, painful truth. "Oh, God in heaven, yes. All I want to know is that someone once loved me."

He reached across the bed and covered her hands with his. A strange, comfortable feeling rolled over her like a great wave. This man, this foreign chieftain who had all but admitted he'd killed his father, somehow made her feel safe and protected and cared for.

"Let us work back over time." He rubbed his thumbs gently over her wrists. "Tell me how you came to be there on the steps of St. Paul's the first day I met you."

He spoke of their meeting as if it had been a momentous occasion. She pulled her hands away and set her jaw, stubbornly refusing to say more. The fright from the storm had lowered her defenses. She struggled to shore them up again. Why should she confess the secrets of her heart to a virtual stranger, a man she would never see again after he left London?

"Pippa," he said, "it's a simple enough question."

"Why do you care?" she shot back. "What possible interest could it be to you?"

"I care because you matter to me." He raked a hand through his hair. "Is that so hard to understand?"

"Yes," she said.

He reached for her and then froze, his hand hovering between them for a moment before he pulled it back. He cleared his throat. "I am your patron. You perform under my warrant. And these are simple questions."

He made her feel silly for guarding her thoughts as if they were dark secrets. She took a deep breath, trying to decide just where to begin. "Very well. Mort and Dove said eventually, all of London passes through St. Paul's. I suppose—quite foolishly, as it happens—I hoped that one day I would look up and see a man and woman who would say, 'You belong to us.'" She plucked at a loose thread in the counterpane. "Stupid, am I not? Of course, that never happened." She gave a short laugh, tamping back an errant feeling of wistful longing. "Even if they did recognize me, why would they claim me, unwashed and dishonest, thieving from people in the churchyard?"

"*I* claimed you," he reminded her.

His words lit a glow inside her that warmed her chest. She wanted to fling herself against him, to babble with gratitude, to vow to stay with him always. Only the blade-sharp memories of other moments, other partings, held her aloof and wary.

"For that I shall always thank you, my lord," she said cordially. "You won't be sorry. I'll keep you royally entertained."

"Never mind that. So you continued to perform as a strolling player, just wandering about, homeless as a Gypsy?" he asked.

A sting of memory touched her, and she caught her breath in startlement.

"What is it?" he asked.

"Something extraordinary just occurred to me. Years ago, when I first came to London town, I saw a tribe of Gypsies camped in Moor Fields outside the City. I thought they were a troupe of players, but these people dressed and spoke differently. They were like a—a family. I was drawn to them."

Warming to her tale, she shook off the last vestiges of terror from the storm. She sat forward on the bed, draping her arms around her drawn-up knees. "Aidan, it was so exciting. There was something familiar about those people. I could almost understand their language, not the actual words, mind, but the rhythms and nuances."

"And they welcomed you?"

She nodded. "That night, there was a dance around a great bonfire. I was taken to meet a woman called Zara—she was very old. Ancient. Some said more than fourscore years old. Her pallet had been set out so that she could watch the dancing." Pippa closed her eyes, picturing the snowy tangle of hair, the wizened-apple face, the night-dark eyes so intense they seemed to see into tomorrow.

"They said she was ill, not expected to live, but she asked to see me. Fancy that." Opening her eyes again, she peered at Aidan to see if he believed her or thought she was spinning yarns once more. She could not tell, for he merely watched and waited with calm interest. No one had ever listened to her with such great attention before.

"Go on," he said.

"Do you know the first thing she said to me? She said I would meet a man who would change my life."

He muttered something Celtic and scowled at her.

"No, it's true, my lord, you must believe me."

"Why should I? You've lied about everything else."

His observation should not have hurt her, but it did. She pressed her knees even closer to her chest and tried to will away the ache in her heart. "Not *everything*, Your Loftiness."

"Continue, then. Tell me what the witch woman said."

"Her speech was slow, broken." In her mind's eye, Pippa saw it all as if it had happened yesterday—the leaping flames and the ancient face, the deep eyes and the Gypsies whispering among themselves and pointing at Pippa, who had knelt beside Zara's pallet.

"She was babbling, I suppose, and speaking in more than one language, but I remember she told me about the man. And she also spoke of blood and vows and honor."

"Blood, vows, and honor?" he repeated.

"Yes. That part was very distinct. She spoke the three words, just like that. She was dying, my lord, but clutching my hand with a grip stronger than death itself. I hadn't the heart to question her or show any doubt. It's as if she thought she knew me and somehow needed me in those last moments."

He folded his arms against his massive chest and studied her. Pippa was terrified that he would accuse her again of lying, but he gave the barest of nods. "They say those in extremis often mistake strangers for people they have known. Did the old woman say more?"

"One more thing." Pippa hesitated. She felt it all again, the emotions that had roared through her while the stranger held her hand. A feeling of terrible hope had welled from somewhere deep inside her. "A statement I will never, ever forget. She lifted her head, using the very last of her strength to fix me with a stare. And she said, 'The circle is complete.' Then, within an hour, she was dead. A few of the young Gypsies seemed suspicious of me, so I thought it prudent to leave after that. Besides, the woman's wild talk . . ."

"Frightened you?" Aidan asked.

"Not frightened so much as touched something inside me. As if the words she spoke were words I should know. I tell you, it gave me much to think on."

"I imagine it did."

"Not that anything ever came of it," she said, then ducked her head and lowered her voice. "Until now."

She watched him, studied his face. Lord, but he was beautiful. Not pretty, but beautiful in the way of a crag overlooking the moors of the north, or in the majestic stance of a roebuck surveying its domain deep in a green velvet wood. It was the sort of beauty that caught at her chest and held fast, defying all efforts to dislodge a dangerous, glorious worship.

Then she noticed that one eyebrow and one corner of his mouth were tilted up in wry irony. She blew out her breath in an explosive sigh. "I suppose that is the price of being an outrageous and constant liar."

"What is that?" he asked.

"When I finally tell the truth, you don't believe me."

"And why would you be thinking I don't believe you?"

"That *look*, Your Worship. You seem as if you are torn between laughing at me and summoning the warden of Bedlam."

The eyebrow inched up even higher. "Actually, I am torn between laughing at you and kissing you."

"I choose the kissing," she blurted out all in a rush.

Both of his eyebrows shot up, then lowered slowly over eyes gone soft and smoky. He gripped her hands and drew her forward so that she came up on her knees. The bedclothes pooled around her, and the thin shift whispered over her burning skin.

"I choose the kissing, too." He lifted his hand to her face. The pad of his thumb moved slowly, tantalizingly, along the curve of her cheekbone and then downward, slipping like silk over marble, to touch her bottom lip, to rub over the fullness until she almost did not *need* the kiss in order to feel him.

Almost.

"Have you ever been kissed before, colleen?"

The old bluster rose up inside her. "Well, of c—"

"Pippa," he said, pressing his thumb gently on her lips. "This would be a very bad time to lie to me."

"Oh. Then, no, Your Immensity. I have never been

kissed." The few who had tried had had their noses rearranged by her fist, but she thought it prudent not to mention that.

"Do you know how it's done?"

"Yes."

"Pippa, the truth. You were doing so well."

"I've seen it happen, but I don't know how it's done in actual practice."

"The first thing that has to happen—"

"Yes?" Unable to believe her good fortune, she bounced up and down on her knees, setting the bed to creaking on the rope latticework that supported the mattress. "This is really too exciting, my lord—"

His thumb stopped her mouth again. "—is that you have to stop talking. And for God's sake don't *narrate* everything. This is supposed to be a gesture of affection, but you're turning it into a farce."

"Oh. Well, of course I didn't mean—"

Again he hushed her, and at the same moment a log fell in the grate. The brief flare of sparks found, just for an instant, a bright home in the centers of his eyes. She moaned in sheer wanting but remembered at last not to speak.

"Ah, well done," he whispered, and his thumb moved again, with subtle, devastating tenderness, slipping just inside her mouth and then emerging to spread moisture along her lip.

"If you like, you can close your eyes."

She mutely shook her head. It was not every day she got a kiss from an Irish chieftain, and she was not about to miss a single instant of giddy bliss.

"Then just look up at me," he said, surging closer to her on the bed. "Just look up, and I'll do the rest."

She tilted her chin up as he lowered his head. His

thumb slid aside to make room for his lips, and his mouth brushed over hers, softly, sweetly, with a sensation that made raw wanting jolt to life inside her.

She made a sound, but he caught it with his mouth and pressed down gently, until their lips were truly joined. His deft fingers rubbed with tender insistence along her jawline, and his lips pushed against the seam of hers.

Open.

Here was something she had not learned from spying on couples pumping away in the alleys of Southwark or groping one another in the shadows of the pillars of St. Paul's.

His tongue came into her, and she made a squeak of surprise and delight. Her hands drifted upward, over his chest and around behind his neck. She wanted this closeness with a staggering, overwhelming need. His mouth and tongue went deeper, and his hands smoothed down her back, fingers splaying as he pressed her closer, closer.

The quickness of his breath startled her into the realization that he, too, was moved by the intimacy. He, too, had chosen the kiss.

All her life, Pippa had been curious about every bright, shiny thing she saw, and loveplay was no different, yet wholly different. It was not a case of simple *wanting*, but the experience of a sudden, devastating need she did not know she had.

Tightening her arms around his neck, she thrust against him, wanting the closeness to last forever. She could feel his heartbeat against her chest, feel the life force of another person beating against her and, in an odd, spiritual way, joining with her.

He lifted his mouth from hers. A stunned expression

bloomed on his face. "Ah, colleen," he whispered urgently, "We must stop before I—"

"Before what?" She reveled in the feel of his wine-sweet breath next to her face.

"Before I want more than just a kiss."

"Then it's too late for me," she admitted, "for I already want more."

He chuckled, very low and very softly, and there was a subtle edge of anguish in his voice. "When you decide to be honest, you don't stint, do you?"

"I suppose not. Ah, I *do* want you, Aidan."

A sad-sweet smile curved his beautiful mouth. "And I want you, lass. But we must not let this go any farther."

"Why not?"

He lifted her hands away from him and rose from the bed, moving slowly as if he were in pain. "Because it's not proper."

Stung, she scowled. "I have never been preoccupied with what is proper."

"I have," he muttered, and turned away. From the cauldron, he ladled himself a cup of wine and drank it in one gulp. "I'm sorry, Pippa."

Already he had withdrawn from her, and she shivered with the chill of rejection. "Can't you look at me and say that?"

He turned, and still his movements seemed labored. "I said I was sorry. I took advantage of your innocence, and I should never have done that."

"I chose the kiss."

"So did I."

"Then why did you stop?"

"I want you to tell me about yourself. Kissing gets in the way of clearheaded thinking."

"So if I tell you about myself, we can go back to the kissing?"

An annoyed tic started in his jaw. "I never said that."

"Well, can we?"

With exaggerated care, he set down his cup and walked over to the bed. Cradling her face between his hands, he gazed at her with heartbreaking regret. "No, colleen."

"But—"

"Consider the consequences. Some of them are quite lasting."

She swallowed. "You mean a baby." A wistful longing rose in her. Would it be such a catastrophe, she wondered, if the O Donoghue Mór were to give her a child? A small, helpless being that belonged solely to her?

She felt his hands, so gentle upon her face, yet his expression was one of painful denial. "Why should I do as you say?" she asked, resisting the urge to hurl herself at him, to cling to him and not let go.

"Because I'm asking you to, *a gradh*. Please."

She blew out a weary sigh, aware without asking that the Irish word was an endearment. "Do you know how impossible it is to say no to you?"

He smiled a little, bent, and kissed the top of her head before letting her go. "Now. We were working backward from your move to London. You met a mysterious hag—"

"Gypsy woman."

"In Ireland we would call her a woman of the *sidhe*."

"She said I'd meet a man who would change my life." Pippa leaned back against the banked pillows. She wondered if he noticed her blush-stung cheeks. "I always thought it meant I'd find my father. But I've changed my mind. She meant you."

He lowered himself to the foot of the bed and sat very quietly and thoughtfully. How could he be so indifferent upon learning he was the answer to a magical prophecy? What a fool he must think her. Then he asked, "What changed your mind?"

"The kiss." Jesu, she had not been so truthful in one conversation since she had first come to London. Aidan O Donoghue coaxed honesty from her; it was some power he possessed, one that made it safe to speak her mind and even her heart, if she dared.

He seemed to go rigid, though he did not move.

Idiot, Pippa chided herself. By now he probably could not wait to get rid of her. Surely he would drag her to Bedlam, collecting his fee for turning in a madwoman. He would not be the first to rid himself of a smitten girl in such a manner. "I shouldn't have said that," she explained, forcing out a laugh. "It was just a kiss, not a blood oath or some such nonsense. Verily, Your Magnitude, we should forget all about this."

"I'm Irish," he cut in softly, his musical lilt more pronounced than ever. "An Irishman does not take a kiss lightly."

"Oh." She stared at his firelit, mystical face and held her breath. It took all her willpower not to fling herself at him, ask him to toss up her skirts and do whatever it was a man did beneath a woman's skirts.

"Pippa?"

"Yes?"

"The story. Before you came to London, where did you live? What did you do?"

The simple questions drew vivid images from the well of her memories. She closed her eyes and traced

her way back over the long, oft interrupted journey to
London. She lost count of the strolling troupes she
had belonged to. Always she was greeted first with
skepticism; then, after a display of jests and juggling,
she was welcomed. She never stayed long. Usually she
slipped away in the night, more often than not leaving
a half-conscious man on the ground, clutching a shattered jaw or broken nose, cursing her to high heaven
or the belly of hell.

"Pippa?" Aidan prompted again.

She opened her eyes. Each time she looked at him,
he grew more beautiful. Perhaps she was under some
enchantment. Simply looking at him increased his
appeal and weakened her will to resist him.

Almost wistfully, she touched her bobbed hair. I
want to be like you, she thought. Beautiful and
beloved, the sort of person others wish to embrace,
not put in the pillory. The yearning felt like an aching
knot in her chest, stunning in its power. Against her
will, Aidan O Donoghue was awakening her to feelings she had spent a lifetime running from.

"I traveled slowly to London," she said, "jesting
and juggling along the way. There were times I went
hungry, or slept in the cold, but I didn't really mind.
You see, I had always wanted to go to London."

"To seek your family."

How had he guessed? It was part of the magic of
him, she decided. "Yes. I knew it was next to impossible, but sometimes—" She broke off and looked away
in embarrassment at her own candor.

"Go on," he whispered. "What were you going to
say?"

"Just that, sometimes the heart asks for the impossible."

He reached across the bed, lifted her chin with a finger, and winked at her. "And sometimes the heart gets it."

She sent him a bashful smile. "Mab would agree with you."

"Mab?"

"The woman who reared me. She lived in Humberside, along the Hornsy Strand. It was a land that belonged to no one, so she simply settled there. That's how she told it. Mab was simple, but she was all I had."

"How did you come to live with her?"

"She found me." A dull sense of resignation weighted Pippa, for she had always hated the truth about herself. "According to her, I lay upon the strand, clinging to a herring keg. A large lurcher or hound was with me. I was tiny, Mab said, two or three, no more." Like a lightning bolt, memory pierced her, and she winced with the force of it. *Remember.* The command shimmered through her mind.

"Colleen?" Aidan asked. "Are you all right?"

She clasped her hands over her ears, trying to shut out the insistent swish of panic.

"No!" she shouted. "Please! I don't remember anymore!"

With a furious Irish exclamation, Aidan O Donoghue, lord of Castleross, took her in his arms and let her bathe his shoulder in bitter tears.

"Act as if nothing's amiss," Donal Og hissed. He, Iago, and Aidan were in the stableyard of Crutched Friars the next day. Aidan had grooms to look after his horse, but currying the huge mare was a task he enjoyed, particularly in the early morning when no one was about.

Iago looked miserable in the bright chill of early morn. He detested cold weather. He made impossible claims about the climate of his homeland, insisting that it never snowed in the Caribbean, never froze, and that the sea was warm enough to swim in.

Absently patting Grania's strong neck, Aidan studied his cousin and Iago. What a formidable pair they made, one dark, one fair, both as large and imposing as cliff rocks.

"Nothing *is* amiss," Aidan said, leaning down to pick up a currying brush. Then he saw what Donal Og had clutched in his hand. "Is it?"

Donal Og glanced to and fro. The stableyard was empty. A brake of rangy bushes separated the area from the kitchen garden of the main house and the glassworks of Crutched Friars. Through gaps in the bushes, Lumley House and its gardens appeared serene, the well-sweep and stalks of herbs adorned with drops of last night's rain that sparkled in the rising sun.

"Read for yourself." Donal Og shoved a paper at Aidan. "But for God's sake, don't react too strongly. Walsingham's spies are everywhere."

Aidan glanced back over his shoulder at the house. "Faith, I hope not."

Donal Og and Iago exchanged a glance. Their faces split into huge grins. "It is about time, amigo," Iago said.

Aidan's ears felt hot with foolish defensiveness. "It's not what you think. Sure and I'd hoped for better understanding from the two of you."

The manly grins subsided. "As you wish, coz,"

Donal Og said. "Far be it from such as us to suspect yourself of swiving your wee guest."

"Ahhh." A sweet, female voice trilled in the distance. All three of them peered through the tall hedge at the house. Slamming open the double doors to the upper hall, Pippa emerged into the sunlight.

The parchment crinkled in Aidan's clenched hand. Aside from that, no one made a sound. They stood still, as if a sudden frost had frozen them. She stood on the top step, clad only in her shift. Clearly she thought she'd find no one in the private garden so early. She inhaled deeply, as if tasting the crisp morning air, cleansed by the rain.

Her hair was sleep tousled, soft and golden in the early light. Although Aidan had kissed her only once, he remembered vividly the rose petal softness of her lips. Her eyes were faintly bruised by shadows from last night's tears.

As spellbinding as her remarkable face was her body. The thin shift, with the sun shimmering through, revealed high, upturned breasts, womanly hips, a tiny waist, and long legs, shaded at the top by dark mystery.

She held a basin in her arms and shifted the vessel to perch on her hip. She descended the steps while three pairs of awestruck eyes, peering avidly through the stableyard hedge, watched her.

At the bottom of the steps, she stopped to shake back a tumble of golden curls. Then she bent forward over the well to draw the water. The thin fabric of the shift whispered over a backside so lush and shapely that Aidan's mouth went dry.

"*Ay, mujer,*" whispered Iago. "Would that I had such a bedmate."

"It's not what you think," Aidan managed to repeat in a low, strained voice.

"No," said Donal Og with rueful envy, his jaw unhinging as Pippa straightened. Some of the water dampened the front of her shift, so that her flesh shone pearly pink through the white lawn fabric. She paused to pluck the top of a daffodil and tuck it behind her ear. "No doubt," Donal Og continued, "it is a hundred times *better* than we think."

Aidan grabbed him by the front of his tunic. "I'll see you do penance for six weeks if you don't quit staring."

Oblivious, Pippa slipped back into the house. Iago made a great show of wiping his brow while Donal Og paced the yard, limping as if in discomfort. The horse made a loud, rude sound.

"The urchin turned out to be a beauty, Aidan," he said. "I would never have looked twice at her, but you looked once and found a true jewel."

"I wasn't looking for treasure, cousin," Aidan said. "The lass was caught up in a riot and in danger of being thrown into prison. I merely—"

"Hush." Donal Og held up a hand. "You needn't explain, coz. Don't you see, man, we're happy for you. Sure it wasn't healthy for you to be living like a monk, pretending you were not troubled by a man's needs. It is not as if you and Felicity ever—"

"Cease your infernal blather," Aidan snapped, pierced to the core by the merest thought of Felicity. His grip on the parchment tightened. Perhaps the letter from Revelin of Innisfallen contained good news. Perhaps the bishop had granted the annulment. *Oh, please God, yes.*

"Don't speak of Felicity again. And by God, if you

so much as insinuate that Pippa and I are lovers, I'll turn blood ties into a blood bath."

"You *didn't* bed her?" Iago demanded, horrified.

"No." Aidan scowled at the polished brown face. "She ran off at the height of the storm and I brought her back here. She seems to have a particular fear of storms."

"You," said Iago, aiming a finger at Aidan's chest, "are either a sick man or a saint. She has the body of a *diosa*. A goddess. She adores you. Take her, Aidan. I am certain she's had offers from lesser men than an Irish chieftain. She will thank you for it."

Aidan swore and stalked over to a stone hitch post. Propping his hip on it, he unfurled the parchment and began to read.

The letter from Revelin of Innisfallen was in Irish. Aye, there it was, news that Revelin expected the hoped-for reply from the bishop regarding the marriage Aidan had made in hell and desperation. But that hardly mattered, considering the rest. Each word stabbed into him like a shard of ice. When he finished reading, he looked up at Donal Og and Iago.

"Who brought this?"

"A sailor on a flax boat from Cork. He can't read."

"You're certain?"

"Aye."

Aidan tore the parchment into three equal portions. "Good appetite, my friends," he said wryly. "I pray the words do not poison you."

"Tell me what I am eating," said Iago, chewing on the paper with a pained expression.

Aidan grimaced as he swallowed his portion. "An insurrection," he said.

* * *

By the time Aidan went back to Pippa's chamber, she had dressed herself. Her skirt and bodice had been laced correctly this time.

She sat at the thick-legged oaken table in the center of the room, and she did not look up when he entered. Several objects lay before her on the table. The morning sun streamed over her in great, slanting bars. The light glinted in her hair and gilded her smooth, pearly skin. The daffodil she had picked adorned her curls more perfectly than a comb of solid gold.

He felt a twist of sentiment deep in his gut. Just when he had thought he'd conquered and killed all tenderness within himself, he found a girl who reawakened his heart.

Devil take her. She looked like the soul of virtue and innocence, an angel in an idealized portrait with her sun-drenched face and halo of hair, the lean purity of her profile, the fullness of her lips as she pursed them in concentration.

"Sit down, Your Serenity," she said softly, still not looking up. "I've decided to tell you more because . . ."

"Because why?" Willingly shoving aside the news from Ireland, he approached the table and lowered himself to the bench beside her.

"Because you care."

"I shouldn't—"

"Yet you do," she insisted. "You do in spite of yourself."

He did not deny it, but crossed his arms on the table and leaned forward. "What is all this?"

"My things." She patted the limp, dusty bag she had worn tied to her waist the first day they had met.

"It is uncanny how little one actually *needs* in order to survive. All I ever had fits in this bag. Each object has a special meaning to me, a special significance. If it does not, I get rid of it."

She rummaged with her hand in the bag and drew out a seashell, placing it on the table between them. It was shiny from much handling, bleached white on the outside while the inner curve was tinted with pearly shades of pink in graduated intensity.

"I don't remember ever actually finding this. Mab always said I was a great one for discovering things washed up on shore, and from the time I was very small, I would bring her the most marvelous objects. Apples to juggle, a pessary of wild herbs. One time I found the skull of a deer."

She took out a twist of hair, sharply contrasting black and white secured with a bit of string.

"I hope that's not poor Mab," Aidan commented.

She laughed. "Ah, please, Your Magnificence. I am not so bloodthirsty as that." She stroked the lock. "This is from the dog I was with when Mab found me. Mab swore the beast saved me from drowning. He was half drowned himself, but he revived and lived with us. She said I told her his name was Paul."

She propped her chin in her cupped hand and gazed at the whitewashed wall by the window, where the morning sun created colored ribbons of light on the plastered surface. "The dog died four years after Mab found us. I barely remember him, except—" She stopped and frowned.

"Except what?" asked Aidan.

"During storms at night, I would creep over to his pallet and sleep." She showed him a few more of her treasures—a page from a book she could not read. He

saw that it was from an illegal pamphlet criticizing
the queen's plans to marry the duke of Alençon. "I
like the picture," Pippa said simply, and showed him a
few other objects: a ball of sealing wax and a tiny
brass bell—"I nicked it from the Gypsy wagon"—flint
and steel, a spoon.

It was, Aidan realized with a twinge of pity, the
flotsam and jetsam of a hard life lived on the run.

And then, almost timidly, she displayed things
recently collected: his horn-handled knife, which he
hadn't the heart to reclaim; an ale weight from Nag's
Head Tavern.

She looked him straight in the eye with a devotion
that bordered discomfitingly on worship. "I have
saved a memento of each day with you," she told him.

A tightness banded across his chest. He cleared his
throat. "Indeed. Have you naught else to show me?"

She took her time putting all her treasures back in
the bag. She worked so slowly and so deliberately that
he felt an urge to help her, to speed her up.

The message he had received still burned in his
mind. He had a potential disaster awaiting him in
Ireland, and here he sat, reminiscing with a confused,
possibly deluded girl.

The letter had come all the way from Kerry, first by
horseman to Cork and then by ship. Revelin, the gentle scholar of Innisfallen, had sounded the alarm
about a band of outlaws roving across Kerry, pillaging
at will, robbing even fellow Irish, inciting idle men to
rise against their oppressors. Revelin reported that
the band had reached Killarney town and gathered
around the residence of Fortitude Browne, recently
appointed constable of the district. And a hated
Englishman.

Revelin was not certain, but he suggested the out-laws would try to take hostages, perhaps Fortitude's fat, sniveling nephew, Valentine.

Aidan crushed his hands together as a feeling of powerlessness swept over him. He could do nothing from here in London. Queen Elizabeth had sum-moned him to force him to submit to her and then to regrant his lands to him. Just to show her might, she had kept him waiting. He battled the urge to storm out of London without even a by-your-leave. But that would be suicide—both for him and for his people. Elizabeth's armies in Ireland were the instruments of her wrath.

Just as Felicity had been.

He would write back to Revelin, of course, but beyond that, he could only pray that cooler heads pre-vailed and the reckless brigands dispersed.

"I must show you one more thing," Pippa said, snapping him out of his reverie.

He looked into her soft eyes and for no particular reason felt a lifting sensation inside him.

Something about her touched him. She reminded him of the hardscrabbling people of his district and their stubborn struggle against English rule. Her determination was as stout as that of his father, who had died rather than submit to the English. And yes—Pippa reminded him of Felicity Browne—*before* the cold English beauty had shown her true colors.

"Very well," he said, trying to clear his mind of the potential disaster seething back in Ireland. "Show me one more thing."

She took a deep breath, then released it slowly as she placed her fisted hand on the table. With a deliberate movement she turned her hand over to reveal a sizable yet rather ugly object of gold.

"It's mine," she declared.

"I never said it wasn't."

"I was worried you might. See?" She set it down. "It looks odd now, but it wasn't always. It was pinned to my frock when Mab found me." She angled it toward him. "It's got a hollow interior, as if something once fit inside. The outside used to have twelve matched pearls around a huge ruby in the middle. Mab said this pin, and the finely made frock I wore, are proof that I came from the nobility. What think you, my lord? Am I of noble stock?"

He studied her, the elfin features, the wide, fragile eyes, the expressive mouth. "I think you were made by fairies."

She laughed and continued her tale. "Each year, Mab sold one of the pearls. After she died, I tried to sell the ruby, but I was accused of stealing it and I had to run for my life."

She spoke matter-of-factly, even with an edge of wry humor, but that did not banish the image in his mind of a hungry, frightened young girl escaping the law.

"So now all I have left is this." She turned it over and pointed to some etchings on the back beneath the pin. "I'm quite certain I know what these symbols mean."

"Oh?" He grinned at her earnest expression.

"They are Celtic runes proclaiming the wearer of this brooch to be the incarnation of Queen Maeve."

"Indeed."

She shrugged. "Have you a better idea?"

He angled the brooch so that the sunlight picked out every detail of the etching. He started to nod his head and gamely declare that Pippa was absolutely right, when a memory teased him.

These were no random designs, but writings in a different alphabet. Not Hebrew or Greek; he had studied those. Then why did it look so familiar?

Frowning, Aidan found parchment and stylus. While Pippa watched in fascination, he carefully copied down the symbols, then turned the page this way and that, frowning in concentration.

"Aidan?" Pippa spoke loudly. "You're staring as if it's the flaming bush of Moses."

He handed back the pin. "It's very nice, and I have no doubt you *are* Queen Maeve's descendant." Absently, he tucked away the copy he had made. "Tell me. You faced starvation many times rather than selling that piece of gold. Why did you never try to pawn or trade it?"

She clutched the pin to her chest. "I will never give this up. It is the only thing I belong to. The only thing that belongs to me. When I hold it in my hand, sometimes I can—" She bit her lip and squeezed her eyes shut.

"Can what?"

"Can see them." She whispered the words.

"See them?"

"Yes," she said, opening her eyes. "Aidan, I have never told this to another living soul."

Then don't tell me, he wanted to caution her. *Don't make me privy to your dreams, for I cannot make any of them come true.*

Instead he waited, and in a moment she spoke again. "This idea has consumed me ever since Mab died. I must find them, Aidan. I want to find my family. I want to know where I came from."

"That is only natural. But you have so few clues."

"I know," she admitted. "But sometimes, when I'm just waking up, lying halfway between waking and sleep, I hear voices. See people. It's very vague and jumbled up, but I know it's all connected."

She put away the broken gold pin and clutched at his hand. "I have to believe I'm someone, my lord. Can you understand?"

He brought her hands to his lips and kissed her fingers softly, all the while holding her gaze with his. She made him uncomfortable with her lost, needy look, because it reminded him of what he could never give her.

She needed the constant, unconditional love of a man to heal her and help her learn to love and value herself. He could not possibly be that man.

Ah, he could love her passionately and well.

But not forever.

ven now, weeks after sending my missive to London, I flay myself for heaping woe upon the right brave shoulders of the O Donoghue Mór. I had hoped to soften the blow with the news that the Harridan—that is to say, his lady wife—is gone from his life, but the bishop equivocates and wrings his fat hands and procrastinates. Sometimes I think he fears the Sassenach more than the O Donoghue Mór, which is a grave mistake.

Although I felt it was my duty to inform Aidan about the insurrection, I hope he will not stray from his course in London. An agreement with Elizabeth, she-king of the isles, is our last, best hope. Especially now, and may the dreadful Almighty bless and preserve us.

All his life, my lord of Castleross has been most cruelly buffeted between forces that claim his loyalty, his energy, his love. His father taught him naught but hatred and war, raiding and rieving. I think I am the only one who sees him for what he truly is—a man torn between desire and duty, a son bound to fulfill the dream of a despised father, a chieftain struggling to meet the needs of his people.

Sometimes, in those half-awake pagan dreams that get me in such trouble with the abbot, I see the O Donoghue Mór striking forth unfettered like Fionn Mac Cool along the Giants' Causeway, walking not into the nest of vipers his district has become, but away, far away, toward a freedom earned with the sweat of his brow and great blessed pieces of his too generous heart.

—*Revelin of Innisfallen*

5

"Your Vast Abundance," Pippa announced in the voice she affected to cry up a show, "fortune favors you today." She smiled eagerly as Aidan looked up from the table where he, Donal Og, and Iago were deep in conversation.

Donal Og sent her his customary "go away" scowl. Unwilling to let him dampen her plans, Pippa stuck her tongue out at him. "I was going to invite you along as well, but I might not."

Iago shot up from the table. "Where are we going?"

She beamed at him. Unlike Donal Og, Iago was always game for an adventure.

With Aidan, she could never tell.

He rubbed the bridge of his nose in a way that spoke of a sleepless night. She wished she could alleviate his worries, but he would not even share the nature of his concerns. Didn't he realize how much she cared? How much she longed to take his beautiful, weary face between her hands and ease the frown from his brow with kisses?

"Come along, my lord Reluctance," she urged, embarrassing herself with her own thoughts. "Even Atlas had to let go with one hand to scratch his arse every once in a while."

Aidan rolled his eyes. "How can I refuse such a charming offer?"

"She bestows more titles than the queen herself," said Donal Og.

"Ah, but I give them much more cheaply, Sir Donal of the Small Wit."

"To what do we owe this honor, Mistress Trueheart?" Aidan asked.

She felt an itchy flush creep up her neck to stain her cheeks. Blushing. *She* was blushing. How ridiculous. She was becoming as soft as a wool merchant's wife.

"You seem to need a diversion, my lord. In the past two days you have done nothing but write letters and yell at your men and pace and swear. And drink sack like it was rainwater."

"The perils of being a chieftain, *pequeña*," said Iago.

She dipped a brief curtsy in his direction. Wearing decent clothes suited her better than she ever would have thought. "I have decided to take you to the public theater."

Iago clapped his huge hands. "Capital!" Then his thick brows clashed in puzzlement. "What is the public theater?"

Pippa spread her arms, wanting to embrace all three of them. "It's anything you want it to be."

* * *

An hour later Pippa stood in the stableyard, staring at a saddled horse as if it were a fire-breathing dragon. "I don't see why we can't walk."

"Ah, it'll be quicker," Aidan said. "You're not afraid, are you?"

"Afraid?" Her voice squeaked up an octave. "I? Pippa Trueborn, afraid of a—a midge-witted beast of burden?"

Aidan regarded her with laughing blue eyes. "I thought your first ride might frighten you, and I was right. I suppose we could both mount Grania—"

"Ha!" She poked a finger at the front of his doublet. "Watch me." In a whirl of skirts and indignation, she seized the saddlebow and attempted to hoist herself on the back of the tall bay. The horse's nostrils flared, and it sidled. "Come here, you flap-eared pestilence," she declared, furious now. She grabbed the saddle and managed to shove her foot into a dangling loop. The midge-wit chose that moment to trot across the yard. Shrieking, Pippa hopped along with the horse. "Oh God, the evil carrion's going to kill me," she yelled. "By all that's holy, save me!"

She had just taken a huge breath, readying herself for another shriek, when a pair of strong arms grasped her around the waist. It was Donal Og, laughing so hard she could feel his vast bulk trembling against her. Iago caught the bay's reins and guffawed. She treated them to a prodigious stream of oaths, which only increased their mirth, while Aidan, equally amused, disengaged her foot from the stirrup.

She staggered against him, then pushed back from his chest to glare at them all. "Braying clog-brains," she said. "I will ride this horse, even though I have scambling clowns for teachers."

To her surprise, it was Donal Og who proved to be most helpful. Though the big man took pains to appear gruff, he failed to hide his air of good-humored patience. It was he who showed her the proper way to hold the reins. He helped her hook one leg over the sidesaddle to keep her balance. Iago calmed the horse with a steady patter of lilting non-sense. Before long she sat proud and beaming, certain she had mastered the art of riding.

As the four of them left the yard, she asked, "My lord, what is this horse's name?"

"Didn't I tell you?" The O Donoghue Mór winked. "He is called Midge."

They rode out into Woodroffe Lane, leaving the narrow byways behind and trotting across Finsbury Fields, scattered with windmills. They passed Holywell, teeming with holiday makers and their pic-nics. In the distance, the playing flag of the theater fluttered on the wind, and she gave a whoop of glad-ness.

Making a loud, urgent noise proved to be a mis-take. The gelding surged out of its bearable trot into a full gallop. Pippa hollered in terror and clung, her fingers twining in the horse's flying mane. She looked down to see the ground racing past at a furious rate. Aidan shouted something, but she could not under-stand.

The knowledge that she was about to die a violent death was unexpectedly and intensely liberating. Acceptance stripped away the terror, and she found that the emotion building inside her was no longer fear, but joy. Never had she moved so swiftly. It was like flying, she decided. She was a feather on the breeze, rising higher and higher, and nothing else mattered but the speed.

Twin shadows encroached upon her. Aidan and Donal Og. They came up on either side, forcing her horse to slow. Like the feather, she settled slowly back to earth, her white-knuckled hands relaxing, her mouth widening in a grin of pure delight.

"We made it, my lord," she said, her voice trembling. "Look." Ahead of them loomed a rambling barn and a horse pond, and beyond that, the theater rose like a citadel.

Still exhilarated from the thrill of the ride, she slid to the ground. With a shaking hand, she gave the reins to a waiting groom. Aidan and his companions did the same, tossing coppers to the grooms and admonishing them to look after the beasts.

"Mind his mouth, then," she called after the boy leading her gelding away. "And give him a good long drink." The very idea of someone actually doing her bidding was heady indeed.

Beneath the playing flag gathered an audience of all manner of persons—nobleman, merchant, beggar, and bawd. She tugged at Aidan's sleeve and led them toward the penny gate. "If you don't wish to pay, we can go stand in the yard, but for a penny each, we can—"

"I want to watch from up there." He pointed to the stairway leading to the curving rows of seats.

"Ah, my lord, it's a higher fare, and besides, the seats are for gentry."

"And what are we?" Iago asked with a haughty sniff. "Groundlings?"

She laughed. "I've always been perfectly comfortable

with the penny public. Actors love us, for we laugh and cheer in all the right places. The Puritans hate us."

"Speak to me not of Puritans," Aidan said. "I have had my fill of such people."

"Ah, have you encountered your share of black crows, Your Reverence?"

Donal Og's reply, in Irish, seemed to indicate concurrence, possibly empathy, but before she could demand a translation, Iago hastened them toward the stairs.

"Wait," she said, balking. "I haven't a mask."

"You have now." Aidan held out a black silk half mask. "It is a curious practice, but the English are a curious race."

As she tied on the mask, she wished he had not spoken like that, pointing out how very foreign he was in the only world she had ever known.

But as she climbed the steps with her remarkable escorts, a sense of wonder filled her. As many times as she had come to stand with the penny public, she had never bought a seat at the theater.

The magnificent building was designed in circular fashion like the bear garden in Southwark. The sloping stage jutted out into the center of the arena. Paint and paste brought to life a colorful world of the imagination.

As they emerged onto the seating tier, people stared at Aidan, Donal Og, and Iago. Flushed behind her silken mask, Pippa tilted up her chin in self-importance, enjoying the slack-jawed looks of awe and admiration. Iago, with his dark skin and colorful garb, was the most striking of the three, but Donal Og and Aidan, towering head and shoulders above the prosperous merchants and gentlemen, also garnered their share of admiring looks.

"*Diablo!*" Iago exclaimed, jumping and turning. "Someone *pinched* me."

Pippa smothered a giggle. A plump woman in a cherry-colored gown winked from behind a feathered mask at Iago. But then another woman, whose bosom all but erupted from her bodice, turned her attention to Aidan, lowering her eyelids halfway and running her red tongue over her lips.

Pippa grabbed Aidan's sleeve and pulled him along the riser. "Stay away from such as that one," she warned.

His eyes danced with merriment. "And why should I be doing that?"

"She is a wanton pestilence. You mark my words."

"I mark them," he said, laughing.

Pippa took a deep breath. "She might give you something you can't wash off."

He made a choking sound. Then he put a gentle hand on her shoulder. "Painted cows have little appeal for me." His voice was low and intimate. "I much prefer the charm of innocence."

She felt wingbeats of joy fluttering inside her. Then he winked. "Not to mention a talent for juggling."

A thrill of excitement chased up her spine. She clung to his arm, so proud to be the favored partner of the O Donoghue Mór that she did not even feel the floor beneath her feet. Like a dry sponge, she absorbed the ways of the nobility, learning to flutter a fan in front of her bosom, to crook her finger daintily as she sampled the fare, to cover her mouth as she laughed at some jest on the stage.

The play concerned a thrice cuckolded husband

and his insatiable wife, and Pippa enjoyed it thoroughly, though the drama was not what she would remember that day. Nor would she recall sampling the pies and nuts and comfits Donal Og bought from the trays of the concession men.

What she would remember was being with Aidan. Hearing the rich music of his laughter. Stealing glances at his magnificent profile. Mimicking the manners and expressions of the noble ladies, even though he protested that such posturing moved him not.

Pippa forgot to perform the ritual she had always done in the past. Every time she found herself in a crowd of people, she searched each face for something vague yet familiar—a tilt of the head, a lift of the mouth, something to mark her connection with another human being; something that would make her a member of a family.

Yet today her usual obsession lay quiet inside her. She wondered why, and answered the question in her heart.

When she was with Aidan O Donoghue, she did not *need* a family, for she belonged, heart and soul, to him.

He wondered how old she was. Some women wore their age like a coat of arms, this or that detail announcing plainly, whether she liked it or not, that she was eighteen, or twenty-six, or thirty-two.

Not so Pippa, bouncing at his side, laughing and squealing in delight at the farce on the stage. One moment he was certain she was no more than sixteen, girlish and breathless and fresh as the dawn. Then the melancholy would sweep like a mist over her, and she would make some observation that was so wise and world-weary that he would swear she was as old as time.

A troupe of clowns scurried out on stage, conking each other on the heads with mallets. Pippa threw back her head and guffawed, slapping her knees and forgetting she was amid noble ladies.

"How old are you?" Aidan finally asked. In the same moment that he spoke, he cursed himself for an idiot. He should not care.

Still laughing, she turned to him, then slowly sobered to that piercing earnestness against which he had no defense.

"I don't know," she said.

"How can you not know?"

She ducked her head. Laughter and applause masked their conversation so that he had to put his head very close to hers in order to hear. "You forget, my lord," she said. "I was not born, I was *found.* Who can say what my age was then? Two? Three? Four?"

He guessed that she was born out of wedlock and abandoned by a mother who couldn't afford to keep her, or perhaps she was orphaned when the mother died. The golden brooch and the expensive frock in which she had been found were intriguing clues. Yet even if she did come from noble stock, that did not change her circumstances now. She was utterly alone in the world. All Aidan knew for certain was that she had been wounded by a horrible force—the wound of abandonment.

The pain in her eyes made him want to flinch. "My lord, I can never keep from wondering. Was I *meant* to be found, or to lie there and die?"

He cupped his hands around her shoulders. "Pippa—"

"It was sheer, blind luck that Mab happened upon me, so I can only think I was not meant to live." She stared down at the tumbling clowns on the stage but did not seem to see them. "Imagine that. I had lived only a short time, and then someone decided it should be over for me."

"You cannot know that," he said, covering his pity with gruffness.

She blinked, and a winsome smile erased her melancholy. "I stayed with Mab for twelve years. One year for each pearl she traded."

"You said she always sold one at Michaelmas." He relaxed his grip on her shoulders and turned to feign interest in the stage.

"And then I came to London. I've been here eleven years."

"That narrows it some. You're between twenty-five and twenty-seven years of age."

She bit her lip. "Old enough to be a spinster."

He brushed a bright lock of hair off her brow. "You don't look like any spinster I've ever seen."

With a soft cry of joy, she clung to his arm and pressed her cheek against him. "Ah, you are kind, my lord. Mort used to say all Irish were savages, but you belie that." She gazed up at him with shining eyes. "No one has ever troubled himself to speak kindly to me."

Aidan felt Donal Og's glare like a brand, and he looked over her head at his cousin. Donal Og had managed to find the second most beautiful woman in the place, and the two of them were sharing spiced wine.

"I worry about you, coz. I really do," Donal Og said in Gaelic. "If you were to simply toss up her skirts and play hide the sausage, I'd understand. That's certainly what *I* intend to do with my lovely friend here."

The "lovely friend" affected a pout. "What secrets do you tell in your savage tongue?"

"That thing he does with lamp oil," Pippa said helpfully, "and a wine bot—"

Aidan placed his fingers over her mouth.

"Pay no mind to this mistress of the gutter," Donal Og said to his lady friend. "She has a twisted sense of the absurd."

Aidan was burningly aware of Pippa's hand slipping down his arm slowly, caressingly. "Please yourself and I'll do the same," he said in Irish to Donal Og.

The crowd roared with laughter at the antics of the acting troupe.

"Faith, Aidan, you're the O Donoghue Mór. Think what you're doing," Donal Og said with a note of warning in his voice. "Whether you like it or not, your destiny was sealed long ago by forces beyond the control of any one man. Even the earl of Desmond has taken to the hills like a common riever. You're charged with keeping the peace for an entire district. Not acting nursemaid to Sassenach street rabble."

"Don't you think I know that?" Aidan said. Her hand slid lower, fingers stroking his wrist, lingering over his pulse. He thought he had found his answer with Felicity Browne, a perfect English rose of a woman, part of the settlement to keep the peace, and the biggest mistake he had ever made.

"It'll do you no good to fall in love with such as

that." Donal Og indicated Pippa with a jerk of his head.

"And why would you be thinking I'm falling in love?" Aidan demanded, hot with irritation. "Sure, and that's the stupidest thing a man ever heard."

Even as he spoke, her hand slid into his and stayed there shyly, like a small wild bird huddling from a storm.

No affinity with this woman was possible, even if he *did* want her. Yet she fascinated him. She gave his natural sense of mastery an unexpected jolt, challenging and contradicting him, making him laugh and breaking his heart all at once. Every moment with her gleamed like a jewel, but the moments were just as fleeting as the flash of the sun on moving water: brilliant, intense, and instantly gone.

Each minute with this woman, he thought with a tightening of his chest, was a glimpse of what could never be.

He forced himself to laugh at the antics on the sloping stage to cover the anguish that twisted his heart. If he were truly his father's son, he would simply bed the wench. God knew, his body kept urging him to do just that. Never, ever, had he so yearned to taste a woman's mouth, to take her in his arms and bury himself in the warmth of her.

The unquestioning trust she placed in him was disconcerting, especially considering his thoughts. Didn't she know the position of an Irish chieftain was tenuous, his life likely to end in blood and fire?

Aidan made his decision. As the acting troupe came out to claim their huzzahs and tossed coppers, he thought of one way to make certain Pippa remained safe, long after he was gone.

* * *

"Absolutely not," she said the next day, trying to look outraged, when inside, her heart was breaking. "I'll never do as you suggest, my lord of the stupid ideas."

She paced the garden walk, sharply aware of the beauty of the day, the foxglove and columbine making a riot of springtime color and scent, the glinting sunlight touching the tops of the yew and elm trees.

"It is a fine idea." Aidan leaned against the edge of the well and crossed his booted feet at the ankles. He looked so indolently handsome that she wanted to slap him. "I think you should consider it."

"Court!" she burst out, almost choking on the word. "I cannot believe you think I could go to court. As a jester, perhaps. But as a lady? Never."

"At least hear me out." He wore his tunic open at the throat, and try as she might, she could not stop from imagining what his chest looked like, broad and muscled, dark, silky hair in the center. . . .

She was instantly impatient with herself. Reaching up, she plucked three small green pears from a tree and juggled them idly, round and round. "I'm listening. I'll try not to snort in disgust too loudly."

He shoved away from the well and clasped his hands behind his back, looking for all the world like a battle commander planning a strategy.

Ah, but he is planning a strategy, said an ugly little voice inside her. A campaign to drive her out of his life.

But I've only just found you, she wanted to say.

"I've not yet met your queen," he said, "but I'm told she values lively company." His gaze followed the whirling pears she juggled effortlessly.

"And I've heard she took away a man's knighthood for farting in her presence," Pippa retorted.

"She would like you."

"How, pray, did you make the leap from farting knights to me? And how do you know if the queen would like me or not?"

"Everyone likes you. Even Donal Og."

"He has such a charming way of showing it. What was it he called me this morning?"

"A nightmare in taffeta." He could not keep the mirth from his voice.

"See?" She kept the pears in motion and pretended nonchalance. "And you, Aidan O Donoghue? Do *you* like me?"

"I am responsible for you. I want to do what is best for you."

"Is that peculiar to the Irish?" she asked.

"What?"

"Pretending to answer a question when you've given me no answer at all." She caught the pears, then tossed him one without warning. He caught it deftly. She took a bite of hers, making a face at the unripe tartness. "And how have I managed to survive twenty-five to twenty-seven years without you?" she demanded acidly.

"You've *survived,* Pippa. But can you honestly say you have lived? You say you want to find your family. You have reason to believe they were of gentle birth. What better place to begin looking than at court? You can find people there who keep bloodlines, census rolls, registers stolen from churches. You can inquire about families that lost a child—presumably to drowning."

She braced herself against a tug of yearning. "I

think we both know what my chances are," she said
quietly. "I don't know my family name, so how can I
find myself in record books?"

He touched her hand. Did the man always have to
be so damned tender?

"Don't say no," he said. "At least not yet. There is a
masque at Durham House tonight. I am expected to
attend. Say you'll come with me. Give yourself a
chance to be with men who might be able to help you.
Meet Robert Dudley—properly—and Christopher
Hatton and Evan Carew—"

The names jumbled up in her mind, strange and
alluring. "No," she said, "I don't belong there. I could
never—"

"Tell me my ears deceive me." He cocked his head.
"I never thought I would see you shrink in fear from a
challenge."

She turned her back on him. Damn him, damn
him, damn him. How was it that he could see into her
heart, even when she took pains to hide it?

"What do you fear?" he asked, taking her by the
shoulders and turning her to face him. "That you'll
never find out who you are—or that you will?"

"What if I turn out to be the by-blow of some gouty
old duke?" she asked.

"Then we'll call you Lady Pippa." Idly he tossed
the pear up and down. "Perhaps this will mean you'll
have to stop thinking of your mother as a princess in a
glass tower. You might learn that she is all too
human, as imperfect as you or I."

She stood staring up at him for a long moment.
How fine he looked, with the glory of springtime
blooming all around him. He was taking away her
long-held dream, aye, but he was offering another

dream in its place—one that had a chance of coming true.

"All right," she said, "I'll go."

"Iago said you sent away the maids," Aidan called in annoyance through her chamber door.

"So I did, Your Splendidness," she called back in a cheerful voice. It was her best, brightest, fool-the-crowd voice, and she had worked for years to perfect it. No one would guess that inside she smarted with wounds that cut to the quick of her pride. "It is beneath me to consort with such a mean class of people."

"They were sent specially by Lady Lumley," Aidan said. "Did you let them stay long enough to dress you?"

She leaned her forehead on a lozenge-shaped pane of a mullioned window and drew a deep breath past the lump in her throat. *I only let them stay long enough to call me the O Donoghue's whore. The laced mutton. The primped poppet.*

"I've decided not to go after all," she called. Ah, damnation. Her voice cracked with emotion. It was too much to hope he would not notice.

He noticed. He pushed open the door and strode into the chamber. He looked magnificent in a dark wool tunic and leather leggings. Iago had added polished silver beads to the long, braided strand of his hair. He looked wild and brooding, faintly danger-ous as he stopped stock still when he caught sight of her.

She wanted to shrivel and die, for she was clad only in an undershift and chemise, stockings pooled around her ankles and the rest of the elaborate costume laid out in confusion across the bed.

But he was not looking at her state of dishabille. He was looking at her face. Into her eyes.

"You've been crying," he said.

"The scent ball makes me sneeze," she insisted, plucking up the pomander by its string and holding it at arm's length.

He took the ball from her and set it on a table. "Is that why you sent the maids away? I went to some trouble to bring them here, with the dressmaker and that frock." He gestured at the garment, a silken fantasy of ice blue and silver. When she had laid eyes on it she had gone weak in the knees, for she had never seen such a beautiful garment. But that was before the maids had started taunting her.

"They say it was originally made for a lady-in-waiting," Aidan said, "but she—" He broke off and lifted one of the sleeves, inspecting it.

"She what?" Pippa demanded.

"She was banished from court."

"Why?"

He dropped the open-worked sleeve and faced her with an honestly baffled expression. "According to Iago, the lady in question petitioned the queen for permission to marry, and the queen refused. A few months later, the lady was discovered to be with child, having secretly wed her lover. He was imprisoned in the Tower, and she was sent from court."

For a moment, Pippa forgot her own troubles. "Why?"

"I asked the same question. One person dared to answer, but only in a whisper. The queen cannot find anyone to marry, and she is past the age to bear children."

"Marrying and having children are not all they're reputed to be," she said.

For a moment, a cold shadow seemed to pass over him. Then, just as fleetingly, amusement danced in his eyes. "And you are an authority on such matters."

"Dove once told me that celibate priests advise people on marriage."

"Ah. Now. About the dress—"

"Surely a frock to bring me good luck," Pippa said sourly.

"It's not to your taste?"

"My lord, the gown is fine. The dressmaker and her assistants were not to my taste."

"Did they offend you?"

"I didn't take offense on my own behalf. I've been called far worse than whore, laced mutton, primped pigeon—or was it poppet?. . ." She sent him her most insouciant grin, then her most outraged scowl. "It's what they said about you, my lord, that enraged me."

He lifted one eyebrow. "Oh? And what might that be?"

"Well, I'm not certain. I've never heard such talk before. What does bedswerver mean?"

His face flushed scarlet, and he ducked his head. "I do not understand the Sassenach, letting their women talk like tavern doxies."

"And what do you 'let' your women in Ireland do?" she asked.

Icy fury replaced the sheepish humor in his face. Then he blinked, and the dark look passed. "We don't let them do anything. They do as they please." He stepped toward her. "I'm sorry you had to endure those harpies. Let me help you dress. I swear I'll not call you names, except, perhaps . . ." He cleared his throat, endearingly discomfited.

"Except what?"

"*A storin.* Or perhaps *a gradh.*" His eyes smiled into her soul, raising a shiver on her skin.

She could not have resisted if she wanted to. "I submit!" she cried out in a theatrical swoon, bringing her wrist to her brow and swaying perilously. "I am yours to do what you will with me!"

Chuckling, he surveyed the elements of the costume on the bed. "I'm not certain I know how all this goes together. Truly, I do not know how you have managed to make the O Donoghue Mór play the handmaid not once, but twice."

"You secretly love it. You know you do."

He picked up an evil, steel-spined object. "A corset?"

"No, thank you. I have never understood why people wish to rearrange the way the Lord made them."

"Let us do this underskirt, then. It is pretty enough."

It was nothing less than splendid, the fine blue fabric shot through with silver threads, the hem worked in the same scalloped design as the sleeves. He pulled it over her head and positioned it around her waist. With his hands around behind her, he began tying the laces.

She experienced an overwhelming urge to lay her cheek upon his chest, to close her eyes and revel in their closeness. What would he say? she wondered, if he knew he had given her the only tenderness she had ever known?

Before she found the courage to confess her thoughts, he added the overskirt of heavier fabric, parted in the front to reveal the dainty underskirt.

Then came the bodice. "This is all backward, my lord," Pippa declared when he stepped behind her to lace it. "What possible use is a garment that laces up the *back*?"

"'Tis of social value. It proves you're rich enough to have maids to dress you."

"Oh. And how rich need I be that I have an Irish chieftain to dress me?"

"For that," he said, his warm breath caressing the back of her neck, "you need only be Pippa." His knuckles grazed her as he worked, and she began to tingle all over.

He gave her a feeling of coming to a roaring fire from out of the bitter cold. If it were possible to actually float, she would have done so. He had a perfect sense of what to say, when to tease and when to be serious. He was magical, his charm so abundant that she paid no heed to the occasional shadow that fell over him.

She laughed at the extra sleeves he laced over her blousy white chemise. Apparently the more sleeves one possessed, the better. She balked, at last, when he picked up the stiff ruff collar.

"You can send that back to the torture chamber it came from," she declared. "I've done time in stocks that are more comfortable than that. Why on earth would someone take forty spans of lace, then crumple it up and make it all stiff with—with—"

"Starch, they call it," he said. "Because someone terribly clever invented starch, I suppose. This is meant to be sewn on after you're dressed."

"Is *that* how the collar stays on? How perfectly ridiculous. No wonder the nobles look like stuffed puppets who spend four hours dressing each day."

He winked at her and set down the ruff. "If you don't wish to wear it, I have a better idea."

"What is that?"

From a pouch on his hip he took a glittering necklace. The stones were rounded and polished, aglow with violet fire. Strange and sinuous knotwork twisted through the silver setting.

"Holy mother of God," she whispered. "It is too precious for me to wear."

"Believe me, you have more worth than a bauble. I had meant this as a gift for another lady, but she's being recalcitrant."

A chill touched her heart. She should hardly be surprised by his preference for another, but that did not dull the hurt. "Surely, Your Serenity, you should save it for that lady."

He paused with the necklace dangling elegantly from his fingers. "Glory be," he said softly, his eyes crinkling at the corners. "I believe you are jealous."

"Ha!" she burst out, her face flaming. "That is but a fond dream of yours, my lord Peacock. Flatter yourself not at my expense."

He laughed softly. "Your protests flatter me."

"Conceit," she said, "thy name is O Donoghue."

When he stopped laughing, he said, "This was not a gift of the heart, but one of diplomacy. It was meant for the queen."

It was the last answer she had expected. "You want me to wear a necklace you brought for the queen?"

"For Gloriana herself." His tone mocked the name. "You would improve on the beauty of the jewel. It's amethyst," he said, "mined from the hills of the Burren." He stepped behind her and fastened the clasp. "The design is Celtic. Very ancient."

And lovely, its facets flashing as she moved this way and that. She whirled around to face him. "Are you magic?" she demanded.

He frowned, his black brows knitting in bemusement. "Magic?"

"You know. Under an enchantment. Mab once told me a story about a fairy prince who comes to life and grants a woman's every wish."

"I'm a chieftain, not a prince," he said, "and I'm certainly no fairy."

She almost laughed at his wry indignation. Then he bent and brushed his lips over her brow. The fluttering wingbeat of his caressing mouth echoed deep inside her.

"But I do confess," he whispered, "the idea of granting your every wish does have a certain appeal."

Diary of a Lady

There is a masque tonight at Durham House, but we have declined the invitation. Richard will go, for Richard is too young to be burdened with my pain. Ah, how hard we labor to protect our children. Richard has never known of our loss; since it occurred before he was born, we saw no point in telling him.

Only my dear husband understands the private ritual I perform each year on this day, the anniversary of the tragedy. At sunset, I shall take a bit of wood and a candle down the watersteps, just there, at the spot where I kissed my tiny daughter good-bye so long ago. I shall remember looking into her wide, trusting eyes and pressing an extra kiss "for later" into the palm of her chubby hand.

Then I'll set the little boat adrift with the candle burning, and I'll stand on the bank and watch it while the tears come, and I shall pray for the strength to bear the unbearable.

—Lark de Lacey,
Countess of Wimberleigh

6

"I'll not be carried in a box like a corpse," Pippa declared.

Annoyed by her mutiny, Aidan took a deep breath. Donal Og and Iago exchanged looks of pure exasperation. Summoning an excess of patience, Aidan said, "Coaches seem strange to me as well. But Lord Lumley assured me that people of fashion ride in them."

Like a wispy blue fairy with a sour disposition, she peered suspiciously into the dark interior of the boxy wooden Mecklenburg coach. "*Dead* people of fashion," she groused. "This is a hearse."

"It is like a pageant-wagon," Iago said.

Aidan scowled at him. "What's a pageant-wagon?"

"They park them on street corners and act out plays on them." Iago folded his arms across his chest. "Right, *pequeña*?"

"This is nothing like a pageant-wagon. It's all

enclosed and dark within," she said. "It must be for people who have something to hide."

Which makes me the perfect passenger, thought Aidan.

"Or people who do not care where they are going." She glared up at the driver, who perched on a narrow railed bench in front of the box. He glared back.

"I'll look after you," Aidan promised. With both large hands fitted snugly around her waist, he lifted her up and in. Then he took a seat on the lumpy horsehair bench opposite her. The interior of the coach was dim and close, smelling of leather and horse. The intimacy seized him, and his breath caught with an excruciating feeling of warmth for the recalcitrant woman scowling at him.

"You *still* haven't bedded the wench," Donal Og remarked in Irish as he and Iago clambered into the coach. "That much I can tell from your pained expression."

"Donal Og," Aidan said with surprising calm, "you are my blood kin, the closest thing I have to a brother. But if you make one more remark like that, I will cheerfully change your religion."

The driver cracked his whip and whistled. The coach surged forward. Pippa swore, nearly lurching out of her seat.

Donal Og slapped his hands on his knees. "What, the ice-eyed O Donoghue Mór is falling in love with a common doxy?"

"I won't hear her insulted, even in Gaelic."

"It is love," said Iago, nodding and rubbing his chin.

Setting his jaw, Aidan stole a surreptitious glance at Pippa. The glow of the sunset gilded her as she sat across from him, her cheek against the side of the unglazed window and her daintily gloved hands clenched in her lap. Moist lipped, wide eyed, her curls a halo, she had never looked more enchanting.

"I can't love her," Aidan muttered, stung by a feeling of futility.

"What makes you think you have a choice?" asked Donal Og.

"Speak English," Pippa said, "else I'll think you're talking about me. But of course you are." She shook an accusing finger. "Aren't you?"

"Yes," Iago admitted before Aidan could stop him. "We are explaining to the O Donoghue Mór that he has fallen in love with you."

"I am blessed by the most loyal of friends," said Aidan, his ears burning.

And after all, it was Pippa who rescued him, laughing. "Don't be ridiculous, Iago. Are such romantic illusions peculiar to the Irish, or to men in general? Now, cease your gossip and pay attention. I shall tell you about this part of London."

"As you wish." Iago put out a strong arm to steady her as the coach swayed around a corner and started down Ivy Bridge Lane.

As she chattered on about famous houses and shops, Aidan wished he could feel for Pippa a simple, healthy, red-blooded lust. Instead, he looked at her and was seized by an emotion so piercing he felt actual pain.

She touched people. Affected them. Iago was her devoted slave. Even Donal Og, as hard and rugged as the Cliffs of Moher, admired her. And when he thought no one noticed, he was patient and kind. She brought out a man's urge to protect, perhaps because she insisted on not being protected at all.

As if she felt him looking at her, she met his gaze. A fleeting, almost shy smile curved her lips. "This is not so bad after all, Your Abundance," she said. "I rather like riding in a coach."

He answered her with a smile, taking pleasure in her enjoyment. *Who are you?* he wondered. The sad truth was, she had probably been born to a trull who could not afford to keep her, didn't want her. The words she had spoken came back to haunt him: *Was I meant to be found, or to lie there and die?*

He wanted to hold her close, to stroke her hair and reassure her, to promise her she had not been abandoned but was simply lost. What sort of creature would leave a child like Pippa? He could almost believe she had no mother at all, but was made by the *sidhe*.

After passing under the gatehouse archway and into an inner courtyard, the coach lumbered and creaked to a halt. Liveried footmen swarmed forth to help the passengers out. Durham House was lofty and stately, with marble pillars and two great turrets. The grace-and-favor residence embodied the very essence of English wealth and privilege. Yet rather than holding it in awe, Aidan felt contempt. The Sassenach labored hard to set himself above his people. Not so Aidan, and his blood was the blood of kings. He held his banquets and councils in broad, open fields, welcoming all rather than walling himself off from the common folk.

He glanced at Pippa and saw that she was impressed indeed, pausing at the main door to finger a silk tassel hanging from a bell pull. But when she began to untie the prize, he realized her intent and chuckled. "I think it would be bad form to be caught nicking the furnishings."

She laughed, too, and followed him inside.

In the anteroom of the gallery, servants gaped in open admiration at Pippa, and Aidan felt a swell of pride. Not so long ago, these awestruck retainers would not have found her good enough to spit upon; now they bowed and stooped, convinced she was a highborn lady.

Bug-eyed stares greeted Iago; there was the usual amount of surreptitious brushing against him to see if his coloring was real or just painted on. He bore it all with his usual charm and aplomb.

At the arched entranceway to the gallery, they could see a whirling sea of merrymakers. Pippa hesitated, her color fading to a chalky pallor. To Aidan's surprise, she looked terrified. But then, before he could reassure her, she threw back her shoulders, lifted her chin, and swept forward proudly, trailed by Iago and a dozen slack-jawed stares.

Donal Og nudged Aidan hard in the ribs. "We have not even been announced yet. What will happen when the guests see them?"

People were staring. Pippa noticed that right away as she walked between Iago and Donal Og, all three of them preceding Aidan, the ranking lord. The first person they encountered was a man in a red silk doublet. His splendid mustache flew outward as he greeted them. Pippa pointed her toe, about to launch into a curtsy.

Donal Og put his hand discreetly on her arm. "That's the majordomo, lass. He'll announce us."

The very idea of being announced was as heady as a cup of fine wine.

The majordomo shouted out their names to the other guests in the crowded room. A mass of people, easily as many as she had seen gathered at St. Paul's, turned inquisitive looks on the Irish party.

Iago, of course, was the most striking, with his dark skin and bright cloak, his ready smile. Like a seasoned performer, he played to the curiosity seekers, flaring his nostrils and pressing his palms together as if performing some exotic, foreign greeting.

Pippa earned her living by making a spectacle of herself, so she found the attention gratifying. Introduced as the mistress of revels of the O Donoghue Mór, she beamed at the watching throng, singling out a few for a special nod or wave—a fat man encased like sausage in an overstuffed doublet and scarlet hose, a lady holding a spangled half mask to her face, a pageboy who nearly choked on a grape when she winked at him.

"So this is our Irish chieftain," a man exclaimed, smiling with ill-concealed fury at Aidan. "You look quite as savage as your father." The smile hardened. "He murdered my own father, you know. I am Arthur, Lord Grey de Wilton."

Pippa stared in astonishment as hatred crackled between the two—the slim, elegant Englishman and the magnificent, black-haired Irish chieftain.

"I am sorry for your loss," Aidan said, his voice toneless, almost bland. "It is a pity your father attempted to drive off a herd of my father's cattle without paying for them." He walked away.

Pippa started after him, but Iago held her back. "Give him time to simmer down. He is not fond of defending his father."

Donal Og joined his cousin, bent his fair head to Aidan's dark one, and whispered something in Gaelic. Aidan gave him a curt reply, then turned and took Pippa's hand, leading her down three steps into the crowd.

A blur of London's elite followed on a whirlwind of introductions: the Lord Keeper and Lord Chancellor, a Swedish princess, three knights from Saxony, an admiral and a bishop, and dozens of grande dames and ladies of rank. Lady Helmsley dropped her feathered mask, raised a pair of spectacles to her eyes, and peered at Pippa.

Pippa, who had never seen spectacles before, leaned forward and peered back.

"Is it customary for an Irish lord to go about with his mummer?" the lady asked. "And a bodyguard of one hundred savages?"

Pippa sent her a dazzling smile. "Madam, do you have a point to make or are you simply trying to convince me you are a horse's backside?"

"Well!" The lady fanned herself in agitation. "In sooth you must be his lightskirt."

"Only in my dreams, Your Ladyship. Only in my dreams."

Iago led her off before she did damage to the woman. The next people she encountered were far more pleasant—a merry poet named Sharpe, a pair of identical twins called Lucy and Letty, a fat woman with a goiter, and the queen's dwarf, Ann. The tiny, stocky lady fascinated Pippa, and they chatted happily for a few moments.

"Get yourself to court," Ann advised her. "It's the only place for the likes of us."

"You are likely correct," Pippa admitted.

High in a railed gallery above the throng, musicians played a dance tune. After an hour of smiling and nodding, Pippa wanted desperately to dance. But Aidan's grim expression and stormy eyes warned her that now was not the time to ask him. Instead, she looked for a way to extract him from the press of admirers and curiosity seekers.

She gripped his arm. "Here comes that foul Lady Helmsley again. Shall I tell her she has a spider crawling up her back?"

The haughty grande dame glared at them and swept past. Pippa looked down into her hand at the diamond bracelet she held.

"Where did you get that?" Aidan asked in an undertone. "Ah, faith, mind your manners." He snatched the pilfered bracelet from her and dropped it on the floor. "My lady," he called after her, "you dropped this." With an exaggerated, courtly flourish, he restored it to her.

If Pippa had not known better, she would have believed the sincerity of his glittering smile and gallant pose. In the blink of an eye, Lady Helmsley's disdain thawed. She thanked him with a disgusting simper before moving off.

"I genuflect to your Irish charm," Pippa whispered.

"No more thievery," Aidan muttered. "I mean it."

She lifted her hand to her heart. "Word of honor."

He glanced down at her, and his expression softened. "Are you hungry?"

"Always."

And then he laughed. It was the most beautiful sound she knew. He led her through the crowd, and she could not help but notice how different he was from the English nobles.

The men in the room wore silken hose and kid slippers. The blousy canion trousers bulged obscenely, as if the wearer had done something disgraceful in them. The form-fitting peascod doublets, all crusted with baubles, added a haughty puffiness to chests too skinny to impress on their own. Just as Iago had said, the English gentlemen had lovelocks bobbing beneath their velvet toques.

In contrast, Aidan wore leather leggings and boots cuffed at the knee, a tunic cinched at the waist by a wide belt decked with polished stones, and the dramatic blue mantle that swirled around him like a king's raiments.

"Colleen." His soft voice near her ear startled her.

"What!"

"You're staring at me rather than feasting your eyes on the cream of English nobility." Bemused, he placed a silver cup in her hand and coaxed her to drink.

She tasted the musky sweet wine and smiled. "In sooth, my lord, you are much more agreeable to look upon than the others."

He muttered something Celtic and dark.

"What?" she demanded.

"Sometimes you are too frank for your own good." He held her by the shoulders and turned her around to face the crowd.

"Now, pay attention," he said sternly. "Look at those I point out. There are those who hold sway over the queen's favor, and their friendship would not come amiss."

Flagrantly disobeying him, she shut her eyes and leaned back against his endless hard length. How good it felt to be held, to have his warmth so close to her, to inhale his scent of leather and man.

"Pippa!" His fingers pressed into her shoulders.

Her eyes drifted open. "I'm listening."

"All right. See that man standing in front of the tapestry?"

Her gaze swept a floral hanging and came to rest upon a man all in black. His thin mustache twitched like tiny whiplashes.

"Yes?"

"Watch him closely. I assure you, his spies are watching us."

"Spies?" she hissed, fascinated.

"That's Francis Walsingham. Hates Catholics with a vengeance and would cheerfully see me roasted alive if he could get away with it. He is the queen's spymaster. Everyone despises him, the queen included, but they have a healthy respect for his abilities. With him are Lords Norfolk and Arundel, both pleasant, neither particularly dangerous."

His hand found the nape of her neck and cradled it gently. She felt giddy from the caress, but he seemed determined to educate her at the moment. He turned her toward a white-haired little man and a tall, fair-haired lady.

"That is the Venetian ambassador. He is shrewd, fair, and knows everyone's business. The woman with him is his widowed daughter Rosaria, the Contessa Cerniglia. She is even more shrewd than her father, but I have heard she does *not* play fair."

"How do you know all this?" she asked, her head swimming with titles.

"The queen has her spies and I have mine. I cannot afford to ignore Sassenach matters of state," he said. "Well? What think you of this esteemed company?"

She sighed. The splendid revelers shimmered in the

setting of gilded halls and endless glass-windowed galleries, the torchlit rambling gardens and fountains outside, the priceless art treasures and tapestries. She studied faces—shining eyes behind masks, smiling mouths—and wondered if one of these ladies had lost a child long ago, and if she had, would she have put it out of her mind, or did she think of it constantly?

"I don't know," she said at last. "In my dreams, I grew up in a place like this, surrounded by cheerful, wealthy people. Yet I don't feel as if I belong here."

"In most of these people, the cheerfulness and sometimes even the wealth are an illusion."

"What about my parents?" she wondered, feeling an anxious tightening of her stomach. The very idea that she could belong to such company seemed ludicrous. "Shall I just go and tap someone on the shoulder and say, 'Pardon me, but did you happen to misplace a daughter once upon a time?'"

He rubbed the nape of her neck. "Don't be hasty, else you go against the wrong person. We should find William Cecil and begin our inquiries with him, for he is one of the few ministers I trust. I'd surely hate to see you accused of being a fraud."

She turned in his arms so fast that for a moment he truly was embracing her. He dropped his hands. She muttered, "I would die if they accused me of being a fraud."

His blue eyes scanned the crowd, lingering on the balding head of Cecil, Lord Burghley. "No one had a particular reaction to hearing your name spoken. Of course, we don't know for certain what your name is."

She sighed again. "Do you know what I would really like?"

"What?"

"For you to dance with me."

She braced herself for ridicule or a rejection. Instead he smiled and bowed from the waist.

"In sooth the Sassenach way of dancing is rather sedate compared to the Irish way. But I'll try to please you," he said.

She could not feel the floor beneath her feet as she followed him to the dancing quadrangle. Couples moved in a circle, their slow, measured steps reminiscent of the pace of a funeral cortege.

Aidan and Pippa fell in, hands clasped and raised, his arm circling her waist.

"Who died?" she asked from the corner of her mouth.

He gave a stifled laugh. "The musicians?"

As they passed Donal Og and Iago, Aidan mouthed a few silent words, then jerked his head toward the railed gallery.

"What are they doing?" she asked.

"Trying to bring the dead to life?" he teased.

Iago and Donal Og disappeared behind a paneled wall. A few seconds later, they emerged into the high gallery. Donal Og took up a skin drum while Iago helped himself to a long flute.

A loud trill from the flute halted the dancers in their path. The master of revels, looking white faced and harassed, went to the rail and gave a forced smile.

"My lords and ladies," he called, "in honor of our noble guest from Ireland, we shall give a musical salute."

Full of a young man's swaggering confidence, the earl of Essex sidled up to Aidan. "That was ill mannered," he said, "but I suppose all Irish are rude, judging by those I have met."

Pippa gave him her biggest smile. "Why, my lord! Did you practice for years to become insufferable or does the talent come naturally?"

He stared at her as if she were a worm floating in his cup. "I beg your pardon?"

She sent him a broad wink. "I suppose, lacking a prick, you endeavor to become one, is that it?"

Essex's eyes flared. "O Donoghue, take your doxy from my sight or I'll—"

Aidan moved one step forward. He stood so close to the earl that no one but Pippa saw him take a fistful of Essex's padded doublet and twist until the starched ruff nearly engulfed his face.

"One more word about her," Aidan said with icy calm, "and I'll wipe the floor with you, *my lord.*"

The music exploded into a lively, almost frenzied reel. Aidan turned his back on Essex, gave a loud Gaelic howl, and started to dance.

His wild spirit engulfed Pippa like a wave. In his aggressive, overbearing presence, she felt swept along on a raft of excitement.

It was easy to dance with him. She simply had to submit. He held her by the waist, lifting her so her feet didn't touch the floor. She spun and laughed; people began clapping and stamping their feet to the rapid rhythm. Round and round they whirled, and the glittering hall turned in a blur. Before she knew what was happening, he smoothly broke away from the crowd and danced her out through a set of tall doors to a dimly lit loggia adjacent to the hall.

The music subsided and they came to a halt. Pippa collapsed, breathless and laughing, against his chest.

"That was splendid," she declared. "A good dance is very much like I imagine flying would be."

A high-pitched giggle came from the shadows of the loggia. She turned in time to see a beautiful lady rush up through the darkened garden.

Like Pippa, the lady was breathless and flushed. Unlike Pippa, this one smiled with lips that were full and bruised by kisses. Her ruff hung askew; grass stains smeared the hem of her gown. Her eyes sparkled with the secret joy of having been loved well and recently.

"Aidan," Pippa whispered, "who—"

"Cordelia, there you are." A man dashed in and snatched her around her wasp-thin waist. "My beloved rodent of virtue has scuttled away!" They both laughed, the lady unoffended, and he led her into the circle of torchlight from the hall.

Pippa froze. For a moment, she thought her heart had stopped beating, but the next instant it lurched into a rapid, nervous tattoo. As from a distance, he heard Aidan speak her name questioningly, but she could not answer him.

She could only stare at the fair-haired stranger.

To call him handsome would be laughable, for so banal a term could not begin to describe the lavish male beauty with which he had been gifted.

Hair the color of the sun crowned a face that would not have been out of place amid a host of angels. Full, bowed lips. A glorious symmetry of high cheekbones and sweeping brown lashes around eyes the color of morning glory. Just to make certain this man would never, ever, find his equal in looks, his Maker in all Her wisdom had added a perfect cleft in his chin, an incomparable set of white teeth, and a look of irreverent humor that made the corners of his mouth turn up.

"Colleen." Aidan spoke with amused tolerance. "If you stare at him any harder, he'll think you're putting him under the evil eye."

She blinked. The image of the stranger shimmered like new-minted gold. He was laughing now, leading his lady into the gallery, head bent toward her as they shared a private jest.

His appearance garnered many stares. Women young and old contrived to pass by him; one dropped a fan and tittered when he picked it up. Another managed to lose her garter. As the golden Adonis replaced it, he murmured the age-old disclaimer: *"Honi soit qui mal y pense."*

"She looks ill," Aidan said with laughter in his voice. "Do you think she'll swoon?"

All at once Pippa, too, was struck by the ridiculousness of it, and she giggled. "Who *is* that man?" she said.

"I don't know. My question is, how can he bear all the simpering?"

She leaned against the door frame and watched the young man, a glowing star surrounded by basking lesser beauties. Not just the women, but the men too seemed drawn to him. He had an air of easy grace; he was comfortable with himself and others. He seemed to have no particular problem with being the most beautiful man in the world.

"Such attention," she said to herself, "cannot be so hard to bear."

Unexpectedly, she felt Aidan's hand at the back of her waist. The gesture was subtle yet full of tenderness.

For a moment she was staggered by an idea so

outrageous that she caught her breath in surprise. This man, this Irish stranger, understood her. He knew her need for attention, for approval, for a gentle touch.

"Aidan," she said, emotion welling in her throat, "I must tell you—"

"—the honor of this dance?" asked a golden voice.

Her mouth dropped open. With infinite patience, Aidan placed his finger under her chin and closed her mouth.

The golden man bowed before her, then held out his hand.

"I daresay my lovely guest would like to dance with you," Aidan said. "Perhaps you would do her the honor of introducing yourself."

The god took her hand. As he led her to the dance floor, he inclined his shining head in Aidan's direction. "My name is Richard, my lord. Richard de Lacey."

A curious change came over Aidan. Until now, he had shown tolerance and bemused patience. Upon hearing the man's name, the O Donoghue Mór all but turned to stone.

Richard de Lacey drew her into a pavane, tilting his head to whisper into her ear, "You are quite the most dazzling creature in here. But clearly, the O Donoghue claims you for his own."

She glanced over her shoulder at Aidan. He had not moved. "You know who he is."

"My little sugared quince, everyone has heard of the lord of Castleross. Under different circumstances, I would endeavor to be his friend. But as things stand, he is bound to despise me." He nodded regally to passing couples. "And not just because I find you dazzling."

"Why, then?" she asked, intrigued by him but missing Aidan's nearness.

"Because I have been granted a commission in Ireland, in the district of the O Donoghue Mór."

By the next morning, Pippa was sick and tired of hearing about Richard de Lacey. The chamber she shared with several other ladies rang with passionate recitations of his charms, both physical and social.

"I couldn't believe it. He *touched* me. He actually *touched* me." Lady Barbara Throckmorton Smythe held out a limp, pale hand.

"Ooh!" Three others gathered around to inspect the favored appendage.

Finally, after hearing Richard de Lacey compared to every mythical and astrological figure the ladies could imagine, Pippa gave an exasperated snort.

Lady Barbara glared at her. "Well, mistress of revels, I did not see you sniffing at his invitation to dance."

"True." Pippa winced; the handmaid who was combing her short hair caught a snag. "I reserve my sniffing for less desirable invitations."

"What was it like?" Bessie Josephine Traylor demanded. "You *must* tell us, for you're the only one he danced with other than that painted tart, Cordelia Carruthers."

"Yes, tell us," urged Lady Jocelyn Bellmore. She studied Pippa's short golden curls, then ran a hand through her own long red hair. "I've been thinking I'd have this cropped short. Richard adores short hair."

Pippa rolled her eyes. What silly gamehens they

were, pecking and squawking after the cock of the walk. But they were looking at her so expectantly that the natural performer in her came out.

"Well, I am far too much the lady to go into detail," she said in a conspiratorial whisper. "But if I were to give Richard de Lacey a nickname, it would surely be the Blond Stallion."

The women collapsed in helpless giggles and the maid dropped her comb. Pippa picked it up, chuckling at her companions, and grew thoughtful as they chattered on.

As beautiful as he was, Richard de Lacey had a different sort of appeal for her. She felt drawn to him, but in a mysterious way that had nothing to do with the wanting she felt for Aidan O Donoghue.

There was something in the way Richard cocked his head, a certain crooked slant to his smile, and a gentle quality in his touch that tugged at her heart. It was not recognition she felt; it could not be. She had never seen him before in her life.

"What sort of boat race?" Pippa demanded, striding down through the gardens at Aidan's side.

"I'm not quite certain." He watched her from the corner of his eye. "I believe it is a sculling race down the Thames." She looked as fresh as a newly opened rose with the dew still clinging to its petals. How naturally she fit into this rarefied setting of aristocrats with their elaborate manners and games. The girl's gift for imitation served her well here. Her courtly graces seemed as seasoned as those of a woman trained from the cradle.

Today she wore a gown of lilac with all the sleeves

and furnishings properly attached and fastened. Her hair was caught back in a coif beaded with gleaming onyx.

"I believe," he explained, "that the race is held for a winner's cup. You and the other ladies will watch the finish line—that would be the watersteps."

"I see." She squinted at the beribboned string that stretched clear across the river.

"Did you get on with them?" he asked, then scowled. He was not supposed to care one way or the other.

"The other ladies?" She looked up, gave him a false smile, and fluttered a pretend fan in her face. "Oh, la, sir, surely you know what deep joy I take in discussing fashion and rose breeding."

He laughed. "They know no better. The Sassenach keep their women on a short leash."

"A charming image. And are Irishwomen kept on a *long* leash?"

"Some would say, in Ireland, the woman wields the leash herself."

She beamed. "That sounds much more sensible."

"I take it they're all deeply smitten with Richard de Lacey."

"Of course. We discussed him in exhaustive detail." She pantomimed a fluttering fan. "The cleft in his chin, his perfectly turned calf, the tenor of his voice, the charm of his manners, all kept us in gossip fodder for half the night."

A stab of feeling he refused to name invaded Aidan. "So you're smitten with him, too."

She blew upward at a curl that had escaped her coif to dangle upon her brow. "I should be. It seems almost a sacrilege not to be."

"But?" Undeniable hope kindled inside him.

"But . . ." A teasing light glinted in her eye. "I don't know, Your Potency. I'm not certain how to put this. I prefer my men to be tall, dark, and Irish." She laughed at his thunderstruck expression. "Richard de Lacey is too perfect to render me smitten and swooning. Does that make sense to you?"

He held a smile in check. "Perfect sense. Being smitten is a serious and sometimes painful business."

She caught her lip in her teeth and gazed at him with eyes so luminescent that he could see his own reflection.

"Aidan!" Donal Og called from the end of the garden. "Reel in your tongue and get down here." His broad Gaelic rang like pagan music through the fussy arbors and knot gardens of Durham House. "The Sassenach sheep-swivers want a lesson in rowing."

"My lord," Pippa called as he turned to leave, "Richard said you would hate him because of his commission in Ireland. Is that true?"

Aidan paused, startled both by her question and by how much she pleased him. He was not accustomed to a woman's empathy, her understanding. "I do not hate him," Aidan said, turning toward Donal Og. "Yet."

He left her seated amid a few dozen spectators at the river landing, then went to hear the particulars of the race.

He was fast learning that the social games of the English had subtle and serious purposes. A man's status among his peers rose or fell with his prowess at sport. Most important of all, the queen herself was given a full report of each man's performance.

They rode a mile upriver to the contestants' boats. Donal Og settled eagerly into one. "It is like a curragh!" he declared, referring to the seagoing rowboats of the Irish.

"They will all drown like dogs in our wake," Iago said with complete certainty.

As he saw the other teams settle into the boats, Aidan felt no need to disagree. Not one of these Sassenach looked as if he had ever exerted himself into an actual sweat. They wore precious clothes and precious, smug expressions on their faces.

Strutting in front of their ranks, Iago put on his scariest I'm-a-savage look, with glowering eyes and protruding lips, muscles flexed until they bulged. The air of English superiority dissipated.

"I think they get the point," Aidan said, smothering a laugh. Already he had decided what to do with the winner's cup. He would give it to the queen as a gift with all the others he had brought for her.

The hoary old bitch. She was beginning to try his patience.

Then the gorgeous Richard de Lacey appeared and Aidan felt his first stab of doubt. The charming young man had two extraordinary retainers in tow. They looked almost as exotic as Donal Og and Iago. Though not as tall as Aidan's companions, they were broad and powerfully built. One had cropped black hair, a black mustache, and black eyes. He wore black boots, old-fashioned trews, and a richly embroidered tunic with a sleeveless red jacket over it.

The other man had a mustache so wide that its stiffened tips extended past the width of his face in the shape of a stout set of bull's horns.

As these formidable challengers scrambled into

their boat, Richard smiled and greeted all his rivals. He was a merry fellow indeed, and clearly it was not just the ladies who thought so.

Richard would need to bring more than charm to Ireland, Aidan thought. He had seen young men, Irish and English alike, made old in mere months by the rigors of privation during the endless, pointless campaigns.

Then Richard spoke to his companions, and an odd chill shot down Aidan's spine. It was a strange language they spoke, guttural and nasal, so wholly foreign he could not pick out a single word of it.

"What are they?" Iago asked. "Demon men?"

"Prussian or Turkish?" Donal Og guessed.

"No matter." Aidan clamped his hands around the oars. "As far as *we* are concerned, they are defeated."

A whistle pierced the air, and they were off. As Aidan had predicted, the Sassenach fell behind immediately. The only serious challenge was from Richard and his cohorts.

Setting his jaw, Aidan threw all of his strength into the race. He rowed with a vigor and rhythm that caused the sweat to pour down his face and arms. His hands blistered and the blisters burst, yet he did not slacken his pace.

He held one clear thought in his mind. Pippa watched from the finish line. He would be less than the O Donoghue Mór if he let her see him lose.

Yet some equally powerful thought was driving Richard de Lacey and his crew, for they too rowed at a furious rate; they were as grim and focused as Aidan and his companions.

Before long, he could hear the low roar of cheering. He blocked it out. He listened only to the thump and splash of the oars, the pounding of his heart, his own steady breathing.

From the corner of his eye, he saw Richard's boat draw even with his. Then, whipping his head around for a split second, he saw the banner of ribbons stretched across the finish line.

The strength that surged through him had deep roots. It was the stubborn ferocity of the ancient Celt that gripped and held him, then shot energy like fire through his limbs.

The last oar stroke flowed from his shoulders to the tips of the oars, and on a surge of speed that drew gasps from the crowd, the boat shot forward. Aidan snatched down the banner. To loud huzzahs and a few anti-Irish boos, he held it aloft.

Richard's boat ran alongside his, and Richard inclined his head. "Well done, my lord of Castleross. I only regret I was not a more worthy opponent."

"You were not so bad for a Sassenach," said Donal Og, examining the raw blisters on his hands.

De Lacey's companions exchanged words in their incomprehensible tongue.

"By my soul, but I've worked up a sweat." Aidan sluiced water over his neck and shoulders. Iago and Donal Og did the same.

The spectators were oddly quiet as the Irishmen drifted toward the river landing. Aidan did not realize why until he set aside his oars and looked up to see the crowd drawn to the very edge of the landing, the women pushing past the men to gape at the drenched savages. Even Pippa went to the brink, her soft eyes wide with interest.

It was more than any man's pride could resist. Aidan exchanged a sly glance with his cousin and then with Iago. All three of them managed to row with the maximum display of flexed muscles that drew murmurs from the ladies.

Unnoticed by Pippa, a grossly overdressed man—Lord Temple Newsome, Aidan recalled—came up behind her.

From a distance, Aidan could not see exactly where Newsome put his hand, but the outraged expression on Pippa's face gave him a good idea. She straightened up and, in the same motion, seized the gentleman by his left arm. In a move that would have done a seasoned wrestler credit, she bent forward, jerking Temple Newsome up and over her head. Screaming, he flopped head over heels into the water.

"So *that* is how she kept her virtue all these years," Donal Og said thoughtfully.

"I wondered that as well," said Iago.

A barked oath burst from the back of the crowd. While Temple Newsome gasped and flailed, his manservant grabbed Pippa by the arm. She pulled away from him. The movement was too abrupt. Her arms made wide circles in the air as she toppled into the river.

For a moment, the skirts spread around her like a bell. "You bean-fed, braying ass," she yelled in a coarse accent, then sank out of sight.

In a heartbeat of time, Aidan experienced a raw sense of panic and loss unlike anything he had ever felt. Neither losing his father in such a horrible manner nor Felicity's betrayal could even approach this sense of dread. He had not realized what having Pippa in his life had given him—until now, when he was in danger of losing her.

In one swift motion, he stood and dove cleanly into

the water. He swam straight past the drowning Newsome, who grasped at him, and when he reached the spot where Pippa had gone under, he dove deep.

Sunlight shone through a blurry filter of silt and river weeds. He saw the vague outline of a waving arm. He grabbed at it; missed. *Hurry!* his mind screamed. *Hurry!* Not until this moment had the survival of another person mattered so much to him. With a strong, scissorslike kick, he surged to the surface, taking mere seconds to gulp air before diving again. A flow of skirts caught his eye. Knowing now the full meaning of wordless, heartfelt prayer, he reached for her. His hand closed around fabric. He tugged, the fabric rent, and she slipped away. He surged toward her, and when he touched her hand— the hand of an Englishwoman, a stranger, a commoner, his heart nearly burst with gladness. He hauled her to the surface.

Pippa gagged and then coughed, spewing river water and vile oaths. He hooked his arm around her and took her to the watersteps. When he reached the shallows, he caught her around the waist and under her knees, sweeping her up into his arms. She clung to his neck and swallowed great gulps of air. He climbed the watersteps with care, for they were green and slimy.

"You're carrying me," said Pippa.

"Aye."

"I can't believe I needed saving."

"Again," he reminded her.

"Well, at least I am consistent."

He reached the landing. The crowd moved back to give them a wide berth, and he set Pippa on her feet. He tried to pretend it was not happening, but he could not hide the truth from himself. He was trembling.

"Utterly hopeless," she said.

He looked into her eyes, seeing anguish and hope and the thing he dreaded most—a love so sweet and clear that it pierced him like a sword thrust.

"We're both hopeless," he said huskily, thinking of Ireland, of Felicity, of all the countless reasons he could not return her love.

Richard de Lacey stood in his boat. Aidan expected derision, but Richard began to clap his hands slowly. Others joined in, and applause rang across the river.

Shaking off her brush with disaster along with bits of river weed, Pippa immediately pulled away from him. She adopted her showman's stance, plucking her sodden, torn skirts and dipping in an elaborate curtsy. Lord Temple Newsome struggled on hands and knees up the slippery watersteps.

"Next time you decide to pinch a lady's arse," she called, "be sure your victim is either too helpless to resist or too stupid to mind."

"You are a common trollop."

"Thank you, my lord *Noisome*," she shot back with a false obeisance.

"Charming," he said, spitting on the ground.

"*You* have the charm of a close-stool," she retorted.

Newsome glared at Aidan. "Where did you find this—this piecemeal maid?"

"Did the first dunking fail to clean up your mouth, Newsome?" Aidan asked, advancing on him.

He said nothing, but squished along a garden path toward the house.

Aidan bent forward and peeled off his tunic and

shirt. He straightened, shaking back his wet hair, to find everyone staring at him. Again.

Female whispers swept the goggling throng. Pippa wore an expression that raised his vanity to new heights. Her eyes were misty, her mouth slightly open; her tongue slipped out to moisten her lips. He held the tunic lower to conceal his body's reaction.

"What are those scars?" she asked with quiet awe.

"That," he said, feeling a flush creep up his neck, "is a long story. We had best get ourselves dry."

"And so you had," said a laughing, friendly voice. Richard de Lacey clambered up to the river landing. "Come with me to Wimberleigh House. It's just there, at the top of the garden." He pointed at a beautiful, turreted mansion bristling with finials, with great bays of oriel windows facing the river. "It would be an honor to play host to such singular company."

Two hours later, Pippa stood at the top of the grand staircase of Wimberleigh House and frowned down the length of steps. The residence was not as big and rambling as Lumley House and Crutched Friars, nor was it as opulent as Durham House.

Yet she felt immediately comfortable here. They had given her clean clothes, and a bashful maid had helped her dress. She inhaled the aroma of beeswax and verbena polish, alien scents to her, so why did they seem so familiar and evocative? She studied the paneled walls and painted cloth hangings. She could imagine Richard de Lacey growing up in this place, a lovely golden child racing through the galleries and halls or cavorting in the garden.

As she leaned on the top newel post, the wooden orb bent to one side. Pippa gasped and jumped back.

"Don't mind that," said a cheery voice.

She spun around to see a smiling maid bustling toward her, holding a lit candle in her hand. "I be Tess Harbutt, come to light the chandelier." She bobbed her coiffed head at the newel post. "There used to be a series of pulleys here to help my own dear grandmum up and down the stairs when she were getting on in years."

Tess clumped down the stairs and slid back a wooden panel to reveal a system of ropes and hooks. While Pippa watched with keen interest, the maid paid out the rope, which caused the chandelier to lower slowly.

"The old Lord Wimberleigh—he be the earl of Lynley now, master Richard's grandsire—was quite the inventor," Tess explained. "Always dreaming up this or that convenience."

Pippa hurried down the stairs to get a closer look. The chandelier hung at eye level now, a great, heavy wheel of candles, each with a chimney of cut glass.

"May I?" She took Tess's candle and touched its burning head to each candle in the fixture. They were thick and white, not all smelly with tallow like the ones she was used to.

"That's him there." Tess pointed to a portrait on the wall along the stairway. "His name is Stephen de Lacey."

She looked up. Ah, there was where Richard got his golden good looks, she noted.

"That next one is Stephen de Lacey's second wife, the Lady Juliana." The matronly dark-haired lady held a fan to her bosom and was surrounded by children. An unusual, long-haired dog lay curled at their feet.

"Juliana," Pippa said. "Pretty name." She was almost to the last candle.

"Some as say she is Russian royalty," Tess explained, warming to her tale. Dropping her voice to a gossipy whisper, she added, "Others as say she was a Gypsy."

Pippa jerked her hand in startlement, oversetting the last candle. The glass chimney fell, but she caught it before it shattered. "What did you say?" She put the glass back.

Tess's face flushed. "Idle gossip, is all. I misspoke, ma'am."

Yet as she lit the last candle and Tess used a crank to raise the chandelier, Pippa frowned up at the portrait.

Juliana. A Gypsy. Some elusive thought hovered at the edge of her awareness, then flitted away. It must be her own encounter with the old Gypsy that jogged her memory, she decided. She pointed to two rectangular shadows on the paneling. "What portraits were removed?"

"Those would be Master Richard's parents, Lord and Lady Wimberleigh. They was taken down for packing. Master Richard's got himself a military commission, he does. He has some miniature limnings of his brothers and sister—Masters Lucas, Leighton, and Michael, and of course Mistress Caroline, the family favorite."

Pippa stared a moment longer at the portraits. A family. How alien the notion was to her. Discomfited by both longing and a sense of awkwardness, she plucked at her skirts. She was ever the misfit, ever the odd man out. "Do I look all right?"

"Oh, aye, ma'am. That's one of Mistress Caroline's

old ones. Perfect for you." The maid eyed Pippa's cropped hair, started to say something, then looked away politely. "You'd best be off to the dining hall. I think they're waiting for you."

Pippa crossed the antechamber, flanked by grand archways, and went through the doors on her right.

"Sorry, ma'am. I didn't realize you'd been here before," said Tess.

"I haven't."

"Then how do you know the way to the dining hall?"

Pippa stood still in her tracks. Again she felt that prickle, that chill. Thoughts teased at her and disappeared, unformed. She looked helplessly at the friendly maid. "A lucky guess, I suppose."

I am a Christian as well as a Celt, which makes for some awkward moments in the confessional. I am not supposed to feel the dark prescience of disaster deep in my bones, for that smacks of paganism and is an affront to Him Who made us all.

Still, there are times when I am forced to admit that the ancients do whisper secrets in my unsuspecting ear, and of late the secrets disturb me.

There is mischief afoot in Killarney town and at Ross Castle. I have no reason to know this except that the chill in my brittle old bones tells me so. That, and the shifty way the bride of the O Donoghue refused to look at me when I went up to the keep to lead the rogation processional. Our "pagan" ceremonies do offend her Puritan sensibilities, but she displayed more than her usual hatred and distrust.

The bishop has promised, at last, to help. It was a marriage that never should have been. In point of fact, it is no marriage at all. I shall send good news to Aidan regarding the annulment.

Meanwhile, the rebellion of which I wrote so urgently to the O Donoghue Mór has been suppressed by Lord Constable Browne; I shudder to think how ruthlessly. A few stray rebels managed to take hostages, including that fat wart-hog Valentine Browne, nephew of the Constable. It is an unfortunate situation that reeks of deception. I think it is a *little too convenient that the rebels seized only men unfit to fight or even govern. The rebels themselves are not Kerry men, but outsiders, masterless men who serve no cause save their own profit.*

A dark, dastardly, and entirely awful suspicion overtakes me when I think about who was truly behind the hostage-taking, and whom the English will blame when they hear of it.

If the she-king in London finds out about the mischief, she will lock up the O Donoghue Mór and throw away the key.

—Revelin of Innisfallen

7

They dined in a lofty hall with a hammer beam roof. A small army of servitors conveyed sumptuous dishes to a table that was so long, Pippa could hardly see Donal Og and Iago. Those two were engaged in an animated, if halting, conversation with Richard's foreign companions.

She discovered two things immediately. She hated eels in mustard, and she adored being waited on. More gradually, she discovered the delights of blancmange and dried figs, the feel of a real silver wine chalice against her bottom lip. Having dining companions who spoke to her politely, in complete sentences, was an unforeseen boon.

"I am expecting my parents from Hertfordshire," Richard explained, "and my aunts and uncles and cousins. I've a large family and they're all quite endearingly mad. We've had wild times together, always have."

Aidan watched him with a charming smile. Pippa suspected she was the only one who knew the meaning of the flinty look in his eyes. He said, "And will you and your family have wild times in Ireland, my good friend? You'd not be the first English family to do so."

"I assure you, my lord, if any of my family were to come to Ireland, it would not be to lay waste to the land," Richard said soberly.

A wave of wistful longing came over Pippa. The very idea of a family filled her with a bittersweet yearning for that warm, unknowable sense of belonging. "Hold fast to them," she murmured. "A family is a blessing some fail to appreciate until they lack one." She blushed and ducked her head. "I reveal too much of myself," she said.

A servant placed a platter of salad greens before her. She stared at them blankly, uncertain how to eat them.

"Use a fork," said Richard.

"Don't speak to a lady like that," Aidan snapped.

"Fork, I said. Use your fork." Richard held up a three-pronged device that resembled a tiny pikestaff.

"Oh." Aidan relaxed against the back of his carved chair. "Sure and I thought you were being impertinent."

Richard threw back his head and laughed, and then he demonstrated the use of a fork.

"Stirrups and forks," said Aidan with his customary rich chuckle. "I have found two useful things among the Sassenachs."

Pippa experimented with her fork and found it much to her liking. In spite of the tension between Aidan and Richard, she found the company much to her liking, too. At the far end of the table, Donal Og and Iago continued to regale their uncomprehending listeners with tales recounted in English, Spanish, and Gaelic. There was an undeniable appeal in watching a group of men in high spirits. The sight of all that lavish handsomeness struck her silent with wonder. She felt as if she had dropped into the very lap of heaven, where God in Her infinite wisdom made every man perfect to behold.

One among them was *too* flawless. Here she sat in the house of the most beautiful man in England, yet she felt no breathless attraction to him. Instead, her gaze kept wandering to Aidan, with his long hair, his craggy features, his piercing eyes, and the mouth that made her shiver when she remembered touching it with her own. She pictured him just out of the river, his hair streaming like black ribbons over his shoulders, his shirt peeled off to reveal his magnificent chest. She pictured the mat of inky hair arrowing down over a ridged stomach. The scars, fanning outward, must have been inflicted long ago and caused him untold agony.

Was it a Catholic matter? she wondered. She would ask him about them soon.

"I think she is smitten with you," Richard remarked laughingly to Aidan.

She sniffed, hoping she would not blush. "Are you unhappy that I'm not smitten with you?"

"No." Richard grinned. "Just surprised."

Her jaw and her fork dropped. "I gather self-love is another of your myriad virtues."

He roared with laughter. "You are a breath of fresh air, is she not, my lord of Castleross?"

Aidan regarded her with such warmth and tenderness

that she wanted to weep. "It is," he said, "a privilege to know her. And sadly, I doubt any of us fully appreciate the gift of her."

She tried to counter with some bawdy comment, but for the life of her, she could not. Saucy words had never before failed her, but they did now. It was as if her tongue would not allow her to pour acid on the sweetness of his comment, to destroy the moment with a flippant remark, to render meaningless his gentle regard.

Just those few words, spoken in Aidan's deep, melodious voice, fired her skin with a blush that blotched her cheeks, her neck, even her bosom. She wished she had worn the ruff the maid had brought with her borrowed gown.

She felt a prickling in her throat, a hot dewiness in her eyes, and at last she realized what had come over her. Somehow these two men, Richard with his humor and godlike good looks, and Aidan with his majestic and mystical Celtic spirit, gave her a sense of belonging.

As soon as the thought struck her, she recoiled from it as if she had been singed. She knew well the price of affection, and it was a price she was not willing to pay. Drawing a deep breath, she became again Pippa the wandering juggler, a clown hiding the tears in her eyes.

"A privilege indeed," she blurted out, jumping to her feet, snatching up three forks and tossing them in the air. "It is not every table that boasts a resident juggler."

Richard leaned forward with his elbows on the table and his ruff mingling with his salad.

"Are you all right?" Aidan asked.

Richard stared at Pippa until she caught the forks
and sat down, certain he had examined her to the last
eyelash.

Then he blinked. "My apologies. I am not usually
so gauche." He flashed his world-brightening smile.
"Just for a moment there, you reminded me of someone. But I cannot think whom it could be. Now, never
let it be said that at Wimberleigh House we make the
guests provide the entertainment." He clapped his
hands, and three musicians appeared, one with a gittern, one with a reed pipe, and a singer. "Perhaps this
will be more to your taste than the noise at Durham
House," he said.

The singer, an effete young man who wore a look of
artistic intensity, pinched out most of the candles on
the table, plunging the room into moody half-light. A
subtle chord rippled from the gittern, and the singer
closed his eyes and swayed slightly, then began to sing
in a perfect tenor. The reed pipe played a haunting
countermelody, and the two blended with a plaintive
splendor that was piercing in its beauty. The mingling
of tones made Pippa feel raw and vulnerable, as if
some part of her had been bared against her will.

She sneaked a glance at Aidan. He was watching
her, not the musicians, and not with the mild, polite
interest with which one listened to a performance.
Despite the dimness she could see him clearly, for the
single candle left burning in the middle of the table
threw a gleam of antique gold across his face. He sat
forward, his face expressionless and his mouth set, yet
the frank passion in his regard was unmistakable.
Despite his unmoving pose, there was a turbulence
deep in his eyes that enraptured her. She was his
spellbound victim, open to him and helpless to resist,

every inch of her flesh burning with the need to touch him. While she looked across the table, she remembered every moment they had shared, from the day she had knelt at his feet and stolen his knife to this afternoon when his strong arms had yanked her from the river. Her thoughts lingered on the night he had kissed her, a night of candleglow and drumming rain when she could hold none of her secret dreams inside her. It was as if they had lived a lifetime together rather than mere weeks.

Only when the song ended did Aidan relinquish her from his stare, leaving her as weak and shaken as if he had actually caressed her.

"God's light," Richard drawled in heavy amusement, "I have heard talk of making love with one's eyes, but until now I have not actually seen it done."

Pippa forced a light laugh. "Your musicians have uncommon talent. You ought to bottle it like wine."

The delighted performers bowed with a flourish and struck up another tune.

Richard drained his wine goblet, waved away a servant who came to refill it, and stood. "Do forgive me. I have many preparations to make before the wild hordes descend."

"Wild hordes?" She was determined to shake off Aidan's spell.

"My family. Parents, aunts and uncles, brothers and sisters. They're all coming to see me off. I do hope you'll have a chance to meet them."

She had, just for a second, tasted the sweetness of belonging, but now it was gone. Richard de Lacey and Aidan O Donoghue were virtual strangers. She almost hated them for giving her a glimpse of another world beyond her dreams.

The entire company left the dining hall. Richard's retainers followed and stood in a formal row before the grand staircase. He turned to his guests. "I'll bid you good night, then." He and Aidan exchanged manly nods; then he took Pippa's hand and pressed it to his lips. The candlelight from the lofty chandelier flickered in his golden hair.

"Good night, my lord." She turned to Aidan, unable to suppress a smile. "Good night."

He took her hand, too, but his manner was completely different from Richard's. Very lightly, perhaps by accident only, his finger skimmed along her palm. His eyes held hers as he slowly brought her hand to his mouth. First she felt the warm flutter of his breath, and that was enough to raise goose bumps along her arms. Then he pressed his lips to her skin. Secretly, his tongue flicked out and touched her.

She gasped.

Richard laughed. "Aidan, I could take lessons from you."

She snatched back her hand. "Please don't. The man is obnoxious." And I am completely mad about him, her errant heart added.

He laughed. "Perhaps it is my Irish blood. There is more than one way to make war on the Sassenach."

Aidan and Richard stepped aside and let her precede them to the stairs. Just before she set foot on the bottom step, she heard a slight, curious sound.

One of Richard's footmen called a guttural warning.

Without thinking, she ducked out of the way. In the same instant, a glass chimney toppled from the chandelier and landed with a clatter on the spot where she had been standing.

"Are you all right?" Richard asked the question, but it was Aidan's arms that went around her.

"Of course." She swished back the hem of her skirt to make certain no shards of glass hid in the folds, then smiled at the footman. "Thank you for warning me."

Richard scratched his head and frowned.

"Is something amiss?" She leaned back against Aidan, liking the solid feel of him behind her.

"Not really, but . . . This is an odd question. Do you speak Russian?"

She laughed. "I barely speak English, my lord. Why do you ask?"

"Because Yuri"—he indicated the footman with a nod—"speaks only Russian. How could you possibly have understood his warning?"

A chill slid through her. There was something strange about this house, something strange about the portraits of the beautiful de Lacey family, something strange about the things she felt when she looked at Richard.

She glanced back at Aidan. He watched her with as much curiosity as Richard.

She shrugged. "I suppose his urgent tone caught me. I have always lived by my wits, Richard."

The broken glass was cleared away, and the entire party climbed the stairs to the upper chambers. In the dimly lit hall, Pippa bade a final good night to Richard and Aidan.

There was no more hand kissing, but what Aidan did was worse, in a way. His searing gaze caressed her like a lover's hands, and he whispered, "Sweet dreams, *a gradh*," in her ear, flooding her with forbidden sensation.

Just as she nearly dropped to her knees in weak wanting, Aidan left to seek his own bed.

Hours later, surrounded by fussy, majestic luxury, Pippa still could not fall asleep. She wore her borrowed shift and a loose robe over that as she paced in the watery moonlight glimmering across the floor of her chamber. She should be reveling in every moment spent here. She should explore every stick of furniture, every pane of glass, every tapestry that graced the walls. This was luxury such as she used to dream of. Now that she was in its lush lap, she could not seem to enjoy it.

Instead, she tormented herself with thoughts of Aidan. Why did she let herself be drawn to him when she knew it could lead only to heartbreak? Why couldn't she keep him at a distance as she did all others?

A shadow flickered in the moonwashed garden below. Drawn by the movement, she went to the window and looked down through the leaded-glass panes.

What she saw gave her a dark surge of satisfaction. Aidan O Donoghue could not sleep, either.

Like a great, hulking ghost, he paced up and down a garden path, pausing now and then to brood at the slick ribbon of river visible at the end of the lawn.

A fever built in the pit of her belly and spread over her skin. She clenched her fists and pressed her burning brow to the glass.

What *was* it about the man?

His aura of masculinity overwhelmed her; of that she had no doubt. He was not as flawlessly handsome as Richard, nor as witty as Sir Christopher Hatton, nor as merry as Iago, yet he drew her. She wanted to be with him, touch him, talk to him, feel his mouth on hers as she had the night of the storm.

"No," she said through her teeth. "I won't care about you. I cannot." She sucked in a breath and held it, willing herself to keep control. Every time she let herself dream of belonging to someone—her unremembered family, Mab, members of troupes she had joined—she had been abandoned.

"You'll abandon me, too," she whispered, her breath fogging the glass. "But I don't care." Aye, there was her answer. Surely there was a way to steal a few moments of splendor with him yet come away with her heart still intact. "It can be done," she said aloud, tugging the robe securely around herself and hurrying out the door. "I shall prove it this very night."

London was never truly silent, Aidan thought, staring out at the Thames. Here it was the very dead of night, and he could still hear voices and horses and the occasional hush of oars—smugglers or clandestine lovers or a party of revelers returning home late.

Sounds of merriment, sounds of suffering, sounds of business being done, crimes being committed. They all surrounded him in a great, discordant chorus that was as strange to him as forks and Protestants.

He had told no one of the summons he had received after the boating race today. A special messenger had delivered it to him at Wimberleigh House. Apparently, news of his performance had reached the queen, and she had decided to favor him with a royal audience.

He was ready for her. Past ready. He both longed

and dreaded to leave London. As soon as he had heard from Revelin of Innisfallen, he'd wanted to sail for home. Donal Og and Iago had convinced him to stay, for if he left London in defiance of the queen, matters would only grow worse. She would tell her military strategists to deploy more troops to Kerry, to evict more Irish people, to burn more Irish fields and raze more Irish forests. That was exactly what he had hoped to prevent by coming here.

Yet a fortnight had come and gone, and what had he to show for his efforts? A few trinkets, a good horse, a meeting with the de Lacey heir, a fork, for chrissake—

"Your Worship, I must speak to you," piped a clear voice in the night.

And Pippa, he thought, turning away from the river. How could he possibly forget Pippa? His burden. His treasure.

"Yes?" he called, searching the shadows. He saw her small shape coming down the path toward him. She disappeared beneath the darkness of an arbor and then reemerged like a wraith.

A feeling coursed through him, a sort of terrible ecstasy and a sudden bright surge of hope. It was as if she were a princess of the *sidhe*, moving from her fairy kingdom into the real world.

Aye, there was something magic and fey about the girl, of that he had no doubt. Still, his ill-governed body reminded him painfully that she was a flesh-and-blood woman. He wanted her with a powerful need he felt in every bone and fiber and nerve. But he could not have her. Not ever. He had not made love to a woman since he had married, and he couldn't, not as long as Felicity drew breath.

"Aidan?" she called softly. "Are you there?"

"Here." Taking a few steps forward, he touched her arm.

She gasped and stiffened. He braced himself. "There now, I'd not want to end up like poor Temple Newsome."

"He deserved worse than the dunking I gave him."

He chuckled. "So he did. Come here. I vow I will not grab you in an inappropriate spot."

"That is exactly what I came to talk to you about."

Ah, God. The words alone shot a jolt of desire through him. "You *want* me to grab you?"

He heard her breath catch. It was too dark to see her face.

"Don't you dare," she said, her voice curiously tremulous. "What I want you to know is that I am exceedingly grateful for all the kindness you have shown me. I don't even know why you decided to take me in."

Wry amusement curved his mouth. "You gave me little choice. How could I resist the sight of you groveling at my hem?"

"I am an excellent groveler," she said.

Though her voice was full of humor, he did not want to hear any more. He simply could not bear knowing what she had endured in order to hone such a skill.

"The fact is," he said gently, "you are well worth saving, and I have no idea why some worthy patron did not see that long ago."

"Stop it!" She made a jerky movement; he realized she was clapping her hands over her ears. "You are making this harder than it has to be."

"Making what harder?"

She lowered her hands and blew out an exasperated breath. "What I came to tell you." She spoke slowly, as if to a man of limited mental capacity.

"And what is that?" he asked.

"That I won't love you. Never. Ever."

He took a moment to absorb the words. He wanted to laugh at her vehemence. He wanted to rage at her and weep for her. But most of all, he wanted to gather her into his arms and never let go. More fool he.

"Ah, colleen," he said on a sigh. "What was it that hurt you so badly that you'd feel the need to say such a thing? It was losing your family, wasn't it?"

She was silent and still for a long time. Finally she said, "All you need to know is that I don't love you and I never will."

He told himself he should feel relieved. He forced out a brief, quiet laugh. "Your love is the last thing I need."

She tilted up her chin. "Fine. I thought as much. It makes things so much simpler."

"So much simpler." He felt hollow and raw. "Now that means we must be friends. The Irish have a saying, 'If you be not mine enemy, then I count you for a friend.'"

"That is lovely." Her voice sounded curiously thick. She sidled away from him and sat down on a marble bench overlooking the river walk. "Would you tell me about Ireland? Is it true there are wee folk in the woods there?"

He closed his eyes briefly, and a sharp yearning gripped his heart. "There are many magical and wonderful things in Ireland. Many dangerous things, too."

Her hands covered his in a gentle caress. He was grateful for the darkness. He could reveal more of himself than he did by light of day, for the night was a great leveler, hiding flaws as well as virtues.

He thought of his homeland with both bittersweet affection and a desperate resignation. Ireland was a place of harsh splendor and alluring danger. It was a place where a man could live close to the land—or so it had been until the English had come.

"Well then," he said, gazing off into the shifting shadows of the garden. "On a sunny day, Lough Leane looks like a blue mirror reflecting the endless sky. The forests are emerald green. There are mountains with raging torrents, rivers teeming with salmon and trout, and in the middle of the lake, there is a place called Innisfallen."

"Innisfallen." She tasted the word. "An island?"

"Aye. The island is home to canons of the order of St. Augustine. My boyhood tutor, Revelin, lives there." Aidan had spent hours on the isle, sitting against the cool stone wall of the abbey and letting the holy silence of the place surround him and cushion his dreams. Revelin was as vast and imposing as the Almighty Himself.

"And Ross Castle?" she asked. "Iago said you displeased the queen by completing the building."

A ghost of the old pain wafted over him. "Ross Castle was my father's dream. But *my* penance."

The words were out before he could stop himself. Curse the darkness and the false sense of security it gave him. When would he learn that no place was safe to bare his soul? Was this strange Sassenach woman enchanted, then, able to draw confessions from a reluctant heart?

He snatched his hands away and drove deep furrows into his hair with his fingers.

"Don't stop talking to me," she said. "Please. I want to know. What do you mean, penance?"

She must be under an enchantment, he decided. For he heard himself say, "After my father died, I felt duty bound to complete the castle even in defiance of English law. My father refused to see that our people were losing the fight to stay free of the Sassenach. Year after year I watched him raise armies and lead them off to die. Year after year I listened to the keening of widows and orphans left to starve because my father refused to compromise with the English."

"Aidan," she said, "I'm so sorry."

"Don't sorrow for me, but for those who fought and died, those they left behind." He dropped his head into his hands and thought of the awesome price he had paid to staunch the bleeding wounds of his people. "Their strength has reached its limit. The English Lord Constable is in place in Killarney town, and so long as we rebel, he'll deal with us harshly. For myself, I would fight to my death, but I cannot ask that sacrifice of my people."

"Your father did," she stated.

"Aye." The flood of memories washed over him: the shouting, the pleading . . . the violence. God in heaven, they had been like mortal enemies rather than blood kin.

"What will you ask of the queen?" she asked.

"Mercy, and some measure of self-rule. If I can negotiate a lasting peace, there will be less bloodshed."

"So you are willing to pay the price of your pride."

"To save lives." He shot up and started to pace. "Damn it, I have no choice."

"My lord, what know you of Elizabeth the queen?"

"That she is intelligent, manipulative, and vain. That she is capricious in her decisions. That she is the most cunning and powerful monarch in Christendom."

"She has a famous temper, I can tell you that. One time, Tom Canty went to beg a favor on behalf of the brewers' guild, and she ended up fining the guild."

"Why?"

"Because Tom went to her with his hat in his hand. My lord, if you humble yourself before the queen, she will scorn you."

"Would you have me declare war?" he asked, giving a harsh laugh.

"No." With a quiet swish of her robe, she got up out of the shadows and came to stand before him. The moonlight limned a strange, pale beauty in her face. By night, her appeal had a wistful quality too subtle to be seen by light of day.

"Aidan," she said, "I know I make sport of you with my lofty titles, but here is the truth. You are descended of ancient kings, a ruler in your own right, the O Donoghue Mór, a chieftain."

He felt a curious melting of emotion in his chest. Words, he told himself. She spoke mere words, yet they affected him profoundly. He told himself she was a homeless waif, her opinions did not matter, but her statement made a splendid sense, and his soul thirsted for the faith she had in him. God knew, he had never gotten it from Felicity.

"I am," he said with his old assurance, "the O Donoghue Mór." He swept her up into his arms and whirled her around. Her laughter floated on the night wind and echoed across the river. Like leaves on a breeze, they subsided and settled to the ground, where the soft, damp grass cushioned them. He propped himself on one elbow and gazed down at her laughing face. Then, casting off the last of his hesitation, he kissed her hard and thirstily, drinking courage and wisdom from her startled lips.

She lifted herself into his kiss, arching her pale throat, winding her arms around his neck. Her loose robe fell open, and he was lost in a world of thoughtless sensation. His hand slipped in between her robe and shift, finding the sweet curves of her body. She had a slim waist and gently flaring hips, strong smooth legs that moved restively when he caressed her thighs.

Yet somewhere, buried deep beneath his passion for her, was a spark of honor that told him to stop. *No.* He squeezed his eyes shut, plunging the spark back into darkness. He would have these moments with her, even if he had to steal them.

She was an innocent in many ways, so open to his caresses, so needful of his affection. And he was a life-scarred warrior, hungry for the trust she gave him, for her complete, unquestioning certainty that there was goodness in him—even though he knew better.

She touched his hard, scarred chest with one finger and drew back to whisper, "I did not come here for this."

"But I'll not let you leave without it." And with that, the last spark of his conscience died utterly. He brushed his hand up over her midsection and cupped one of her breasts. She made a whimpering sound in the back of her throat and raised herself higher so that her breast fit into the palm of his hand. Desire scalded him.

"God, Pippa," he said in a choked voice. He had not

anticipated the force of his passion. He shared the same terrible wanting he sensed in her. Suddenly his own desire, his own pleasure, became that which pleasured her. He slid his tongue down the side of her throat, lingering over her gently fluttering pulse, tasting the faint spice of sandalwood on her soft, creamy skin.

He moved lower still, using one hand to brush aside the laces of her shift. The garment gaped wide, baring her breasts to the night air. She caught her breath, then whispered, "It's cold."

"I'll warm you, love." He lowered his head to one breast and his hand to the other. She made no sound, but her flesh seemed to sing to him as she arched into his embrace. He wanted to cover her like a stallion, to lose control and draw cries of ecstasy from her. God, it had been so long . . . too long. . . . And then the spark of honor flared back to life, as he had known it would. No matter what the reason, he had made a vow to Felicity, and his insidious correctness reared its self-righteous head.

As gently as he could, he stopped kissing Pippa and pulled the robe back around her. In the shadows and moonlight, her eyes looked huge, bewildered.

He sat up. For a moment, he could not speak. It hurt too much, and not just in his aching loins. In his heart. For that was where he wanted to bring Pippa, and—God help him—he could not.

He touched her cheek. "Colleen?"

"What?" She sounded wary, like a child who knew she was about to be punished.

"I want to make love to you," he said. "You know that, don't you?"

"I sensed it as soon as you threw me on the ground and started ravishing me."

He tried to smile at her cocky words.

She sat up and hugged her knees to her chest. "I have one question, Your Excellency."

"Aye?"

"Why did you stop?"

Tell her, he urged himself. *Tell her the truth.*

Instead, he brushed a curly lock of hair from her forehead. "I don't want to hurt you. Can you believe that?"

"Of course," she said, and faith shone in her eyes. She looked away. "But it hurts when you stop."

"God!" His chest felt ripped in two by a devastating struggle. Before he could talk himself out of it, he grabbed her by the shoulders. "I do want you."

He fumbled for words. Other men made adultery look so easy, and in his case it was justifiable, some would say. Donal Og and Iago had been urging him for months to indulge himself. "I want you for my mistress."

She clutched his arms with her hands. "Mistress!"

"You'll wake the household." He dragged himself to his feet and pulled her up with him. "I desire you, Pippa. You desire me. I'll be good to you. I swear it. You'll want for nothing."

"Except for my pride. But of course, someone of my station should be honored by your offer. In fact, I *am* honored. Look at me. I'm all choked up." A humorless laugh burst from her, and he heard her desperation. She laughed to keep from weeping. That was how she had survived this long.

"I'm sorry," he said in a low voice. "I should have thought—I'm sorry."

"You need not apologize," she said, "for you see, you can't hurt me, Aidan. Don't you remember why I came out here to find you?"

"To tell me you don't love me."

"Exactly so. I do not love you. I will not. Ever."

He took a step toward her, cradled her face between his hands, and glided his thumbs gently over her warm, damp cheeks. "Then why the tears, *a gradh*?" he asked quietly.

"I'm just . . . just . . . "

"Just what?"

"Trying to get used to not loving you. And you're not helping one bit."

She was so revealing, so honest with him. "Colleen—"

"This is going to sound insane to you, but I do not feel honored after all. I feel insulted, Your Stupidity. Let go of me. Don't hold me like this."

He wanted never to let her go. It felt so good, so right, to hold her.

"Aidan, if I have to do serious damage to your codpiece, I will. *Let go.*"

He dropped his hands to his sides. It was the hardest thing he had ever done.

The second hardest thing was to let her walk away.

After a week passed, Pippa realized that she was not going to die of a broken heart.

She was going to live with it.

And what was more, she was going to ignore it, try to find her family, and meet the queen of England.

She meant to use the opportunity to find herself another rich patron. One who appreciated her. One who didn't insult her. One who didn't break her heart.

Standing at her chamber window, she looked

down into the central cloister of Crutched Friars. It resembled an innyard just before a play, with men running to and fro, fussing with their hair and weapons.

Only this time the hair was long and wild, and the weapons were real. Aidan had certainly taken her advice to heart. All one hundred of his kerns or gallowglass or whatever he called them were girding themselves for battle.

Shortly they would march on Whitehall Palace into the presence of Queen Elizabeth. Then what? What if the plan went awry? The queen would have them all put to death.

Pippa forced herself to calm down and moved away from the window. She stopped to study her reflection in the sheet of polished brass that served as a mirror.

"A face not even a mother could love," she said, poking sullenly at her hair. "I look like a mop standing on end."

"I would not say that." Resplendent as a Turkish sultan, Iago sauntered into the room. "You have more curves than a mop."

For a moment, she could do no more than stare at him. He wore loose trousers of blue silk and knee boots that laced up the sides. His chemise gaped open to reveal a broad, hard-muscled chest bearing scars similar to those she had seen on Aidan. Rather than a doublet, Iago wore a short, sleeveless coat and a brilliant sash around his waist. A long, thin rapier traced the length of his thigh.

She could not help smiling. "Truly, Iago, you should have been a showman. You have such presence. The women will be on you like flies on honey."

He grinned back at her. "Is there a court lady in my future, I wonder?"

"If you smile at everyone like that, there might be more than one. Perhaps the queen herself."

He shivered. "No, thank you. Her admirers do not always fare so well."

She scowled back into the mirror. "At least I won't have to worry about being plagued by pernicious admirers."

He stood behind her and rested his hands on her shoulders. "*Pequeña*, why do you not let the maids help you dress? Are you modest? Hiding some secret deformity?"

She leaned against his chest and tilted her head back to look at him. "I do not like the maids of Lumley House. They're not like the ones at Durham or Wimberleigh. They say ugly things about me."

He made a hissing sound of anger and squeezed her shoulders tighter. "*Putas.* Why didn't you say something?"

She lowered her head. "They were right. Except for the part about me being the lover of the O Donoghue Mór." *The only part I wish could be true,* she thought, cursing her wayward heart.

Iago said something else in Spanish, then turned her to face him. With hands as deft and gentle as any skilled costumer's, he began to dress her, layering garments over her shift and chemise. First came the back-laced corset, then the belled petticoat and underskirt.

As he worked, he spoke in the low, melodic patois she found so fascinating. "I do not understand you," he muttered. "You have everything—charm, youth, beauty, humor—and yet all I see when I look into your eyes is sorrow."

She bit her lip as he made her hold out one arm for a sleeve. "Then you have a wild imagination. What have I to grieve about? I've had you and Aidan both for my handmaids. Can any other woman in London make that claim?"

"I know what sorrow looks like. You cannot hide it from me."

She studied his face, sculpted and grave, the eyes snapping with lively intelligence, and yes, there it was. A pervasive, soul-haunting melancholy that burdened him even when he smiled.

"Save your pity for homeless beggars. *I* have a plan for my life."

"Fine," he said. "But tell me. As long as I am playing lady's maid, I should play the confidante as well."

He finished with her sleeves and started on her hair with a wooden comb. She took a deep breath. "Iago, it is this. I don't know who or what I am. One day I convince myself I am a princess lost by mistake. The next I am certain a fishwife spawned me and left me to die or to be succored by strangers. I could accept either explanation, as long as I knew it was true. I think what hurts is not knowing."

He took out a net coif decked with seed pearls. It had been in the chest with the other things, but she had not known what to do with it. He scooped up the loose curls at the back of her neck and fitted on the coif. Its draping folds gave the illusion of length. She was heartened by the improvement.

"Listen, *pequeña*," he said, "I am hardly the one to complain to about that. Look at me."

She looked. "You are an uncommonly beautiful man."

He shook his head, beaded braids clicking. "My father was a rapist, and my mother a murderer."

She blinked. "Your stories are almost as outrageous as mine."

"No, I tell you the truth. My father was a Spanish hidalgo who owned a huge hacienda in the islands. My mother was a mestiza house servant."

"Mes—what?"

"Mestiza. Of mixed blood—island native and African slave."

She saw it all in his face, then, a magnificent blending of haughty Spanish nobility, rich African coloring, and the exotic native bone structure.

He finished pinning on her coif. "My father raped my mother, and she killed him. So you see, *pequeña*, there are worse things than not knowing who you are."

"Ah, Iago. I am so sorry."

He kissed her brow, and she marveled at him. He had been born of sin and rage, had been beaten and enslaved, and yet here he was, bathing her in the radiance of gentle friendship and understanding.

"Aidan was my salvation," he said suddenly.

"What?" Just the sound of his name raised prickles on her skin.

Iago smiled. "There is such goodness in him as the angels would envy. But—" He looked away and distractedly plucked at her hem.

"But what?"

"Too many depend on him. He is like the poui tree in the islands. It is a tree so large that its top branches brush the clouds. It supports everything that comes to it—monkeys and parrots, lizards and snakes, beetles and bees. The natives use its branches and leaves for shelter, its bark and sap for building *canoas*. But finally, the poui cannot support all who demand life from it, and the tree dies."

He turned her to face the brass mirror. "Now, look at yourself. The fishwife's daughter is a princess, no?"

"No," she said, yet a thrill chased up her spine. "But let's see if we can fool the royal court."

*S*ometimes at night, when he thinks I am asleep, my husband arises and paces the floor. Oliver does not want me to see his worry; ever has he been protective of me.

It is concern for our son Richard that stirs my beloved husband from his slumber. Richard is as young and golden as the morning—and in many ways as innocent. He does not know what it means to go to war. He thinks only of flying pennons and blares from trumpets, thundering hoofbeats and grand, dramatic gestures.

Oliver knows better. He has seen the face of war; he has looked death in the face, and it is not a thing he wants his son to encounter.

But this is a matter of state, and women are not supposed to concern themselves with such things.

That I find to be a grand fallacy. For the person most concerned of all is a woman—Elizabeth of England.

—*Lark de Lacey,*
Countess of Wimberleigh

8

The queen had finally summoned the lord of Castleross to court. All the way to Whitehall Palace, Pippa had not been able to catch a glimpse of him, for Iago insisted on keeping her at his side, ahead of the bodyguard. Like a king from a mythical realm, Aidan remained invisible, remote, holding himself back, waiting to appear suddenly with dramatic impact.

As his escort of one hundred armed Irishmen tramped along the Strand, she understood the full impact of marching. The sound of feet pounding on the road had a profoundly visceral effect, like a sinister heartbeat.

The citizens of London and Westminster seemed to share her opinion. People tripped over each other to move out of the way. Men plastered themselves against walls or slipped into side alleys. Women gathered children into the shelter of their skirts and retreated into doorways. Pale young students of

Westminster School clutched their scholars' scrips and stared with wide eyes.

Iago had been sent ahead to act as herald, and he arrived early with Pippa in tow. The entrance to the palace was an arched portal overburdened by a forbidding gatehouse. Iago and Pippa waited in an open court called the Preaching Place. She felt the pricking eyes of guards and pensioners and palace officials, but like Iago, she held her chin aloft and ignored them.

Iago stood in the middle of the Preaching Place, staring the onlookers into silence. "Aidan, the O Donoghue Mór," he shouted after a long pause. "Chieftain of the sept O Donoghue, and known in these parts as the lord of Castleross."

After some minutes, she heard again the pulsebeat of marching. The iron portico of the court gate gaped open to admit the Irish chieftain. So that his escort would not be shut out, he came in last, mounted on his fully caparisoned mare.

Grooms and ministers and lesser folk of the palace rushed out to look. The crowd jostled Pippa back against a thick wall. She craned her neck but lost sight of Aidan.

"Never mind," whispered Iago. "You'll see him when he greets the queen. If he gets his way, the whole world will see him."

From a distance, she watched him dismount with a blue flutter of his mantle. Then Donal Og called something in Irish and the troops formed two lines. A piper and drummer began to play a strange, minor-toned march, and the entire assembly crossed the court to the Privy Gallery.

"This is an outrage," blustered a liveried, soldierly

looking man stationed at the entrance. "The O
Donoghue might as well fling down a gauntlet and
declare war."

"May his cursed Irish head roll," said another
guardsman.

"It may indeed. Watch him dig his own grave."

Iago and Pippa exchanged dubious glances. Then
they, too, hurried into the long, elegant building.

The main gallery seemed endless, with stone walls
and stone floors that made the marching footfalls
reverberate like thunder. At the end, a soaring doorway opened to the Presence Chamber.

Pippa entered with Iago. He led her along the side
of the chamber where it was less crowded. They continued toward the light-flooded end of the room
where there was a dais with a canopy so high that it
resembled a great tent.

"Where are we going?" Pippa demanded.

"This will do." Iago stepped to the middle of the
gallery, bowed low, and repeated his announcement.
Then he returned to Pippa's side and escorted her to
the end of the room. "Can you see now?"

She peered past a thick stone column and felt as if
the very hand of God had frozen her in place, stricken
her so that she could not move.

It was her first glimpse of Queen Elizabeth, and
Pippa was awestruck. Here, she thought, was majesty.
It was a quality far more rare and fearsome than mere
beauty, noble grace, or lively intelligence, although
the queen possessed all three in abundance.

Elizabeth sat on her throne of state, a huge box
chair carven and canopied and draped with hangings.
An array of shields were hung along the wall behind
her.

Wearing the most elaborate costume Pippa had ever seen, the queen appeared tiny, yet her diminutive size was like the very heart of a flower, the nectar surrounded by lavish petals.

A starched white collar framed her face, and braids of pearls and jewels adorned her cloud of fading reddish hair. From where Pippa stood, the queen's face looked stark white, her eyes a shining, canny black.

Fascinated, Pippa moved away from the pillar and began edging closer to the dais. Iago hissed something at her, but she ignored him. She found a spot in the shadows where she could observe the queen in profile as well as the grand aisle leading to the dais.

The thump of drums and the scree of pipes sounded from the antechamber. The deadly tramp of marching feet never faltered.

Elizabeth's black eyes flashed like moonlight on water. She leaned over to the man standing at her side. "Robbie, what *is* the meaning of this?"

"The earl of Leicester," Iago whispered to Pippa. "Her lord chancellor."

"I know. He tried to have me arrested the day I met Aidan."

Essex, the preening lord she recalled unpleasantly from the masque at Durham House, bent to whisper to the queen. The feather in his ridiculous velvet hat brushed the queen's cheek. "Out of my sight," she barked. "I have not forgiven you for winning at mumchance." Flushing, Essex stepped back a safe distance.

The heavy doors parted. Even Pippa, who had expected the ploy, caught her breath and gaped in amazement. The unsuspecting courtiers simply froze and stared.

In came Aidan's escort of one hundred gallowglass, looking more savage than a pack of wolves. They wore their rough beards and wolfskins like trophies of conquest, and each man bore full arms. She doubted that the Presence Chamber had ever seen such an array of battleaxes and broadswords, maces and pikes, and clubs.

The queen's guards bared their own swords, but the Irish made them look like toy soldiers, dressed for show rather than action.

The sound of the pipes shrilled and expanded, rolling out to each corner of the room before falling silent. The gallowglass formed two long lines, the sheer numbers of their bodies sweeping aside the palace guards.

Then a shadow loomed in the arched portal. Backlit by a blaze of sunlight from the antechamber, Aidan appeared massive and godlike, his gleaming cloak rustling and belling out like a huge set of wings.

His mane of hair flowed with his movements, the single decked strand looking defiantly pagan. His face wore an arrogance and pride Pippa had never seen before.

Somehow, the light managed to pick out every glorious angle and plane of his remarkable face: The broad, intelligent brow. The high cheekbones and square jaw. The sensual lips and fierce eyes. He was more than beautiful, more than remarkable. He radiated authority and majesty.

He was the O Donoghue Mór.

No one who saw him today would fail to know that. No one would ever forget him. Not even the queen of England.

He stood there long enough for the impact of his appearance to peak. Then he strode into the room, past frozen sentries and the Irish escort, directly to the base of the dais.

To her credit, the queen did none of the gasping and whispering and bosom fanning that erupted among her ladies, who stood in a group near Pippa. Elizabeth merely sat still, pale as ivory, unsmiling, her eyebrows barely lifted.

Aidan flung his cloak back over one shoulder. His silver rowan brooch flashed. Then, with a movement so abrupt Pippa feared he had been shot, he prostrated himself on the floor before the dais.

He lay facedown with his arms spread wide, looking like a fallen angel.

Clearly the queen had not anticipated this show of submission. No doubt, like everyone else, she was wondering just what it meant.

Submission? Even in this prone pose, the O Donoghue Mór radiated power. Fealty? That was doubtful indeed, given his distrust of things English.

"Rise, my lord of Castleross," the queen said at last. She had a rich, loud voice, the vowels round as cultured pearls.

Aidan stood before her. Sunlight streamed down through the high, arched windows, cloaking him in translucent gold. He could not have arranged for a more dramatic setting.

Pippa felt a tightness in her throat. She had never seen such a man, and she had sneaked her way into dozens of plays and revels in which men transformed themselves into birds and angels and Greek gods. But this was no playacting, no illusion of costume and character. There was something intensely moving about such a princely man confronting the queen in this manner.

He broke the silence then—with a howl so loud it caused people to jump in startlement. With savage fury he flung back his head and bellowed an ancient war cry—at least it sounded so to Pippa.

Then he began to pace, his hands clasped behind his back, his boots and spurs ringing on the flag-stones. His speech was in Gaelic, delivered with such passion and conviction that the foreign words did not matter. His tone said it all. He was an Irish chieftain, a ruler in his own right.

Beside Pippa, someone stifled a chuckle. She glanced over to see Iago nearby, cloaked in shadow.

"What is he saying?" she whispered out of the corner of her mouth.

Aidan ranted on, sometimes pausing in his pacing to gesticulate while the tirade never ceased.

"You do not want to know," Iago whispered. "But the *least* of what he is saying could earn him a penalty of death."

"God have mercy," murmured Pippa, thinking of the comments she had overheard in the antechamber. Chills swept over her skin.

As Aidan paused to draw breath, the gentleman pensioner on the queen's right thumped his halberd on the floor.

"My lord," said Sir Christopher Hatton, "Her Majesty desires for you to address her in English."

Pippa held her breath to see how Aidan would respond.

He faced her directly and bowed his head. "Madam," he said, "it is an honor to address you in your native tongue."

"Ooh," whispered a lady-in-waiting. "He has the most gorgeous Irish brogue!"

Pippa rolled her eyes. Clearly, Aidan O Donoghue had the desired effect on these ninnies. The question was, did his powers affect the queen?

"I wonder if he is in need of company," the lady's companion said. "Surely he is lonely, so far from home."

"He has plenty of company," Pippa hissed at them. "So back off!"

The ladies gasped and fell silent.

Iago chuckled softly. "You are always so discreet, *pequeña*."

". . . my absolute authority as lord of Castleross," Aidan was saying. "And furthermore, whilst I am in London, I shall attend mass at the Spanish embassy. These matters are required of my station as the O Donoghue Mór, good madam, a station that must carry equal respect as your own."

"I see," Elizabeth said in a loud, unpleasant voice. "But I have not challenged you in matters of faith, my lord, have I?"

He sent her a grin that started the ladies' fans fluttering again. "Nay, in this you are the soul of tolerance. I come to you on far more immediate matters, madam."

She tilted her head, clearly intrigued. "Go on."

"My people are suffering. Their crops have been burned. The women raped. Men hanged for made-up offenses."

"Your people have defied their English ruler," she countered.

"We would rule ourselves and send a tithe to Your Majesty," he shot back. "Under present conditions, you will receive nothing, for our lands are in ruin, thanks to Lord Constable Browne and other greedy opportunists. Keep on your present course, and there will be nothing left to claim."

The queen seemed, uncannily, to swell and grow in size. Pippa knew it was impossible, yet as Elizabeth's temper flared, so did her presence.

She was like a thin flame goaded to a brightness by a blast of wind. In her intense, diminutive way, she matched the powerful presence of the Irish chieftain.

But she did not exceed it.

"Are you quite finished, my lord of Castleross?" she asked at last.

"Madam," he replied, "I have barely begun."

Her nostrils flared. "My lord, if you seek to impress us with your defiance, you have succeeded."

Pippa cocked her head to one side. She heard a quavering thrum in the queen's voice. "Oh no," she whispered to Iago. "She is absolutely furious."

"Therefore, my lord," Elizabeth said, "we would ask one thing of you. It is a small matter, but one you might be hard-pressed to give."

"And what is that, Your Majesty?" asked Aidan.

"We should like you to give us one reason why we should not have you clapped in irons."

Aidan O Donoghue did the unthinkable. He threw back his head and laughed. It was that banner of dark mirth Pippa had heard the first day she had met him, and the rich, sultry sound of it echoed through the chamber.

The queen's eyes flared brighter. Leicester bent and said something to her in a pleading tone, but she waved him away.

At last Aidan's mirth subsided. "Madam, to answer your question."

Pippa wondered if the queen could detect the steel beneath the smooth silk of his tone.

He swept his arm back to gesture at the Irish soldiers. "When you mow down one blade of Irish grass, two more sprout in its place. And there are men far less cooperative than I. They would not hesitate to take my place if you remove me."

Silence fell, and within that silence thrummed a strain so taut that Pippa lifted her shoulders, ready to flinch when the tension snapped. Aidan was a dead man. She could read his fate in the eyes of the queen, in the grim whispers of her courtiers, on the outraged faces of her guards.

Then, like an arrow out of the blue, came an idea. Before she could talk herself out of it, she charged forward, breaking through the ranks of courtiers and gallowglass.

"Make way," she called, mimicking the major-domo's bell-like tones. "Make way!"

All were too startled to stop her. After stepping in front of Aidan, she curtsied deeply before the dais.

"Your Majesty, I must *insist* that you let this man go. You see, he has promised to do something for me, and he has not yet delivered."

Deliberately, she stumbled back against MacHurley, one of Aidan's troop leaders. "Ye gods!" she shrieked, clapping her hands to her cheeks and springing back to stare at him. "It is a lamb in wolf's clothing!"

Nervous titters drifted from the ladies, followed by a subtle murmur of male laughter from the group of courtiers beside the dais. Aidan scowled and hissed a warning under his breath, but she ignored him.

She stroked MacHurley's war tunic. "I do like a

man in fur," she announced, and looked pointedly at Essex's foppish hat. Aye, the lordling was in trouble with the queen, so it was safe to torment him. "It's so much preferable to feathers."

"See here now," Essex burst out, red faced with rage.

Pippa sidled up to him. He was so overdressed with trusses and shirt stuffing that he never felt her relieve him of his purse. With a flourish, she dangled it in front of his horrified face.

"Ah, see *here*," she said in a teasing voice. "What is it, my lord, that purples your complexion? A lock of hair from your lady love?"

The other courtiers burst into guffaws.

"What," the queen said, silencing the laughter, "is the meaning of this?"

Pippa turned back to the queen, to that pale, unreadable face, those snapping black eyes. "Your Majesty, I am but a humble strolling player in the employ of Lord Castleross. If he is clapped in irons, I shall be idle." She gave the queen a broad wink. "You know the perils of a woman in idleness, surely. I might actually have an intelligent thought. And *then* where would mankind be?"

The queen's mouth tightened. For a moment Pippa thought she might smile. "I take great pains to avoid idle thoughts," she said.

Pippa laughed, but no one else did.

"Guards! Remove her at once," said Leicester.

Two guards came toward her.

"Wait!" called the queen. Everyone froze. She looked from Aidan to Pippa and back again. "My lord of Castleross," she said.

"Madam."

"Get you gone from my sight, and take this—this *player* with you. On the morrow shall you return, and *then* I will render my decision regarding your defiance and the people of your district. Is that clear?"

"Abundantly." He did not wait for her to dismiss him. He swung around, bellowing a command in Gaelic. The pipes and drums started up. Grabbing Pippa by the arm to pull her along, he led his entourage out of the Presence Chamber.

Once he had reached the great quadrangle outside, he paused. "Well," he said, "I presume you have an explanation for your little performance."

"My performance was nothing compared to yours," she retorted. "You could have had yourself arrested for treason. I owe no explanation to you."

He caught her other arm and brought her around to face him. She could feel the heat emanating from him, could see the flecks of silver in his blue eyes.

"Ah, but you *will* talk to me, *a stor.* Tonight, I will have what I want from you."

She was late. The contrary female was deliberately making him sweat and pace and fret.

He went to the hearth in the great hall of Lumley House and savagely poked at a flame-eaten log. Sparks flew up the chimney. The infernal woman consumed him. He could think of naught but her, with her impish smile and lush body. His passion for her was like a fever for which he knew no cure save one— to have her on *his* terms, in his own manner, and damn the consequences.

Unfortunately, Pippa had a mind of her own and no fear of asserting her strong will. It was a quality that both drew and repelled him. Why couldn't she be more tractable? He answered his own question: because weak, compliant females held no appeal for him.

A terrible thought occurred to him. What if she had run off?

Ah, but she would be better off if she did leave. He could bring her only heartache.

A sense of loss clogged his throat. He slammed home the iron poker and strode for the door, flinging it wide open and pounding up the steps to her chamber. Without pausing to knock, he jerked the door open.

Empty. No trace of Pippa lingered save a light, elusive floral scent. He should feel relieved, he thought, closing the door with exaggerated control. She took the decision away from him. It was wrong to desire a woman who could never be his. Wrong to avoid telling her about Felicity. But then, what could he say to anyone about Felicity? He never spoke of her. There was simply no explaining about her, especially to Pippa, who had grown to trust him implicitly.

He stalked to his chambers and jerked open the door. He almost smacked into Pippa, who was on her way out. She gazed up at him, an ironic smile quirking her mouth. "There you are, Your Worship. You were late, and I came looking for you."

"I was late!" he yelled. With a curse to cover his relief, he drew her into the room and kicked the door shut. He had told himself to be stern with her. To censure her for interfering with his audience with the queen.

Instead, unable to stop himself, he gave a great

whoop of triumph, lifted her up, and swung her around gleefully.

"By the blessed heart of Saint Brigid," he declared, setting her on her feet and giving her a great smacking kiss on each cheek. Though he wanted to let his lips linger over the smoothness of her skin, he pulled back and said, "We were *good* today. We walked into the lion's den and lived to tell the tale."

She took a moment to recover herself. Then she grinned. "I told you so. Admit you were afraid, just for half a second. Admit you feared she would have you arrested and locked up."

"I was *not* afraid for half a second," he said in a blustering tone. "I was pissing scared the entire time, you saucy baggage."

She laughed. "You forced the queen to see you as a man, a worthy rival, rather than a beggar seeking favors. It was better that you risked all."

"Including my people. That was stupid of me."

"Nay, it was bold. Your people would think so."

"Perhaps. Now what, pray, was the meaning of your little performance?"

She gave an elaborate shrug. Feigned innocence, but ah, faith, she was wondrous. Her spilling curls looked as if they had been gilt by the fairies. She still wore her court gown, though without the coif and extra set of sleeves.

"Someone had to divert the queen's attention so she'd forget about punishing you." She went to the sideboard and poured herself a goblet of wine from a stoneware decanter. She turned around and took a bracing gulp. "Not that I give a rat's furry arse," she amended.

"Ah." He stared at her, remembering what she had

said. *I don't love you. . . .* The memory wrenched at his heart and tweaked his conscience, too. What a fool he had been to ask her to become his mistress. What made him think he could possess any part of her without giving all of himself?

"Pippa, about what I said yesterday. . . ," he began, desperate to ease the hurt that knit her brow.

She tossed her head. "Badger me no more about it, my answer is still the same. You are an overwhelming male specimen. Your touch is magic. When you kiss me, the world seems to melt around the edges. But I don't love you, and I won't be your mistress. You'd not want me, anyway. I would spend all your money, drive you mad with all my chatter and bad singing. So it is best for us to—"

He strode across the room, stopped her with a hard, lingering kiss, and did not let up until he felt her all but collapse in surrender against him.

"I meant to say I'm sorry," he whispered into her ear. Then he let her go and moved away, out of her reach. "That's all I wanted to say. And you sing beautifully."

"S-sorry?" she said in a dazed voice.

"To dishonor you with my request."

She stared at him until he grew uncomfortable under her stern regard. She continued to stare even as she lifted the wine goblet to her lips and drank. She did not flinch as the strong draft went down.

Finally she said in all solemnity, "Dishonor me?"

"I spoke without thinking, in the heat of the moment."

With exaggerated care, she set down the goblet. "You're not listening, my lord. I refuse to be your mistress. I do not want to be your arm ornament at revels. I do not want you to dedicate songs and poems and—God forbid—jousts and tourneys to me."

She paused, took a deep breath, and said, "But I do want you . . . I invite you . . . I *implore* you to dishonor me."

Her intensity, her candor, tore at his heart. "Colleen," he said, "you don't know what you're asking."

She pushed away from the sideboard and crossed the room toward him, her brilliant skirts and petticoats whispering on the flagstoned floor. She stood before him, close enough for him to feel the warmth of her, to catch her scent of silk and fresh air.

"I know exactly what I'm asking." She spoke softly but with conviction and an edge of defiance. "I want the whirlwinds and bonfires they sing about in ballads. I want the feeling I get when you touch me."

It took much strength to keep his hands fisted at his sides when all he wanted to do was take her in his arms. "You've been saying you don't love me—"

"And pray you, remember that," she snapped. "This has naught to do with love."

"Then what has it to do with?"

She swallowed. Though it seemed to require some effort, she kept her gaze steadily on his. "It has to do with need, my lord. The need of a young girl on the road, making her way to London with nothing but a dream to sustain her. The need of a strolling player in St. Paul's, making strangers laugh at her and pretending to laugh with them, when sometimes all she wants to do is cry."

Her desperation seemed to reach down inside him and clasp his heart until he could no longer separate her pain from his own. "Pippa—"

"No, let me finish. I'm not asking for your pity. I'm

simply telling you these things so you'll understand.
Please, may I continue?"

He did not want to hear any more, for he already
understood all too well the source of her heartache. In
one way or another, she had been deserted all her life.
Now she had some notion that he could heal her, and
in that, she was dead wrong. But he nodded, almost
against his will, and said, "I'm listening."

"By now you know everything there is to know
about me, except for one thing."

"And what is that?" he asked. It took all of his
resolve not to touch her, to feel her softness, to inhale
her scent.

"It's this." She took a deep breath. "I have never
been touched in the way you touch me."

"In what way is that?" he asked, dry mouthed.

"You touch me as if you care."

He could not help himself then. He did not even try
to stop his hands as they came up, slowly, brushing
over her wrists and traveling up her arms, finally
cresting at her shoulders and, so gently, as if she were
as fragile as the spun glass of Crutched Friars,
cradling her soft, flushed cheeks.

"I do care," he confessed. "That is why I must ask
you not to tempt me. Cling to your honor, Pippa. It is
the only thing a person has that cannot be taken
away."

She smiled grimly. "You think I care about honor?
I?" She closed her eyes, and for a moment her mouth
thinned as if she were in agony. Then she looked up at
him. "I have lied, cheated, and stolen in order to survive. For the right price, I would have sold my body."
She took his hands away from her face and clung to
them. A bitter, mirthless laugh escaped her. "The

funny thing is, no man ever considered me worth paying for. A few tried to simply help themselves, but even I had the sense to rebuff them."

She paused, and silence hung in the room. Evening was deepening to twilight. Soon it would be time for them to go to the hall for supper, but neither moved.

Finally she spoke again. "So you see, I have no honor. You cannot take from me something I never possessed in the first place."

"Faith, Pippa, you have more honor than a legion of Sassenach nobles."

"Don't ply that Irish charm on me. Words just get in the way. I want you, Aidan. All of you. Everything. But if I can have you for tonight only, then that is what I will settle for."

He pulled his hands out of her grip. "You're asking me to hurt you."

She caught the front of his tunic, twisting her fingers into the heavy silk. "Have you not heard a word I've said? I hurt *now*, Aidan! How much worse can it be?"

A curse of frustration erupted from him. He grabbed her and hauled her close, crushing her against him. He slid one hand down to cup her backside, pressing until she felt the full force of his desire. The other hand he buried in her hair, tilting her head back until his mouth was a mere whisper away from hers.

"Is this what you want, then? Is this no worse than the pain you already feel?" Before she could answer, he plunged his mouth down on hers, taking her and tasting the wine she had drunk, violating her with his tongue, hearing her whimper and forcing himself to ignore the sound of her distress.

Her hands slid up over his chest. He expected her to try to push him away. Instead, she clung to him. She stood on tiptoe so that their kiss grew even deeper. She willingly pressed herself against him, mad with wanting, driving *him* mad. Somehow she had sensed that his rough embrace was only an act designed to discourage her. He had not fooled her in the least.

Somewhere, buried deep in a corner of his mind, was a reason he should not let this continue, should not build this emotional bond with her.

Deliberately he closed his mind to it.

And when she made a yearning, straining movement with her hips against him, he could not even remember his own name.

Still kissing, still embracing, they moved like a pair of dancers toward the chamber door. It opened with a push of his foot, and they entered the bedchamber.

No candles had been lit. The twilight gleamed dully through the wavy panes of the mullioned windows. A few coals breathed faintly in a brazier.

He guided her backward until, with a sweet, surrendering sigh, she sank onto the bed. He leaned over her, watching the way the curls spilled around her face like the gilded petals of a flower.

The stark need in her eyes reached for him, caught at him. Ah, that need. It was the one thing he could not resist about her.

"Turn over," he whispered.

She obeyed unquestioningly. He took hold of her bodice laces and tugged, then peeled away the stiff garment. Beneath, she wore only a chemise of fabric so thin that even in the dull purple light he could see the shape of her breasts, the darkness of the aureoles.

He leaned down, brushed his mouth over her lips, and then leaned lower to nuzzle aside the chemise and kiss each breast lingeringly, trying to hold his own sharp need at bay while giving her the sweetest pleasure he could impart.

He lifted his head and looked at her. The sight of her bare breasts, moist and budded from his kisses, nearly made him come out of his skin with wanting her.

She shifted restlessly, and he caught the hem of her skirt, drawing the garments up and over her knees to reveal knitted stockings, hugging her shapely legs. These he peeled away slowly, with relish, kissing and tasting each bit of flesh he revealed. His hands blazed a tantalizing path up her bare thighs, finding at last the treasure at their crest. Ah, she was ready for him, warm and moist and pulsing already, offering no resistance, only welcome. He bent his head and kissed her there, and grew drunk on the heady essence of her.

She lay as if frozen by shock, but then her hands clutched at his shoulders, and her breath came in thin, shallow gasps. She gave a startled cry and grasped at him, pulling him up and kissing him almost frantically.

He felt her tongue enter his mouth, and without volition, his hand went to unlace his codpiece, his only goal to bury himself in her, to ease the intolerable ache she created in him. He had never known a desire as piercing, as all-consuming, as this. She had lit a wildfire in his blood, and the heat surged through him until he lost all sense of who he was. Then her hand crept down to help with his codpiece, and against his mouth, she whispered, "If this be dishonor, then what is the point of honor?" She kissed

him again, her mouth soft and moist, her body arching toward his.

What is the point of honor?

In the dimmest reaches of his conscience, a sense
of guilt flickered dully. He forced himself to remember who he was. What he was. A chieftain. A foreigner. A husband.

Stopping himself from making love to Pippa was
like keeping the waves from pounding at the shore.
His passion flooded in all directions, exploding
through him until he nearly surrendered. What
stopped him was no loyalty to his married state, but a
thought of Pippa. She trusted him, admired him,
even. He could not bring himself to shatter her image
of him, to disappoint her as she had been disappointed all her life.

He forced himself to lighten their kiss, all the while
cursing inwardly. Very gently, he lifted his mouth
from hers.

Her eyes fluttered open. "Oh, Aidan, Jesu, that
was . . . we . . . you . . . "

He smiled, touched her cheek, tried to ignore the
ravaged state of his body. "I know, lass. I know."

A tiny frown puckered her brow. "How can you
know? *I* had all the pleasure."

His smile broadened. It was amazing that she
could make him smile when an inferno burned inside
him. "There you are wrong."

"You mean you . . . we . . . "

He brushed a tendril of hair off her temple. "For
someone who talks so much, you seem to be at a loss
for words. There is more than a little enjoyment in
this for me as well." With hands both discreet and
tender, he drew her bodice up and her skirts down.

Her eyes narrowed. "I think you're lying."

"And I think," he said, "that you have failed to understand something. You matter to me. Your pleasure matters to me. Giving you pleasure is my reward."

"Well, then, what about *my* reward?" She reached for him.

He laughed softly and stopped her. Before tonight, he had no idea it was possible to be as hard as bog oak and still be able to laugh. "Don't get greedy on me."

"I said I wanted you to dishonor me," she said. "I don't feel dishonored yet."

Her words froze his blood. Suddenly the whole world rushed back at him. He was no longer detached, remote, free. For he remembered it all now, remembered why he had no right to be here, with Pippa, taking joy in her joy.

With stiff movements, aching as he did on the day after a battle, he pulled away from her and stood.

"You're wrong," he said, passing a weary hand through his hair. "We are both dishonored."

She lay awake that night, trying as hard as she could to die of a broken heart. It wasn't working. She was beginning to think these things happened only in tawdry love ballads.

Even when she pictured Aidan, glorious and mysterious as a dark angel, turning from her and leaving her cold, she could not will her heart to stop or to shatter or to do whatever it was hearts did when someone broke them.

When she thought of the way he had held her and

whispered in her ear, when she remembered his intimate kisses and caresses, she wept, but she did not
die.

She took out her brooch, fingering the warm gold
as she thought about her plan to find her family.
What a foolish notion, to fancy she could accomplish
such a feat. Even her own mother had abandoned her.
Why should Aidan be any different? And how could
she have thought an Irish chieftain could love a girl
off the streets?

By dawn she had decided that she was going to survive after all. The question was, what was she going
to do with herself?

She got up and stepped over the clothes she had
left in a heap on the floor. After Aidan had—what
had he done? Made love to her? No, it was something
more controlled and cold-blooded than that, for he
had refused to give her the one thing she needed—his
heart.

Just for a moment, he had opened a window into
his heart. But before she could truly peer inside, he
had closed back up, shunted her away.

"Damn your Irish eyes, Aidan O Donoghue," she
muttered, stepping into her petticoat and skirts. She
could not avoid remembering the way he had helped
her dress, laughing at the absurd complexities of
Sassenach clothing. She tugged on her bodice, defiantly lacing it in front, and then she went to the basin
and bathed her face in cool water.

In the stableyard, she found Iago. Just the sight of
him, putting a horse through its paces, was a balm to
her heart. He had become that rarest of treasures, a
true friend.

He tugged at the lunge rein to stop the horse.

"What happened to you?" he demanded. "You look terrible."

"Thank you," she said mockingly. "How very kind of you to point that out."

He led the palfrey over to a drystone wall and tethered it. "You were with Aidan last night."

"Yes." To Iago, she could deny nothing. "But he . . . didn't stay."

The mare sidled restively. He patted her neck with a soothing hand. "Ah. I feared—" He suddenly seemed very interested in inspecting the horse's bit.

"What?" She leaned her elbows on the rough wall and scowled down at him. "What do you fear?"

He took his time adjusting the bit. Then he regarded her with placid melancholy. "I feared that Aidan's conscience and his sense of duty would get the best of him. He ignores the call of his heart."

"I don't understand."

"It is not my place to explain. Soon, we will all go back to Ireland. None of this will matter."

In the back of her mind, Pippa had always known Aidan O Donoghue did not belong here in London amid the littered streets and wreaths of smoke and pervasive sewage smell. She envisioned him in his native Ireland, a place as clean and dramatic and wild as the O Donoghue Mór himself.

Ireland was his home. He was never meant to be here, never meant to pick up a penny player from St. Paul's and steal her heart. It should not have happened, but it had.

The mare nickered and stamped the ground.

Pippa looked at Iago, studying his remarkable face and beaded hair, his sensitive, long-fingered hands, and his black liquid eyes. Knowing he was so far from his own native land calmed her and underscored her conviction.

"In all my wandering years," she told him in a surprisingly steady voice, "I have learned one important thing."

"What is that, little one?"

"To leave first. So I am not the one being left."

He touched her hand, ever so gently, and his tenderness made her weep inside. "That is not such a bad plan."

She gave him a tremulous smile. "You're supposed to talk me out of it."

"That would only postpone the inevitable."

She dragged in a shaking breath and patted his hand. "I suppose so. But now the question is, where do I go next?"

His smile flashed like silver in sunlight. "*Pequeña*, I thought you would never ask."

FROM THE ANNALS OF INNISFALLEN

I worry that the nine-fingered courier seen taking ship out of Dingle Bay is up to some mischief.

At least, though, I have a smidgen of happy news to record. By now, the O Donoghue should have received my letter about the marriage, saying he is a free man, and a high praise be to all the saints and angels for that blessing.

The question that plagues my poor soul now is, can the damage wrought to his heart ever be mended?
—*Revelin of Innisfallen*

9

"She left?" Aidan stood with Iago outside the Crutched Friars glassworks, where they had gone to fetch a gift for the queen. He had commissioned it from the glassblowers, but Iago's news made him forget his purpose.

Pretending only idle curiosity, he had asked after the whereabouts of Pippa, who had been conspicuously absent last night at supper and this morning at breakfast.

"Yes, my lord," Iago said evenly, "she has departed."

Aidan stopped next to a hive-shaped glass forge and tried to absorb the shock of losing her. It was not supposed to matter to him, but somehow she had embedded herself in his heart, and her absence left a gaping void.

Especially now. A message had come from Revelin, claiming his ordeal with Felicity was over. Aidan felt cautious, though, and would not believe the truth until he was certain.

In a brusque voice he said, "I should have known she would leave, inconstant female."

Something strange and unexpected was happening inside him. A fiery ache started in his heart and then rolled outward along his limbs to his hands and feet and head. If he did not know himself to be in hale good health, he would have thought the sweat was coming over him.

He choked out a curse and turned away from Iago, clenching his teeth and pressing his palms together on the plaster outer wall of the hut. The forge heated the wall, but not enough, not nearly enough to warm the cold empty place carved out by Pippa's departure.

When had he begun to love her, he wondered, and how had he managed to deny it for so long?

Images of her shone like sunlight in his mind. He remembered his first glimpse of her, insolent and exuberant upon the steps of St. Paul's. He remembered her belting out a bawdy song as she took her first bath, banishing the maids with heartbreaking pride, diverting the queen's wrath with reckless courage. And finally, begging him to make love to her—begging him and then recoiling in the face of his rejection.

"God," he whispered with a harsh breath, "she's gone."

"She went to court," Iago said quietly.

Aidan stopped breathing for a moment, then started again with a great heave. "To court."

"That is best for her, no? She will live in decent quarters, will be safer than she was scrounging about St. Paul's."

He closed his eyes and pictured her at court, moving with perfect ease amid nobles and diplomats and jurists. Perhaps she would find another man to charm, a protector who could give her his heart as Aidan never could. He pushed away the intolerable thought. "If anyone can succeed at court," he said, "Pippa can."

"Indeed. And of course, she might actually find her family, just as you suggested."

Aidan gave a bark of humorless laughter. "I merely suggested it to dissuade her from risky living among thieves and pimps."

"I think she believed you, my lord. I think, in her heart, she dreams she will find her family. She needs to know she is loved."

A shiver passed like the winter wind over Aidan. "She needs me," he said, half to himself.

Iago made a *tsk*ing sound with his tongue. "But what of the future? Can you give her the constancy she needs?"

Futile rage boiled up in Aidan, and he pushed away from the hut to glare at Iago. "I cannot. You know that." In the wake of the rage came a gray tide of bleakness. "Do you ever just want to turn your back on it all? To simply let go of everything and walk away?"

"I have done that." Mischief gleamed in his eyes. "Only in my case, I swam."

Aidan forced a smile. At the same time, his errant heart led him to a decision. "Go and fetch the queen's gift. I must get myself dressed."

"*Diablo!*" Iago said. "Do not tell me—"

"Yes." Aidan started back toward the house. "I am taking the gift to court myself."

* * *

". . . and so," Pippa said with a confidential wink at the queen, "the brewer's daughter could only make one choice. To poison the keg!"

Queen Elizabeth's smile was slow and filled with pleasure. Other listeners took their cue from the queen and chuckled.

Pippa curtsied and surreptitiously released her breath. Her Majesty's moods were capricious. Stories she found amusing one moment might land the teller in the stocks the next. So far, Pippa had been lucky.

Of course, it was only her second day as the royal fool. Thus far, the queen had made no decision regarding the O Donoghue Mór, but Pippa kept an ear cocked for any whisper of his fate.

"Well told," the queen said. "In sooth, virtue and innocence do not always triumph, do they?"

"Not nearly so often, ma'am, as old age and cunning," Pippa blurted out, then froze.

The queen stared at her for a long moment. Her face, already smooth and pale with its coating of ceruse and powder, seemed to whiten even more. Then she let out a hoot of laughter, and the courtiers joined in.

"You are a tonic, my poppet," she said. "I am pleased indeed that you petitioned me for a player's warrant. I do like to nurture talent. And you are well rid of that foreign chieftain."

"Ma'am." Hiding her regret, Pippa sank to one knee and snatched up the hem of the queen's gown. "I am so humbly grateful."

"Yes, yes." Faint impatience underscored the queen's words. "Do stand up and let me look at you."

Pippa stood. The queen's bird-black eyes flicked over her, and she said, "That gown is familiar to mine eyes."

"I am told it belonged to Lady Cheyney," Pippa said baldly, knowing the truth was safer than lying and then being found out. "But here's the fact, ma'am. The gown does not a fool make. I have worn this for two days and have not felt the slightest urge to invite a gentleman to my chambers."

The queen tapped a long finger on the arm of her chair. "You are a fool in name only." Her smile tightened. "Still, you should consult the master of revels for the proper mode of dress. My sister Mary, of honored memory, did make her fool shave her head and wear striped garb."

Pippa lifted a hand to the curls escaping her coif. "There are worse things, madam, than shaving one's head," she said bravely. Still, she felt a heavy disappointment. Her hair was finally beginning to grow out to a more becoming length.

"Fear not, for I—" The queen glanced at the distant doorway of the Presence Chamber. "Yes?" she called.

"The O Donoghue Mór, lord of Castleross," intoned the majordomo.

Elizabeth waved away the other courtiers clustered round the canopied throne. Pippa found herself standing next to the Contessa Cerniglia. Of the many people Pippa had met at court, Rosaria was her favorite. Fair and tall, she had a pleasantly cynical view of life and a keen ear for gossip.

With her heart pounding wildly, Pippa trained her gaze on the door. Aidan!

Why had he returned? Part of her prayed he had come for her, while another part dreaded seeing him again, feeling that twist of raw wanting and the sting of his indifference.

She stood as still as a marble pillar and waited.

With the dramatic suddenness of a darkening storm, he filled the doorway, flanked by Donal Og and Iago. Looking like mythical giants, they made their unhurried way down the center of the room.

He wore his princely garb, the stone-bedecked tunic and rich blue mantle. Pippa felt a lurch of pure yearning. His masculine beauty was so powerful, it made her want to stare at him and never look away.

He knelt before the queen. Iago and Donal Og did likewise; then simultaneously the three of them stood.

"We bring gifts, my queen," Aidan said formally. He kept his gaze straight ahead, but Pippa had an uncanny sense that he was aware of her in the room.

"Ah, and he speaks English today," Elizabeth said with wry humor. "We are making progress."

Iago and Donal Og placed the gifts at her feet. One was the most elaborate salt cellar Pippa had ever seen, a tall fantasy of spun glass. It resembled a stylized castle, its slender turrets reaching upward, the tiny chamber where the salt was held surrounded by thin threads and coils of glass.

The other gift was a bracelet of cut amethyst that caught the light and seemed to shine from within. Pippa remembered wearing the matching necklace, remembered the magic of that night, and she blinked back tears.

"That is lovely." The queen held out her hand for the bauble and lifted it to spin on its gold chain in the light.

"The jewels were mined by Irish hands in the Burren," Aidan said.

"Indeed. For that honor, I thank you, my lord." She spoke pleasantly and smiled, yet at the same time her small, slippered foot pushed at the base of the salt cellar.

Pippa gaped in horror as the perfect glass tower shattered on the flagstone floor. Tiny shards and needles of glass scattered every which way.

The O Donoghue Mór did not flinch. The bright, wasted glitter covered the floor all around his feet.

"Such a pity." The queen fixed her black-eyed stare on Aidan. "You see, my lord, when a man builds a castle without proper consent, accidents are bound to happen."

The Contessa Cerniglia gave a soft murmur of dismay. Delicately she plucked at her skirt. A small cut marred her ankle. Instantly Donal Og knelt at her feet and touched the tiny bright bead of blood that seeped through her stocking. The lady's dismay changed quickly to romantic interest as she gazed down at Donal Og. She had large bosoms, which she displayed proudly with a low-cut, jeweled bodice. The effect was not lost on Donal Og.

"It is also a pity," Aidan said, "that accidents are capricious by nature. Sadly, it is often the innocent who suffer." He directed a meaningful look at the blond contessa.

"Sometimes the strong suffer, too." The queen rose from her throne. Leicester and Hatton moved in fast to escort her out of the Presence Chamber. Before she left, she said, "My lord of Castleross, I trust you'll join us at supper and revels tonight."

No. Pippa tried to will him to refuse. It was dangerous

for him here. The queen was playing some cruel game with him. He ought to leave while he had the chance.

The O Donoghue Mór bowed from the waist. "Madam, I am most humbly honored."

The revels that night consisted of wild, skirling music and a troupe of Italian acrobats. Donal Og and Iago watched with rapt attention.

Aidan watched Pippa. She sat at one of the lower tables amid minor officials and the queen's lesser ladies. Court, he noted with a pang, agreed with Pippa.

She laughed with practiced charm and wielded her fork and knife as if she had dined at table for years. Though he could not hear what she said, he guessed that she was in rare form. She looked animated and flushed. Everyone nearby listened to her and laughed.

Yet he began to notice an almost feverish desperation beneath her chatter. Her gaze darted about the hall and searched every noble face.

He knew what she was looking for. The mother and father whose image she had tended so lovingly in her imagination. When, he wondered, would she realize the futility of her dream? Not only had he hurt her, but she was bound to suffer when her impossible quest failed.

As soon as the dancing began, he sought her out. She was standing beneath the musicians' gallery with Donal Og and the Venetian contessa, urging them to dance the volta.

Aidan could not help smiling at the picture they made, giant Donal Og gazing in helpless adoration at the blond beauty.

Pippa shooed them out onto the dance floor, then watched them with a satisfied air.

"In Ireland," Aidan said softly, coming up behind her, "we do leave matchmaking to crones and tanists."

She turned and caught her breath. He stopped walking toward her, wanting to freeze the moment, to hold this image of her forever in his heart. She had that look of timeless beauty, her face smooth, eyes wide with a startled look, a crown of curls gleaming in the rushlight.

How had she done it? he wondered. How had she managed to stay so winsome and innocent when every day of her life had been a struggle to survive?

Finally she spoke. "I'm sorry about the salt cellar."

He smiled. "Revelin used to say 'When you sup with the devil, you need a long spoon.'"

She laughed and said something, but her words were drowned by a brassy blare of trumpets from the gallery above.

"Come with me." He steered her by the elbow toward a side exit. Within moments they had gone through a low-ceilinged passageway and emerged into a garden. At the end of the sloping yard, the river gleamed with starlight. Aidan took a deep breath of the cool night air. "That is better," he said.

"No one is supposed to depart until the queen gives leave," said Pippa.

"Is that so? I wonder how I dared."

"Must be your long spoon. Aidan—"

"Pippa—"

They both spoke at once, both laughed awkwardly.

"Go on," he said. "What were you going to say?"

She strolled down a walkway, her slippered feet

silent on the path. Then she stopped and turned to him, leaning back against the rail of the knot garden. "I wanted to explain why I left."

"Without a word," he reminded her, staring at the slim, pale column of her throat, the tops of her breasts where they pushed up from her bodice.

"This was all your idea," she said. "You said I might find a way to discover who I am, where I came from." Her eyes narrowed. "Or was that another of your lies?"

Her distrust cut at him like a blade. "I never—"

"You did," she shot back before he could finish. "You asked me to be your mistress. You had me *begging* to be your lover, and then you denied me." She fixed him with an insolent stare. "I tell you, my lord, I have had better days. *Much* better days. Such as the time I was set upon by dogs at the bear-baiting ring."

"You were attacked by dogs at the bear-baiting ring?" He felt sick. He had seen the curs kenneled outside the ring at Southwark. Slavering, vicious beasts, they were.

"No," she snapped, "but if I had been, it would have made for a better day than being cast off by you."

Aidan swore in Gaelic. She had managed to singe his temper, and he was glad. It was the only way to keep his desire in check. "You're a fine performer indeed. Tell me, was the queen as gullible as I was when you came to beg a place in her household? If you had said your loyalty was for sale, I would not have worried so much."

"The queen's offer tempts me far greater than yours," she retorted. "I would have paid for yours in heartbreak."

If her voice had stayed firm, he could have stood it. But it did not. Instead, her speech quavered with a bitter hurt that seared his soul. "Ah, Pippa. You were right to leave me. I can't give you what you need."

She squeezed her eyes shut. He had a powerful urge to kiss her, to use mouth and tongue to change her expression from pain to pleasure. But he resisted.

"We should not quarrel. It serves nothing." She drew away from him. He folded his arms to keep from pulling her back into his embrace.

"There is a dream I used to have of a dark-haired woman bending to kiss me," Pippa said. "'Mind Mama's brooch, darling,' she would say. 'Don't prick your finger on it.'" Pippa plucked at the head of a rose. "I don't know if it's a flight of fancy or a true memory, but I do know that last night I dreamt it again. And I dreamt of a man's merry laughter, and a grandmother singing to me in a strange language."

"Singing what?" he asked. "Do you recall the tune?"

"The song lingers still." She sang, the words so unfamiliar they sounded like gibberish, but she seemed quite sure of herself. "I feel close to them here, Aidan. As if I might spy a face in the crowd and recognize it. Recognize *myself*."

For long moment, he did not—could not—speak. What must it be like, not to know one's family? Aidan O Donoghue had known from the cradle who he was. It had brought him little pleasure and much pain, but at least he had known. Again he ached for her. The chance of finding her family was too painfully slim. She could walk right past her mother and not know it.

"I think I understand your hunger," he said at last.

"And I am Irish. I would never be so foolish as to underestimate the power of a dream."

"Thank you for saying that," she said. "All I want to know is that someone once loved me. And perhaps then I can believe someone could love me once again."

Someone wants to love you, *a gradh*, Aidan thought, biting his tongue to keep from blurting out the words. The problem is, the wrong man wants to love you.

Wimberleigh House, the soaring Strand residence of Richard de Lacey, teemed with activity. The garden doors of the house had been flung wide open, and servants paraded down a path to the river, carrying parcels of all shapes and sizes to a commodious river barge.

And there was the low-bellied bastard Aidan was looking for.

"Lord Castleross!" From the river landing Richard waved in greeting.

Feeling grim as winter, Aidan stalked down to the landing where Richard stood amid parcels and barrels.

"You just missed making the acquaintance of my parents, the earl and countess of Wimberleigh," Richard said. "They've taken themselves off to Hertfordshire. We did celebrate a grand farewell. My aunt Belinda set off colored fire and rockets, ah, that was a sight to see, and—"

"I'm certain it was." Aidan wasted no time in idle talk. "Why didn't you tell me your commission was a post in Kerry?"

Richard's ears reddened. "In sooth, my lord, I did not know. I expected a post in Ireland, but my assignment to your domain came as a surprise to me."

"But you accepted it," Aidan said tautly. All during his wild ride through the streets of London, he had hoped the gossip he'd heard the night before was wrong.

Richard made no attempt to deny it. He planted his feet wide. "The queen gave me no choice. No more than you had about coming to London."

"Aye," Aidan lashed out, "but I did not come here to butcher the citizens, steal their land, rape their women, and raid their livestock."

"And that is not my purpose in Ireland." Richard cursed and flung his velvet hat to the ground. "I am being sent to keep the peace."

"Ah, that is rich," said Aidan. "Did you ever think, my young lordling, that if the Sassenach would stay out of Ireland, then we would be at peace?"

"If we were not there, the Irish would fight amongst themselves."

"Then give us that freedom, man!" Aidan roared. "Let us destroy ourselves at our own discretion, with no help from you." He flung out his arm in agitation. His fist hit a canvas-wrapped parcel, toppling it. There was a tearing sound, and the corner of a crate ripped through the parcel.

"God's teeth." Richard bent to pull aside the wrapping. A large portrait of a lady, now pierced by the wooden crate, stared up at the gray morning sky.

"I'm sorry," Aidan said brusquely. "'Twas an accident."

The woman in the picture was remarkable—dark and serene with misty eyes the color of winter rain.

"Your betrothed?" he asked, picking up the ruined painting.

"My mother, Countess Wimberleigh. God knows when I shall see her again." Richard called out in a foreign tongue. The burly servant with the mustache hurried over and reached for the portrait.

"Wait a moment." Aidan held up a hand and frowned at the picture. The countess wore a rather plain gown of dove gray. Her one ornament, a brooch, looked out of place pinned to her bodice.

His heart lurched. The ornament was large and unusual, cruciform in shape, decked with a huge red stone encircled by twelve matched pearls.

He swallowed past a sudden dry heat in his throat. "When was this painted?"

Richard shrugged irritably. "Sometime in the first year of my parents' marriage, about twenty-five years ago."

"Does your mother still wear that jewel?"

He frowned and shook his head. "I've never seen it." He exchanged words with the foreign servant who then carried off the portrait.

"I'll pay to have it repaired."

"Never mind," said Richard. "My lord, I'm sorry to part with you on these terms. I would that we could—"

"How did you come to have Russian servants?" Aidan's mind was starting to pull together the fragments of an amazing puzzle.

"My family has ties to the kingdom of Muscovy. The Muscovy Trading Company was begun by my grandfather Stephen, Lord Lynley. He and my grandmother still live in Wiltshire."

"Did she sing to you?"

Richard regarded him with a confused scowl. "Sing?"

"You know, ballads. Lullabies. In Russian."

"I don't know. Perhaps. I don't remember."

Aidan saw that he was rousing Richard's suspicions. He cut himself short and said, "I have no quarrel with you until you set foot on Irish soil. Then, it will be as if our brief friendship had never occurred."

If Richard replied, Aidan did not hear him. He had sudden pressing business at Whitehall with the queen's fool.

Pippa pretended to be totally absorbed in the game of chess she was playing with Rosaria, the Contessa Cerniglia. In reality, her attention was secretly trained on the travel-weary courier who claimed he had urgent news from Ireland.

The crowded room buzzed with activity. The courier, a man with long cheeks and sunken eyes and a clear tenor voice, pressed his hands on the petitioner's table in frustration. Pippa noticed that he was missing a finger on his left hand.

"What do you suppose his problem is?" asked the contessa.

Pippa smiled at her across the chessboard. "Who, my lady?"

The contessa's lips thinned. "You know very well who. You have been staring at him since he walked in. You have also been cheating at chess, but I like your company, so I'm letting it pass."

Pippa stared at her. No one—*no one*—had ever caught her cheating.

The contessa laughed softly. "I am the daughter of the Venetian ambassador," she reminded Pippa. "My father built his life around observing people, seeing what is in their minds by watching what they do, particularly with their hands and eyes. I learned all I know from him."

"Sorry about the cheating," said Pippa. "It is a habit with me."

The blond contessa gave her a brilliant smile. "Never mind. Are you interested in learning the news from Ireland?" She nodded toward the courier, who was still arguing with a palace official. Leicester and his stepson, Essex, went to join in the discussion.

"Certainly not."

"Of course you are." The contessa rose from the table. "The news might concern your lover."

"The O Donoghue Mór is not my—" Pippa clapped a hand over her mouth, furious at herself for letting the contessa trick her into blurting out his name.

The cool, beautiful woman patted Pippa's arm. "I thought as much." She led Pippa through the packed room, exchanging polite snippets of greeting with the courtiers they passed. "Now, what about the other one—is he a brother?"

"No, Donal Og is Aidan's cousin."

"Donal Og." The contessa's mouth stretched into a smile. "Has he a wife?"

"No, he—" Pippa stopped walking. "You're smitten with Donal Og!"

"Smitten is too chaste a word, *cara*." The contessa winked and took her hand. "My feelings have progressed well past smitten." When they drew close to the petition table, she paused and took out her fan, fluttering it in front of her face.

Pippa held back. "They'll see us," she said. "They'll know we're trying to listen to them."

Rosaria smiled. "Here is a basic truth about men. When their minds are not on lusty matters, women are invisible to them. They will not even notice us."

It was true. The messenger spoke in low, agitated tones to Leicester and Essex and did not even pause for breath when Pippa and the contessa moved in close, pretending to have a whispered conversation behind their fans.

". . . an emergency. The danger is barely under control," he was saying. "His kinsmen kidnapped six Englishmen while they were on maneuvers. I fear they mean to kill the hostages."

"Have the rebels made any specific demands?"

"None that I know of. I strongly suspect they will contact Lord Castleross and await his instructions. In fact, a letter to a priest or monk called Revelin was seized at the port of Dingle."

Pippa's blood froze.

"Then you know what we must do," said Essex.

"Don't crane your neck so," the contessa warned Pippa. "It is too obvious."

"We must make certain the O Donoghue Mór does not receive word from—"

"Pippa!" The contessa's harsh whisper failed to stop Pippa's sudden departure. She raced to the end of the hall and fled past the ever-present gentleman pensioners flanking the doorway. Beyond the hall lay a sunlit passageway with tall slender windows and a soaring arched ceiling.

Courtiers and petitioners milled around the area. Robed barristers, minor noblemen, and the occa-

sional hard-eyed Puritan could be seen. She rushed
past them all with only one thought in mind. She had
to find Aidan and warn him.

When she was halfway down the corridor, she saw
a large man striding toward her, his midnight hair
flowing out behind him.

Aidan. It was as if her frantic thoughts had summoned him.

She lifted her skirts, heedless of the disapproving
glares of the Puritans, and hurried on, skidding to a
tottering halt when she reached him.

"My lord!" The sight of him was, as always, a
shock to the senses. He possessed, in extravagant
excess, every male charm conceived of by God in Her
wisdom. Being away from him for a few days only
made him that much more fascinating.

For a few seconds, she stared in rapture at his perfectly hewn Celtic features.

"Mistress Pippa." He took her hand and lifted it in
formal greeting to his mouth. When his flame blue
eyes met hers, she saw her startled face reflected in
their depths and remembered her purpose.

"My lord, I just found out—"

He touched a finger to her lips. Perhaps it was her
imagination, but he seemed to be studying her
intently, drinking in the sight of her. Could it be that
he had missed her, too?

"*A storin,*" he said, "a most singular thing has
occurred."

"*Seize him! Seize the rebel O Donoghue!*"

The call came from the arched doorway of the
Presence Chamber.

Aidan's head snapped up. "What the—"

She grasped his thick, muscular arm and tugged

with all her might. "Run!" she said desperately. "They mean to arrest you!"

Instead of fleeing as she begged him to do, he planted his feet and glared at the oncoming guards and pensioners. The captain of the guard bellowed his orders again.

"Seal the doors! Seize the rebel Irish lord."

Strong hands grabbed Pippa and dragged her away from Aidan. She screamed a curse. The roar of raised voices and thundering footfalls drowned her protest. Reverting to tactics she had learned from street fighters, she lashed out at those who detained her, kicking and elbowing, looking for something vulnerable to bite.

There were too many of them. This was the queen's chief residence, after all. It was more heavily guarded than the royal treasury. Firm hands subdued her. Furious, she stopped struggling long enough to look at Aidan.

He towered over the guards, but at least a dozen surrounded him, making escape impossible. He was like a great noble stag cornered by snapping curs.

His gaze found hers, and she felt her heart turn to ice. For the eyes of the O Donoghue Mór were filled with hatred and accusation.

Dear God. He thought she had betrayed him.

So this, thought Aidan grimly, was the great Tower of London.

He had been given a room in Beauchamp Tower where, years before, Guilford Dudley had suffered and pined for his Lady Jane before being led off to die. The room was hexagonal in shape, with walls of

light colored stone, narrow windows giving a view of
the Thames on one side and Tower Green on the
other.

Tower Green, where the heads of traitors were
lopped off.

He paced like a caged lion. Three days and nights
had passed, and no one save the warden and guards
had come to ease his isolation. No one had told him
the precise reason for his arrest.

Ah, but he knew.

He continued to pace, noting that the furnishings
in the room, though sparse, were of good quality. The
low bedstead had rails of carven oak, and the thick
tabletop was covered by a chessboard. His noontime
meal—untouched—sat upon a tray of silver.

He had all the amenities of a prisoner of rank.
That was something, he supposed. But it was not
enough.

He swore under his breath, went to the window,
and braced his palms on the ledge. Fury boiled
silently inside him. He did not know who made him
angrier—Revelin of Innisfallen, for advising him to
stay on in London, himself for heeding that advice, or
Pippa for her part in his arrest. There, in the gallery of
Whitehall, she had given him the Judas kiss. How
quickly she had deserted him.

News from Ireland had arrived like an ill wind. The
rebels had fired flaming arrows at the Browne residence in Killarney. Most of those involved were violent men of little honor and lesser sense.

His reply had been an express and urgent order to
withdraw and await the chieftain's return. Obviously,
Revelin had either not received the message or was
ignoring it. The rebels had seized English hostages.

Panic clawed at Aidan's throat. He was afraid—but not for himself. The past few years had stripped him of all fear of dying.

Nay, he feared for the people of his district, what would become of them if the Sassenach host took it upon themselves to avenge the insult dealt by the rebels. Aidan had seen Sassenach justice at work in Ireland.

It took the form of wanton, wholesale slaughter.

Old women and babies were dragged from their cottages and gutted like pigs. Men were hunted in the forests and spitted on swords and pikes. Women were raped and left to die or to bear the children of the men who had brutalized them.

The barrier between the atrocities and a peaceable solution was thin and fragile. For now, there was a standoff. Six Englishmen were prisoners of the rebels. Aidan was likewise a prisoner of the Crown.

Nothing would happen until one side or the other lost its hostage.

Stricken cold by an idea, he turned away from the window. For many long moments he stood unmoving, staring at the table with its hearty meal of meat and wine laid out for him.

A wave of fatalism rolled over him. With glass-edged clarity he saw a way out.

Perhaps the most useful thing he could do for his people now was to die.

Diary of a Lady

We had a most singular visitor today— Rosaria, the Contessa Cerniglia. I found her to be delightful and unfettered in her conversation. I was early taught that women should press down their frank opinions and bold ideas; what a mercy my dear Oliver showed me otherwise!

Worldly (as most Venetians are), the contessa took a great fascination in the Russian retainers in Richard's service, and even found merriment in trying to read words written in that alphabet.

Ah, Richard! My son! The very thought of him mars my pleasure in recounting the contessa's visit.

For tomorrow, he takes ship to Ireland.

—Lark de Lacey,
Countess of Wimberleigh

10

Bits of litter, buffeted by an unseasonably chilly wind, rolled along the street in front of Pippa. She clutched her shawl tighter around her and lowered her head, hurrying on.

The queen's ladies, eager to train the newest royal plaything, had cautioned her not to stray from the palace without formal leave.

"Formal effing leave," she muttered, her words swallowed by the wind, "my pink backside."

"Come with us, sweetling," called a rough voice.

She saw a pair of wet-mouthed soldiers clutching flasks and ambling toward her. "We'll keep you warm."

In the weeks she had spent with Aidan, she had almost forgotten the ugly sensation of being threatened by brutes. But she would never forget how to dispense with them.

As she had dozens of times before, she bit the

inside of her lip until she tasted blood. The routine was so familiar that she didn't even wince. She spat blood on the street in front of the soldiers. "Want to take your chances with me, lads?"

Cursing her, they stumbled off, cramming themselves through the doorway of the nearest tavern.

She nursed her cut lip with her tongue and quickened her pace. Her heart was pounding by the time she reached the street gate of Lumley House.

Please be here, she thought.

But no one greeted or challenged her at the gatehouse. She pushed through to the inner courtyard and went around to the kitchen garden behind the main house.

The entire place echoed with emptiness. Shivering, she leaned against the well sweep to catch her breath. Memories crept up and seized her unawares.

"No," she whispered, but the feelings raged like the wind, unstoppable, impossible to ignore. She had no idea memories could be so sad and so sweet all at once.

There was the pear tree where she had juggled for Aidan, easing the frown off his face and finally coaxing laughter from him. There was the arbor under which she had shown him the cut-and-foist technique of a seasoned thief and the eastern way of self-protection, taught to her by a tumbler from the Orient. At the top of the steps she had sat with Aidan and explained the intricacies of dicing while shafts of sunlight had bathed him in radiant splendor.

He had touched her that day, as he did so often, with gentle solicitude, his long fingers brushing back a curl of her hair and then lingering, for perhaps just a heartbeat too long, upon her cheek. He had taught her things as well, good things, valuable things, magical Gaelic words to describe the color of clouds at dawn and the feeling one gets while watching children at play. He had taught her that she did not always have to measure her value with the applause of strangers. And he had shown her that families could take many forms and that some of the strongest bonds were forged not by blood, but by the heart.

Tender leaves and blowing petals drifted down, littering the pathway. The herb garden had burst into bloom, and the pungent dry aroma of lavender and mint hung in the air.

She swallowed past a welling of grief in her throat. The house and garden stood still and silent, empty and desolate, as if her weeks with Aidan had never happened. As if the halls had not rung with laughter, with Pippa mimicking Donal Og's accent or singing an island ballad in Spanish with Iago.

They had been, for one brief, shining season, a family.

Dashing away a stinging tear, she went to the back wall of the garden and entered the adjacent priory of Crutched Friars. The only sign of life was a thin trickle of smoke from the glassworks.

She stood in the doorway of the foundry and waited for her eyes to adjust to the dimness. A lone artisan worked at the forge, heating molten glass into a glowing blob at the end of a steel rod. With several deft twists, he transformed the shapeless mass into a goblet, expertly using tongs to break it off when he was finished.

"Hello," said Pippa.

The goblet slipped and shattered on the packed

earth floor. The area was already littered with broken glass.

The artisan let loose a stream of invective that impressed even Pippa.

"I'm sorry to startle you," she said.

He set aside his rod and yanked off his thick gloves. "It's not your fault," he said in disgust. "Actually it is, but you ought to tell me it's my punishment for working on the Sabbath."

She had forgotten it was Sunday. "I thought that was against the law."

He propped a hip on the worktable and spat on the floor. "I fell behind. The earl of Bedford wanted his goblets yesterday."

The dull glow of the forge lit his face, and she saw that he was a mere boy, beardless and soft cheeked, a troubled frown puckering his brow.

"You're an apprentice?" she inquired.

He nodded.

"What happened to the guests at Lumley House?"

"All gone away, and good riddance, I trow."

"Do you know where they went?" She tried to show only casual interest. She had come dreading the worst— that Donal Og and Iago and Aidan's men had been rounded up and arrested or, Jesu forfend, put to death.

"They just sort of slipped away in the night," he said. "Odd, that." The youth smiled. "I think it were *her* idea."

"Her?"

"The foreign mort. Blond, she were. Big . . . dimples." He winked. "A mite bossy, but after she yammered at them for a while they all up and followed her. Never came back."

Pippa sagged with relief against the door frame.

The contessa. Somehow she had warned Donal Og and Iago of impending danger.

Perhaps they were in hiding or on their way to Ireland. Once there, Donal Og would know what to do. He would free the English hostages and put down the rebellion. The queen would have no further need to detain Aidan in London Tower.

Pippa thanked the apprentice and left, taking Petty Wales Street south toward the river. Nearby loomed the Tower, handsome and imposing, pennons flying from each corner tower.

Aidan, she thought. The merest thought of him made her turn weak and warm.

The idea that he was in danger filled her with a fear that ripped like the thrust of a sword through her. She stood across from the grim edifice for a long time, staring and thinking while the evening closed around her and deepened into night.

After a while, she heard the Ceremony of the Keys being called out. A scarlet-coated and feather-bonneted warder appeared with a lantern and a massive escort. Bemused, Pippa crept through the shadows of Water Street, watching their progress. As each gate of the fortress was locked, a sentry called out, "Halt! Who comes there?"

"Queen Elizabeth's keys," the warder answered. "All's well." At the end of the ceremony, the men removed their massive hats and cried, "God preserve Queen Elizabeth!" A bugle signaled the end of the ceremony.

Pippa wanted to laugh at the determined formality of it all, but the thought of Aidan drove all mirth from her.

She had to find a way to get him out.

But first, she had to find a way to get herself in.

* * *

The queen was in a fine rage. The usual lavish nightly feast lay uneaten before her, and her attendants scurried to clean up the plate of comfits she had just swept to the floor.

Standing amid the queen's ladies, Pippa looked on goggle eyed as Her Majesty darted up from the table and began to pace. She was spry despite the weight of her jeweled and embroidered court dress. She paused to glare at Sir Christopher Hatton, who stepped forward to offer her a cup of spiced wine.

"Begone, Sir Mutton," she snapped. "I need wise counsel, not strong drink."

He bowed from the waist and stepped back. Distinguished by steel gray hair and long, elegant legs, Hatton was one of Elizabeth's most seasoned courtiers. Pippa suspected he was used to braving the storm of the queen's temper.

"The O Donoghue Mór means to shame me," wailed the queen. "How dare he?"

How dare he what? Pippa wanted to yell back. A Tower official had scurried in, and the moment the queen had gotten the report, Pippa had known it was something serious.

She pressed her hands together and squeezed her eyes shut. Please let this mean he has escaped, she thought with all her might. Please please please.

"He'll make me out to be more of a monster than Czar Ivan," Elizabeth bit out. "I ought to have him beheaded at once."

"Madam," William Cecil pointed out, "that would serve his purposes quite well."

"I know that, damn your feeble eyes." She glared

at her ladies, who pretended, like well-trained parade horses, that nothing was amiss. "But the insolent foreigner has angered me enough to move me to murder."

Pippa gritted her teeth to keep from choking in horror.

Elizabeth swung around to glare at the constable of the Tower. "Tell me, sir. Did the O Donoghue Mór explain precisely why he has decided to starve himself?"

Pippa did not hear the mumbled reply. Starve himself! Had Aidan gone mad?

No, she realized with a sick lurch of her stomach. He knew precisely what he was doing. There was a terrible, cold logic to it. He meant to die in the custody of the English Crown.

If he did, Elizabeth would be shamed, disgraced, vilified in the eyes of the world even more viciously than she already was by her enemies.

"Make him eat," the queen snapped. "I won't have it said that I allowed an Irish lord to starve. I won't lose my one bargaining lever against the Kerry rebels. If you have to, tie him down and feed him by force."

The image made Pippa ill. "Ma'am!" She spoke before she lost her nerve. She sank to one knee in front of the dais.

"What is it?"

"With all due respect, perhaps there is a better way than forcing him."

"Ah." The exclamation dripped with sarcasm. "And I suppose you have just the answer. If you dare to suggest I set him free, then you shall find yourself in custody as well."

"I can persuade him to eat," Pippa said recklessly.

The queen's black eyes flashed in the candlelight. "Since you came to court you have done nothing unforgivably foolish. This would be a very bad time to start."

"I am asking you to let me try, Your Grace. If I fail, then punish me."

Silence lay over the gathering like a heavy cloak. The queen stood motionless, expressionless, an icon carved of stony power. "You think you can make the Irish chieftain eat," she said at last.

"Yes, ma'am." Pippa's face burned. Her wits lagged far behind her quick tongue tonight.

"Your success would mean a great deal to me," Elizabeth said with soft steeliness. "A great deal indeed. In fact, if you do as you promise, I would be inclined to grant you the favor we discussed this morning."

The floor pressed hard and cold against Pippa's bended knee. This morning, the queen had questioned her about her background and Pippa had confessed her earnest wish to find the parents who had abandoned her so long ago. A word from Elizabeth could summon every noble in the land, could send officials poring over census rolls and records. The possibility shone like a beacon in her mind.

"Oh, madam," Pippa said, rising as if buoyed by hope alone. "I could ask for no greater boon."

"You could," the queen said wryly, "but you're wise not to. Very well, visit the prisoner. Talk sense into his thick Irish head. And pray you, don't fail me, mistress."

With each successive meal, the fare looked better—more succulent, more plentiful, more delicious.

Or so it appeared to Aidan.

The current meal was dainty enough to grace the royal table. A large bowl of shining black olives, a delicate poached trout, cheese, and smoked meat. The bread was nearly white and looked as soft as a cloud.

More tempting to his empty stomach than the food was the jar of deep red wine set beside a stoneware goblet. It took all the powers of his will to resist the wine. He imagined its harsh, hot bite and the numbing oblivion that would come over him, blotting out his frustration.

He cursed and went to the hard, narrow bed, flopping down to glare at the chipping plaster on the ceiling. Correspondence was so slow between London and distant Kerry on the far western peninsula of Iveragh. He wondered how long he would last.

A bitter smile thinned his mouth. What an unpleasant predicament for Queen Elizabeth, to have the death of the O Donoghue Mór on her hands. It might force her to unbend in her policies regarding Ireland.

A pity the cost might be his own life.

He heard the patter of footsteps and an incessant, familiar voice.

". . . and don't give me any of that blather, for I've a paper right here that says I, Pippa Trueheart, have a warrant to visit him."

Aidan stood so quickly that he nearly bumped his head.

"Where?" demanded the nasal voice of Smead, the sentry. "Show me where it says that."

She laughed. "Ah, that's an old ruse, sir, to keep me from finding out that you don't know how to read."

"Of course I—good God!" Smead's voice rose an octave. "What are you doing with that knife?"

Something bumped against the cell door. Aidan would have paid in gold to see what was happening outside.

"Nothing," Pippa said, "yet. But what a pity if I should be so dismayed by your recalcitrance that my poor hand should slip."

"Now, look, mistress—"

"No, *you* look." Her voice had an edge to it Aidan did not recognize. "This is a very sharp blade, and it happens to be perilously close to your puny codpiece. Now, open that cell immediately."

"Jesu!" Smead squeaked. "Very well, but I shall report to the constable that you coerced me."

"Oh, that should make a pretty story. Coerced by a mere slip of a girl."

A key ground in the lock. The door swung open to reveal a white-faced Smead. Pippa had one dainty, slippered foot propped on the doorjamb. She yanked back her skirts to reveal a shapely leg with a small sheath fastened by a garter. Into this she slid the bone-handled knife she had stolen from Aidan the day they had met.

"Mistress?" Smead's gaze stayed riveted to her leg.

"What?"

"You cannot take a weapon in—"

"Smead?" She straightened and shook out her gown.

"Aye, mistress?"

"Kiss my backside, Smead." With that, she kicked the door shut and faced Aidan.

Neither spoke. They both stared. He drank in the sight of her curls escaping their coif, wide eyes, sweet angel face that haunted his dreams. He was in a delirium, he thought, as a greater hunger overtook him—a hunger of the soul. "To God," he whispered, in spite of himself, "I have missed you."

A soft, involuntary sound came from her. Just for a moment, she looked as fragile as an ornament of spun glass, and he feared she would shatter.

Then she tossed her head and the artful change came over her. A cocky glint appeared in her eyes and she set her hands on her hips. "Is that so? Well, I haven't missed you."

By now he saw through her facade. He strolled toward her, past the shadows that hung in the corners of the cell. He touched her cheek, almost wincing at its soft purity.

"No, *a gradh*," he whispered. "You do not want to miss me. That is different."

"I did not come here to debate with you," she snapped, pulling away. "I wish to make certain you know I had nothing to do with your arrest."

"I know that now." And in his heart, he did. She had no reason to wish him ill. "When I was first brought here, I thought the worst."

"I tried to warn you." She touched his sleeve, her fingers perched there like a shy bird. "If it gives you any comfort, I have news of your men."

His mouth dried. "Arrested?"

"Quite the opposite. The contessa helped them leave London rather quietly. Only Donal Og and Iago remain, and they are in sanctuary aboard a Venetian galley."

He looked away, his eyes and throat burning. "*Cead mile buiochas*," he whispered. "Thank God." He wanted no more innocent blood on his soul.

Feeling as if a weight had been lifted from him, he said, "It is a blessed thing for you to come and tell me this."

"I owe you that and much more." She shivered. The meager brazier that heated the room stood near the bed. Since there was nowhere else to sit, he led her there, pressing gently on her shoulders until she sat on the thin, hard mattress.

Time froze in the oddest way. He felt himself being swept into an elaborate fantasy. He was not Irish, nor was she English. Nothing existed beyond the charmed circle formed by the two of them. They alone made up the entire universe.

He shook off the thought. Beyond this cell, the world awaited. And for each of them, for different reasons, the world was a dangerous place.

With sharp clarity he recalled his visit with young Richard de Lacey. The image of the lady in the portrait haunted him. How lovely she was, this Lady Lark, countess of Wimberleigh, wearing a brooch of gold and pearls and rubies.

The days in prison had given him time to think. Perhaps the resemblance of the brooch was purely coincidental. Perhaps Lark had lost or sold the piece.

Or maybe, his mind kept whispering to him, *Pippa is kin to the countess of Wimberleigh.*

He knew one thing for certain. He would say nothing yet. He did not want to raise her hopes only to have them dashed. Besides, he knew nothing of Lord and Lady Wimberleigh. If they were as haughty and intolerant as the other Sassenach nobles, they would not welcome a rollicking street performer like Pippa; indeed, they would surely not believe she belonged to them.

She had been rebuffed so many times in her life. He would not make her suffer yet another betrayal.

Unbeknownst to Pippa, Aidan had been in contact with another lady—Rosaria, the Contessa Cerniglia. Only to her had he confessed his suspicions about the connection between Pippa and the de Laceys. Long ago, he had copied the foreign symbols from the back of the brooch. Two days earlier, he had bribed a guard to deliver the message to the contessa. She had promised to make discreet inquiries.

"You look so far away," Pippa said, breaking in on his thoughts. "Where were you?"

He sat beside her and pulled her into his arms. "My sweet, I was closer to you than you can imagine."

She tucked her cheek against his shoulder. "You were thinking of me?"

"I was."

She pressed closer, her hand slipping into his and warming itself there. In a movement as thoughtless and natural as breathing, he bent his head and laid his lips carefully over hers, tasting her, feeling the softness of her mouth, his tongue seeking the moist heat of hers. She lifted herself against him as if to meld their bodies. Her hands tangled in his overgrown hair; her breasts pushed against his chest; her legs shifted, brushing his thighs with unknowing, scorching intimacy.

He pulled back before it was too late, and he tried not to see the joy and the yearning in her upturned face.

"It is so hard not to love you," she said with her customary stark honesty.

"You'll find it easier once you come to know me." His voice was gruff with frustration. Only a fool would observe his marriage vows now, when he would likely never breathe the air of freedom again. Pippa was here, she was ready, she wanted him. His every instinct urged him to take her. And then, like a wall of stone, his sense of honor held him back.

He must not compromise her, not now, not when he was powerless to protect her from the vicious world. If she were to have a child—an Irishman's bastard—the queen would banish her in disgrace. She and the babe would be set out to starve.

She lifted her free hand to his stubbled face. "I do know you, Aidan. That is why I came. Can we—" She bit her lip. "We must talk about it."

"About what?"

"Do not pretend you don't know."

"The fast."

"Aye. You look pale and thin already. You must end it."

He thrust her away and stood to prowl through the confines of his cramped quarters, ignoring the now familiar dizziness that swept over him. "Did they send you to tell me that?"

"No." She looked delectable, her clothes and hair charmingly rumpled, her full mouth moistened by his kisses. "The next person they send to you will be a team of sentries who will force you to eat."

The idea chilled his blood. He did not doubt that the Tower officials would carry out the barbaric plan. Neither did he doubt his ability to fend off the attempt.

"Please eat," she whispered with a tremor in her voice.

The sight of her, so wide-eyed and concerned, took him apart inch by inch, each word a chisel to his will.

"I can't," he said. "Don't beg me to compromise myself. They have taken everything from me except my convictions, and I'll die before I surrender that."

"You place a high value on your will," she said. "What of your people who need you?"

"I'll serve them better by dying."

"No!" She shot up from the bed and flung herself at him, pounding her fists on his chest. "Don't speak of dying. I won't let you die."

He caught her hands. Her tears came freely, streaming down her cheeks. "You must not die. I'll kill you if you die."

"An interesting thought," he said with black humor. "It is the way these things work. I am a useful hostage for now. But what if the rebels in Kerry murder their English hostages? What if the English army retaliates and takes over my lands? What if the name of the O Donoghue Mór comes to mean nothing? The English will not need me. I'll die. Either quietly, comforted by a cup of poison, or with much ceremony, at the hand of an expert axman before a crowd of Londoners, so that I am an example to others."

"How can you speak so calmly of this?"

"Because my demise is not going to happen the way they planned it." He dragged in a deep breath. "It is going to happen the way *I* plan it. I shall die on my terms, not theirs, and the shame will be on the queen."

She absorbed his ultimatum like a woman bracing herself for a storm. Her head was slightly bent, shoulders hunched, arms wrapped protectively around her middle. Then she looked up, and the storm burst.

"You are the most idiotic, bull-witted, stubborn,

white-livered embarrassment to manhood I have ever met."

He could not suppress a smile. "What sort of persuasion is that?"

"Is it working?"

"No."

She blew out her breath. "What if you were to be freed?" She went to the only window and pressed her hands on the ledge. Daylight fell over her dainty features, and the sun glistened in the long sweep of her eyelashes.

"And who would be freeing me," he asked softly, "when they went to such trouble to lock me up?"

She turned and stared him in the eye, and although she was clean and wore beautiful clothes, she resembled the bundle of bold energy he had first spied on the steps of St. Paul's.

"I could do it," she stated.

"Break me out of the Tower of London."

"Yes."

"No one has escaped the Tower in this century."

"The century is not over yet. At least, I don't think it is."

If the proposition had been made by anyone other than Pippa, he would have discounted her for a fool. But she was the most resourceful person he had ever met.

"Very well," he said quietly, cautiously. "You get me out of here and I'll eat a whole roasted pig."

She grinned. "I thought you'd like that idea." She took his hand and tugged him over to the table. "Now," she said, picking up the soft loaf of bread. "Eat."

He pulled his hand from hers. "No."

Fear and anger blazed in her eyes. "You must. You'll need your strength."

"I have strength for another day or two. So if you mean to carry out your promise, you'd best make haste."

"But you have to eat now," she said. "You see—"

"No, I don't see," he roared, then remembered to lower his voice. "If I eat, and the escape fails, then I am set back on my plans, and I'll look like a weakling."

"It won't fail," she said through gritted teeth.

"So long as I am a prisoner of Mother England, I will not touch a bite of food. You had best act quickly, or you'll be dragging out a corpse."

"He'll wish he was dead before I finish with him," Pippa muttered under her breath as she crept along the slimy river wall of the Tower.

It was deep night, and she worked solely by touch and memory. Here was a jut of the wall; around the corner would be a shaft with an iron grate over it. She had seen workers using this little known portal to carry out garbage and muck from the stables.

She knew it to be a place of rats and filth, but she would have to bear the unpleasantness. The O Donoghue Mór wanted to escape, and he expected her to do the work.

The insufferable jack-dog.

She took a deep breath, pulled her cloak of filched rags around her, and wedged herself into the portal. It was a close fit; the damp stone scraped her. At the end, she encountered an iron grate.

Her speech was larded with curses as she picked at the mortar. By the time she twisted one of the iron bars away and squeezed through the opening, her hands were raw and bleeding and she had run out of oaths.

Carrying the iron bar, she stole past Devereux Tower. A bellman called out the hour of nine. Pippa hurried. Soon the Ceremony of the Keys would begin.

Why couldn't Aidan have eaten? She would have looked like a heroine to the queen, Elizabeth would have summoned her nobles, and Pippa's family would be found. In her heart she knew it was unlikely, yet it had given her the sweetness of hope.

But the stubborn Lord Castleross had no faith in her abilities. He refused to eat until he was a free man. She tried to feel angry at him, tried to curse his obstinance, but instead she felt sick with worry. What if he died?

Her triumph at court would mean nothing if Aidan was gone. If she lost him, there would be nothing left of her heart to share with a family even if she were to find them.

Pippa spied the first guard. Reeking of ale, he loitered in a circle of torchlight, whistling between his teeth. She edged closer. He stopped whistling and sniffed the air like a hound on the scent.

Damn. She should have ditched the cloak.

Before she could move, he blinked blearily at her. "You there!" he said. "What—"

"Evening, sir!" Before he could reply, she clasped his hand in both of hers and twisted. Bless the troupe of tumblers she had traveled with through Lincolnshire. They'd taught her how, with the proper momentum, she could land a large man flat on his back.

The guard's ale-sour breath left him in a rush. She

clucked her tongue in sympathy. "Just keep silent and all will be well."

He wheezed as she secured a gag around his mouth and tied his hands to a gatepost. She roundly cursed Aidan O Donoghue. For his sake, she was putting her only chance in jeopardy. Still, in her heart she knew that all she truly wanted was for him to survive.

To that end, she thought of Mort and Dove, her accomplices waiting at the Galley Key. If indeed they were. She had surrendered a gold crown and promised two more if they were still there, acting as lookouts, when she and Aidan arrived.

She intended to see him off, wish him godspeed, and then return to her new life at court.

So why did she feel so empty when she thought of going on without him?

The question did not matter. She could not let it matter. The guard growled something through the rags she had stuffed in his mouth. She snatched his shortsword from its sheath. "I'm afraid I'll be needing this," she whispered. "Your trousers as well."

He made a garbled sound of protest. She ignored him, slicing away the buttons that held his canions in place. They fell down around his ankles. With trembling hands she pulled them on, tied the drawstring snug, then plucked his coat from a peg on the door. Finally, she left him tied in the dark and went to take his post at Bloody Tower archway.

The long scarlet coat and huge bonnet engulfed her, but she would have to hope no one noticed. Swinging his candle lantern, the chief warder went from gate to gate, followed by a sergeant and three other guardsmen. She stood stiffly at attention, the way she had observed while formulating her plan.

"Halt!" she said in a deep voice. "Who comes there?"

"The keys," replied the warder.

Pippa could not remember what came next. "Keys? Whose keys?"

"Queen Elizabeth's keys." He delivered the reply in a bored voice.

"Advance the keys. All's well." She held out her hand, praying it would not tremble.

The warder hesitated. "Are you falling ill, Stokes?"

"Mayhap, sir." She scratched her throat.

When the keys were passed to her, she neatly substituted those she had pilfered from the pantler at Whitehall. After the ceremony, she marched off to the guardroom with the others. At the door, she stopped.

"Problem, Stokes?" someone asked.

She tugged down the brim of her hat. "I have to take a piss."

Her fellow guard took down a torch from a wall sconce. "You seem strange tonight, Stokes."

She snatched the torch from him. "Nay, what is strange is making prisoners of innocent men." With that, she tossed the torch onto the thatched roof and fled, praying for a miracle as the guards screamed in fear and rage.

She raced to Beauchamp Tower, bounded up the winding stairs, and unlocked Aidan's cell.

"Don't think for a minute," she said to the darkened room, "that I have forgotten your promise about the pig."

He made one of those Celtic exclamations she so dearly loved, and then he hauled her in his arms, squeezing her so deliciously hard that the breath left her. He whispered something heartfelt and Gaelic.

"And what does that mean?" she asked tartly.

"It means you are a shining little miracle."

"Also an idiot," she said, pretending his words meant nothing. "A brainsick idiot."

Mortlock and Dove surprised her. Like a pair of watchdogs they stood at the Galley Key, waiting patiently; it had taken Pippa and Aidan most of the night to steal out of the Tower and make their way to the riverside. The flaming thatch on the guardroom had provided enough of a diversion to get them out onto Petty Wales Street, but they had narrowly escaped a party of guards by hiding in an abandoned well. Though she would never admit it, she had loved every minute of the adventure.

"So you showed up after all," Dove said. "Did you bring the rest of our pay?"

"You'll have it after I see that you've done as you promised," Pippa said.

Both Mort and Dove subjected Aidan to a long inspection. "So who's the toff, anyway? He's the same one what saved you from the pillory, eh?"

"And that's all you need to know." She was getting nervous. These two had never been trustworthy, and she did not like the way they were eyeing the fine needlework of Aidan's shirt and the quality of his leather boots. He looked weary, his cheeks hollowed by his fast. While they had hidden in the well she had made him eat a loaf of bread she'd brought with her, but it would be days before he regained his strength.

"Did you get the boat?" she asked Mort and Dove. Mortlock's eyes narrowed. "What's your hurry?"

Aidan took a step toward him. Despite his lack of food and sleep, he towered like a mountain over Mortlock. "I believe," Aidan said softly, "the lady asked you a question."

Mort's crooked nose twitched, a sign of fear Pippa recognized. "A lady, are we now?" he asked, his tone derisive even as he edged away from Aidan.

"Ooh!" said Dove, fluttering a make-believe fan.

She touched Aidan's sleeve. "Ignore them. They have always been obnoxious."

"Ob-nox-shus," Dove said, trying the word.

She tried not to let her irritation show, tried not to let her gaze stray to the middle of the broad river, where the Venetian galley lay at anchor, waiting. "A pity you failed to accomplish the simple task of securing a boat. I'll have to find a ferryman—"

"It's here." Mort jerked his thumb upriver. "In the boathouse yonder."

She paid them. They bit the coins and bobbed their heads but did not leave. "Look," she said, "I've nothing more to spare." She shrugged out of the voluminous guardsman's jacket and dropped it on the ground. "We're off, then," she said, and started toward the boathouse.

Muttering, Mort and Dove slunk off into the shadows. At the watersteps of the rickety structure, she turned to face Aidan. "You understand what you must do."

"Take the lighterboat to the Venetian galley." He pointed to the shadowy hulk at anchor in the deepest part of the river. A hint of dawn colored the smoky sky.

"The contessa assured me you'll have diplomatic sanctuary there. Once you're aboard, the English can't touch you." She could barely speak past the lump in her throat. "It is so hard to say good-bye."

He caught her against him. "I know, my sweet. If I live a thousand years, I should never forget you."

Weeping, she lifted her face and waited for his kiss. His lips brushed hers and then their mouths clung, breath and tears and hearts mingling until she almost cried out with the pain of it.

She broke away and stepped back. "Even though I do not love you," she whispered, "I shall miss you as I miss the sun in winter."

"Pippa—"

"Seize them!" shouted a voice from the gloom. "Seize the fugitives."

She glanced back at the galley key, and her heart plunged to her knees. In the blink of an eye, she realized her mistake. Mort and Dove were supposed to keep an eye out. Instead they'd taken the money and run.

Straight to the Tower guards.

Her curse echoed across the river. The pounding of footsteps came from the black maw of an alleyway in front of them.

"It appears your friends found a higher bidder," Aidan said in a disgusted voice. "Now what do we do?"

She grabbed his hand. "Run!"

Her stolen, overlarge boots made running clumsy. She stumbled along the quay, then clutched Aidan's arm while she shook off the boots and left them behind.

She was glad for the predawn darkness, for it concealed her smile of pure pleasure. There was little that she missed about her former life on the streets, but every now and then a good chase was exhilarating.

Few people—certainly not the night bellmen or Tower guards—knew the rabbit warren maze of London streets as well as Pippa did. She prayed Mort and Dove had not offered their services as guides. "Just stay hard by," she said to Aidan, ducking her head beneath a brick archway to enter the underworld of the East End.

It was gratifying to be running for her life with a man like Aidan. He was swift and strong despite his fast, and he didn't ask stupid questions. If they stayed ahead of their pursuers and kept to the shadows, they should have no trouble eluding the guards.

She ducked down a cramped alley, tearing off her baldric as she ran and tossing the belt into a sewage conduit. At the end of the alley, they emerged into a small market square awakening to the business day. The spire of St. Dunstan-in-the-East loomed against the lightening sky. Even at this early hour, traders had arrived with rickety carts and hastily set up booths. A deafening roar of music, laughter, and general hubbub filled the air.

"Ah, this is splendid," said Aidan. "We've come to the one place where they'll be sure to spy us."

"Ye of little faith," she scolded. "We'll just go back the way we came."

The moment she spoke, excited shouts issued from the alley. The soldiers had found the baldric.

A nasty thorn of worry pricked at Pippa. They needed to hide. She shoved her elbow at a side doorway of St. Dunstan's. It swung open to reveal a set of dank, sagging stairs.

"What do you hope to accomplish by trapping us in a spire?" Aidan demanded.

"Trust me," she replied. "They won't look here."

The stairs groaned ominously beneath their weight. The smell of rot hung thick in the air. At a high landing, a platform gave access to the large, heavy bell on one end and a low opening in the stone spire on the other.

They burst outside and found themselves on a wall walk surrounding the steeple. The surface was perilously slanted. A low murmur burbled from a dovecote in one corner.

Across another corner, someone had pegged a few articles of clothing out to dry.

"Ah, luck," said Aidan, plucking down a plain jerkin. He pulled it over his shirt. The garment fit taut across his chest, so he left the lacings open. Just for a moment, Pippa stared at his chest and all thought fled.

He cracked a smile. "There's something for you here, too." He took down a threadbare brown skirt and held it out for her. She yanked the skirt on over her breeches and used a square of linen to tie over her hair.

"How do I look?"

"Like an angel. Any moment now, I expect you to sprout wings."

"Very funny."

He grazed her cheek with his knuckles. "I was not trying to be funny. I—"

"There they are!" exclaimed a voice far below. Four armed men ducked into the stairwell.

"I wish you'd been right about the wings," she said.

He did not answer, but untied one end of the clothesline and made a loop in the rope.

Bumps and thuds and curses sounded hollowly in the old stairwell.

"Hang on to me," Aidan said. "Put your arms around my neck."

Falling from a church roof in the arms of the O Donoghue Mór, she decided, was as good a way as any to die. She latched her arms around his strong neck, reveling for a moment in the firmness of his flesh. Thank God he had not starved himself to death after all.

Brandishing pikes and long-handled axes, the soldiers emerged from the stairwell and stormed across the roof. Three sharp prongs from a pikestaff drove toward them. Aidan turned to shield her body with his own. She squeezed her eyes shut and buried her face against his chest.

He took one step backward, then swung out in a wide arc. They dropped so fast, her stomach seemed to rise to her throat. The rope sang as it paid out, hissing across the eaves of the building.

They stopped with jarring abruptness and swung helplessly, bumping against the wall of the church tower.

"Now what, Your Loftiness?" she asked in a voice that was little more than a squeak of fright. She clung to him harder, winding her legs around his waist and locking her ankles. He mumbled something in Gaelic, and she peered at his face. Dear God, he was dizzy with weakness from fasting.

"I wonder how far it is to the street," he said.

She peeked at the alley below. Many feet below. Many perilous, bone-crunching feet below.

"Too far to jump." She dared to look up. "Uh-oh."

"What is it?"

She stared speechless as the dawn light glinted off the curved ax head of a soldier's halberd. It swung down once, twice, thrice.

Pippa screamed. They plummeted, breaking apart, her skirts billowing. Her mind emptied in anticipation of the end. Instead, she struck something and stopped falling. She heard a grunt from Aidan.

They had landed in some sort of canvas awning. Before she could catch her breath, an ominous ripping sound began and they were plunging downward again.

This time, they had not far to fall. They landed in a tangle of canvas upon something soft and rather strangely warm. She apprised the situation through her dazed senses. Her nostrils flared, and she choked. She and Aidan lay atop a pile of manure in a cart.

Aidan muttered in Irish and bounded out of the cart, pulling her after him while the carter looked on, amazed. The canvas awning had shielded them from the worst of the muck.

They rushed along through the cloth sellers' booths and peddlers' carts. Slowly, gradually, they caught their breath, and Pippa conquered her shaking knees. Somehow she found the presence of mind to steal a roll of cheese.

"Eat," she said. "It's not a whole roasted pig, but chew on that."

He devoured the cheese in three bites. Pippa began to breathe more easily. But when they started toward the east exit of the square, two soldiers came toward them.

Aidan gave a short, lusty laugh. Instead of setting upon the soldiers, he took Pippa in his arms and kissed her, long and hard. She made a little whimper of surprise and then simply gave herself to him.

He kissed her until the soldiers had passed, apparently discounting them as a pair of eager lovers. Then, just as abruptly as he had grabbed her, he let her go and started hurrying again.

She almost stumbled as she tried to keep up. He acted completely unaffected by a kiss that had all but singed her eyelashes, damn him.

Shouts rang from the steeple walk. The men there, black crows against the gentle pink sky, gesticulated wildly to their compatriots.

Pippa and Aidan ran through Fowler Street and turned back down toward the Thames. When at last they reached the galley key, both were nearing the end of their strength.

The lighterboat was gone. Gray rivers of fog swirled around their knees as they called to the ship's master. A tender broke away from the long galley and rowed silently toward them.

She squinted at the two men in the tender. She did not recognize them. Still, the contessa had assured her that the crew of the Venetian ship could be trusted.

She shivered. "It is good-bye again, my lord. You should have taken my word for it in the first place."

One corner of his mouth lifted in a self-deprecating grin. "I needed a new set of clothing anyway. And of course"—he touched the tip of her nose—"it is fitting that our parting was as perilous as our meeting."

"Our parting," she whispered, despising the finality of it. "Ah, Aidan, I shall never forget you."

"A touching sentiment," said a melodious, accented voice. "You can tell her on the voyage." Out of the mist stepped the contessa, wrapped in rich black silk velvet. Behind her stood an escort of Venetian bodyguards. "You're late," she added. "The tide is up, and they were about to leave without you."

The tender bumped gently into place. Aidan hesitated. "A moment, Your Ladyship—"

"You don't have a moment, and neither does Pippa," snapped the contessa. "If you're caught now, I'll offer no more help. Now, get in, both of you."

Pippa gasped. "I'm not going to Ireland!"

"You must."

"My lady," she whispered past the tears that burned in her throat, "you don't know what you're asking. I have a place at court now, and the queen—"

"She's asking you," Aidan snapped, "to get in that boat before I hurl you in. The contessa is right. If you stay, you could be arrested for helping me escape."

"But—"

"Your role in the flight of the O Donoghue Mór will be found out," he declared. "Perhaps if the dodge had been quieter, we might have eluded attention. But you've been seen with me."

The contessa handed something to Aidan. He pushed Pippa toward the boat. "You would be treated not as a prisoner of noble rank, but as a common traitor. Do you know the punishment for that?"

The contessa made a slashing gesture across her throat.

Pippa felt cold inside. What a fool she had been. She had bought his freedom at the price of her dreams.

The contessa kissed both her cheeks and whispered, "Go with the O Donoghue Mór. It is better to run toward the future than cling to the past."

Pippa turned to Aidan. He stood poised with one foot braced on the quay and the other in the service boat, his large hand held out for hers, his face utterly inscrutable.

The rising sun set fire to the sky behind him, and for a moment he looked as splendid as a painting on a church wall. His black hair drifted, a long ripple on the breeze. His eyes were penetrating, yet impenetrable.

"Come with me, Pippa," he said at last. "I'll make it all right, I promise. Come with me to Ireland."

PART TWO

It is sweet to dance to violins
When Love and Life are fair:
To dance to flutes, to dance to lutes
Is delicate and rare:
But it is not sweet with nimble feet
To dance upon the air!

—Oscar Wilde
The Ballad of Reading Gaol, st. 9

It is only now, days later, that I am able to dry my tears and take pen in hand. Yea, I do grieve as any mother would that my son has gone to war, but that is not the reason for my distress.

Oliver is like a madman, pacing the halls of Blackrose Priory and laying curses upon anyone who has the ill fortune to cross his path.

Neither of us can sleep at night; we have not been able to sleep since the message was delivered from London. Cruel trick or honest report; I know not which it is.

I know only that someone penned me a message, copying the inscription from the back of the Romanov brooch. That singular object was given to me by Oliver's stepmother, Juliana. I thought it had been lost forever.

The last time I saw the precious jewel, I had pinned it to the bodice of my beloved little daughter, just before I said farewell to her, not realizing I was never to see her again.

—Lark de Lacey,
Countess of Wimberleigh

11

Aidan sought shelter in an abandoned fortress by the sea. Dunloe Castle once housed the O Sullivan Mór, but he had died, like so many others, in Desmond's great war against the English.

The windy hall stood as bleak and empty as a plundered tomb. Aidan tried not to think about the slaughter that had occurred here as he awaited word of Ross Castle and thought about Pippa.

She had hated the voyage. She had spent the entire time in a cramped private berth, doubled over by seasickness and shivering with fright. He had expected her to perk up once she was on dry land, but she was more subdued than ever.

He went to a window and looked out, and his heart lifted. The rounded hills, greener than the green of England, wore sturdy necklaces of drystone tillage walls. Sheep and cattle grazed upon the verdant abundance, and cloud towers swept toward the heavens.

This was Ireland—a tragic beauty blithely unaware that she was doomed. The thought filled him with the sharp, sweet ache of loving something, knowing in his heart it was hopeless.

Hearing a footstep, he turned. Iago and Donal Og strode into the hall. "Has the news come yet?" asked his cousin.

"No." He returned to the table and poured heather beer into cups for each of them. "If O Mahoney doesn't return by daybreak, I'll send someone after him."

"Where is our guest?" Iago asked. "Is her sickness passed?"

"She went to walk out in the fields." Aidan pinched the bridge of his nose. "Would that I could ease her melancholy."

"Can you?" asked Donal Og.

"Yes and no." Aidan drew out the letter the contessa had pressed into his hand at their parting. "The symbols on the back of Pippa's brooch are from the Russian language. The contessa found someone to translate the words. 'Blood, vows, and honor.'" He shivered, remembering Pippa's story of the dying Gypsy woman.

Donal Og stroked his beard. "Someone's motto?"

"It is the motto of a clan called Romanov, far across the seas. They are associated with a family we know well." He took a sip of ale. "The de Lacey family."

Iago and Donal Og exchanged a glance. "Richard de Lacey?"

Aidan set down his cup. "He could be her brother."

"*Diablo!*" whispered Iago. Donal Og gave a low whistle.

Aidan had worked it all out from the information gathered by the contessa. Years earlier, plague had stricken the de Lacey household, and Oliver de Lacey was not expected to live. His wife, fearing their only child would fall ill too, had sent their tiny daughter on a voyage to the kingdom of Muscovy to stay with the kin of her grandmother.

"The ship was lost," Aidan told his listeners. "No survivors were found."

"You think there was a survivor," Donal Og said.

"And that her name is Pippa," Iago added.

He felt that odd lift of nervousness in his gut. "Philippa," he said. "The lost child was named Philippa."

Iago stroked his chin. "It is Pippa. It has to be."

"Imagine." Donal Og quaffed his ale in one swallow. "The ragamuffin's got noble blood. Have you told her yet?"

"No!" Aidan stood and prowled through the musty hall. "You're to say nothing. Nothing."

"But it's her family. Her heart's desire. Surely, coz, it's a grand and wanton cruelty to withhold the information."

"Call me cruel, then," he snapped. "I'll say nothing until I am absolutely certain."

"It all fits," Iago said. "She looks like Richard—the hair of gold, the brilliant smile, the lack of reverence for her betters—"

"You didn't notice that until I told you what I learned," Aidan pointed out. "I don't want her hurt. You saw what insufferable snobs the English nobles were. The de Laceys accepted their loss more than two decades ago. What if they do not want the old wound reopened? What if they are ashamed that their daughter lived as a common street performer, a thief?"

Donal Og nodded, understanding dawning on his face. "What if they call her a pretender who stole that brooch?"

"Or what if," Iago chimed in, "they decide to accept her, only to learn she is an outlaw for helping the O Donoghue Mór escape London Tower?"

Aidan looked from one to the other. "Now you see why I hesitate."

Iago walked to the window and seated himself in the embrasure, where weak sunlight trickled over him. "Ah, why do we bother so with this toilsome life?"

Donal Og snorted. "Is there another choice?"

Iago turned and gripped the edge of the embrasure. "Upon my soul, there is."

Donal Og made a heart-thumping gesture with his hand on his chest. "The islands in the great western sea of the Caribbees." He mimicked Iago's round-voweled accent and musical timbre. "Where the sun shines all day, where food falls from the trees, where the water is warm enough to swim in naked."

"It is all true, you large Irish ogre. Ah, I am the first to admit there are a few problems—"

"Slavery, disease, the Inquisition—"

"But a man can live free if he is smart enough. There are uninhabited islands by the thousands. A man can make what he wants of his life. With *whom* he wants."

"Ah, Serafina!" Donal Og pretended to swoon.

"No wonder you have no woman." Iago curled his lip in a sneer. "You have the mind of a jackass. No, that is an insult to the jackass. The mind of a brick of peat."

"A brick of peat *has* no mind," Donal Og roared.

"Precisely," said Iago.

As their conversation deteriorated into bickering, Aidan spied a movement on the slope leading down to the sea. A flash of gold, a flutter of brown skirts. For a moment he stood transfixed. The hills and the crashing sea were so vast. Pippa looked as vulnerable as an autumn leaf on the wind.

She found a sheep path leading down along a crumbling cliff. Below her, treacherous breakers bit at the shore. In one heart-seizing instant he remembered something else the contessa had told him about Oliver de Lacey.

In his youth, Wimberleigh had a reckless reputation. His moods swung from giddy to melancholy. Some—even his half brothers and sisters—swore he harbored an earnest wish to die.

Iago and Donal Og were too busy arguing to note how quickly Aidan left the hall.

A dark fascination with the sea drew Pippa. Now she felt strong enough to move close to the seething ocean, to witness the violence and drama of the battering waves.

She clambered down a path. The slope was pocked by large gray rocks around which grew clumps of grass and wildflowers. Ireland was surely the loveliest place she had ever seen. It was stark and wild and uncompromising—just like Aidan O Donoghue.

The path ended at a great cleft between two hills. Within the fissure, a fall of broken boulders and old driftwood tumbled into the roaring sea. She teetered

on the edge, tasting the sharp salt air and feeling the
wind rush over her like a great, sweeping, invisible
caress. The boom of the waves exploding on the
rocks below filled the air. Beads of spray touched her
face and clung in her hair. Then, without warning,
she was lost, swamped with memories. Uttering a
low cry, she tumbled into the dream world inside her
head.

*Up and up and up she climbed, battling her way
through the rushing water on each successive deck.
She could no longer see Nurse nor hear her saying
Hail Mary Hail Mary. The sailors were all gone. But
for the dog, she was alone now.*

*She poked her head up through a square hatch and
was out in the face-slapping rain with thunder shouting and a burning bolt of lightning turning night to
day.*

*It stayed light only for an instant, but she saw the
man in the striped shirt who had been shouting
about battening hatches and shortening sail. He lay
all tangled in thick rope. His face was gray, his lips
were black, and his eyes were wide open like the
eyes of the stag head that hung in Papa's hunting
lodge.*

*She clung to a ladder while the dog scrabbled and
lurched on long, skinny legs. The boat began to tilt
and groan, riding up one side of a wave that was bigger than a mountain. Higher and higher they went,
like the forward arc of her garden swing. The big boat
hovered at the peak and seemed to freeze there, waiting, before it fell over.*

*Down and down and down, barrels crashing
everywhere, toppling one against the other like
ninepins. The lightning flashed again. In the distance*

a shape rose out of the sea like a great rock or perhaps one of the towers in the palace where her godmother lived.

She wished she could remember the name of her godmother, because she surely needed help now. But all she could recall was that the lady had blazing red hair, mean black eyes, and a loud, bossy voice. Everyone called her Your Majesty.

Then she lost all thought. A big wooden barrel broke loose and rushed straight at her as if someone had hurled it—

The breath left her in a *whoosh* as she was flung to the ground. She had no voice to scream as a hard body covered her and pinned her against the grassy turf.

At last she regained her breath. "Jesus Christ on a frigging crutch!" she yelled. "What do you think you're doing?"

The O Donoghue Mór had his body pressed to hers. She could feel his heart beating rapidly against her chest. Somehow that pleased her. He had run all the way to see her.

"Well?" she asked, sounding more annoyed than she felt. She was still slightly dazed by the— What was it? A vision? A waking dream? A true memory? Then the images faded and dispersed.

Aidan lifted himself by bracing his hands on the grass on each side of her. This was, she realized with a heated thrill, the time-honored pose of lovers. She had seen it depicted in a book of disgusting sonnets Dove had stolen from a St. Paul's bookseller.

The wind caught at Aidan's ebony hair, and sunlight glinted in the single beaded strand. Ah, he *was* Ireland, in all its pain and splendor; like the land, he was rugged and beautiful, untamed and untameable. She had the most indecent urge to run her fingers through his silky, rioting hair.

"Do you often attack unsuspecting females?" she asked. "Is this some Irish ritual?"

"I thought you were getting too close to the edge. I wanted to stop you before you fell."

"Or jumped?" she asked. "By my troth, Your Highness, why would I do such a thing as that?"

"You would not?"

"That is the act of a madwoman or a coward. Why would I want to die? Life is hard. Sometimes life hurts. But it's all so blessedly interesting that I should not like to miss any of it."

He chuckled and then laughed outright. There was something deliciously intimate about the way his body vibrated against hers. She pressed her fists into the grass to keep from winding her arms around his neck. Part of her longed to give in to impulse, but another part held back, resisting, wary.

"Are you going to remove yourself sometime between now and eventide?"

"I have not decided. You are very soft in certain places."

He placed his lips close to her ear. With a warm gust of breath, he said one of the sweetest things she had ever heard. "It is a rare thing indeed for a man to feel so perfectly comforted by a woman."

She forced herself to scowl. "I know what you are doing."

"Getting ready to kiss you?" His mouth hovered above hers.

Lord, but she wanted to draw his taste inside her.

She used all of her willpower to say, "I don't think you should."

He lowered his mouth and then, quite deliberately leaving her hunger unsated, he turned his head to nuzzle her neck.

"Why not?" he whispered.

"You're trying to make me forget how vexed I am with you."

"Vexed? Why?"

She was stunned. "Because, you arrogant stuffed doublet, you gave me no choice. Do you think I *wanted* to come here? *Wanted* to be dragged along on that horrid ship for an endless sea voyage?" She scrambled out from under him and sat back on her heels.

"I thought you wanted to help me," he said. "As I helped you, once upon a time."

"That was once upon a time. All I wanted," she said, "was the chance to earn the queen's favor." To her shame, her voice cracked. "The queen was going to help me find my family. I broke you out of the damned Tower! All I wanted was for you to end your hunger strike, and you wouldn't give me that."

"I could not," he said. "I had to stay firm."

"You could have given in just so the queen would reward me."

"And if the escape had failed?"

She had no answer, so she scowled at him.

"Pippa," he said, "if it means that much to you, we can make it appear that I forced you to come along as hostage."

"That," she said, "would not be so far from the truth."

"We could arrange for you to be rescued by the English."

The idea of being taken in by strangers was repellent to her, but she could not let him see that. She drew herself up and said, "Ha! You'll not be rid of me that easily, my lord."

Aidan saw that she was close to shattering. It was a terrible thought that Pippa, sturdy survivor of the London underworld, was about to be driven to weeping by the only man who cared about her.

He wanted to touch her again, to gather her to his chest, but that was dangerous. His blood was still on fire from their embrace. He might not be able to stop himself a second time.

"Tell me more of this reward, *a gradh*," he said, brushing a curl away from her temple.

"The queen made me an offer. If I got you to eat, she'd help me. All you could think of was your fast, and your honor—your stupid, precious honor."

The lash of anger was sudden, unexpected. "You and the queen made a bargain? That's why you wanted me to eat?" As quickly as the fury had seized him, it fled. So she had made a bargain, using him as leverage. It was no worse than what he had done.

"Ah, Christ." He grabbed her and pulled her against his chest. "I didn't know."

"She was going to summon all the noblewomen of the realm, get an army of clerks to search the records." She clutched at the front of his shirt. "Nothing would have come of it. I know you're thinking that. But it was my only chance. And now it is gone."

"You should have explained it all," he said. "Nay, it would have made no difference. I would not have compromised myself even to give you your most cherished wish. The true cost would have been exacted from the people of this district."

She blew out a disgusted breath. "I wouldn't have been able to live with myself if something terrible happened here."

He ground his teeth together to keep himself silent. He knew in the very marrow of his bones that she was Philippa de Lacey.

Instead of telling her, he forced himself to think matters through. The lofty de Laceys might reject her, which would be more painful than never knowing.

"I'm sorry," he whispered into her hair. "Somehow I'll get you back to England. You'll be blameless, I swear it."

She pulled back to look up at him. "If all of your eloquent speeches were solid gold, I should be a wealthy woman indeed."

He stood and helped her to her feet. "I never promised I would be good for you."

The breeze tousled her curls, which by now had grown nearly to her shoulders. "You were good to me. Never doubt it."

He took her hand, and they started up the hill together. If someone had told him that one day his best friend in the world would be a Protestant Sassenach street waif, he would have laughed them out of his presence.

Yet the most unlikely of circumstances had come true.

At the top of the hill, O Mahoney met them. His face pinched and white, the scout sat upon a lathered Connemara-bred mount.

"What news?" Aidan asked. "Have you been to Ross Castle?"

"I have seen it." O Mahoney glanced at Pippa and switched to Gaelic. "Ill news. The ramparts are flying English colors."

By the time the party rode into Aidan's district, Pippa had ceased complaining. She was still terrified of riding on horseback, but all her protests fell on deaf ears.

The sharp sea air gave way to the rich green scents of woodland and pasture. The forest thickened, and in some places, branches and debris lay across the path.

"'Tis plashing," Donal Og explained, gesturing at a heap of broken trees. "The Irish damage the paths through the woods to slow the advance of the Sassenach."

She shivered. This war was real here, imminent. Not just some vague idea murmured about at court. The trees soared to the sky, the trunks like massive pillars, the leaves a translucent canopy. Velvet moss grew on the forest floor. Sunlight, filtered through the leafy awning, glowed with a verdant luminescence. A hush hung in the fecund air.

No wonder the Irish believed in enchantment. Only magic could have created a place so holy and silent. It was like standing in a cathedral; the star-shaped leaves, shot through by sunlight, were glass panes in the most glorious of windows.

"It was a fine, grand place to be a boy, long ago," Donal Og said, kneeing his mount to draw abreast of Pippa.

"This is where you and Aidan played?" She

thought it extraordinary for a person to have ties to a particular spot on earth. That was an alien notion to her.

"Playing? Nay, it was all serious business. I was always the bigger lad, but he was the braver and the better thinker, though if you tell him I said so, I'll damn you for a liar."

"Your secret is safe with me." She pictured them, one dark, one fair, darting through greenwood groves or leaping across one of the many burbling springs or hiding in the cleft of a rock.

"No wonder London seemed so strange to you," she said. "This is a place apart. A wild, magical world."

"Like all magic, it has its perils." Donal Og clicked to his horse and trotted to the fore to fall in step with Aidan.

They had reached the edge of the forest. The shadowy woods opened out like a set of lofty doors flung wide. With a cry of wonder, Pippa shaded her eyes. The forested hills surrounded a misty blue-and-green valley. Lakes dotted the landscape, and here and there little rock-bound bits of tillage hugged the shores.

Very far away, on a jut of land pushing out into the largest of the lakes, stood a castle. The massive tower was built of light colored stone, surrounded by lofty battlements near the top. Small, defensive windows pierced the walls and ramparts.

High atop the tower flapped the banner of England.

"That is Ross Castle," she said.

"Aye, it is." Aidan's voice sounded strained.

They rode the rest of the way in silence. Aidan's

one hundred soldiers were already encamped on the shores of the middle lake, awaiting orders.

The main tower of the castle shone like alabaster, the foundations formed by a great upheaval of ancient rock. A narrow neck of land led to an imposing gate with an arching guardhouse. The iron teeth of the raised portcullis gave the menacing look of an evil grin.

A guard stepped out to challenge them. "Halt, while I summon the master."

Aidan barely glanced at the guard. He rode straight on through the arched gate while the Englishman spluttered and gesticulated wildly. "Attack!" he called. "Invasion! The barbaric hordes are upon us!"

Donal Og's fist swung down like a hammer and clobbered the guard on top of the head. The man staggered against a wooden rail, clung there briefly, then sank in a daze.

Two faces peered from a half door at the front of the stables. "Come along, then," Aidan called in an exasperated voice. "Since when do you fear the O Donoghue Mór in his own house?"

One lad shoved the other along in front of him, and they emerged from the stables. Aidan dismounted and tossed his reins to the taller boy, a skinny lad with flame red hair. "And how are things with you, Sorley Boy Curran?"

The boy hunched his shoulders and let the reins fall without catching them. "Begging your pardon, my lord, we've been told we must serve a different master now."

The other lad, like enough to Sorley Boy to be his brother, nodded fearfully. Pippa held her breath and watched Aidan, even though she wanted to shield her eyes from the expression on his face. She recognized it, the numb shock of betrayal. There was something especially poisonous when treachery came from children.

The boys would never know what it cost Aidan to smile at them and hold out the reins once again. He spoke in Gaelic. The lads exchanged a glance, replied to Aidan with relief in their voices, then set to putting up the horses.

"This way." Aidan led them to a stairway that spiraled up the outside of the main keep. Aidan seemed a stranger to Pippa. His face was set and grim, his strides long and purposeful.

As they climbed the lofty tower, she could smell boiled cabbage and roasting meat, and in a few moments they found themselves in a huge hall with an arched ceiling made of plastered wicker. At one end of the gallery was a broad hearth and table where a host of enemy invaders sat eating their midday meal.

All four of them saw the face of the new master of Ross Castle. Pippa blinked at him in astonishment. "God's holy nightgown," she whispered.

Aidan made a dangerous sound in his throat, a combination of growl and Gaelic curse. The expression raised prickles on her arms. She could only wonder what it did to the folk in the hall.

The O Donoghue Mór strode to the high table. His huge hand shot out and lifted the usurper off his bench. "Enjoying your stay, my lord?" he asked in a voice Pippa had never heard before.

Even growing red faced and goggle eyed from lack of air, Richard de Lacey still managed to look ridiculously handsome.

"I . . . can . . . explain," he choked out.

Four English guards rushed forward.

Richard made a quelling gesture with his hands, and the guards subsided. Aidan loosened his hold a notch. "Talk," he barked.

"*I* shall explain," said a strong female voice.

A remarkable woman stepped down from the dais. She was dressed from neck to toe in unrelieved black, and she kept her head covered by a thick, heavy cloth.

The lack of adornment made her beauty only more apparent. It was like seeing the face of the moon in a cloudless night sky. She had perfect, smooth cheeks and expressive eyes, a bowed mouth, and small white hands. A prayer-book pouch hung from her waist.

"Felicity," Aidan said in a cold voice, "be quick with your explanations, or dear Richard might expire from lack of air."

Felicity? Pippa looked to Donal Og and Iago for a hint, but both of them studiously avoided her eyes.

"I invited Lieutenant de Lacey to occupy Ross Castle," said the mysterious Felicity.

Aidan relinquished his hold on Richard, who sank to the bench and loosened his collar.

"Oh, that is fascinating," Pippa burst out, unable to contain her outrage. "By what right do you offer the home of the O Donoghue to strangers?"

The silence in the hall was absolute. Felicity stared at Pippa, giving her a look so full of false pity and false tolerance that Pippa wanted to choke her.

Felicity walked with measured paces to stand directly in front of Aidan. She held out her dainty porcelain hand. She stared up at him, although she directed her answer at Pippa.

And somehow, in some remote place in her mind,

Pippa felt it coming, the thunderhead of emotion hurling like a storm toward her. She braced herself for agony beyond enduring, already knowing what she would hear.

"What right have I? By my right," said the poetically lovely Felicity, "as Aidan's wife."

*T*he day Aidan O Donoghue agreed to wed Felicity Browne was a day like any other—with one exception.

It's true that the abbot frowns on superstition, but I, Revelin of Innisfallen, do swear on the heavenly bosom of my own sinless mother that I heard a fairy horn blow that fateful morn.

To God, Aidan felt he had no choice. Fortitude Browne, the father of Felicity, came up from trade and had what the Sassenach would call Ambitions. He wanted his daughter to marry a lord. Even an Irish lord would do.

Constable Browne required the marriage as part of the peace he made with Ronan. Of course Ronan refused, but Aidan saw a way to bring about peace in the district. Ah, but it was a fine rage that came on Ronan. He did, quite literally, have a "fit" of temper.

Aidan is convinced he slew his father by his own hand. Still, he wed her—a Protestant and Puritan to boot—just as he had promised.

She was beautiful in the flawless fashion of a marble saint—holy, remote, untouchable. It was that quality, perhaps, that drew young Aidan. The challenge of her. The promise that beneath her porcelain Sassenach surface lay a loving heart.

It was the one time Aidan should have listened to his father. It was the one time the instincts of Ronan O Donoghue were right.

—*Revelin of Innisfallen*

12

If Aidan could have slain a person with his eyes, he would have done so, and cheerfully. He hated Felicity with a virulence so sharp and toxic that he wondered how she could still be standing at this moment.

"What the devil are you doing here?" he murmured for her ears only. "You're supposed to be gone."

"Did you think, my lord, that Revelin's feeble annulment petition to Bishop O'Brien would drive me off?" Her hand in his felt cold as stone.

He pulled away and looked at Pippa. There she stood with her heart in her eyes, and in that instant he understood.

She loved him. No matter what she said, no matter how loudly she protested it, she loved him.

And now his betrayal had struck a fatal blow to her soul. He looked into her eyes and could see her love for him dying by inches.

"His wife," Pippa said in a small, clear voice. "You are the wife of the O Donoghue Mór."

Felicity's smile softened to perfect sympathy, and only Aidan could see the hard falseness in her expression. "We have been married nigh on a year. And who might you be?"

"Nobody." Pippa took one step back, then another. "No one at all."

And with that, she turned and fled.

A curse wrenched from Aidan's throat as he followed her out of the hall and up another flight of the stone steps. Clearly unfamiliar with the layout of the castle, Pippa came to a cramped landing, hurled her shoulder against a low door, and burst through it.

This led along the open-air battlement overlooking Lough Leane. She paused between two square-topped merlons.

He froze several feet away from her. For a moment a horrible terror seized him, the same fear he had felt when he had seen her on the sea cliffs, swaying as if in a dream world. She had only to thrust herself forward a few more inches, and she would plummet to her death hundreds of feet below in the rock-bound lake.

"Surely I'm not worth dying for," he said softly.

She looked at him with dazed hurt glazing her eyes and her face pinched and pale. "Never think it," she said.

He chanced a few steps forward and leaned against the wall. "See that island out there?"

He pointed, and she looked out across the blue glass surface of the lake. "Innisfallen?" she asked.

"Aye."

"I can see the roof of a church through the trees.

Do you think your friend Revelin is still there, or do you suppose Richard de Lacey ousted the canons as well?" She spoke with perfect, understated acid.

"I imagine they are all still there. The place is of little strategic value."

"I will be interested to meet Revelin," she said. "To meet the man who was your tutor, charged with turning you into a man of honor." She regarded him with piercing sympathy. "What a disappointment you must be to him."

"That," he said, hating himself, "is no doubt correct." He forced himself to look at her when all he wanted was to hang his head in shame. "Pippa, what shall I say to you? Shall I tell you I'm sorry? Tell you how she came to be my wife and why she is no wife to me at all?"

That, at least, sparked a flicker of interest. "Telling me all of those things explains nothing. Not why you deceived me. Not why you took me in and gave me gifts and treated me with more kindness than anyone ever treated me before. Not why you held me in your arms and kissed me, caressed me, made me—" She bit her lip and turned her face away.

"At least hear me out," he said.

Other than the weary sigh of the wind, he heard no sound. He held his breath until she looked back at him and asked, "Why?"

"Because I care about you, Pippa. God forgive me, I have from the very start."

The breeze corrugated the lake with shimmering ripples. She stared at him, her mouth agape. She looked as fragile and beautiful as a new-made flower, uncertain of her position or what to do next.

Finally, after a long, windy silence, she kicked her

heels against the castle wall. "Why should I believe you?"

"You should not. You should be able to hear the truth in my voice and feel it when your very touch makes me burn, *a gradh*."

"Lust. That's what I see in you. Lust and deceit." She raked a hand through her wind-mussed hair. "I can't think of a single reason I should believe a word you utter."

"Don't believe words. Believe what you see and feel."

"I don't know what I feel," she said. "I wish I could rage at you and throw things, but I feel too numb for that." She looked at him over the top of the merlon. Her face was soft with suffering and bewilderment. "Why didn't you tell me?"

A shudder of self-disgust passed over him. "At first, there seemed no reason. You were a stranger who did not need to know my business. Later, I thought I would leave you at Queen Elizabeth's court, never to see you again. I did not even speak of Felicity to my friends, much less acquaintances I didn't expect to last."

He winced at the stark pain in her eyes. "But you lasted. You came to mean the world to me. I would have done anything not to hurt you, Pippa. I said nothing because I knew the day would come that I would have to leave you. Selfish as I am, I wanted to leave you with a fondness for me in your heart, and so I said nothing. By the time I realized you were coming to Ireland with me . . ." He hesitated and studied the broken-backed line of Macgillycuddy's Reeks in the distance, outlined by the marbled blue sky.

"After that, I just couldn't find the words. I hoped

I would never have to speak of her to you. I had a letter from Revelin stating that an annulment would be granted. She was supposed to have gone back to her father. Even so, there is no excuse. I should have told you about her."

"Then tell me now."

He got up and then sank to one knee before her, holding out one hand. "Please come down."

She hesitated, and that brief distrust cut at him. He had lost her. The old Pippa would have leaped into his arms. At last she took his hand and stepped down.

"I wish we could be alone somewhere, far from the rest of the world," he said.

"You wish for the impossible. The world will never go away." She shivered and hugged herself. "Neither will your wife."

He stood, dropped her hand, and gave a harsh laugh. "Aye, here she is, having surrendered my castle to the enemy." He propped a shoulder on the stone wall and listened for a moment to the wind off the treetops. "Still, that does not excuse my deception."

"She is the reason you never made love to me, isn't she?"

He nodded. "For the very worst of reasons, I pledged a vow to her. I am bound to keep that vow."

Pippa gave a self-deprecating smile. "At least that's a crumb for my vanity. Each time you stopped and put me aside, I thought something about me repelled you."

If she had not been so gravely earnest, he would have laughed. Instead he said, "Quite the opposite, *a stor*. There is nothing in the world I find more beautiful than you." He smiled. "Does that surprise you? Don't look so pale, love. From the first time I saw you performing at St. Paul's, I found you completely captivating. I even liked it when you sang in the bath. Ah, Pippa, you worked so hard to entertain me so I would keep you close. What you didn't know is that I wanted to keep you forever. But I could not." He slid a glance at the archway leading back into the keep.

"Why did you marry her?" Pippa asked.

"For the sake of my people." He gave a bitter laugh. "How noble that sounds. I wed Felicity in order to form a much needed alliance with the English constable in Killarney town. My father had been working feverishly to finish building Ross Castle. I was given a choice of offering for Felicity or suffering an attack on the stronghold."

"But that is not so unusual," she said with touching credulity. "Don't the gentry always marry for reasons of expedience?"

"That is the reason I told the world. The truth is, I wed Felicity in order to spite my father." There. After all this time, he admitted it. He felt again that hot stab of emotion brought on by thoughts of his father. He closed his eyes and let the wind rush over his face.

He remembered it all with razor-edged clarity: his father's snort of disbelief, followed by a bellow of outrage, and then the blows, two of them, open-handed slaps across the face, so hard that Aidan's head had snapped from side to side. These went unchallenged, and more blows followed, until Aidan had sunk to the floor and put up a hand to staunch the ooze of blood from his split lip.

Ronan O Donoghue would have murdered his son bare-handed, Aidan was certain of it. As the older man hammered away, and as Aidan all but sat on his hands to keep from fighting back, the long buried truth had come out.

"You are no son of mine," Ronan had roared, "but a Sassenach mercenary's get, a bastard. Your faithless mother tricked me into believing I had sired you, but I finally beat the truth out of her."

The old sickness built in Aidan's throat. He pressed his back against the wall and inhaled through his teeth. He would never know for certain if his father had spoken truly that night. The rumors that Máire O Donoghue had died by her husband's hand seemed likely. Ronan had never sired another child, so perhaps his accusation was true also.

"Blood will tell," Ronan had bellowed. "I thought I could make a true warrior of you, but the moment I turn my back you crawl into the lap of the Sassenach."

The beating and bellowing had gone on. Hatred formed like a ball of ice in Aidan's chest. He would not let himself fight back, for his rage was too strong. He could not trust himself not to kill his father.

And then, after all, he did kill him. Ronan had stopped screaming midsentence, his arm raised for yet another blow. His purplish face contorted, his eyes bulged, and he pitched forward.

His heavy bulk had landed on Aidan. Slowly, on fire with agony from the barrage of blows, Aidan extracted himself and stood. He remembered looking at his father for what seemed like a long time. He remembered walking—not running—down the winding stone steps of the tower to find someone to send for the barber surgeon.

"Aidan?" Pippa's soft voice rescued him from the hellish memories. "Go on."

Aidan surprised himself. He told her. For the first time, he revealed to another person every hideous, humiliating detail of that night.

"My defiance was the ax that killed my father," he concluded. "He died while raging at me about Felicity. His death did cause me considerable guilt, so I finished building the castle according to his plans."

She listened without taking her eyes off him. She looked at him as if he had become a stranger. She was pale and still, yet rather than disgust or accusation, she regarded him with sympathy. "I thought people who had families were happy," she said at last.

Clasping his hands behind his back, he paced the wall walk. "Within hours of marrying Felicity, I knew I had made a mistake."

"Within hours?" She blushed. "You mean the wedding night."

He stopped walking. "I suspected something was amiss when she barred me from the marriage bed. Just in case I misunderstood, she declared she would remain a virgin until I and all my subjects renounced the Catholic faith and embraced the new Reformed religion."

"She placed a high price on her virtue."

He smiled at Pippa's dark but ready humor. "It proved to be little incentive. Call me strange, but I find nothing attractive about smashing icons and cursing the pope." His smile vanished. "In every sense that counts, I have never been married at all. Yet I am consumed with guilt over my feelings for you."

She gave a soft moan and stepped back as if to resist going into his arms. "What do you intend to do now?"

His heart beat slowly, heavily. He allowed himself

to smooth his hand lightly over her cheek. "When I married her, I had no idea it was possible to care for a woman the way I have come to care for you." He wanted to say he loved her, but he couldn't. Not now. Not when he had no idea what he could offer her.

She tilted her head so that his hand cradled her cheek, and he could feel the warmth of tears. It proved to be his undoing. He gathered her gently into his arms and pressed his lips to her hair.

"It is too late for us, isn't it?" she whispered.

"That is what common sense tells me. But my heart tells me we will find a way."

"Aidan—"

"We were never properly introduced," Felicity called from the arched opening of the stairwell. An icy sheen of hatred gleamed in her cornflower blue eyes.

Aidan and Pippa broke apart to see her standing there, as perfect and beautiful as a marble statue. An odd turbulence seethed in Felicity's eyes. She had always been strange and fanatical. She appeared tense, as if she were a tautly coiled spring.

Pippa put her hands on her hips and faced Felicity unflinchingly. "You may call me Mistress Trueheart."

"Mistress?" Felicity hissed out the word. "Don't you mean leman, or perhaps *whore*?"

Pippa lay awake that night, fuming about Felicity. At Richard's insistence she had been given a private chamber as a guest of honor.

Deep down, she reluctantly admired Felicity. Being married to the O Donoghue Mór and staying chaste was an exercise in greater willpower than Pippa could ever hope to possess.

"He has but to crook his finger, and I come running," she muttered, punching her pillow. "At least the intolerant bitch has the courage of her convictions."

Meanwhile, Aidan was trying to negotiate a treaty with Richard. His men wanted war. Pippa had heard them arguing in the guardroom. They spoke in Irish, but she now understood enough of the language to glean some of what was said. She understood enough to know how desperately Aidan loved his country and his people.

"You foolish, foolish woman," she whispered to the windy darkness. "You have no idea what you are missing."

If he put Felicity aside, Aidan reasoned, then the terms of surrender she had signed as lady of Castleross would be null and void. There would be no agreement with the Sassenach. But he knew the power of the Browne clan. Their rage could set a torch to wholesale slaughter.

Standing at the window in an upper-story room he had occupied since boyhood, he felt a lifting of his heart. The battle would come to a head whether he kept Felicity or not, and according to Revelin, he had permission from Rome to set her aside. He should send her to her father in Killarney.

The shame would slay her. But she was the one who had betrayed her marriage vows and barred him from her bed.

The thought of being free intoxicated him. Free to show Pippa what was in his heart. It was like a blessing from heaven. God, how he wanted her!

He would tell Felicity first thing in the morning. She might have driven Revelin away, but she would not deter Aidan from carrying out the annulment.

A latch clicked and the chamber door swished open. He turned, reaching for his shortsword.

A cloaked and hooded figure entered the room. "Stay your hand, my lord," said a soft, female voice. "Please, I beg you." She sank to her knees in a pool of pale moonlight.

"Felicity?" His hand relaxed. "What are you doing here?"

She dropped back the hood and opened the cloak to reveal that she was wearing naught but a translucent linen shift beneath.

He froze, transfixed. For the first time ever, he saw her unbound hair, sleek and rich as polished wood. He saw the dark tips of her generous breasts thrusting against the thin garment. He saw the ivory skin of her throat, with the pulse beating gently beneath the surface.

She raised her perfect face to his, and he saw the disquieting turbulence in her eyes, more pronounced than it had been earlier.

She took a deep breath. "I came here to do what I should have done the very night we were wed. I should have given myself to you then. But the Lord spoke to me and told me I must wait."

"I see. And now the Lord tells you it is all right to spread your legs for me?"

She flinched at his crudeness. "It was wrong for me to refuse you. I know that now. I realized it the moment I saw you tempted by the evils of lust for another woman."

"Nay, Felicity. You realized it the moment you

knew I would set you aside and invalidate your treaty with the English."

Her expression remained serene, empty of emotion. He lauded her self-possession, though there was a quality about it that discomfited him.

"I think not at all of the treaty," she insisted. "Greater matters are at stake. Matters of the soul."

"Madam," he said, "you are a huge and constant liar."

"No!" She glided to her feet. The gown wafted against her as she rushed to him. Her figure was outlined in silver moonlight. "I want you, my lord, my love. I always have. Surely you know how hard it was to keep from begging you to take me. I am begging now, Aidan. I can give you children—"

"Felicity," he said softly, regretfully, "you will never get the chance." Before she could protest he went on. "Life is short, and life does not wait for us to decide when and how to live it."

He had a bleak, fleeting thought of how dazzled he had once been by her beauty, her purity. And by the idea that their union would also unite their two peoples. "We both made the mistake of trying to seize control of something that is out of our grasp."

She flung herself at him and covered his face with kisses. Taken by surprise, he stepped back. "Felicity, please. Don't make this worse than it already is."

"All will be well," she whispered huskily. "Aidan, you are my husband!"

She moved nearer, and to avoid her, he stepped through the doorway to the stone-railed balcony. The cold air of a clear night blew over him. She followed and clung to him, whimpering and kissing his mouth, his chin, wherever she could reach.

"You never understood," she said, her voice a chilling whisper in his ear, her grasping arms curving around behind him. She was clumsy yet insistent, and again he felt a pang of regret that any sweetness they might have shared had been doomed from the start.

"I did love you much, my lord," she said.

"Nay, Felicity, nor did I ever truly love you." Her arms still imprisoned him; he wished she would let go. "We must end this. Now. Tonight. Revelin has the papers all ready."

"I will not let you shame me!"

At first he felt nothing; then a searing, sharp pain stung him. He froze, too amazed to move. The bitch had stabbed him in the back. She raised her arm to stab him again.

He gave a wordless cry and thrust her away. The wound sent icy tingles of shock and agony down his back. She lifted the small knife and rushed at him.

He caught her by both wrists. Images skipped past his blurring vision, and he realized he was on the verge of falling unconscious. "Don't do this, Felicity. It's mad, do you hear me?"

She tried to thrust down with the knife, but he tightened his grip. "You're destroying yourself, woman, not me," he said through his teeth. With a little more pressure, he could snap her wrist, but he did not want to hurt her. "Just go back to your family. Blame it all on me. Tell them I'm an ogre, tell them I beat you or made you say the rosary. We can claim our barren state is my fault, we can say anything—"

"Never! You papist bastard!" The blade quivered in her hand.

He pressed his thumb into her pulse point, finding the nerve. She dropped the knife and went limp against him. Hot blood seeped down his back. He felt airy, without substance, as if he could float away. He needed to sit down, put his head between his knees, call for Iago to dress the wound.

But first he had to deal with Felicity. "It's over," he whispered. "The whole ugly farce is over. Let us end it now before we hurt each other anymore."

She gazed up at him. "But I love you. And you love me."

He was certain she missed the irony of the words she had said to the man she'd just stabbed in the back. "I wanted you in order to anger my father and please yours," he explained. "You wanted me in order to further your Reformed crusade. We were wrong, both of us. It's over."

"No," she said, stepping back. She leaped up onto the stone railing. The wind caught at the hem of her cloak and tossed her beautiful long hair in a dark nimbus around her tormented face. "Not quite over, Aidan."

"God, Felicity!" He took a stumbling step forward. "What are you doing? Please come down." He heard himself repeating words he had said to Pippa just a short time ago. But Pippa had not been determined to destroy him no matter the cost to herself. Pippa's eyes had not shone with that silvery, manic light.

A grating sound came from somewhere above, the creak of hinges, perhaps. He ignored it and held out his hand. "I didn't mean any of it, darling," he cajoled. "I'll take you to bed tonight, make love to you, make you so happy."

"Your lies come too late." She grasped the front

of her shift and rent it asunder so that her pale breasts spilled out. She raked a hand across her chest, scoring her flesh with ugly red stripes. "Your lies will not save either of us now. Your lies will damn you to hell. By morning, they will all know you killed me."

He lunged for her, but she was quicker, stepping back and then falling, falling, her hair and cloak billowing, her face a stark white oval that disappeared into blackness.

Aidan clung to the railing and vomited. Sweat beaded his forehead as anger built in his chest. Even in death, she controlled him. By morning they would call him a murderer.

Unless he left now, in secret, and did not return until he had an army at his back.

Richard de Lacey handed Pippa a handkerchief. She dried her eyes and glanced up at him. "How many of these do you have?"

"Four more, I think."

She gave a long, miserable sniff. "I shall need more than that."

The sun had not shown its face. A dull rain drummed on the eaves of the small corner office where she sat with Richard and a woman named Shannon MacSweeney.

Shannon had come at dawn to see if the rumors that flew about Killarney were true. With her vivid red hair and tall, proud bearing, she resembled a flaming torch as she patted Pippa's shoulder and watched Richard with sharp green eyes.

"So she is dead for certain," Shannon said.

"She is."

"And did the O Donoghue attack her and fling her over the wall? That is what her father claims, and that is what her cousin, Valentine Browne, announced at the village well."

"Completely untrue," Richard said furiously. "I saw it all. I heard voices, and looked out my window, which is directly over the terrace. She stabbed Aidan, then leaped up on the rail, rending her gown to make it look as if he had attacked her." Richard's voice thickened with horror and grief. "He tried to get her to come down, but she jumped."

Pippa crushed the handkerchief to her eyes, wishing she could scrub away the image his words made. "Why did he flee?" she whispered. "That only makes him look guilty."

"He was right to flee," Shannon MacSweeney said. "He'd be hanged by sunset if he stayed."

"I would speak in his defense," Richard insisted.

Shannon gave a bitter laugh. "Do you think that would matter? Fortitude Browne is looking for any excuse to be rid of Aidan O Donoghue."

Filled with cold fury, the O Donoghue Mór swept down the Iveragh peninsula, mustering rebels from every hamlet and town. It was not hard to find violent, discontented men to follow him on his quest to take back Ross Castle. For a generation now, English rule had bowed their backs beneath greed and injustice. The recent hanging of rebels by Fortitude Browne in retaliation for Felicity's death had pushed them to the breaking point.

Willingly they took up arms, and within a month a

formidable army was camped on the far shores of
Lough Leane.

Pippa, who had spent most of the time at
Innisfallen in the company of the canon Revelin,
arrived by rowboat at sunset. She spied Iago working
with a company of archers. Watching their arrows
thunk into straw, man-shaped targets made it all
chillingly real. They meant to kill every last
Englishman.

"Where is Aidan?" she asked Iago.

Iago's eyes widened. "You should not be here."

"Just answer me, Iago."

He looked at Revelin, who had come with her.
"She should not be here."

"Sure and who's going to stop her?" Revelin asked
in his thick brogue. "Like a battering ram, she is,
pounding away at a man's good sense until he all but
begs her to do as she wills."

Grim humor flashed in Iago's smile. "I see you
have gotten to know our Pippa."

"Well?" she demanded, speaking brusquely to
cover her nervousness. "Where is he?"

Iago pointed. "Just there, at the edge of the woods,
at the source of the spring." He touched her shoulder
and regarded her with troubled brown eyes. "There's
a shrine to his mother there. And *pequeña*, he has
been at the poteen, I fear."

She tossed her head and struck out for the spring.
"I've seen drunken men before." Yet anxiety
pounded in her chest as she passed through the
encampment. The soldiers were silent, their anticipation palpable, like invisible taut threads strung across
the camp.

The past weeks had been a turbulent time for the

whole district, the English crying foul in the death of Felicity Browne O Donoghue, the Irish passionately proclaiming Aidan's innocence, and Richard de Lacey himself, still entrenched at Ross Castle, strangely silent. No doubt preparing for war.

She climbed a short, muddy pathway to the spring. A beautiful stone Celtic cross stood beside the burbling waters.

Aidan did not seem to hear her approach. He sat upon a large rock, his elbow resting on his knee, a deerskin flask dangling from his fingers, and his hair, longer than ever, falling forward in unkempt hanks.

Despite his haggard appearance, he still looked every inch the chieftain, fierce and strong and unconquered, yet oddly reluctant, as if he played a role for which he was ill suited.

"Aidan," she said softly.

He looked up at her. She saw the terrible rage and reckless defiance burning in the bluer-than-blue centers of his eyes. In that instant she understood, saw his torment as if he had laid it all out before her. He considered himself a dead man now. Getting himself killed in the siege would be a mere formality.

"Please," she said, stepping into the glade. "Please don't do this. Find another way, Aidan. I beg you."

"Find another way." His harsh, drink-roughened tone mocked her. "What would you suggest? Marrying a Sassenach to keep the peace? Or murdering one when she becomes a burden?"

She caught her breath to keep in the horror. "You blame yourself, don't you?" Her voice shook. "Revelin said you would."

"Revelin is seldom wrong."

The anguish she heard in his voice touched her. At his core, Aidan O Donoghue was a kind and decent man with too many responsibilities and too few choices. She dropped to her knees beside him and sat back on her heels.

She picked up the flask and touched it to her lips. It was still warm from his mouth, and she tilted it back and drank deeply, watching him from beneath her lashes. He stared back, looking skeptical. The strong drink lit a bonfire in her stomach, but she would not allow herself to gag or even flinch.

As calmly as she could, she set down the flask.

"Well?" he asked.

"That would put a plowhorse under."

He favored her with a quick, bitten-off laugh, and then the shadows fell over him again.

"It was not your fault," Pippa insisted. "Not your father's death, nor even Felicity's. Both were victims of their own hatred."

He stared at the carved stone cross. A Gaelic inscription was etched at the bottom.

"I wish to God I could believe you." He took a long, comfort-seeking pull on the flask and wiped his sleeve across his mouth. He looked debauched, hopeless, remote.

Pippa had never seen him like this, and she did not know how to reach him. He was so bitter and tense that she feared he would explode at any moment. "Your mother was called Máire," she said, her finger tracing the letters and whorls carved into the stone. "Is this her name here?"

"Aye."

"Tell me about her."

"Ah, another happy subject." He drank again, then

flung the flask onto the grass. The sharp fumes of poteen made her eyes smart. "Supposedly she was unfaithful to my father, and I am half Sassenach. At least that is what my mother confessed while my father was beating her for the last time."

Shaken, she put her hand lightly, tentatively, on his forearm. His muscles were coiled. "A woman in torment will say anything. Revelin said that Ronan was a hateful and hated man."

She drew a deep breath for courage and finally said what she had come to say. "If you take these men to storm the castle, you will be acting just like him. Is that what you want? To become your father?"

He snatched his arm away and glared at her. "You don't know what you're talking about."

She wanted to shrink from his anger but forced herself to stay there, pinned by his glare. "I do, my lord. You told me yourself. Ronan O Donoghue offered up men's lives without regard to the widows and orphans they would leave behind. If you so desperately need something to feel guilty about, then feel guilty about that. Not about your father keeling over in a fit of pique or Felicity taking her own life."

He moved so quickly that she did not even have time to cry out. Grasping her by the shoulders, he hauled her to her feet. His fingers bit into her.

"Enough," he said through his teeth. "I'll hear no more. These affairs are none of your concern. Begone now, and leave me to do what I must do."

She stared down at his fingers. "You said you cared about me. Is this how you show it?"

He muttered something anguished and Irish, then let her go. It was all there in his face, the determination, the desolation, the cornered look of a man who had run out of choices. "Pippa—"

She wrenched herself away and fled.

He had decided to take the castle at dawn. By now, Richard de Lacey would have gotten word that an army was gathering, but there had been no time for reinforcements to arrive.

Ross Castle was reputed to be impregnable, and perhaps it was. But not to Aidan. He had personally overseen the design of its defenses. With luck, he and his men would cross the narrow causeway unchallenged and make it at least as far as the guardroom before engaging the enemy.

The fog-laden chill of dawn settled into his bones. He kept hearing Pippa's voice. *Is that what you want? To become your father?*

Hard questions. Things no one else dared to ask him. Things he dared not answer. Couldn't she see he had no choice?

He turned to the silent, waiting men behind him. Dressed in traditional tunics and fur, barefoot and crudely armed, they exuded an anger honed by generations of subjugation. They wanted this fight, Aidan reminded himself. They were ready. More than ready.

Iago and Donal Og caught his eye and nodded to signal their flanking troops.

"God be with us all, then," he said in clear Gaelic.

Donal Og winked. "And may we all get to heaven before the devil knows we're dead."

Nervous laughter rippled through the assembly. Aidan turned and led the way to the stronghold. He expected to see scouts melting from their lookout posts and slinking back to warn de Lacey, but in the forest they met with nothing more fierce than a badger and a flock of birds.

His hopes rose as they crossed the natural causeway formed by the peninsula projecting out into the lake. The Sassenach host did not lift a finger to stop them.

When he found the main gate unbarred, he felt the first prickle of apprehension. He turned to Donal Og and whispered, "It's a trap."

Donal Og nodded grimly. "Bound to be. Shall we go on?"

"Aye." Aidan went first, despite offers from some of the men. He wanted to prove himself different from his father.

They crossed the inner courtyard and entered the guardroom. The dim, unsteady light revealed six hulking shapes stationed at the windows and stairwells. He braced himself for a fight but quickly surmised that something was wrong.

He motioned for the men behind him to stop and entered the guardroom alone. Good Virgin Mary, were the guards dead?

A long, blubbering snore filled the air.

He nearly came out of his skin. When he realized what the situation was, he blew out a sigh of relief. "See that they're disarmed," he said to his men.

"My lord," someone said in an incredulous whisper, "they've already been disarmed."

"Their hands and feet are bound," Iago noted.

Beyond the guardroom, they climbed the stairs. At each separate landing, they found a sleeping Englishman. It was uncanny, as if the *sidhe* had cast a spell over the entire household.

By the time they had reached the great hall, Aidan had begun to believe victory was in his grasp.

But from the landing of the staircase, he heard voices and froze. He cocked his head to listen.

"All right, then," said a sweet, feminine voice, "what about this one?"

Revelin's distinctive silvery chuckle wafted on the foggy air. "Not quite, my dear. I believe you are surrounded."

"Oh, geld and splay you—" She broke off as Aidan stepped into the room, followed by Donal Og, Iago, and the first troop of men. She stood and grinned at him, and it was the sweetest smile he had ever seen. "Welcome, Your Eminence," she said.

He strode to the table, where a *fidchell* gaming board had been set out. "What in God's name is going on here?"

Revelin stroked his long white beard. "Well, my lord, it looks as if the young lady is about to surrender her key pegs and lose the game."

"I mean *here*." Exasperated, he gestured at the men strewn about the room.

"Ah, them." Revelin dipped his head in a sage's nod. "We drugged them."

"We did," Pippa confirmed. She pointed to a stack of shortswords and shields and stabbing daggers at the base of the dais. "We put their weapons here. Does that suit you?"

"We also sent the strongbox of Ross Castle to the coast for safekeeping." Shannon MacSweeney spoke from a corner of the room where she sat placidly doing needlework. "I had to tell them about the chest of gold, Aidan," said his childhood friend. "I hope you don't mind."

She stroked the golden hair of Richard de Lacey, who lay on a cushion beside her. "I hope *he* doesn't mind, either."

For a moment, Aidan could not speak. When he found his voice, he said, "You drugged them."

"That's right," Pippa said.

"A bit of Tristram's knot in the poteen," Revelin said. "Well, perhaps more than a bit." He went back to studying the *fidchell* board.

"And also in the porridge and ale," Pippa added. "And I'm quite afraid I added some to the wine and ale just for good measure. But you had better hurry up and defeat them or do whatever it is you do when you conquer a castle. Once they wake up, they are bound to be most unhappy fellows."

Aidan walked over to the table. He stood very still, looking across at her, drinking in the sight of her face, all soft in the morning mist. He stared at her for so long that she blushed.

"You really should make haste, my lord."

"I shall." For the first time in more than a month, he smiled. It felt good to smile. "There is one thing I must do first."

"What?"

"This." He slid his arms around her and leaned down to place a long, lush kiss on her startled mouth. Ah, he had forgotten what she meant to him.

But never, not for a moment, had he forgotten how much he loved her.

"If you mean to thank me in the same manner," Revelin said, "you'll find yourself highly unappreciated."

Aidan straightened, his eyes never leaving Pippa's face. "I'll save my kisses for her, if it's all the same to you."

The tension among the men dissolved into loud guffaws. Donal Og beat his chest like a warrior of yore. "Come, lads!" he bellowed. "Let us make short work of the prisoners before they awaken and make us sweat for our victory!"

We had a most perturbing report from Richard in Ireland. It seems he and his forces were compelled—by means he did not explain in his letters—to abandon Ross Castle and retreat to Killarney. Even more disconcerting is the news that he has fallen in love with an Irishwoman and means to marry her before the ban on Irish and English unions takes effect. Imagine! My Richard, a bridegroom.

I fear his duty to England will dim his joy. He has called for reinforcements, but Oliver says more men are unlikely to be sent, as the queen's forces are already taxed to their limit.

However, Oliver himself is quite capable of raising an army and a fleet of ships as well, for the Muscovy Company has grown unimaginably rich on the trading begun by Oliver's father.

Perhaps a voyage to Ireland would allow us to investigate the truth of the mysterious message we received that dredged up such a sweet, aching wealth of memories.

For now, I shall put aside my cares. The delightful contessa is coming to Blackrose Priory for another visit. She is always full of the most deliciously shocking gossip.

—Lark de Lacey,
Countess of Wimberleigh

13

"Will you marry me?"

Aidan looked up from the document he was studying. The bewilderment on his face disheartened Pippa, but she forced herself to stand calmly in the middle of the counting office, waiting for his answer.

He gave her a soft, distracted smile, his eyes hazy with distant thoughts. "I'm sorry. I didn't hear you correctly. I thought you just asked me to marry you."

"I did."

His eyebrows shot up. "You did?"

"I did."

The eyebrows descended in a frown. "Oh." With his thumb, he curled the corner of the letter on the desk, then frowned and turned the document face-down.

An awkward silence stretched out between them while the afternoon sunlight, streaming through a narrow window, painted lazy patterns on the stone floor.

Fool, she called herself. All her life she had lived in dread of rejection, so much so that she had learned to shield herself from any kind of intimacy. Now here she was inviting the ultimate rebuff—from the one person who could wound her the most deeply.

It was too late to retract her question, so she took refuge in a cocky pose, with hands on hips and a challenging lift of her chin. "Well? Will you?"

"Will I marry you?" He tasted the question as if it were some exotic drink. How maddeningly attractive he looked this afternoon. Three weeks after signing terms of surrender with Richard de Lacey, the O Donoghue Mór seemed a new man, hale and assured, lord of his domain.

Richard and his army had withdrawn to the northern shores of Lough Leane, near Killarney. Aidan was home now, truly home for the first time since she had known him, and he looked at ease.

Also puzzled, as he sat with his elbows resting on the table, fingers forming a steeple. "Forgive me, but isn't it the usual way for the man to ask the woman?"

"I don't know anything about the usual way. I only know my way." She tossed her head as if his reply did not truly matter. "I know that marriage is a grave business, and for a chieftain to wed an outsider is unheard of, but—"

"How do you know these things?"

"Revelin told me."

"Ah. Revelin the all-wise. What else did he tell you?"

"That you would say yes." She was so embarrassed, she could barely choke out the words.

He rose slowly, with a predator's grace, and moved past the writing table. "Revelin misunderstands."

Through sheer force of will, she kept herself from melting of shame. She summoned a sparkling smile and winked at him, pretending the whole thing had been a joke. "Of course," she said briskly. "The whole idea is quite preposterous. You are absolutely right to refuse—"

"I adore you with all my heart," he said softly.

She let out an involuntary sigh. His declaration sent warmth rushing through her, raising a flush on her skin and lifting her hopes until breathing became painful.

"And I cannot marry you," he continued. "Not now. Perhaps not ever."

Her heart turned to stone in her chest. The old torment stormed through her, the all-too-familiar feeling of abandonment. It was the numbness that had come over her when she had stood on a windswept strand in England while they buried old Mab; it was the freezing sense of isolation she had experienced each time a troupe of players melted apart; it was the forced aloofness she cultivated even in the teeming yard of St. Paul's.

She thought she had prepared herself for the hurt, but she had underestimated its strength. If his words had been blows, they would have killed; they were that lethal.

Turning away, wanting to get out before he saw her pain, she managed to mumble, "I see." There would be no quick recovery for her this time, no blithe laughter to hide her tears.

He stood to bar her from leaving and reached for her hands. "Nay, my love, you do not see. Come here." He led her out a low doorway and up a short spiral of stairs, then through a tower door. They emerged onto the west section of the wall walk. It was a perfect day, the sun soft upon the treetops and the lake reflecting a clear blue sky.

"Look well upon the beauty," he said, standing behind her and speaking intimately into her ear. "Who knows when you shall see its like again? It is too lovely, too piercing, to last."

She was not sure if he meant this kingdom or the feelings between them. "Why do you say that?"

"Because we won't be left alone here, to live and love and make bairns and do all the things ordinary people dream of doing."

Her hopes began to sink beneath the weight of his logic. "You mean Richard will return."

She felt his broad shoulders stiffen as if preparing to bear a great burden. "With reinforcements. And he won't stop at taking Ross Castle. He'll have to take me as well."

"No," she said. "Could you not just come to terms with him? Why should he need you as a prisoner?"

"If it were only Richard, I would not worry. For all that he's a Sassenach, he has acted with honor." Aidan turned her in his arms so that she faced him. "Felicity has a powerful family."

The mention of Aidan's late wife sent a dark chill rippling over Pippa's skin. She clung to his arms, feeling suddenly sick and dizzy. "Her father continues to insist you killed his daughter, doesn't he?"

Aidan nodded, and his gaze strayed to the letter lying on the desk. "He will not rest until he sees me hanged."

The chill deepened to an icy sting. She wanted to

clap her hands over her ears, to close her eyes, to make the feeling of dread go away.

But Aidan was right. It would not go away. A man had lost his daughter. How could he rest until he felt justice had been served?

"I still want to marry you," she whispered.

Aidan smiled sadly and touched his lips to her brow. "Perhaps today you do."

"I think I wanted to the first moment I saw you. So don't try to tell me this feeling will fade away."

He seemed to have to work to keep his embrace gentle; she sensed a strained tension in him. "If you have even a fraction of the desire I feel for you, then your wish is understandable."

"It is more than mere desire," she insisted. "It is like wanting to find my family, only stronger than that. One thing I have come to realize is that if I have you, I don't need them. It is probably impossible to find out the truth anyway."

"But if you were to learn who they are?" His voice sounded taut, the words forced.

"I might be curious about them. But I don't care anymore. I don't wish to know."

He closed his eyes, and a look of torment shadowed his face. Yet when he opened his eyes, he was smiling. "My sweet, entirely adorable colleen," he said, lowering his mouth to kiss her, "is there anything you won't say?"

"I think not." She shuddered as his tongue flicked out to taste her lips. "Not to you." His kiss deepened, and she felt the love and desire flowing so richly through her blood that she moaned with the urgent pleasure of it. She was shaking when he pulled back. "You know," she whispered, "I'm certain there are worse reasons to marry than rampant lust."

"I'm certain you're right," he said, some of the old laughter creeping into his voice. But then, as he studied her upturned face, he sobered. "Sweetheart, you need a reliable husband, not someone who is likely to end at the gibbet."

She clenched her hands into fists and struck his chest. "Don't talk like that!"

"But what if I were to be seized by Constable Browne?" he persisted. "What would you do then?"

She forced a laugh. "I suppose, my lord, I would be a rather wealthy widow."

He laughed, too, and bent his head again to kiss her. Just before their lips met, she fancied she saw a flash of crazed desperation in his eyes. But when his warm mouth closed over hers, she forgot all about their macabre conversation.

I suppose, my lord, I would be a rather wealthy widow. Her words, though spoken in jest, clung in Aidan's mind like a burr in a horse's mane.

Late at night, when all the household lay at rest, he climbed to the topmost point of Ross Castle, where he could brace his foot on the wall and look out across the moonlit lake to the far mountains.

How simple life had been for his forebears, he reflected. Simple and brutal. A chieftain ruled the domain for as far as he could see.

Now the Sassenach had come, preserving the brutality, heightening it, creating complications for which Ireland was unprepared. The Irish would lose much of themselves in this war; Munster was in pieces, and even the great rebel earl of Desmond had been driven into the misty mountains of Slieve Mish.

Aidan thought of the flurry of furious letters, warrants, and proclamations he had received since making peace with Richard. He could not say how long he could keep the force of Constable Browne's fury at bay—a month? half a year? He knew only that they would come for him; it was the way of the Sassenach.

So there it was. Felicity had won. She had defeated him.

Except on one matter.

A soft, heartfelt smile unfurled on his lips as the night wind lifted his hair. She had not managed to destroy his love for Pippa.

His clenched fist came down hard on the top of the wall. He noticed a smear of blood but felt no pain, only a deep, quiet exultation as he came to his decision.

Aye, he would marry Pippa. He would steal joy from the jaws of despair. And secretly, without her knowledge, he would prepare her for a future without him.

I suppose, my lord, I would be a rather wealthy widow.

"And so you shall be, my beloved," he whispered to the quiet night. "So you shall be."

They were married by Revelin of Innisfallen. The canon beamed as he held out his book for Aidan's offering of silver for the Arrha; his voice rang with triumph as he blessed the knotwork wedding ring of the O Donoghue.

During the celebratory mass that followed, Pippa sat in wide-eyed awe. The sacred mysteries intrigued her. She wondered why the Reformers found such things as Latin prayers and songs, clouds of incense, and unshakable faith so threatening. The little windy chapel of Ross Castle hardly dripped with decadent riches, and Rome seemed several worlds away. The people gathered here exuded a simple piety that was bound to change the mind of any Reformer.

Or perhaps not any. To her dying day, Felicity Browne O Donoghue had dedicated herself to converting these people to the Reformed faith. More stubborn than their mistress, the people of Ross had resisted, driving her to unbearable frustration. What a foolish waste, Pippa thought. God was God, no matter what church a person worshiped in, no matter how prayers were offered.

Even as memories of Felicity chilled her, a small, evil exultation nudged into her mind. Pippa was here, wed to the man she adored, because Felicity had taken her own life.

Filled with guilt, Pippa stole a glance at Aidan. He knelt with his head bent. His raven hair fell forward, the single beaded strand catching a glow from the candlelight. His face looked strong and intense, curiously determined, and so beautiful it made her heart ache.

She was stricken by a terrible fear. What in God's name was she doing? She, a common street urchin, marrying an Irish chieftain. It was madness. *Madness.*

She must have made some subtle sound or movement of distress, for he closed his hand around hers and caught her eye. "*Pax vobiscum,*" he said, echoing the words Revelin had just spoken.

She closed her eyes and swayed toward him. Aye, peace. It settled around her like a golden mantle, enveloping her, comforting, healing her. All her life, she had sought the peace of knowing she was loved. Aidan O Donoghue was giving that to her. The magnitude of his gift struck her, and a tear seeped out from beneath her eyelashes.

With a touch as light as a moth's wing, he brushed away the tear. She opened her eyes to see him looking at her with an intensity that stole her breath.

"Those had best be tears of happiness," he whispered.

"So you should hope, or it is going to be a very long night," she whispered back, trying to lighten the moment and resisting the urge to sniffle loudly. "I am now your wife. What more could I want?"

His smile held such promise that a wave of shivers slid over her. "That," he said, bending to secretly trace the shape of her ear with his tongue, "is something we will explore tonight."

The maids spoke in rapid Gaelic, but their broad winks and friendly tweaks and pats delivered a universal message of good-humored bawdiness. Pippa realized that even for the older married women, there was something inherently exciting about readying a new bride for her husband.

With much giggling and sighing, they stripped her naked and bathed her in warm spring water steeped in fragrant herbs. One girl explained, in a dense brogue, that morning dew had been added to the bathwater in order to keep her skin beautiful. Pippa luxuriated; baths were still a novelty to her and the gentle care of womenfolk even newer yet. Sibheal, the local midwife, had strong, capable, cosseting hands. With wry laughter, she told of assisting the birth of the O Donoghue Mór, pantomiming hilariously the prodigious size—in all aspects—of the future chieftain.

The merriment continued to surge and lull like a friendly breeze. When Sibheal helped her from the tub to dry her and comb her hair, Pippa sensed a soft shock of memory. Just for a moment, she felt cosseted in a way that evoked the faint bittersweetness of a distant dream. Was it the barely remembered touch of a mother? The sensation fled quickly, and Pippa smiled, but her heart pounded with the realization that she had almost recalled her mother.

The other two maids rubbed her with rose oil until her skin was soft and supple. They draped her in a gauzy garment of fine white linen. It fit loosely, sliding down over her collarbones.

Sibheal pulled it up at the neckline and clucked her tongue. "We need a jewel to fasten this."

"I have just the thing." Pippa fetched her bag, which looked worn and paltry in the clean, well-swept chamber. She took out the broken ornament of gold. "This will hold it."

Sibheal pinned up the shoulder of the tunic, and Pippa sent her a grateful smile. Though plundered of its jewels, the brooch was the only link she had with a past she did not know. Even so, she drew a measure of comfort from wearing it on her wedding night.

The women fussed with her hair a little more until it was a mass of springy curls crowned by fresh marigolds. Then, curtsying and backing toward the door, the two younger maids left.

Sibheal took her to a lofty private chamber high in the main keep above the great hall. A wreath of hawthorn adorned the door. The women had decked the bridal chamber with garlands of fragrant wildflowers. The bedstead was huge and luxuriant, a carved oaken headboard and great linen swags cloaking the interior in fragrant mystery. In the hangings and bedclothes, the women had tucked small offerings—bundles of herbs and dried petals—to bring luck and bounty to the newly wedded couple.

After Sibheal had left, Pippa stood in the middle of the room and simply stared. "Bedding is a serious matter," she said faintly.

"That it is, my dear." With his raiments flapping loose like broken wings, Revelin stepped into the room, followed by two barefoot acolytes who tripped over their robes as they peered at the bride.

She blushed but gave them a smile of pure happiness. Let them look their fill. Let them know what a woman looked like when her dreams were finally coming true. She was the wife of the O Donoghue Mór.

One of the lads circled the room, swinging a censer that gave intermittent puffs of richly perfumed incense; the other held a basin of holy water. Revelin took a green rowan branch, dipped it in the water, and sprinkled the bed while calling down blessings. "Our help is in Thee, O Lord, who made heaven and earth. Bless this bed, that all lying in it may rest in Thy peace, and preserve and grow old and multiply in length of days, amen."

Then, looking sheepish, he turned to Pippa. "I suppose the rowan branch is a mite pagan."

She drew in a nervous breath. "I'll take all the blessings I can get."

Revelin came and stood before her, tall and straight, his white hair and beard giving him a lordly dignity even as the twinkle in his eyes belied the severe look. "I never had a daughter," he whispered, "but if I did, I would pray God she was like you."

She raised herself on tiptoe and kissed his cheek. "I never knew my father," she confessed, "but now I feel as if I do. Thank you, Revelin."

He laid the palm of his hand on her forehead and murmured something in Gaelic. Then he was gone, and she stood alone in the room.

Two candles burned in holders attached to the bedstead, and a few coals glowed in a brazier. Everything looked rich and golden. She felt pampered and delicate, a princess in a charmed tower, the air heavy with promise. All was just as she had dreamed it would be, except for one minor detail.

She had never imagined that she would be afraid.

She was afraid; that much he could see right away.

Aidan stood in the doorway of the tower chamber and drank in the sight of her. Or at least what he could see of her. With her back turned, her head slightly bent, she lingered near the window.

Garbed in gauzy white fabric and intriguing shadows, she looked as slim and straight as a beechwood sapling. Her hair spilled over her shoulders and neck, and a circlet of flowers rested on the springy mass.

"You left the feast early." His throat felt strained. "The harper dinned us for at least another hour." A small lie, that. He had not been in the hall, either, but closeted in his office with Donal Og and Revelin, working out the documents that would govern

Pippa's future when he died. He would leave her with the Ross Castle treasure and a safe conduct to England, to Blackrose Priory in Hertfordshire, the home of Oliver and Lark de Lacey.

"Aidan?" She broke in on his musings, and he was grateful, for they were melancholy thoughts.

He had not anticipated being so aroused by her appearance, but he was. By now he should know that the unanticipated was commonplace where Pippa was concerned.

Her only reaction to the sound of his voice was a stiffening of her spine.

"It's all right, *a gradh*," he said, crossing the room to stand behind her. "You can turn around. It's only me, remember? Aidan."

She moved as if an opposing force held her back—slowly, painstakingly, until finally she was facing him. "Only you?" she asked. "As in, only the O Donoghue Mór, lord of Castleross, descendant of kings? I must be out of my mind. I don't belong here."

Despite her challenging speech, he could not answer her right away. He was too busy staring. She was perfect. Too beautiful. It was not the remote perfection of a marble statue, but the vibrant appeal of a bride of the *sidhe*. She was warm and glowing, her lips full, the lower one vulnerable, her eyes wide and uncertain.

"My lord?" She folded her arms across her middle as if to shield herself. "Why do you look at me so?"

He sank down on one knee. "To God, you are lovely, lass. You look like a fairy maiden, all white and gold and pure as the rain."

She bit her lip and gazed at him with a worried look. "And that's supposed to put me at my ease?"

He laughed softly, coming to his feet. "I was being honest, my love. You have a curious effect on me. It's not often I burst out with dramatic poesies or tributes to beauty."

"Being considered a beauty is very new to me." A shy smile flirted about her mouth. "It didn't happen until I met you."

It was all he could do to hold his hands at his sides, to keep from devouring her with his eyes. "And now. May I touch you, my lady of Castleross, or are you going to make me suffer?"

Her smile widened, changing from wistful to impish. "You mean I have a choice?"

He nodded, wondering where he found the strength to endure his need. "By rights I should fling you on your back and have my way with you, regardless of your preferences. However, you bring out an honor I never knew I possessed."

"Really?"

"Truly. I will do nothing to hurt you. I will touch when you say touch and stop when you say stop."

She took a deep breath and moved toward the bed, halting in the pool of candlelight by the headboard. "Why would I say something so foolish as stop?"

He swallowed past a painful dryness in his throat. "It will be your prerogative. And my challenge."

Just then, one of the fat white candles on the headboard sputtered and flared higher, brightening the room. Her gown was, in a way, more enticing than total nudity. It clung to the tips of her breasts, and the light shone through, revealing the high, rounded shapes. The draping fell to her hips, where it clung once more, outlining the shadow of her womanhood.

A groan burst from him. "Pippa, for the love of God, tell me I can touch you! You're taking me apart."

She stepped toward him and pressed her small, warm palms to his chest. Her eyes widened when she detected the racing cadence of his heart.

"There is something so appealing about frankness," she said.

"I could not possibly hide my desire for you," he admitted. Ah, God, he was hard. Hot. Aching for her. Was this her idea of torture? "Well?" His voice rasped like a rusty hinge.

She kept her hands in place. The heat radiated from there, burning him. "I do not want you to touch me."

A groan of frustrated outrage ripped from him. "For Christ's sake, woman—"

"Touching is not enough," she continued with almost painful honesty. "I want more than that, more than touching. I want you around me, inside me, all through me. Do you understand?"

He could only nod. What good had he done, what marvel had he performed, that God had given him this woman?

He would be a fool to tempt his good fortune, so he left the question unanswered and slipped his arms around her. His embrace was deliberately restrained; he teased and enticed them both with what was to come. Slowly he traced his finger down the side of her cheek, ran it along her jaw, stopping under her chin to turn her mouth up for his kiss.

Like a flower in full bloom she was, her lips damp and ripe, unfolding for him, falling open to receive him. His mouth devoured her, drank from her, and she was the sweetest delight he had ever tasted.

He had kissed her before, aye, but always those kisses had been marred by creeping guilt. This was the kiss of a new husband to his new wife, of a man who adored the woman in his arms.

She pressed herself against him, making a sound of startlement when she encountered the evidence of his need. He slid one hand down her back and cupped her closer still. After long moments, his mouth left hers to trail down her throat. She arched back to give more of herself to him; she hooked one leg around him. If not for their clothes, they would be fully joined.

"Ah," she whispered, "Aidan . . ."

"Are you all right? Am I . . . is this uncomfortable?"

She straightened and dug her fingers into his hair. "I had no idea a man was—" She flushed and looked away.

He was intrigued now. He kissed her ear and whispered, "Was what? Go on with what you were saying."

"Well, of course I heard bawdy jokes about it, but I simply didn't realize your—his—you know—"

He chuckled softly, though given his present state, mirth was slightly excruciating. "You're not making yourself clear, my sweet."

She took a deep breath. "I was just startled to find that what I thought of as a rather benign body part could turn into such an interesting, uh, tool."

He pulled back, all but shaking with laughter. "Tool," he repeated.

She thrust up her chin. "I have heard it called more ridiculous names than that. Some men even christen theirs."

"We wouldn't want a total stranger making all our decisions for us."

Her embarrassment dissolved into giggles, which then relaxed into a dreamy, comforted smile, this one totally devoid of the fear he had sensed in her when he had first come into the room.

Thank God, he thought. He had banished her fear. Now there was room for nothing but pleasure. Even so, he knew her state of trust was fragile. It took all his restraint to move slowly.

He touched the ugly golden brooch at her shoulder. "May I?"

She nodded. "Of course."

Just for a moment, the meaning of the brooch stung him with guilt. He forced away the feeling and unclasped the pin. The garment slid, with a whisper of protest, to the floor. He felt a fresh blast of heat. "You may call me interesting," he said, "but that doesn't begin to describe what I see when I look at you."

"It must have been the bath. Or the oil of roses."

"Ah, love," he said, "it's you. Simply you." He was surprised to hear a catch in his voice. The truth was, she moved him—to something beyond need and passion. When he looked at her, standing quietly in the candlelight, he felt an emotion so pure and sweet that his soul trembled.

With unsteady hands he removed his shirt, then stood looking at her while she looked back, and the silence, thick with desire, hung between them.

"Now what?" she whispered after a time, her gaze traveling over his scars. "Why do you hesitate?"

"Because I don't know what to do with a woman like you." He cradled her cheek in his palm. "You conquered your fear of this night, but it seems mine is just beginning."

"You're afraid?"

"Aye." Her cheek felt like satin against his rough hand. "I want tonight to be perfect."

Her breath caught, and he was shocked to feel the heated dampness of a tear on his hand. "Don't you see?" she whispered. "It's already perfect. I knew it when you said you'd never been with a woman you loved."

A groan tore from his throat as he slid his arms around her, reveling in the warm, silky feel of her unclad body and burying his face in her hair. "You make it all so simple, *a gradh*." He pushed her gently back so that she reclined upon the bed, watching him through a golden haze of candleglow while he bent to remove his boots and trews.

Ah, she did make it simple. She, who had never belonged to anyone, now belonged in his heart. And he, who had never been loved, now looked into her eyes and saw that she adored him.

So why was he still afraid?

As he lay beside her and felt the glorious length of her curl against him, the answer flashed like a spark through his mind.

He knew the truth about her past; he knew the answers she craved. Yet he dared not give Pippa her heart's desire for fear of losing her sooner than he had to.

Then she draped her slim arms around his neck, and the spark died, and he knew only the need to bring her joy. And ah, she made it easy. Slim and supple and warm, she was like a tender sapling in springtime, drawn to him, basking in his touch as if he were the sun.

He braced himself up on one elbow and settled his mouth over hers. His hand skimmed downward, circling her breasts and belly, outlining the curve of a hip and then the smoothness of her inner thigh. At his gentle pressure, her legs parted slightly, shyly, and he stifled a gasp at the excitement that singed him.

Something about her coaxed tenderness from him. Long after most men would have flung her down and plunged in, he loved her with his mouth and hands and endearments whispered in Gaelic. His tongue wrote love words on her skin, and each time she gasped with pleasure or cried out with a burst of joy, he felt his passion building and building until his chest ached.

"Ah, sweetheart," he said, "I want to touch you so deeply. But I don't want to hurt you."

She clung to him and moved her legs restlessly so that her hips formed a cradle for him. "It's the wanting that hurts," she said, "not the touching."

He covered her with the whole hard length of his body. "How deliciously naive you are," he whispered, nipping at her earlobe. In Gaelic he added, "And I mean to take shameless advantage of that."

"But you are such a good teacher," she said, and then, also in Gaelic, "And I am a fast learner."

For a moment he was too stunned to react, and then he laughed softly into her ear. "Wench. How long have you spoken Gaelic?"

She lowered her head and licked a ridge of scars on his chest. Her mouth and tongue seared him, and he gasped with the pleasure of it. "I'll let you wonder."

"Then I'll leave you to wonder . . ." He lapsed back into Irish, and using terms she could not possibly know, he described in explicit, loving detail exactly what he wanted to do to her.

"I haven't a clue what you said," she admitted, her hands drifting down, lingering over his hips, "but I wish you would hurry."

"Nay, I'll not hurry. We have all night."

"But—"

"Hush. Trust me."

"I only meant—"

He pressed his fingers to her lips. "You talked all the way through our first kiss and nearly ruined it. And wasn't it so much better once you fell silent?"

Her mouth gaped beneath his fingers. "I cannot believe you remember our first kiss."

"How could I not? It changed my life."

With a choked cry, she flung her arms around his neck. "Mine too. Ah, Aidan, I do love you so much."

He felt no surprise to hear her say it at last. He had known for a long time that she loved him, but he had also understood why she had resisted telling him. She feared abandonment. The fact that she would confess her love now could mean only one thing. She believed that he would never leave her. And he never would, not willingly.

But there were some things he could not control.

Pushing away the thought, he indulged his every urge to kiss and caress her, preparing her so thoroughly to receive his love that a flush swept her entire body. She lifted herself against him and rocked her hips in an unconscious, impatient rhythm.

Nearly mindless with desire, he knew he could not hold himself in check much longer. He tested her with a gentle, questing hand, loving the warm velvet smoothness of her, the flower-petal softness of her untried flesh, and the rush of damp heat that told him she was as ready as he.

He settled himself over her, stirred to near madness by the brush of her breasts against his chest and the wholly natural way her legs opened and then enclosed him as if their two bodies were parts designed to fit perfectly to form one whole. He lifted himself and paused, gazing down into a face that looked more beautiful to him than the sun, and then he kissed her softly, letting his tongue show her what their bodies would do. She whimpered and clasped him with her legs, drawing him closer. The need and the heat lit his soul with fire.

"More," she whispered between kisses, and then she sucked on his tongue, nearly causing him to lose control. "More," she murmured. "All of it. *Now*."

He drew closer still, yet hesitated, so reluctant to cause her pain that he nearly shook with the effort. He felt an almost blasphemous urge to worship her. Whatever he had expected of her, it was not this absolute and unquestioning generosity, nor this frank and compelling passion. Yet she gave him this and more with a selflessness that left him speechless with wonder. She had sparked a fire in the dark night of his soul, and every move he made, every touch and kiss, was designed to show her what she meant to him.

For a moment longer he held off, drawing back to look at her one last time in innocence.

Finally he buried himself in her giving warmth, and she cried out and surrounded him. When her maidenhead broke, her eyes opened wide, and her unsteady sigh was one not of pain, but of welcome, as if she understood that the moment bound their hearts forever.

He began moving with slow strokes that took him to the very limit of his control. She tilted herself with an instinct driven by love and desire, and his hand drifted down to help her, for he knew what she was reaching for even if she did not.

He touched her in a place that made her gasp and shudder, and then she dug her fingers into his back while long, silky spasms closed around him. Her abandon and pleasure would have coaxed a response from a stone, and Aidan, being flesh and blood, was far less resistant. He cupped her churning hips with his big hands and pressed himself home, indulging the need that had scalded him. His rush of pleasure was so intense and prolonged that it felt a bit as he imagined ascending to heaven would be—he saw naught but a blinding brilliance behind his eyes, and the entire universe seemed to shrink until it was encompassed by the small, passionate woman beneath him, who clasped him as if she would never let go.

He relaxed and settled over her and waited for his pulse and breathing to return to normal. Instead, he felt as hot and driven as ever.

"Ah," he said, nuzzling aside a sweat-damp lock of her hair so that he could whisper in her ear. "Are you all right, my love?"

"No," she said in a small, frightened voice.

He raised his head and stared down at her. "You're hurt? Do you need your maids, or—"

"Aidan, calm yourself." She brushed his cheek with a trembling hand. "All I need is you."

Worried that he had damaged her in some way, he lay beside her carefully and drew up the covers. He smoothed the wild, tumbled hair from her face to find that her cheeks were wet with tears, her eyes wide and haunted.

"My love, talk to me, please."

She gave him a wobbly smile. "I never thought I would hear you beg me to speak."

"I love to hear you talk. I always have. I even like your singing."

She sighed. "You are so good to me. So good. Please don't let my tears upset you. It's all so over-whelming. I'm not sad and I don't hurt. It's just that I never realized, never imagined, how sweet it could be for a man and woman to make love."

He pressed his lips to her temple. "You give me much relief."

She tangled her fingers in his long hair. "If I had known it would be like this, I would have worked harder to seduce you long ago."

"Ah. Then we shall have to make up for lost time."

"I agree completely, Your Eminence."

Ah, she was a joy to him in this dark time. Thus far, he had succeeded in avoiding thoughts of the future. What he had done was best for her. She would understand that when the time came.

She stroked him boldly with her hand, and his instantaneous reaction took his breath away.

"Again?" His whisper was a harsh, disbelieving rasp. "Now?"

"Yes," she said. "Show me that the first time was not a mischance, Aidan. Show me that it will always be like this for us."

"But it won't, *a stor*."

Her face fell. "It won't?"

"Nay." His hand coasted down the length of her body, discovering softness, dampness, readiness. "I shall find as many ways to love you as there are stars in the sky."

And while the harper played in the hall below, Aidan blew out the candles and made good on his promise.

*A*nd may the Almighty King of Heaven strike me entirely cold and eternally dead if I have done wrong.

I have known Aidan O Donoghue since the moment he took his first living breath, holding him in my grateful hands and weeping like a maiden aunt while the birth blood still clung to him.

When I dared, when Ronan O Donoghue was looking the other way, I gave the lad the father's love Ronan denied him. Never has it been my wont to question this, but I have always felt responsible for the boy's happiness.

Some would say I overstep my bounds, that I should sit back with a distant chronicler's eye and let the events of his life unfold. Ah, meddlesome knave that I am, I lost my objectivity decades ago.

So they are married. So they will snatch a little joy from the hard troubles that await them. Is that such a bad and wicked crime?

—Revelin of Innisfallen

14

Pippa became superstitious about counting the days or even the hours of her life with Aidan at Ross Castle. Some apprehensive, small part of her said not to tempt fate by examining her contentment too closely or questioning her worthiness of it.

She refused to look to the future, to dwell on the fact that Richard de Lacey's forces had withdrawn to Killarney town, obviously to regroup and await reinforcements.

Like a dreamer borne on a cloud, she drifted through each day, singing until the other residents cringed. She learned, with clumsy earnestness, her duties as lady of Castleross.

Hands that could juggle anything from pears to dead fish could not seem to master the intricacies of spinning and sewing. Finally Sibheal took pity on her and told her the household would be better served if she would simply supervise the work. Preferably from a great distance.

The comments were made in high good humor, and Pippa flung her arms wide while Sibheal and the others laughed in relief.

Aidan found them thus one morning after breakfast. His booted steps rang ominously on the stone floor of the hall. "What is this?" he shouted.

The women froze and gaped at him. Without warning, he grabbed Pippa around the waist. "I never thought to hear ladies' laughter in my hall ever again," he said.

The women dissolved into giggles and whispers. Pippa's heart seemed to fill her chest, expanding with rampant happiness.

"My lord, Sibheal was just commenting on my skill at spinning."

"If it is anything like your skill at singing, she has my sympathy."

Forcing herself to scowl, she pushed away from him. "You're a bad and cruel husband, Aidan O Donoghue," she said, imitating his brogue.

"Am I, now?" His brows lifted over eyes bluer than Lough Leane. "That is a sad pity, then, my lady, for I suppose it means I cannot show you your surprise."

She clutched the front of his tunic. "Surprise! Ah, what a quick, sharp tongue I have. I am your adoring wife, and you are the grandest of husbands."

He thumbed his nose at her flattery. The maids who understood English all but fell off their stools with mirth. Aidan caught her against him. "See them smile on us, my love. Now that you are here, it is like the spring again after a long, bleak winter."

His words touched her like a caress. Her mirth

disappeared, for she understood that his winter was his marriage to Felicity. "Come, my lord." She drew him toward the steps leading out of the hall. "You promised me a surprise."

"So I did," he said.

His presence was like an invisible buoy beneath her, lifting her up and sweeping her along, filling her with a warmth she had never felt before.

She did not know it was possible to feel all the things she was feeling. It was like discovering a new color in a rainbow or seeing a falling star—unanticipated, utterly thrilling.

As they crossed the bawn together, waving to Sorley Boy Curran and his brother, she squeezed his hand and said, "In sooth I don't need surprises, Aidan. I can think of nothing that could make me happier than I am now— Oh!"

She stopped and stared. There, in front of the stone and thatch stables, stood a boy holding the reins of a horse, saddled and ready to ride.

"It's a mare from Connemara, my love," said Aidan. "She is yours."

Pippa took a step toward the horse. She was magnificent, dun colored with shadowy black furnishings.

"Well?" he asked with endearing eagerness. "What think you?"

"She is the most beautiful horse I've ever seen. But you know what a poor rider I am."

"Not a poor rider." He walked her to the horse and placed his hands at her waist. "Just inexperienced."

Before she knew what was happening, he lifted her up and placed her in the lady's saddle. After she had hooked her leg around the bow, the seat felt as comfortable as a chair in a dining hall.

As always, the great height took her aback, and she clutched at the mare's mane. A groom brought out another horse, and Aidan mounted and smiled across at her. "Shelagh was bred and trained to be a lady's mount. I think you'll be pleased."

"Where are we going?"

He didn't answer, but the brief, smoldering look he gave her provided a hint. He had an uncanny ability to speak through his eyes alone; she could look at him and hear him telling her without words that she was beautiful, that he desired to please her, and that she made him happy.

Only occasionally did she notice secretive shadows in his eyes, and she dared not speak of them. For the first time in her life, she was truly happy, and though she knew it was selfish, she wanted nothing to disrupt the delicate balance of their lives.

She refused to see the English forces camped outside Killarney, refused to acknowledge the worried looks Revelin had shot her last time she had visited him at Innisfallen.

With a guilty start, she thought of the letter that had been delivered from Dublin the day before. O Mahoney had looked so grave and hopeless when he had handed it to her, explaining that the lord deputy had learned that a thief was diverting Crown revenues from Kerry. No doubt they would hold Aidan responsible for that as well.

She would worry about that later, she vowed. But not now. Not when he was gazing at her with such sweet promise in his eyes. She wanted their idyll to last forever.

No, admitted a little voice inside her head. *It is not as simple as that.* She wanted an answer to the one question she was afraid to ask: Did Aidan truly love her?

Part of her had to believe that he did, for she felt protected and cherished when she was with him. But another part, a small, cold, dark place inside her, whispered doubts through her mind. What did she know of love? No one had ever loved her; how could she possibly know what it was?

That same evil whisper planted another doubt. All her life, she had been abandoned by every friend she had found. How could she be certain Aidan was different?

She couldn't.

Let the marriage bond be enough for now, she scolded herself. Let it be enough.

They rode across the causeway and along the shores of Lough Leane. It was high summer, and the woods were canopied and carpeted by leaf and moss and fern and lichen in a vivid, glowing green. The rich, earthy smell of the forest filled the air. The lake was as blue and deep as a sapphire jewel.

"So much beauty," she said. "It almost overwhelms the senses."

"Aye," he said, and he was looking not at the lake, but at her.

They headed up a twisting, sloping path, and after a while it seemed they were the only people on earth, so remote were they. She heard the *churr* of a pheasant and a rustle of leaves as some small animal scuttled for cover, but other than the thump of hooves and the occasional snort of a horse, the forest was silent.

They followed a stream over a bed of rocks, and after a time she detected a low, distant roar. Intrigued, she craned her neck to look ahead. Aidan reined his horse and motioned for her to ride on.

The change was so dramatic that it took her breath away. On either side of the path, trees clad in emerald moss soared like pillars. The high branches formed a vault overhead, where sunlight filtered through and filled the air with hazy warmth. Then, farther up the path, the branches opened up to the summer sky, and she saw a surging cataract. It sprang from a great cleft in the mountain and hurled outward with such force that the stream was pure white, spraying and tumbling down from the heights. On the rocks below, a fine mist filled the air and made rainbows in the great bars of sunlight.

"This is Torc Falls," he said, dismounting and then helping her down. "Some will tell you it's a place of powerful magic."

As her feet touched the loamy mat of leaves and moss, she smiled up at him. "I do not doubt that in the least."

He chuckled as he tethered the horses to a branch, where they could browse in the tender shoots beside the roaring stream. "A Sassenach who believes in Irish magic?"

"Absolutely." She ran and hugged him, loving the solid feel of him against her. He was her gentle protector, everything she had always thought a man should be and everything she had never dared to dream a husband could be.

She lifted her face to his. "Is this not powerful magic?"

"It is." He kissed her tenderly, his big hands holding her as if she were a treasure. "And aye, my lady, you have become my favorite form of enchantment."

"Aidan!" She lifted herself on tiptoe to kiss him. "I do love you beyond words."

"Ah. I've never seen you lack for words. And aren't you the saucy wench who said she did not love me?"

She sniffed. "If that is what you prefer, then no. I do not love you." She pushed her hands inside his mantle and splayed them across his chest. "Is that clear, my lord?"

He took in a sharp breath. "Aye, that it is. You have a very powerful way of not loving me."

"Wait till you see what I can do when I *do* love you."

She removed his cloak and then her own, spreading them on the springy ground in a golden green haze of sunlight. "Come here, and I'll show you more."

Intoxicated by the rarefied air, she felt brazen and unfettered, as free as a bird soaring from a cliff. Item by item, she removed his clothes, laughing at his astonishment and then soliciting his help in disrobing.

There was something pagan and delightful and, aye, magical about standing naked in the open forest, with sunlight and mist swirling about them. She had an uncanny feeling of rightness, as if heathen powers had ordained their union, as if the very elements themselves sanctioned their love.

They stood facing each other, and she could see that he, too, felt the extraordinary invisible forces pulsing around them. Perhaps aeons ago, when the world was young, two different lovers had come together in this silent, mist-filled sanctuary.

"Aidan," she said, the single word heavy with emotion. She put her hands upon his chest and feathered her fingers over the thick, long-healed scars there. "You have never told me about these."

He lifted one side of his mouth in a half smile. "I thought Iago would. He tells you everything else."

"He has the same pattern of scars."

"It's part of a manhood rite performed by the people of his mother's tribe. I was at a very impressionable age when I first met him. I found his scars most interesting."

She brushed her fingers over him and felt a surge of wanting. "I think I understand."

Low laughter rumbled from him. "To make a long story short, my own scars are the result of a boring sea voyage, a large flask of poteen, and an excess of male pride."

She took a step closer. "It must have hurt terribly."

"Not half so much as the hiding my father gave me when he saw what I had done."

He spoke lightly, but she heard the undertone of resentment in his voice.

"You're much like me," she said. "You were abandoned, too, in a way."

"Only the one who abandoned me stayed near, so that I felt his displeasure every day of my life."

"It is a wonder we even know how to love," she said.

"You make it easy."

She leaned forward and pressed her lips to the ridge of scars that ran along the broadest part of his chest. She flicked her tongue out, and he gasped and went rigid. The idea that her touch could hold him filled her with a heady sense of mastery. The feeling of liberation drove her to boldness, and she swirled her hands around and over him, her caress an eloquent statement of her love. Lower she went, eliciting a delicious gasp from him as her hands and then her lips found him. Unfettered by timidity, she loved him with a boldness she had never thought herself capable of. She carried on until he loosed a hoarse sound—a cry of pleasure, a cry for mercy. He pulled her up and kissed her hungrily, and then they lay back upon the spread-out cloaks and she impaled herself upon him. She found the rhythm he had taught her, and while his hands traced her breasts and shoulders, she lifted and rode, controlling the pace until at last it controlled her, possessed her, and she could do no more than ride the crest.

She poured her love out to him, and she was like the great cataract surging from the heart of the mountain, exploding outward and splintering into a rainbow-hued mist.

When he pulsed into her moments later, she collapsed onto his chest and lay still, listening to the thud of his heart and feeling dazed.

Finally, with the gentleness she had loved about him from the start, he brought her to lie beside him, cradling her in the circle of his arms.

"You are," he said at last, "quite remarkable."

She gave a shaky laugh. "I am acting by instinct alone. Thank God you are a patient man." She smiled as latent pulses of pleasure coursed softly through her. She felt the warmth and passion all through her, at its deepest where her heart was. Out of her dazed contentment came a stunning thought, and she lifted her head to look at him.

"I wonder if we have made a baby yet."

His reaction was unexpected. Although he still held her in his arms, he seemed to withdraw ever so slightly. "I suppose we won't know that for some weeks."

She kissed his jaw. "I used to long for a child," she said. "I always told myself if I had a babe of my own, I would never, even abandon him. I would love him and lavish attention on him and hold him so close to my heart that he would never fear I'd leave him."

"Ah, Pippa." He stroked her cheek. "And do you still feel that longing?"

"Well." She turned over and cupped her chin in her hands. "It is not so much a longing anymore. It is an expectation." A flush crept up her throat. "After all, we are both quite healthy, and we've been—that is, each night—"

"And day," he reminded her.

"Aye, we have most faithfully done our duty—" She stopped and broke into peals of laughter. "You know exactly what I mean, Aidan O Donoghue, so I'll not continue that awkward speech. We *will* have babies, and they'll grow up strong and happy—"

She broke off again. The change in him was so subtle that she almost missed it, but she saw a somberness come over him. His eyes darkened to the color of the lake in shadow.

A chill shot through her. "Aidan?"

"Aye, beloved?"

"You don't think this can last, do you?"

He fell still and studied her for long moments. Torc Falls crashed ceaselessly into the silence that hung between them. At last he pushed himself up with the heels of his hands. "We had best be getting back." Very tenderly, he helped her don her clothing, then put on his trews.

She sat back on her heels and clutched his hand.

"It is worse for you to ignore my question, Aidan. You're frightening me."

He sat down, facing her directly. Shirtless, his chest marked, his hair flowing back over his shoulders, he looked like a savage god, the lord of the grove, who had the power to change the seasons.

As she gazed into his deep, sad eyes, she understood at last.

"Damn you," she whispered.

"Pippa—"

She wrenched her hands from his grip. "You've been deceiving me. *Again.*"

"Ah, beloved, I—"

"You never spoke to me of your worries. And I, fool that I am, never let myself ask. You made me believe everything would be all right."

Her tirade elicited a weary smile from him. "Is that not what a husband should do? Pippa, listen. You are so spritely and clever. Always with you I feel clumsy and inept. My heart tells me to protect you. Is that so wrong?"

"Yes. It is when something is eating away at you inside. You cannot keep things from me. When I wed you, it was to share your sorrows as well as your joys. Anything less is not fair to me. Anything less relegates me to the status of a child—an ignorant, spoiled child."

He rested his hands atop her shoulders. "So what shall I do, Pippa? What is it that you want to hear from me?" A tempest stormed in his eyes. "You want to share my fears, is that what you want?"

His passion took her aback. She felt a niggling of fear, but she looked him in the eye and said, "Yes."

"I tried to explain this when you first said you

wanted to marry. Our victory in reclaiming Ross Castle is only temporary. The Sassenach will return to take it back. Fortitude Browne holds me responsible for Felicity's death, and who is to say I am without guilt?"

"The woman took her own life," Pippa said desperately.

"Because of me. That is not something I can shrug off. Nor will Constable Browne."

"You can't be sure. Perhaps—"

"Ah, deny it, then," he said. "You asked. You insisted on knowing."

She turned away, feeling as if she had been struck.

He stood and finished dressing. When they were both ready, he lifted her onto her horse. By that time, all the anger had left him.

And all the magic had left the grove.

He gave her a rueful smile. "Do you see why I kept my fears in?"

She kissed him. "Aye, but you shouldn't have. This news doesn't mar my love for you. It deepens it. Can you understand that?"

He brought her hand to his lips and kissed it. "Then we'll speak no more of it."

One morning in early autumn, the news arrived with a cruel swiftness that took Aidan like a blow to the stomach. Donal Og arrived with the tidings.

Aidan was with Pippa in the counting office, showing her ways to reckon the winter stores. Though she knew it not, he foresaw a day when she would have to carry on without him, and he wanted her well prepared. Each day she grew more precious to him and more beautiful to his eyes. There was an aura about her, a glow; she was like a rare jewel with the light behind it, sparkling and gorgeous to behold.

Aye, that glow. That had been missing when he had first met her. He considered it a small miracle that his love had put it there.

He went cold inside when Donal Og approached. His cousin took long, loose strides, looking ever the giant of legend, his shoulders stiff and hunched.

Aidan bent to kiss his wife and then stepped outside into the guardroom. He and Donal Og stopped and stared at one another. It was painful for Aidan to read defeat in his cousin's face.

"What news from Killarney?" he asked, bracing himself.

Donal Og leaned back against a wall. "It's not good. Fortitude Browne has slapped a heavy fine on all the cottagers. A punitive act due to the insurrection last spring. And he has banned mass for seven weeks."

Aidan swore. "The jack-dog. Faith is the only thing those people have left."

Donal Og glanced inside the counting office. Pippa sat at the exchequer's table, her head bent, absorbed in Aidan's ledgers and counting rods. He jerked his head toward a path that led out of the keep to the shores of the lake.

"So it gets worse," Aidan said once they were outside.

Donal Og, the largest, strongest, most fearless man in Kerry, sank to the ground and buried his face in his hands. "'Tis over, Aidan. No matter how hard we struggle, they will break us. There are too many of them."

Aidan's heart pounded. He had never seen his cousin so full of grim fatalism. "I think you'd best start at the beginning. What do they plan?"

"To crush us like ants beneath their boots. The reinforcements have arrived. It's a fleet of eight ships, Aidan. And more soldiers marched in from the Pale."

"Coupled with the forces of Richard de Lacey, that gives them an army at least five times the size of our own," said Aidan.

Donal Og picked up a rock, stood, and flung it so far into the lake that Aidan did not see it drop. "It's clear they want a surrender without resistance."

Aidan stood listening to the roar of blood in his ears. His world was crumbling; he could lose Pippa. When he thought of never again hearing the sound of her laughter, seeing the morning sun on her face, holding her while she slept, he felt like a man on the verge of dying. "Surrender without resistance." He raised grim eyes to Donal Og. "This is a bit of a change for the Sassenach, is it not?"

Donal Og nodded. "In the past they took high delight in putting the Irish to the sword. What do you suppose this new offer of mercy means?"

"I fear it's as you said. It is over. The Sassenach will come whether we fight or surrender. The dilemma now is to hope for terms that treat the people as men, not slaves." Unbidden, an image of Richard de Lacey flashed in his mind. He was Sassenach, aye, but he possessed a core of humanity that was rare in an Englishman living in Ireland.

More hopeful than that was the news that Richard had taken an Irish wife. Shannon MacSweeney was a sturdy, stubborn woman; Aidan believed her fully capable of conquering the heart of her English husband. He almost smiled, thinking of little Gaelic-speaking de Lacey children.

After a time, Iago found Donal Og and Aidan at the lakeshore. "There are some days," he said dangerously, "that I am tempted to get into a curragh and strike out for the horizon."

Aidan tried to smile. "That is quite a thought, my friend. To simply set sail and let the wind take us where it will."

Iago winked. "I would hope for San Juan. My Serafina still waits for me."

Donal Og snorted. "After all these years?"

Iago glared at him. "The heart does not count the years."

"That depends on what the lady has in mind."

"What news?" Aidan broke in impatiently.

Iago sobered. "A herald from the new English forces has arrived and waits in the hall."

Aidan did not stay to hear more. Filled with an icy calm, he hurried back to the keep.

A lone woman waited within. He stopped and stared at her in shock. She turned to him slowly, her face as serene as that of a goddess in a Florentine painting.

"My lady." He bowed over her extended hand. "It is an honor to welcome you."

The Contessa Cerniglia heaved a resigned sigh. "I know this is unusual, but I wanted to be the one to tell you. Is Pippa here?"

"Aye, my wife is in the counting office."

The contessa smiled. "Now there is news. I'd wager she is radiant."

He glanced at the parchment scroll she held in

both hands. "For now." He led her to a chair and gave her a cup of mead.

She began to speak, and nothing she said surprised him. The English required total surrender. Whether he resisted or not, Ross Castle would fall to English hands and he would be forced to either leave or govern as an English vassal.

"So my only real choices," he said, "are to fight back or capitulate."

"Both will end the same," she said with true sympathy. "And if you surrender, there will be no loss of life."

None but my own, he thought. He said, "How can I trust the promises of the Sassenach?"

She took a long drink of her mead, then carefully set aside her goblet. "Because of the man who leads the English forces."

"Oh? And who is that? Surely not the rouged poppet Essex?"

"No. It is the earl of Wimberleigh, Oliver de Lacey."

When Pippa was sound asleep that night, Aidan slipped away from the bed they shared. In silence, in the dark, he donned his tunic and trews, then carried his boots until he was outside. In the bailey, a wolfhound growled at him; he silenced the dog with a low, reassuring word.

He passed the cool, bleak hours the way he had passed many a troubled night. He took a boat and rowed himself to Innisfallen.

In the sanctuary of the chapel there, while the wind sang through the tall, narrow windows, he fell to his knees and tried to pray.

But instead of entreaties to the Almighty, his mind seethed with the news the contessa had brought.

Pippa still did not know, and the contessa had agreed that it was not her place to tell her. That decision, that agony, was for Aidan and Aidan alone.

The fact that Oliver de Lacey had come—and that he had brought his wife—confirmed what Aidan had suspected upon seeing the portrait of Lark. He had been waiting for the moment ever since sending them the message that their daughter lived.

Philippa de Lacey's parents had come for her.

But it was up to him to decide the terms of surrender.

Ah, surrender. Such an ordinary-sounding word. And now it encompassed his duties not only as the O Donoghue Mór, but as the husband of Lady Philippa de Lacey.

He reviewed what he and the contessa had learned. The family were of an ancient, respected line. Judging by the terms offered, Lord Oliver was more fair minded than his peers. According to the contessa, the lord's wife was utterly beloved of all those who knew her.

"Ah, Christ." He brought his fists crashing down on the altar rail.

"An eloquent prayer, to be sure," said a wry voice.

Aidan stood and looked back toward the nave of the sanctuary. The gray predawn light picked out a tall, slim figure. "Don't you ever sleep, Revelin?"

"I'd not like to miss anything."

"It's my guess that you've missed nothing."

Revelin nodded, his long beard brushing his chest. "When I learned the name of the man leading the reinforcements, I knew he was the last missing piece to the puzzle. Have you decided what you'll do?"

Aidan glanced at the shadowy cross above the altar. He was glad he had confided in Revelin. "Almost."

"Ask yourself this," Revelin said. "What can the de Laceys give her that you cannot?"

"The security she has never known." The words came quickly, as if they had been waiting to be spoken. "They could spoil and cosset her. If she were free of me, she might one day find some proper English lord who would offer her the solidity of a settled life rather than sweeping her along on impossible adventures."

"So you're saying you can't stay at Ross Castle?"

"And be the pet spaniel of the Sassenach, performing for scraps?" With a sense of icy certainty, Aidan realized that every day Pippa stayed with him would sink her deeper into peril.

Revelin hesitated, then cleared his throat. "At least it would be a way to keep Philippa."

Aidan clenched his jaw. He had to force the words out. "Why would she even want me then?"

Revelin touched his shoulder. "Sometimes the most courageous thing is to know when to surrender, when to let go."

He threw off the comforting hand. He stalked past Revelin and rowed with savage strokes back to Ross Castle. Taking the stairs two and three at a time, he climbed to the highest parapet and burst out onto the walkway just as dawn was breaking.

This castle was the glory of the clan O Donoghue. It should represent the very pinnacle of his achievement.

How he despised it. He had from the start, when it had only been a minor peel house on the shores of

Lough Leane. His father had been determined to turn it into a monument of defiance.

"You left me a legacy of hate," Aidan said between his teeth. He stepped up between two merlons and gazed outward from a dizzying height.

The dawn was blood red. The bellies of the clouds beyond the mountains were heavy and swollen with a coming storm. But for now, the morning was clear and crimson. Already he could see the corrosive power of the English landlords. Fields that used to roll on forever were becoming enclosed into neat, cold parcels. Churches stood empty except for the wind howling through them. Sacred images had been smashed, priests put to the sword or exiled to sea-scarred islands. Smallholdings and crofts disappeared like dust on a breeze.

For a moment the landscape parted like a curtain, and he saw the perfect oval face of Felicity as clearly as if she stood before him. She had died, and no one had paid the price.

How had she felt, falling all that way to her death?

Aidan imagined it was the way he felt now—wild, out of control, flung toward a destiny so certain it seemed almost preordained.

He took a last long look at the red dawn, and in his heart he knew there could be only one choice.

Pippa smiled in her sleep as Aidan's arms went around her. With her eyes still closed, she took a deep breath. The scent of the lake winds lingered in his hair.

She blinked herself awake and saw that it was barely dawn. "Where have you been?" she asked.

"Out on the parapet. Looking. Thinking." He reached past the bed hanging and handed her a cup of cold water. She drank deeply and gratefully.

There was no reason she should have felt it, but she sensed an edge of desperation. She put down her cup and hugged him, pressing her cheek to the warm hollow of his chest.

"I love you, Aidan," she whispered.

He plunged his fingers into her hair and turned her face up to his, kissing her thoroughly and hard. Within moments they were making love with a fervor that filled her with a strange sense of panic and joy.

He was not tender with her; she did not want him to be. He was intense and restless, like the waves pounding on the rocks at the shore. His love was a storm of raw emotion, and she wanted it, all of it, no holding back, no shielding her from its ruthless power.

There was a harsh beauty to his lovemaking. He turned her this way and that, his mouth and hands finding places of agonizing sensitivity. His excitement seemed to fill the entire room. The sky through the open window was on fire, and he was on fire, and his touch set her on fire.

He stroked her, and his mouth and tongue seared her until she cried out, first begging him to stop and in the next breath imploring him to go on.

When at last he mounted her, the sun had risen fully and the light glowed behind him, outlining his untamed, long hair and the raw desperation on his face.

"Now, yes, now," she said, lifting herself against him and sweeping their bodies together, completely engulfed by the maelstrom of his passion.

They clashed and separated, clashed and separated, loving enemies locked in loving battle, one that had no outcome save total surrender for both. He bent his head and kissed her neck, then kissed lower, harder, his teeth biting her. Some remote, observant part of her looked on in surprise. It was as if he wanted to brand her with the stamp of his passion. As if he wanted to mark her with an image that would never fade.

And ah, she wanted it, the rough pleasure, and she told him so with a harsh whisper in his ear. She crested higher and higher like a feather on the wind, and each time she thought he could not take her farther, he did, sweeping her so far she was afraid to look down, so high she was afraid the fall would kill her.

And then it didn't matter. She looked into his eyes and saw a flame of devotion that would never die, and her fear dissolved.

She cried out his name and flung her soul to the wind.

The fall was long and fast, and it ended with a strange crimson darkness that only later she discovered was created by her tightly closed eyes.

"Ah, Aidan." Her own voice sounded alien.

"Aye, beloved?" His did, too.

"I thought after all the times we've made love, you had shown me everything."

"And now?" A smile lightened his tone.

"I was wrong. It is new every time you make love to me. But particularly just now."

He kissed her, carefully settling his mouth on hers, gentle now and tender. "Did it disturb you?"

"No." Yet she could not deny a slowly awakening

sense that something between them had changed. "I love you. Part of my love for you has to do with times like this. But—"

"What is it?" His gaze pierced her.

"It's silly. Never mind."

"Just tell me."

She hesitated, struggling to deny the thought. Finally she forced herself to speak. "You made love to me as if it were the last time."

Diary of a Lady

Ireland is more beautiful than I had ever imagined a place to be. The reports we heard in London concerned only the burned fields, the painted, shrieking warriors, the starving populace driven to violence.

Perhaps it was good fortune alone, for we saw only blue and green vistas, towering cliffs, sapphire lakes, and emerald mountains. Ireland is a place where the unexpected comes true, so I suppose this is as good a place as any to face what I must face now.

Though Oliver pleaded with me to stay back in England and wait for word from him, I insisted on coming. The contessa was good company during the voyage, and she did her best to prepare me for the events to come.

Aye, she did her best.

But can a mother ever truly be prepared to meet, face to face, the daughter she had given up for dead twenty-two years before?

—Lark de Lacey,
Countess of Wimberleigh

15

"There is no easy way to tell you this," Aidan said. After breakfast, he had brought her to the most beautiful spot encompassed by Ross Castle. It was a lakeshore garden, wild with cattails and reeds, ducks and terns darting in and out of the marshes.

She looked up at him with the sweet, lazy smile of a woman who had been well and thoroughly loved and had, without regret, been awakened by a kiss before dawn.

A woman who had no idea she had been deceived.

"What is it, my love?" She bent and plucked a flower and tucked it behind her ear.

He hesitated, giving himself one last look at her while she still loved him. After he spoke, she would never regard him with such adoration again. It was like knowing he was seeing her for the last time. The total, open trust and acceptance would be gone in a few moments, so for now he gave in to selfishness, taking time to bask and indulge in her affection.

As he watched her watching him, he reflected that there was a sort of magnificence about their doomed love. A majestic, sweeping scope to it. Their passion was too huge and all-consuming to last as long as his dreams.

"Aidan?" She tilted her bright head to one side. "Why do you look at me so?"

"I have news," he said. "It concerns your family."

She sent him a melting smile. "You are my family."

"I mean the family you have been seeking."

An odd distress flickered in her eyes. He realized it was denial. "You are all I want or need," she said.

"Nay, it was your search for yourself that led you to me. Long ago, you asked me to help you find out just what occurred, how you happened to be lost at such a vulnerable age."

She paled. "What have you learned?"

He became very aware of the cool shadows, the blue scent of the lake, and the way the morning light gilded her.

"I believe you are Lady Philippa de Lacey," he said. "Daughter of Oliver and Lark de Lacey, the earl and countess of Wimberleigh."

She made absolutely no movement. After several moments passed, he feared she had not heard.

Then finally she spoke in a dull, quiet voice. "Philippa de Lacey."

"Aye, my love."

"My parents are the earl and countess of Wimberleigh."

"Aye."

"And Richard?"

"Your younger brother." Now that he knew the truth, he wondered how he had failed to see the resemblance earlier. In looks, Richard de Lacey was a model of golden perfection, with an angelic smile and laughing eyes and a deep, unexpected cleverness. Donal Og was right. Pippa—or Philippa, as he should think of her now—was Richard's female equivalent.

"How did you find this out?"

"It started with the brooch you have. After you first showed it to me, I made a copy of the markings on the back. With the help of the contessa, I learned they were letters in the Cyrillic alphabet. The words are Russian. They mean 'blood, vows, and honor.' It is a family motto."

He raked a hand through his hair. So much time had passed since that revelation.

Her breath caught. "That's a lie!"

"The words are the same as those spoken to you by the Gypsy woman."

"How did you decide it's a motto of the de Lacey family?" she inquired, her voice growing stronger.

"I saw a similar brooch in a portrait of the Lady Lark. It was painted twenty-five years ago. It had the ruby and twelve pearls, just as you told me." He wanted to pace but forced himself to stand still and continue. "The contessa learned that Lord and Lady Wimberleigh lost a daughter—their first child—in a storm at sea. They gave her up for dead."

"When did you find this out?"

"The day I was arrested and taken to the Tower."

"You've known since then." Her voice lifted in wonder. "How perfectly evil of you not to tell me." She pressed both hands to her stomach as if to quiet its churning.

"Pippa—"

"Of course you couldn't tell me," she went on, speaking in deadened tones. "Just as you couldn't tell me about your wife. You needed me to help you escape the Tower of London. You had to keep me in a helpless state of slavish devotion so I would do your bidding."

Her words, though spoken quietly, lashed out at him. He accepted their sting, absorbed it like the burn of a hot brand. "I deserved that. But truly, I was concerned for you. I wanted to be certain, so you would not raise false hopes. I wanted to be sure the de Laceys would accept you, not accuse you of being a fraud. And by the time we got here, I saw no point in telling you. For all I knew, you would never have the chance to meet your mother and father."

"Because after I helped you escape, I became an outlaw who can never return to England."

"True," he said.

"You made me an outlaw."

"True again. Pippa—"

"No!" For the first time, she shouted at him. "I want no more excuses. You found the answer to my dreams, and you didn't tell me."

"I'm sorry, beloved. I wanted to shield you from hurt."

A bitter laugh escaped her. "I find that odd, for I have never suffered such hurt as I have since meeting you. Tell me, why have you decided, all of a sudden, to reveal this to me now?"

It was almost too dramatic that, just as she spoke, a cloud obscured the sun and plunged the morning into a yellow gray haze.

"They want to see you," he said. He had to trust

that Lark and Oliver were as kind and loving as the contessa claimed. "They are in Killarney, waiting to meet you."

She shuddered. "My parents have come for me."

"Aye, my love."

"They gave me up for dead, and now they want to see me. To see if I am worthy of them. To see if my blood is blue enough."

He took a step forward, reaching to comfort her. His hands touched her shoulders. She pulled away, making an agonized sound in her throat.

His prediction that the revelation would destroy her love for him had come true. There was only one thing left to do to sever the ties completely.

"I think you should go to them."

Her head snapped up, and she gasped. Aye, that was the killing blow. The coup de grace. Her love for him was dying before his eyes.

"Sweetheart," he said softly, "Oliver de Lacey has brought an army large enough to put all of Kerry to the sword. I am forced to come to terms with him."

"Am I part of those terms?"

"He would not be so crass as to state it."

Of course, she would know as well as Aidan did that it was one of the unspoken demands.

"Would you do something for me?" she asked in a small, cold voice.

"Yes, my love?"

She flinched at the endearment. "Would you please leave me be? Would you please today get out of my sight?"

He understood all too well what she needed. Her manner and countenance brought to mind a battle-shocked warrior, so emotionally devastated that thinking and feeling were dulled to sensation or constructive thought.

He watched her for a moment longer. She looked the same, yet not the same. She was his beloved golden Pippa, but something was different. The spark that lit her soul had died. She looked hollow, empty. A cold, beautiful vessel.

"Good-bye, my love," he said, and turned and walked away.

"I'm beginning to believe there's no such thing as dying of a broken heart."

It was much later that day, and Pippa had rowed herself to Innisfallen to seek sanity and wisdom from Revelin.

He handed her a linen cloth to wipe her eyes and blow her nose. More than a dozen such handkerchiefs lay at her feet in the garden in front of the island sanctuary.

"Why do you say that, my child?" he asked.

"I have tried several times to die of a broken heart, and each time, I just have to live with it."

"Then no doubt you were not meant to perish," he said. "You were meant to heal and go on."

"Ah. How noble that sounds. How simple."

"The words are simple. Not the deed." A strong breeze blew back his cowl to reveal the snow white fringe of his tonsure.

She forced a weak smile. "You're good to me. I have no right to expect you to make up my mind for me. I suppose there is no decision. I must go to the de Laceys." Speaking the words aloud sent a shiver coursing through her.

"By the sound of it, they won't reject you."

Fresh heat came to her eyes, and she blinked back another onslaught of tears. "I don't suppose they will, since they came so far and brought an army with them. It is Aidan who cast me off," she added bitterly.

"Do you think he wanted to, lass?"

"He made it so neither of us has a choice."

"There is a choice to be made," the old canon said. "The choice of whether or not to trust. You have to be the one to make it."

He left her alone then, in the garden beneath the gray sky, breathing the heavy air. Very deliberately, aware of every movement, she got up and walked to the rocky shore of Innisfallen. She stepped into the light rowboat and cast off the rope, then sat back and closed her hands around the oars.

She did not row but drifted, lost in thought. She was in no hurry to go anywhere. Her gaze touched the bag containing all her belongings. She had dragged it along through all the years of her life, along all the miles she had traveled, filling it with objects that had meaning only to her. With a shaking hand, she took out the ruined brooch and pinned it to her shoulder.

How often she had imagined this day. The day she would meet her family. How different it had been in her imagination. Her heart skipped a beat, and she took a deep breath.

Steady. Think of things one at a time. Think of Richard.

The family connection explained much about him—why he appealed to her, why she was so comfortable with his servants, why she had understood a warning in Russian about a falling candle, why she seemed to know his house on the Thames.

A wave of wonder hit her as she realized the red-haired lady from her dreamy memories, her god-mother, was Queen Elizabeth herself.

And Richard de Lacey, the most beautiful creature in the world, was her brother.

A pity he was the enemy, she thought with a sting of regret. Or was he? If she went to the de Laceys in Killarney town, would she be joining the English cause? Would she be any better than the Sassenach, the outsider come to invade the district?

Nay, she would always be like this boat, churning aimlessly, swept up by a storm of happenstance. Perhaps, she thought with a glimmer of hope, something good could come of this. She could appeal to the powerful de Laceys, possibly win sympathy for the Irish. She seized the oars and began to row, thinking harder.

The de Laceys were strangers to her. She had only other people's evidence that she was Philippa de Lacey. She could never know the truth for certain until she felt it in her heart.

Fat droplets of rain pelted her and pocked the surface of the lake. At first she felt no fear, only annoyance at being caught in the chilly rain. The weather, she thought bleakly, seemed somehow tied to the state of her heart. The weeks following her marriage to Aidan had been the golden days of high summer, days of sailing clouds and bountiful sunshine, nights of moonlit splendor in his arms.

Then the wind picked up, raising whitecaps on the surface of the water. She shrank from remembrances of how they had loved one another—deeply, with complete sureness . . . or so she had thought. In sooth their love had been built on his lies. She had been blissfully oblivious, a wanderer in the sunshine, unaware of a gathering storm in the distance. Ignorant of the destruction it could wreak.

A spear of lightning cleaved the sky, briefly illuminating the majestic, cloud-draped heights of Macgillycuddy's Reeks. The rain came faster, harder, in dense icy sheets that blew her sideways and caused the boat to list.

"No. Oh God, no!" Her teeth chattered; she clenched them and prayed through them. "Please God, no . . . Hail Mary . . . "

She plunged into the chaos inside her head.

Hail Mary . . . Nurse's words pounded through her, even though Nurse was gone, sucked under the rushing river of seawater belowdecks. The dog kept barking and whimpering and staggering, but he was the only one left alive, so she clung to his soggy neck.

The ship bobbed, a little cork spilling this way and that. But after a while came a great cracking sound like the time the oak tree had fallen in Grandfather Stephen's garden.

When the lightning flashed again, she could see why the boat had stopped. A great sharp rock, tall as a church spire, had punched a hole in the hull. She clung to a fat wet rope until another big wave came. When the next lightning struck, she could see another wave rising like a mountain of black glass.

The ship was lifted up and then plunged under. A whole army of stout barrels broke loose, rolling toward her along the crazily slanting deck. Something—the wind? a wave?—picked her up and hurled her into the sea. She flew through cold black space, and the water smacked her hard when she hit it. . . .

A scream gathered in Pippa's chest as lakewater swamped the boat. She could barely make out the misty shoreline. The boat sat lower and lower in the water, finally tilting out of control before it began to sink.

She stopped screaming, for above the storm she heard the faint, hoarse yelp of a dog. Then the wind roared in her ears and she slid into the cold water, clinging only to a single oar as the boat was sucked out of sight.

She felt a twinge of regret, for the de Laceys had come a long way to see her. Then she felt nothing at all. The water closed over her, and beneath the surface she could not hear the storm. Beneath the surface it was quiet as a crypt.

At the height of the storm, two horsemen met at an abandoned shepherd's hut in the hills overlooking the lake. Aidan dismounted and led his horse into the dim shelter while Fortitude Browne, the lord constable of Killarney, did the same.

Aidan had come alone, even though he knew full well a troop of rain-drenched English soldiers waited below the hill. Browne was a man of great caution when it came to his own safety.

Aidan had disbanded his army and sent them into the hills, for that was one of Browne's first demands.

For a few moments they stood facing each other, not speaking, letting the cold rain drip down their faces. Even in the faint light of the storm-darkened evening, Aidan could see the hatred in Browne's lean, ascetic face. He had thin lips and high cheekbones, a cruel set to his jaw, and hard eyes. Browne kept his hand on his sword, but Aidan did not fear he'd use it. Not here. Not now.

"You'll not believe this from me," Aidan said, "but I am sorry Felicity died."

"You should have thought of that when you murdered her."

Aidan had expected the fierce accusation. "Nay, sir, I did not, but my guilt runs deep. Felicity would be alive today if we had never met, never married."

Browne made a strangled sound in his throat and turned away, bracing his arm on the sagging lintel of the doorway and glaring out at the lashing storm. "You wanted to marry that beggarwoman. That is why you pushed Felicity to her death."

Aidan took a breath between his clenched teeth. "My lord, we both know she lost her reason. She took her own life. There was a witness, an Englishman like yourself."

A light mist of steam rose from the sod walls of the hut. "Perhaps," Aidan went on, "I am responsible for failing to see her madness."

"You *drove* her mad, you murderer! The state of her mind is your fault!"

Aidan felt no anger, only a great weariness. "Did you ever think of the state of her mind when you were forcing Felicity to kneel on stones or recite scripture through sleepless nights?"

Silence. The rain came so hard that it almost obscured the lake. Pippa hated storms, and now that Aidan had learned about her past, he understood why. He was glad she had gone to Innisfallen while the weather was still fair. As he himself had done, she sought solace on the lake island. Revelin would give her warmth and shelter; he would counsel her to go to the de Laceys.

Clenching his jaw against the searing pain of losing her, Aidan waited for Browne to speak again.

The older man turned back, running a hand through his thick, wet hair. "Do not sully my daughter's name by speaking it aloud. According to the letter you sent with the Venetian woman, you are prepared to accept my terms."

Aidan sent him a humorless smile. "I would not go so far as to call your demands for my surrender *terms*."

"You deserve to be drawn and quartered, made to die by inches." Browne's voice shook, and Aidan felt a stab of sympathy. The man had lost a daughter, after all. She had been beautiful, unearthly, and rare with her pale, perfect skin; in her lucid moments, before she had begun to hate Aidan, she had been pleasant and mild.

"So long as you agree to uphold your side of this devil's bargain," Aidan said, "I will come along as your prisoner."

"Excellent." Browne went to the door and waved his arm. Four men approached, shoving Aidan up against the sod wall and clamping cold, iron manacles around his wrists and ankles.

Browne led his horse out into the driving rain. He smiled. "I shall take great pleasure in sending the O Donoghue Mór to hell."

A subtle scent hung in the air. Pippa shuddered, amazed and frightened by a dream so vivid that it would include smells.

It was a scent that her every instinct recognized and responded to, for it was the sweet, unique scent of her mother.

Her mother.

Had she drowned? Was she in heaven? Philippa dragged her eyes open to banish the dream. She wasn't dreaming, but lying in a strange bed. How had she gotten here?

She blinked in the candlelight and noted, just in passing, the rich yet unfamiliar bed hangings.

Then she turned her head on the pillow and saw the woman.

Mama.

Her heart knew at last she had come home.

Seized by horror and joy and dread and relief, Philippa pushed herself up and drew her knees to her chest. She stared, and the small, dark-haired woman stared back.

Candlelight flickered at the edge of Philippa's vision. She caught her breath and closed her eyes, and from out of the darkness surged a memory so clear, it might have happened only yesterday.

Mama clasped her to her breast, and Philippa inhaled the nice laundry-and-sunshine scent of her.

"Good-bye, my little darling," Mama whispered in a curious, broken voice. "I want you to take this with you to remind you of your mama and papa while you're away."

Mama pinned the gold-and-ruby brooch to the front of Philippa's best smock. Then she removed the little knife that fit inside it. "I'll keep this part. It's safer that way, Philippa—"

"Philippa," the woman said.

Her eyes flew open. "I am Philippa," she said in a soft, wondering voice. "Your daughter."

"Yes. Oh, yes, my darling, yes." The dark-haired Englishwoman wrapped her arms around Philippa.

The scent of laundry and sunshine was as evocative now as it had been more than a score of years ago. It was the smell of comfort, of love, of Mama.

But between them gaped decades of estrangement. Philippa broke away. Lark de Lacey seemed to sense her need to adjust and let her go.

A moment later, a man stepped into the room. Lark went to meet him, taking his hand and bringing him to the bedside. At first Philippa thought it was Richard, but then she saw that this man was older, though golden and handsome as no other man she had ever seen.

Papa.

She sat perfectly still, while they stood unmoving, staring at her as she stared back. A storm of feelings swept over her: shock, confusion, disbelief, rage, helplessness, and a terrible impotence.

But no love.

When she looked at them, she simply saw two handsome strangers with tears coursing down their cheeks.

Finally she found her voice. "You are Lark and Oliver de Lacey, the earl and countess of Wimberleigh."

"We are." Lord Oliver's eyes were blue. Not the deep flame blue of Aidan's, but a lighter color, shining with tears as he took her hand and pressed it to his heart. Then he gave her his special kiss: cheek, cheek, lips, and nose, always in that order. And her heart began to remember the gentle touch of this man.

"Welcome home, Philippa, my darling daughter."

* * *

"He's been condemned to die?" Donal Og asked the contessa in a low whisper. He had ridden fast and hard from Ross Castle, and the smells of rain and wind clung to his clothing and abundant blond hair.

She regarded him silently, solemnly, unable to speak until she conquered the lump in her throat. She did at last, swallowing with effort, and took his big hand in hers. "I tried my best. Wimberleigh tried. Fortitude Browne refuses to retract his accusations against Aidan."

Donal Og ripped his hand from hers and drove his fist into his palm. She winced at the force of the blow. The lamp hanging from a hook in the stables lit him strangely, making him appear even larger and more forbidding than usual. She had arranged to meet him here, in secret, near the Killarney residence of Oliver de Lacey.

"All my cousin ever wanted," Donal Og said slowly, "was to be left in peace. His father would not permit that. Nor would Felicity. Even now that they are dead, they grip him in a stranglehold."

Her heart wept for him, wept for them all. "My love, I am so sorry."

He grasped her shoulders, pulling her against him. "I must go to Aidan, break him free of his confinement—"

"No!" she broke in. "Ah, Donal Og, I feared you would try this. It is the one sure way to get both yourself and Aidan killed. He won't go with you, and you will be caught."

"I'll force him to go with me. I'm bigger than he, always have been."

"You are bigger than everyone. But think with your brains, not your brawn. If you spirit Aidan away,

Fortitude Browne will water all of Kerry with innocent blood."

Donal Og clenched his jaw savagely and glared at
the roof. "God, ah, God, kill me now so I do not have
to see this through to the end."

She pressed a shaking hand to his cheek. "Find
your strength, beloved. You will need it." A wave of
frustration broke over the contessa. She had used all
her skills, all her charm, all her considerable powers
of duplicity, to convince the constable to show mercy.
"All I could wrest from Fortitude Browne," she confessed, "was his assurance that no one else would be
put to the sword."

He paced the floor. "I should put *him* to the sword.
Consign him to hell with his crazy daughter."

"Stay the impulse. Fortitude Browne is crooked;
we simply need proof." And we need it, she thought
urgently, before he carries out his sentence against
Aidan. "I will write again to the lord deputy in
Dublin."

Donal Og released his breath in a deflated hiss. He
opened his arms and gave her a weary smile. "Come
here, my sweet."

She went willingly, finding comfort in the embrace
of a man unlike any other she had ever known.

"What is to become of us?" he whispered into her
hair. "Shall I disappear like a wounded wolf in the
wilds of Connaught, where even the Sassenach fears
to go?"

"I have a better idea. Wimberleigh has outfitted
one of his ships for you and all the others who wish to
leave. It's provisioned for six months, and an expert
crew will take you anywhere you choose."

He chuckled. "Iago will be pleased to hear that.

He'll have us bound away for the West Indies before the week is out."

"Is that such a horrible fate?"

He held her tightly. "It is if it means leaving you, my sweet."

From the dregs of despair, she summoned a ray of hope. "Is there some law that says I cannot come with you?"

He stared down at her, thunderstruck and finally, cautiously, joyful. "You would do that? You would follow me into exile?"

"I would follow you to the ends of the earth if need be," the contessa said.

"Ah, sweet Rosaria. That is probably where I shall take you," said Donal Og.

In the morning Pippa rose and dressed after a surprisingly sound sleep. As she washed and dressed, she pondered the extraordinary events of the day before.

Her muscles ached from battling the storm, and her mind was filled with all that had happened. According to Oliver, an English patrol had spied her fighting her way to the shore. Alerted by the hounds, one man had dived in just as she'd gone under. She had been half drowned, unconscious. They had brought her directly to the manor house.

After seeing her parents, she had taken a little broth and wine, then fallen into a deep sleep.

The hall of the Killarney house was lofty and sun washed. The aftermath of the storm left the surrounding gardens glistening and green. She was not surprised to see a tall, long-coated hound cavorting in an orchard. A borzoya. Papa raised them. And now she remembered that the handsomest of each litter was called Pavlo.

All three of them—Oliver and Lark and Richard—shot to their feet when Philippa entered the room. Her gaze took them in with a slow, troubled sweep.

"Will you break your fast with us?" Lark asked.

"I'm not hungry." Philippa heard impatience in her voice, so she tempered it with a forced smile. "Thank you." With cold hands she unpinned the brooch and pushed it across the table toward Lark. "I'm told this was once yours."

With an unsteady hand, Lark took out a small, sharp dagger with a jeweled hilt and slid it neatly into the sheath formed by the brooch. "Before me, it belonged to the Lady Juliana, your grandmother."

Philippa nodded. "She used to sing to me. I remember snatches of a Russian song."

Lark moved to hand back the brooch, but Philippa shook her head. "There was a time when that pin was the only thing I treasured. The only thing that belonged to me. The only thing I belonged to."

Richard asked, "Were the jewels stolen from it?"

"I sold them. To survive."

He reddened and looked down at his hands. Oliver made an anguished sound in his throat. "Philippa. My daughter. God, when I think how you have suffered, I despise myself. Somehow I should have sensed you were alive. Should have scoured all of England to find you."

Her throat felt tight, yet she remained distant from these three lovely, well-fed, well-bred people. "You know nothing about me," she said. "Nothing about the pain I suffered, nothing of the loneliness that ached inside me for so many years."

"We ached, too, Philippa," Lark said softly. "More than you know. We grieved for the daughter we thought we had lost."

Philippa hardened her heart. Long habit made her resist loving them. "Circumstances, it seemed, were not kind to any of us."

"We were deprived of each other's love," Oliver said, "but a miracle brought us together again."

"Not a miracle," Philippa said. "Aidan O Donoghue." It hurt just to speak his name. "My husband."

Her pronouncement caused Lark's face to pale and Oliver's to redden. Richard raked a hand through his glossy, golden hair. "So you married him."

"An Irish rebel lord," said Oliver.

"A Catholic," said Lark.

"A man!" Philippa slapped her hands down on the table. "You speak to me of love simply as something that exists between us due to blood ties. That is not love. That is kinship. Love is something that is earned by constancy and caring and attention and devotion, the very things Aidan—not you—gave me."

"Philippa," Lark began, "we would have—"

"But you did not." She felt no anger, just exasperation. "It was no one's fault. The point is, Aidan loved me when I was dead to you. He loved me when I was at my most unlovable. When I was poor and crude and homeless and hungry. When I cared about nothing save who my next gull was going to be."

Lark wept, making no sound, the tears falling from eyes so like Philippa's that it was like looking in a mirror.

"I'm sorry for your grief," Philippa said. "No one is to blame. I love my husband." Aye, that was true. The shock of learning about the de Laceys had made her lash out at Aidan, but she knew she had never stopped loving him. "Nothing you can say will change that."

Richard cleared his throat. "Then why were you on the lake, fleeing toward Killarney?"

His question made her blood run cold. She touched her throat and began to pace. She trembled inside, wondering if she had destroyed Aidan's love by leaving him with such bitter words.

Finally she faced her parents and brother. "He told me of your summons."

"It was a summons of the heart," Oliver said. "I wanted to see my daughter." He smiled. That smile brought back all the magic of her earliest years. For a moment he was no stranger, but her loving Papa who made her laugh. He formed shadow puppets on the nursery wall at night. He showed her how to hide her porridge from Mama when she didn't want to eat it. He gave the most special good-night kisses in the world— cheek, cheek, lips, and nose, always in that order.

"I haven't yet told you," Oliver said, "how beautiful you look to me."

The words tugged her heart in one direction, but thoughts of Aidan pulled her in the other. "Perhaps," she said, "we will have plenty of time to visit one another in the future, but I must get back to Aidan. Your troops have threatened his people. I intend to stand at his side and fight—"

"My sweet," Oliver said, coming around the table and holding out his hands for her, "I can't let you go back to him."

"Don't touch me!" She snatched his dagger from its sheath.

He held out his hands, palms up in supplication

and surrender. "Philippa, you misinterpret me. We have no objection to your marriage to Aidan O Donoghue, no more than we object to Richard's marriage to Shannon, hasty though it was. I admire your loyalty to the Irish."

"Then why do you try to keep me from Aidan?" She set down the dagger. "I'm going to Ross Castle within the hour."

"Philippa," said her mother, "he isn't there. He isn't at Ross Castle."

Dread pulsed at her temples. "What do you mean? What has happened? Have you killed him?"

It was Richard who spoke. He sank to one knee before her. "Philippa, the Browne family believes Aidan murdered his wife. Everyone knows Felicity was mad. She took her own life, but her father is demanding retribution. Fortitude sent Aidan an ultimatum. He was ordered to surrender Ross Castle to me and himself to Constable Browne."

She lifted her chin. "Aidan would never capitulate to Fortitude Browne."

Oliver clenched his jaw, then spoke with obvious distaste. "The constable promised to burn out one Irish family a day until the O Donoghue Mór surrendered."

"Can't you do something?" she asked her father. "You're a lord, a noble. Intervene, restrain Mr. Browne—"

Oliver pressed his hands on the table and took a deep breath. "I have tried. I was up all night writing letters, sending riders to Cork and Dublin and London, but I have no authority here. In Browne's district, I have little more influence than a common soldier."

Looking heartsick, Richard rose to his feet. "The O Donoghue Mór knows he is outnumbered, low on provisions, facing a starving winter."

"What are you saying?" Philippa asked in a harsh voice she did not recognize.

Oliver clasped her hands in his. "My sweet, he had no choice. Last night he disbanded his army and surrendered to Fortitude Brown."

She wrenched her hands from his and fled to a window seat, wishing she could curl up into a ball and make the world go away. "He knew," she said, whispering to herself, beginning to shake. "He knew this would happen." Yesterday morning, she had almost guessed. He had loved her as if it were the last time.

She felt Lark's hand on her shoulder. "God," Philippa said, "oh God, he wanted me to leave in anger, wanted me to come to you. He had it all planned. Why didn't I see it?"

"He didn't want you to guess," Lark said.

Philippa looked up. *Make it better, Mama.* But no one could make this hurt go away. "What happens now?" she asked. "Will they send him to trial at Dublin Castle?"

Lark and Oliver exchanged a glance.

"Don't lie," Philippa said. "I'll never forgive you if you lie."

It was Oliver who told her what she had dreaded in her heart all along.

"They're going to hang him."

The ominous pulsebeat of a drum broke the morning quiet. The air held a chill as Aidan walked along the *boreen* toward the scaffold on a hill a mile distant.

In deference to his rank, his hands and feet were unfettered, and he wore his deep blue mantle to ward off the early autumn cold. His hair blew long and loose over his shoulders.

A troop of twelve soldiers surrounded him: three in front, three in the rear, three on each side. Constable Browne rode in grave, black-clad Puritan dignity in the fore. There was no real danger of his trying to escape. With sharp, well-honed cruelty, Browne had ensured his cooperation.

Irish people lined the roadway, slowing the pace of the death march. Their weeping was loud and unabashed and filled with a uniquely Celtic mix of curses and blessings.

The sound of his grieving people was curiously affecting. He tried to feel nothing, but they made it so hard. He had done his best for them.

At least he would not have to face Pippa today. More than ever, he was certain he had made the right choice—forfeiting her love and driving her into the bosom of her family.

"God bless you, my lord!" The cries came from all quarters, each side of the road, in front and behind, even above, for a group of defiant youngsters had climbed the trees to call to him and to hurl beechnuts at the soldiers.

"And a blessing on all of you as well." His voice rang strong and clear, and despite a bone-deep weariness he held himself tall. He had not slept the night before, had spent the entire time hammering out the terms of surrender.

Ross Castle and all its dominions were to fall under the jurisdiction of Richard de Lacey. Iago and Donal Og and the O Donoghue hundred were to be granted

clemency and sent into exile. Iago swore he would
find paradise. Donal Og challenged him to do so.

Fortitude Browne had agreed to all this readily
enough. What he truly wanted was the death of the O
Donoghue Mór.

And that was what he would get.

They were yet a quarter mile or so from the scaf-
fold on a lonely hill high above Lough Leane when he
heard the sound of galloping hooves.

He looked over the heads of his escort and saw a
lone rider coursing toward him down a green hill. He
knew of only one person who sat a horse and rode
with such reckless clumsiness.

Pippa.

Ah, Christ, why had she come?

She barreled headlong through the crowd of
onlookers. Fortitude reined his tall horse. "See here
now—"

"Bugger off," she said, plowing her mount boldly
across the *boreen* and forcing the soldiers to halt. She
dismounted in an awkward billow of skirts and
pushed past the escort.

How lovely she looked, flushed and golden as a
ripe peach, her eyes moist, her lips parted. She
stopped before Aidan, choked out a wordless cry, and
flung her arms around his neck.

All the love he had ever felt for her came flooding
back, rising through him like a fountain of sunshine.
He kissed her and tasted her and called himself seven
times a fool for loving her so much.

"Your trick didn't work," she whispered against
his mouth. "You tried to destroy our love. So losing
you would not hurt me."

As she spoke, the soldiers stopped, shuffling their

feet and staring at the amazing spectacle. But Aidan forgot them, just as Pippa had seemed to.

"You should have known better than that, Aidan. I will love you till the end of time."

Heat built in his throat, and his eyes smarted. He cupped her cheek in his palm and pressed her head to his chest. "What a selfish brute I am," he said. "To hold you in my arms. One last time." Yet he did not want her to see him die, to see the cart kicked out from beneath his feet, to see the noose tighten and his body jerk and his feet dancing helplessly in the empty air.

"Say farewell to me here and now. I beg you, don't finish this journey with me."

She pulled back and stared up at him. "How can you do this? How can you choose death rather than running for your life?"

He gestured at the crowd of Irish people. "If I fled, they would pay the price."

He could read on her face the words she would not speak: *Then let them pay!* And some small, selfish part of him agreed with her.

But he felt oddly invigorated now, holding the woman he loved. He even managed to smile.

"Beloved," he said, "it's too late for us. Ironic, isn't it? When first we met it was too early. Now it is too late."

She drew in a long, tremulous breath. "I begged my father and brother to intervene on your behalf."

"It is useless. Do not hold the de Laceys responsible for this. They have no authority to stop Constable Browne."

"So you have given up on everything. On Ross Castle. On us. On life. I won't let you!"

He skimmed his knuckles down her flushed cheek and nearly winced at the sweetness of touching her. "Not on us, beloved. Never on us. My faith has undergone many tests, but here's something I believe with all my heart. Love never dies. I'll never find a love so perfect as ours in this world or the next."

"Oh, God!" She turned her head and pressed her lips desperately to his palm.

"I will be with you always," he said. "That is my pledge. That is my promise. I'll be in the warm breeze when it caresses your face. In the first scent of springtime, in the song of the meadowlark, in the flutter you get in your heart when you feel joy or sorrow." His hand slid down to cup her chin. Bending, he laid his lips over hers solemnly, silently, while in the background his people sobbed.

"Do you trust me, Pippa?"

She stared at him, looking as if the slightest movement would cause her to shatter. Yet deep in her eyes, deeper than the grief, deeper than the despair, he saw the strength of her love burning like a bright, steady flame.

"Thank you," he whispered, knowing she would understand his gratitude. "Thank you for that."

It was her last gift to him. A pure, shining love that would carry him across whatever time and space was doomed to separate them.

Fortitude Browne barked an order. Gently but firmly, a soldier drew Pippa out of the way. For a moment, wild panic flared in her eyes, but Aidan steadied her with his gaze.

"Let go, my darling, my beloved," he whispered. He drank in a last image of her—wide eyes, soft lips, wind-tossed curls. Hand outstretched toward him. He wanted to take her hand, wished it could pull him into a magical, invisible world, but he made himself say again, "Let go."

She stepped back out of the way. The soldiers reprised their formation around him. To the steady thump of a drum, the O Donoghue Mór was led off to die.

How does a man tell of a life that is ended before the best part has begun?

I, Revelin of Innisfallen, find it impossible to pluck the words from my grieving, sad brain this day.

Likewise I find it impossible to pray, a grave problem for a man who has devoted his life to study and prayer. But what good is faith when injustice triumphs in this evil world? What good is prayer when the Vast Almighty is eternally deaf to my pleas on behalf of the best man I've ever known?

I had hoped the letter from Dublin and my efforts—and those of the contessa—to act upon it would bear fruit, but alas, it is too late.

It is time for me to go now, to be with the O Donoghue Mór in his most desperate hour.

And may the Almighty—deaf or not—have mercy upon the soul of my lord Aidan.

—Revelin of Innisfallen

16

"It's called a *what*?" Donal Og demanded, looking at the object Iago had drawn on the ship's deck with a bit of charcoal.

"A pineapple," Iago said. "*Anana*." He looked with exaggerated patience at the contessa. "Señora, you should tell your husband to pay closer attention. There are many new things for him to see in the islands of the Caribbean. He will be lost without my guidance."

The contessa sent an adoring smile to Donal Og. "My husband had a long night. Give him time. We are only one day out of Ireland. We have weeks of sailing ahead of us."

Iago shook his head in mock desolation. "Woe betide us all," he said. "This ship will sink 'neath the weight of all your sappy sentiment."

"This ship is unsinkable," the contessa said with a superior sniff, watching a pair of dolphins leap near the high bow. "It is a barque of the Muscovy Company Line. Lord Oliver assured me it is completely seaworthy and provisioned for up to six months."

"It will take us less than six weeks to reach San Juan if the winds stay as fair as they are today. Ah, San Juan! Amigos, a new life awaits us!" Iago threw out his arms to encompass the gallowglass and crew and all those from the castle who had chosen to sail with them into exile.

The heavy tread of boots on wooden planks rang down the decks. Everyone looked toward the lofty sterncastle quarters.

There, gripping the gilded rail, his black hair flying on the trade winds, stood the O Donoghue Mór.

Huzzahs went aloft like signal flags. Aidan smiled, but it was an empty smile, one he did not feel in his heart. His heart was grieving for the woman he had left behind.

With mystifying abruptness, his captors had marched him not to the scaffold on the hill, but to a well-provisioned ship docked in Dingle Bay.

The deliverance had been arranged, he had learned, by Oliver de Lacey. Aidan would never know what pressure Wimberleigh had brought to bear, but the lord protector in Dublin had learned the name of the man who had been diverting Crown revenues for his own use. Only moments before Aidan's sentence was to be carried out, soldiers had raced in from Dublin with the lord deputy's decree. Fortitude Browne was sent in disgrace back to England.

It proved to be a bittersweet triumph. Though Browne was gone, so was Aidan's domain. He could never reclaim Ross Castle, for another Irish-hating constable would take Browne's place. Aidan was alive, yet without Pippa, a part of him was cold and dead. He knew he would never see her again. Doubtless her father did not consider an exiled Irish chieftain to be a suitable husband. Aidan did not blame him. A daughter like Philippa was to be cherished and kept close, not sent adventuring to an unknown land.

Did she realize he had been spared, or had her family deemed it best to let her think he had died? He pictured her, couched in the splendor provided by her father's riches, wistful with memories of him. He wondered how long he would last in her heart. A year? Two? She was young yet; perhaps she would learn to love another. But surely—please God—not with the wild, all-consuming love she had shared with Aidan.

The very thought tore into his heart, and he winced with the pain of it. Yet he did not wish her ill. One day, when the pain dulled to a persistent ache, he would allow himself to picture her with another man, a conventional Englishman who would offer her a safe, quiet affection for years to come. A man she could trust never to leave her.

But could she forget the incandescent passion that had lit their world for one magical summer season?

"Sail ho!" A boy shouted the alert from the topmast. "Fine on the port bow!"

All hands rushed to the rails. Sailors scrambled up the ratlines. Two colored flags flapped from the sterncastle of the approaching ship.

"They're signaling us to come about," the ship's master said. "They want to reconnoiter."

Aidan's instincts took fire with apprehension, but he deferred to the captain.

"It's a law of the sea," the wind-battered Englishman declared, and orders were whistled down the deck. "We must parlay with them. God help us all."

Aidan stayed where he was, gripping the rail on the high deck while the two ships drew closer. He braced himself for the worst. Somehow, Browne had found a way to haul him back to the gibbet.

Then he blinked in the bright glare of the autumn sun, thinking his eyes deceived him. A woman stood on the midships deck of the other vessel, waving her arms while the sunlight shone down on wild curls the color of beaten gold.

"Pippa!" His shout rolled like thunder across the water. It seemed an eternity before the two vessels drew close enough.

He paced and swore, certain the moment would never arrive. Even when the ships came within boarding distance, time seemed to crawl.

"Patience, my lord," said Iago. "It takes time to steady the ships for a boarding plank."

"By God, I don't have time." He seized a rope that hung from a yardarm. Despite protests from all quarters of the ship, he tied on a grappling hook and sent it swinging toward the other ship. The hook caught on the third try, and without the slightest hesitation he looped a pulley over the rope and swung across.

He smacked against the midships rail, bounced off, and hit the archers' screen. Heedless of his bruises, he scrambled over and landed on his feet in front of Pippa.

Her eyes sparkled like the brightest stars. "I can't believe you're here," she said.

He gave a whoop of pure joy and captured her in his arms. They kissed long and so lustily that it took a firm, fatherly clearing of the throat to interrupt them.

Aidan pulled back to face a grinning older man who stood with his arm around a petite woman. Lark de Lacey wore Pippa's brooch pinned at her shoulder.

"You are Lord and Lady Wimberleigh," he said. "My thanks. I owe you my life."

"Ah, for our daughter, that was not enough. She would give us no peace until we brought her to join you on this wild adventure."

"That is true," she said, tucking herself against his chest. "I can't imagine why any of you thought I would be content to sit and embroider handkerchiefs while you sailed the world." She pressed a hand to Aidan's broad chest. "I was born to go adventuring with him." She glanced at the companion ship, where all the men and the contessa had gathered at the rail.

Taking a deep breath, she broke away from Aidan and kissed her mother and father. All three of them wept and pretended not to notice. "Give Richard my love, and embrace my other brothers and the sister I've yet to meet," said Philippa.

"With the Muscovy fleet at our disposal," Oliver said, "I'll bring them for many visits." Shamelessly, he wiped his face with his sleeve.

Lark touched the ugly gold brooch. "Are you sure you don't want this as a keepsake?"

Pippa smiled up at Aidan. "I don't need it, Mama. Not now. I have all that I need."

"I could have it reset with jewels and bring it to the Indies."

"Mama, I would welcome a visit from you," Pippa

said. "But as for the brooch, keep it for your grandchildren."

Aidan's chest ached with hope. "We'll see to it that you have plenty of those."

"Then take our love, and nothing more," Oliver said.

"That is all we need," said Pippa.

Aidan caught the pulley and swept her up in his embrace. Her arms went around his neck, clinging as he stepped to the rail. With a laugh of pure exultation, he leaped. They were suspended for a moment over seething open water. Then, on a great gust of wind, they swung across to the other ship and landed with a lurch on deck.

"You're carrying me," she said breathlessly.

"Aye."

"I can't believe you're carrying me."

"Again," he reminded her.

"Yes, again," she said, and laughed.

*S*ure and it's a high blessing entirely to clap my poor old eyes on such a thing as Lord Richard has brought me this day, two years after he came on as master of Ross Castle. It's a sheaf of letters and sketches from an island in a sea called Caribbee. It was delivered by Lord and Lady Wimberleigh, who have just returned from a visit to the islands to see their first grandbabe.

Imagine a place so littered with green islands that men of purpose can simply land on one and claim it as their own! That is exactly what Aidan O Donoghue and his merry adventurers did. Iago was their guide; they provisioned at San Juan—Iago had a bride waiting for him there, heaven be praised!—and set off on their own. They founded a great plantation where they grow enormous, tall cane that yields sugar, of all things. I'd never have believed it, except Wimberleigh's ship was fair crammed with sugar syrup when it arrived.

In addition to the blessing of a fat, black-haired baby boy, my Lady Philippa is increasing again. She and the contessa are both due to be delivered in the same month, and may the Great Almighty protect them and the bairns.

The O Donoghue Mór says I'm not to call him the O Donoghue Mór any longer and that I'm to stop chronicling his life. He tells me that all this constant, unremitting bliss makes for very boring reading these days.

And so I close this thick tome, built with laughter and tears, on a life well lived, on a triumph of the heart. I shall write no more of Aidan O Donoghue because he asked it.

But I shall think of him often, aye, and that is a thrice-made promise. I shall ever think of him as the O Donoghue Mór, last of the great chieftains, the twilight lord.

—Revelin of Innisfallen

Dear Reader:

For the past three books, the de Lacey family has consumed me, giving me more hours of laughter, frustration, tears, and pleasure than I can count. When I finished *Dancing on Air* and gave Pippa and Aidan the happy ending they'd fought so hard for, the idea for my next book started nagging at me, demanding my attention, and keeping me awake at night.

I dove into my imagination to mull it over, and what emerged was the sort of story every writer prays for each time she begins a new project. All the right elements were in place: a glittering jewel of a setting—Regency England; an English war hero and wild Scot; and, most intriguing of all, a beautiful woman emerging from a burning warehouse, only to discover that she has no idea who she is.

According to the locket around her neck, her name is Miranda. She has absolutely no recollection of her past. And no notion of why someone—a shadowy man with a deadly purpose—is after her.

She meets not one but two strangers—a handsome English lord, and a dark and brooding Scotsman—who fascinate her. One of them wants to marry her. The other intends to murder her.

And she doesn't know which is which.

Miranda is a race against time as well as a harrowing journey of the heart. All of Miranda's beliefs—about herself, her world, and the nature of love and trust—are tested to their utmost limits. Spiced with intrigue and set against the backdrop of the most extraordinary summer of the Regency era, this novel was both a challenge and a joy to create.

I hope you'll look for *Miranda*, coming from HarperPaperbacks in mid-August. Happy reading!

Warmly,

Susan Wiggs

Home Fires by Susan Kay Law

Golden Heart Award-Winning Author. Escaping with her young son from an unhappy marriage, lovely Amanda Sellington finds peace in a small Minnesota town—and the handsome Jakob Hall. Amanda longs to give in to happiness, but the past threatens to destroy the love she has so recently found.

The Bandit's Lady by Maureen Child

Schoolmarm Winifred Matthews is delighted when bank robber Quinn Hawkins takes her on a flight of fancy across Texas. They're running from the law, but already captured in love's sweet embrace.

When Midnight Comes by Robin Burcell

Time Travel Romance. A boating accident sends detective Kendra Browning sailing back to the year 1830, and into the arms of Captain Brice Montgomery. The ecstasy she feels at his touch beckons to Kendra like a siren's song, but murder threatens to steer their love off course.

Harper Monogram